Letters from Ancient Egypt

Society of Biblical Literature
Writings from the Ancient World

Edited by
Burke O. Long

SECOND PRINTING

Volume 1
Letters from Ancient Egypt
translated by Edward F. Wente
edited by Edmund S. Meltzer

Letters
from
Ancient Egypt

Translated by
Edward F. Wente

Edited by
Edmund S. Meltzer

Scholars Press
Atlanta, Georgia

SECOND PRINTING

LETTERS FROM ANCIENT EGYPT
Copyright©1990
Society of Biblical Literature

The Society of Biblical Literature gratefully acknowledges grants
from the National Endowment for the Humanities, an independent
federal agency, to underwrite certain editorial, research, and publication
expenses of the Writings from the Ancient World series. Published
results and interpretations do not necessarily represent the view of
the Endowment.

Library of Congress Cataloging-in-Publication Data

Letters from ancient Egypt / [edited by] Edward Wente.
    p. cm. — (Writings from the ancient world ; no. 01)
    Includes bibliographical references and index.
    ISBN 1-55540-472-3. -- ISBN 1-55540-473-1 (pbk.)
    1. Egyptian letters—Translations into English. 2. English
letters—Translations from Egyptian. I. Wente, Edward Frank, 1930-
II. Series.
PJ1947.L4   1990
932--dc20   90-41202
                                         CIP

Printed in the United States of America
on acid-free paper

Contents

Editor's Foreword   vii

Chronological Table   viii

Map of Egypt   x

Abbreviations   xi

Explanation of Signs   xii

INTRODUCTION   1

TRANSLATIONS   13
    I.   The Book of Kemit   15
    II.   Letters to and from Royalty   17
    III.   Letters to and from the Vizier   41
    IV.   Letters from the Old and Early Middle Kingdom   54
    V.   Later Middle Kingdom Letters   68
    VI.   Eighteenth Dynasty Letters   89
    VII.   Papyrus Anastasi I: A Satirical Letter   98
    VIII.   Ramesside Letters   111
    IX.   Letters of the Ramesside Community of Deir El-Medina   132
    X.   Late Ramesside Letters   171
    XI.   Twenty-First Dynasty Letters   205
    XII.   Letters to the Dead and to Gods   210

Sources   221

Bibliography   238

Glossary   251

Indexes   255

Editor's Foreword

This book is the first of many in the series Writings from the Ancient World (WAW), which will present up-to-date and felicitous English translations of important documents from the ancient Near East. Covering the period from the beginning of Sumerian civilization to the age of Alexander, WAW provides access to the fullness of major cultural areas of the ancient world. The editors have kept in mind a broad audience that includes, among others, scholars in the humanities for whom convenient access to new and reliable translations will aid comparative work; general readers, educators, and students for whom these materials may help increase awareness of our cultural roots in preclassical civilizations; specialists in particular cultures of the ancient world who may not control the languages of neighboring societies. The series thereby tries to meet research needs while contributing to general education.

The editors envision that over time this series will include collections of myths, epics, poetry, and law codes; historical and diplomatic materials such as treaties and commemorative inscriptions; texts from daily life, including letters and commercial documents. Other volumes will offer translations of hymns, prayers, rituals, and other documents of religious practice. The aim is to provide a representative, rather than exhaustive, sample of writings that broadly represent the cultural remains of various ancient civilizations.

The preparation of this volume was supported in part by a generous grant from the Division of Research Programs of the National Endowment for the Humanities. Significant funding has also been made available by the Society of Biblical Literature. In addition, all those persons involved in preparing this volume have received significant financial and clerical assistance from their respective institutions. Were it not for these expressions of confidence in our intentions, the arduous tasks of preparation, translation, editing, and publication—indeed, planning for the series itself—simply would not have been undertaken.

BURKE O. LONG

Chronological Table

Archaic Period: Dynasties 1-2	ca. 3050–2720 BCE
Old Kingdom: Dynasties 3-8	ca. 2720-2200
Third Dynasty	ca. 2720-2645
Djoser	ca. 2705-2685
Fourth Dynasty	ca. 2645-2510
Fifth Dynasty	ca. 2510-2373
Djedkare-Izezi	ca. 2437-2393
Sixth Dynasty	ca. 2373-2220
Pepi I	ca. 2361-2326
Merenre	ca. 2326-2319
Pepi II	ca. 2319-2225
Seventh/Eighth Dynasty	ca. 2220-2200
Neferkauhor	
First Intermediate Period	ca. 2200-2050
Ninth/Tenth Dynasty (Heracleopolis)	ca. 2200-2050
Eleventh Dynasty (first half)	ca. 2120-2050
Middle Kingdom: Dynasties 11-14	ca. 2050-1650
Eleventh Dynasty (second half)	ca. 2050-1979
Sankhkare Mentuhotep	ca. 1998-1986
Twelfth Dynasty	ca. 1979-1801
Amenemhat I	ca. 1979-1950
Senwosret I	ca. 1959-1914
Amenemhat II	ca. 1917-1882
Senwosret II	ca. 1884-1878
Senwosret III	ca. 1878-1859
Amenemhat III	ca. 1859-1814
Amenemhat IV	ca. 1814-1805
Thirteenth Dynasty	ca. 1801-1650
Khendjer	

Second Intermediate Period	ca. 1650–1570
Fifteenth Dynasty (Hyksos)	ca. 1650–1560
Apophis	ca. 1610–1569
Seventeenth Dynasty (Thebes)	ca. 1650–1570
Nubkheperre Iniotef	ca. 1650–1640
Kamose	ca. 1573–1570
New Kingdom: Dynasties 18–20	ca. 1570–1070
Eighteenth Dynasty	ca. 1570–1293
Amenhotep I	ca. 1551–1530
Thutmose I	ca. 1530–1518
Hatshepsut	ca. 1498–1483
Amenhotep II	ca. 1453–1419
Amenhotep III	ca. 1386–1349
Amenhotep IV/Akhenaton	ca. 1350–1334
Nineteenth Dynasty	ca. 1293–1185
Ramesses I	ca. 1293–1291
Seti I	ca. 1291–1279
Ramesses II	ca. 1279–1212
Merenptah	ca. 1212–1202
Seti II	ca. 1199–1193
Siptah	ca. 1193–1187
Twentieth Dynasty	ca. 1185–1070
Setnakht	ca. 1185–1182
Ramesses III	ca. 1182–1151
Ramesses IV	ca. 1151–1145
Ramesses V	ca. 1145–1141
Ramesses VI	ca. 1141–1134
Ramesses IX	ca. 1126–1108
Ramesses XI	ca. 1098–1070
Renaissance	ca. 1080–1070
Third Intermediate Period	ca. 1070–650
Twenty-First Dynasty	ca. 1070–945
High Priest Masahert	ca. 1054–1046
High Priest Menkheperre	ca. 1045–992

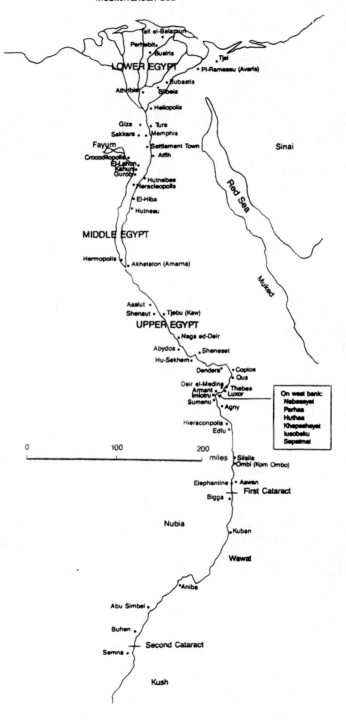

Mediterranean Sea

Tell el-Balamun

Perhebit

Busiris

LOWER EGYPT

Tjel

Pi-Ramessu (Avaris)

Bubastis

Athribis

Bilbeis

Heliopolis

Giza

Tura

Sakkara

Memphis

Fayum

Settlement Town

Crocodilopolis

Atfih

El-Lahun

Kahun

Gurob

Hutnebes

Heracleopolis

El-Hiba

Hutnesu

MIDDLE EGYPT

Hermopolis

Akhetaton (Amarna)

Assiut

Shenaut

Tjebu (Kaw)

UPPER EGYPT

Naga ed-Deir

Abydos

Sheneset

Hu-Sekhem

Dendera

Coptos

Qus

Deir el-Medina

Armant

Thebes

Imiotru

Luxor

Sumenu

Agny

Hieraconpolis

Edfu

Sinai

Red Sea

Muked

On west bank:
Nebeseyet
Perhaa
Huthaa
Khepesheyet
Iusobeku
Sepatmat

0   100   200

miles

Silsila

Ombi (Kom Ombo)

Elephantine

Aswan

First Cataract

Bigga

Nubia

Kuban

Wawat

Aniba

Abu Simbel

Buhen

Semna

Second Cataract

Kush

Abbreviations

ASAE	*Annales du Service des Antiquités de l'Egypte*
BAe	*Bibliotheca Aegyptiaca*
BdE	*Bibliothèque d'Etude*, Institut Français d'Archéologie Orientale du Caire
BM	British Museum
BMFA	Boston Museum of Fine Arts
CG	Catalogue Général
DFIFAO	*Documents de Fouilles*, Institut Français d'Archéologie Orientale du Caire
DM	Deir el-Medina
GM	*Göttinger Miszellen: Beiträge zur ägyptologischen Diskussion*
JAOS	*Journal of the American Oriental Society*
JARCE	*Journal of the American Research Center in Egypt*
JE	Journal d'Entrée
JEA	*Journal of Egyptian Archaeology*
JNES	*Journal of Near Eastern Studies*
LRL	Jaroslav Černý, *Late Ramesside Letters*
MDAIK	*Mitteilungen des deutschen archäologischen Instituts*, Abteilung Kairo
MMA	Metropolitan Museum of Art
O.	Ostracon
P.	Papyrus
RdE	*Revue d'Egyptologie*
RIDA	*Revue internationale des droits de l'antiquité*
rt.	recto
SAK	*Studien zur altägyptischen Kultur*
UCL	University College, London
vs.	verso
ZÄS	*Zeitschrift für ägyptische Sprache und Altertumskunde*

Explanation of Signs

Single brackets [ ] enclose restorations.

Angle brackets ‹ › enclose words omitted by the original scribe.

Parentheses ( ) enclose additions in the English translation.

A row of dots ... indicates gaps in the text or untranslatable words.

Introduction

The purpose of this volume of translations is to provide the nonspecialist and general reader with a broad selection of letters written during the major periods of pharaonic history from the Old Kingdom to the Twenty-first Dynasty. The letters that have survived from this span of nearly a millennium and a half were written by a fairly wide range of people, including the king, his high officials, lesser bureaucrats, priests, army officers, necropolis workmen, and landholders. There are as well a number of letters from women, or to women.

While there are many hieroglyphic texts from pharaonic Egypt, including royal and private monumental inscriptions, such texts are generally composed with reference to ideals regarding the divine kingship or the proper functioning of an official. The rhetoric of such formal and often laudatory compositions renders it difficult for us to discern fact from fiction. Among the documents from ancient Egypt that can bring us closer to the realities of daily life and make the ancients more comprehensible to us moderns are letters. Although letters may contain certain formulae that are repeated, particularly in their introductions, the bulk of a letter is addressed to specific situations that demand the attention of the recipient. Naturally a diversity of subjects is treated in the letters: economic matters, commerce, agriculture, law, administration, family life, and religion, to mention a few.

In contrast to formal hieroglyphic inscriptions, letters, which were written in the cursive hieratic script, provide one with the opportunity to observe Egyptians reacting to specific problems arising in the course of pursuing daily activities, and letters are among the best documents for revealing the workings of the living language of ancient Egypt. They thus can provide an important means for penetrating the psychology of the Egyptians and determining something of the logic of their minds in dealing with immediate situations as well as the values that underlie their approach to problems. In the spontaneous writing of letters one can find Egyptians giving vent to various emotions without the restraints imposed by the more carefully edited royal and biographical inscriptions.

The accidents of preservation have in large measure dictated the scope of this corpus, making it possible to include most of the letters that have survived reasonably intact. With the exception of some model letters that have been translated to illustrate what the aspiring student scribe should master

1

in the way of epistolary conventions and style, the correspondences in this volume are primarily genuine letters or copies thereof. Within a body of pedagogical texts known as Late Egyptian Miscellanies, edited by Alan H. Gardiner (1937) and translated by Ricardo A. Caminos (1954), there exist numerous model letters, but because Caminos has provided such felicitous translations of the Miscellanies and also because it is not always easy to determine which of these letters are copies of real letters and which ones are entirely fictitious, I have opted to omit them from this volume.

Papyrus was the preferred material for writing letters in ancient Egypt. Using a rush brush, the scribe would write his letter in black ink in the cursive hieratic script. Hieratic had already been developed in the archaic period as a means of written communication paralleling the more formal hieroglyphic writing, reserved for monumental inscriptions and for religious texts such as the Book of the Dead (Goedicke 1988: vii–ix). While in ancient Mesopotamia the clay tablet letter was frequently contained within a clay envelope that was sealed, in Egypt papyrus letters were not inserted into envelopes. The scribe simply folded his inscribed sheet of papyrus into a neat little packet, around which he tied a string and applied a mud sealing to ensure the integrity of the letter within. Normally the scribe would write the addressee's name and sometimes the sender's name on the exterior of this easily transportable packet.

Most letters written in ancient Egypt concerned the affairs of people living in the fertile Nile Valley, held vise-like between the desert plateau on either side of the Nile in Middle and Upper Egypt and fanning out into the verdant Delta of Lower Egypt in the north. The vast majority of settlements, in particular those of the Delta, were located in the flood plain. Many cities and towns of antiquity are today either mounds of habitation still occupied at the higher levels or are simply areas that have been denuded over the ages by *sebbakheen,* native diggers who have destroyed the site by carting away disintegrated brick for fertilizer. The impressive remains of temples built of stone and the vestiges of mud-brick houses and city walls are still to be found on the moist alluvium, but small documents of perishable materials, such as letters on papyrus, have scant chance of being recovered intact by the modern archaeologist who painstakingly sifts through the debris of ancient settlements on the flood plain. Although papyrus was substantially more robust and durable than our paper, it does not survive at all well when subjected to the dampness encountered in a site that has been inhabited over long stretches of time. Papyrus documents have rarely been discovered in town sites located entirely on the alluvium. No letters on papyrus, for instance, have been recovered from the main settlement areas of such major cities as Thebes, Memphis, Heliopolis, or Pi-Ramessu, the Delta capital of the Ramesside pharaohs. The only towns yielding substantially intact letters written on papyrus are those few which were not situated on the flood plain, or which had a significant portion of the settlement built on land that remained unirrigated such as the island of Elephantine (Letters Nos. 65, 67, 153), El-Lahun (Letters Nos. 78, 84–110), Gurob (Letters Nos. 17, 34), and El-Hiba (Letters Nos. 332–38). Even when the conditions of a site are relatively dry, as at the Middle Kingdom Nubian fortresses of Uronarti and Buhen, the evidence for extensive communications by letter is limited to many fragments of papyrus and the mud sealings once affixed to papyrus letters. In fact, at the Eighteenth Dynasty Malkata palace of Amenhotep III in western Thebes the testimony for letter writing consists solely of more than eleven hundred mud sealings from papyrus letters that have perished entirely (James 1984: 164).

Much of our information about the daily life of the ancient Egyptians derives from tombs, whose chapels were decorated with scenes depicting people engaged in the activities of this life and whose burial chambers have yielded objects and materials used by the tomb owner while he was alive. This same cemetery environment has also been the source of many papyrus letters, even those whose contents are entirely related to affairs of daily life. From the vast Memphite necropolis of Sakkara come such papyrus letters as Nos. 40, 64, 66, 131, and 133–35, while the necropolis of western Thebes is the source of Nos. 68–72, 79–83, and 111. Letters Nos. 41–43 were copied in a papyrus roll found atop a Middle Kingdom coffin in a tomb at Naga ed-Deir, and Nos. 123–24 derive from a tomb at Tell el-Amarna.

With the exception of the letters to the dead (translated in Part XII), which were deposited by living persons in the tomb chapels of deceased relatives for the purpose of communicating with someone in the beyond, it is difficult to determine how it is that letters sent to living individuals found their way into a desert cemetery—and in fact the reasons may not all be the same. In the latter part of the Old Kingdom the Djoser Step Pyramid complex had become the administrative center for work relating to the building of tombs in the Sakkara necropolis, and Letters Nos. 40 and 66, both discovered at the southern end of the great court of the Djoser complex, were probably sent to this destination since they are both concerned with tomb construction. On the other hand, the Hekanakht letters (Nos. 68–71) seem simply to have been discarded in the tomb of a certain Emsah either by Hekanakht's eldest son, Merisu, who had taken the papyri along with him to review in his free time while he was substituting for his father as a mortuary priest in the Theban necropolis (James 1962: 2) or possibly by thieves, who had waylaid the messenger and robbed him of the goods he was carrying (Goedicke 1984: 6). There is an extensive archive of papyri, including Letters Nos. 52, 59–60, 149, 164(?), 178, 179, 209–11, 262(?), 280, and 282–87, that appears to have been assembled over some period of time and deposited for safekeeping in the cemetery of the New Kingdom workmen's village of Deir el-Medina (Pestman 1982). In one of the Late Ramesside Letters (No. 313) reference is made to papyri being stored in a tomb at Deir el-Medina, and it may be that most of the Late Ramesside Letters, translated in Part X, were recovered from

Deir el Medina (Černý 1939b: xv–xvii). In the case of Letters Nos. 41–43,
mentioned above as being found in a roll placed on top of a coffin, one can
only surmise that these documents of administrative nature served to
enhance the deceased's position in the netherworld because of his loyal par-
ticipation in the state-sponsored dockyard activities that the papyrus is concerned with. The Semna dispatches (Nos. 79–83) had been copied on the
recto of a papyrus whose verso was subsequently inscribed with magical
texts. This document ultimately formed part of the burial equipment of a
magician who was interred in the vicinity of the Ramesseum in western
Thebes. Such is the diversity of circumstances that have contributed to the
preservation of letters of the living in the world of the dead.

There are numerous papyrus letters that have reached museums and private
collections without known provenience, acquired as a result of illicit digs. In
such cases one can make only an educated guess about the provenience of
these documents. It seems likely that Letters Nos. 22–30, 132, 140, 143, 144,
and 147 derive from the Memphite necropolis of Sakkara, while the necropolis of western Thebes is the probable source of Letters Nos. 11, 12, 35–38,
73–76, 113–17, 146, 151–52, 154, and 339.

Although rolls of papyrus were not exorbitantly expensive (Janssen 1975:
447–48), they did have monetary value, which is reflected in the considerable
number of letters, especially private letters, that are palimpsest. In the writing
of letters it was common practice to use a sheet of secondhand papyrus cut
off from a roll that had previously been inscribed for some other purpose.
Since papyrus rolls could be manufactured only from freshly harvested
papyrus plants, there were probably also seasonal shortages of papyrus that
led to the practice of erasing an older text so that a letter might be inscribed
on the same sheet (James 1984: 156–64). The fact that the Hekanakht letters
(Nos. 68–71) were palimpsest may account for the ease with which they were
discarded, for it would have been difficult to reuse these sheets of papyrus
which had already been inscribed twice and folded, making erasure difficult.
It was only rarely that a scribe would reuse a sheet of papyrus previously
inscribed with a letter.

It should be stressed, however, that not all papyrus letters are the originals
that were transmitted, for some have survived only as copies of letters sent
or received. Occasionally a number of related letters were copied on a single
roll, as, for example, Nos. 11–12, 41–43, and 79–83. There is one roll that
consists of several original letters (Nos. 35–37) that have been glued together
and attached to a copy of a letter from the high priest of Amon (No. 38).

Both the cost and the possible unavailability of even discarded documents
on papyrus without a doubt contributed to the frequent use of alternative
media for the writing of letters: flakes of limestone that were readily obtain-
able at no cost in areas where tombs were being excavated, and potsherds that
resulted from the constant breakage of pottery vessels. Like papyri, these
documents, called ostraca, were inscribed in black ink with a rush brush in

the cursive hieratic script. As a medium for inscribing a letter the ostracon lacked the possibility for maintaining the confidentiality of the message, for there was no way of sealing it and preventing its being read by others than the intended recipient. Another drawback in the use of ostraca for correspondences was their weight and other physical properties, which would tend to restrict the distance over which they could be sent. Thus, original letters on limestone flakes or potsherds were generally hand-carried only over short distances. Letters on ostraca bear no external address apart from what may be provided in the first sentence of the letter, and sometimes there is no indication at all of the recipient's identity. In such cases the letter carrier was simply told verbally to deliver the document to a specific individual. Ostraca were more clumsy to store than small packets or rolls of papyri, which could be conveniently filed in boxes. Indeed, at Deir el-Medina many ostraca were simply discarded in pits once they had served their purpose.

The ostraca that were actually sent as real letters tend to be briefer than papyrus letters, many being simple requests for supplies — short orders that did not require a high degree of confidentiality. Most letters on ostraca that are known to us are from the Ramesside workmen's village of Deir el-Medina and its environs, including the Valley of the Kings and the Valley of the Queens, where the citizens of Deir el-Medina were employed in the excavation and decoration of royal tombs. These documents form the bulk of the material translated in Part IX. There are a few Eighteenth Dynasty ostraca letters that come from other parts of the Theban necropolis: No. 112 is from Deir el-Bahri, and Nos. 119 and 120, purchased in western Thebes, may not have come from Deir el-Medina. Letters Nos. 125–27 were excavated at Tell el-Amarna. Of the Ramesside ostraca translated in Part VIII, No. 136 was found at Abydos, but the provenience of Nos. 141, 142, 148 and 150, which are probably copies of original letters, perhaps used as models in the scribal education, is unknown.

The Ramesside ostraca that are translated in Parts II and III, are not likely to have been the actual letters sent to the king or the vizier, for the exalted status of these individuals would have required a letter to be inscribed on a new sheet of papyrus. Some of these letters were certainly copies of real letters. The large Toronto ostracon, for example, actually contains copies of several letters (Nos. 45, 47, 48, 49) written to two viziers who were not contemporary. These letters were perhaps used as models in the scribal education at the Deir el-Medina school. There exist other ostraca bearing either drafts of letters that were to be inscribed on papyrus for mailing over some distance or "carbon copies," retained by the writer of an official letter. To distinguish between a draft and a copy retained for the files or possibly to serve a pedagogical function is difficult, especially when only one version is preserved.

One means of ensuring the preservation of an important letter, such as one from the king to a loyal official, was to have it recorded in stone in the hieroglyphic writing, transcribed from an original hieratic version on papyrus. A number of Old Kingdom copies of letters from the king actually preserve the same format as their hieratic originals (Goedicke 1964). Writing boards, which could easily be erased, were used in the scribal education, and one document of this sort (No. 77) may possibly be based on an original letter that was adopted as a model. Letters to the dead were most commonly written on bowls that were deposited at the tomb, but there is one example of a bowl used to inscribe a letter to a living person (No. 128).

In surveying the corpus of genuine letters, the question arises as to how many were actually penned by the writer and literally read by the recipient. Two possible situations would allow for the actual inscribing of a letter by someone other than its author. The individual writing the letter may himself have been entirely literate but, like a modern executive, may have utilized the services of one or more secretaries who wrote letters from dictation, or the author might have been illiterate and sought out someone possessing scribal talent to write a letter on his or her behalf. There is reasonable evidence to suggest that most kings were able to read and write (Baines and Eyre 1983: 77–81), but we also know that the pharaoh had letter-writing scribes, who took care of much of the royal correspondence. King Djedkare-Izezi of the Fifth Dynasty was able to write and read documents presented for his perusal, and it is probable that the originals of his letters sent to his viziers (Nos. 2–5) were actually penned by this king. From the content of his letters it appears that he was something of a stylist, possessing considerable appreciation for the deft turn of phrase. Is it by chance that the oldest letters we possess, both royal and nonroyal (Nos. 62 and 63), come from his reign? One can surmise that Djedkare-Izezi was instrumental in fostering the epistolary genre.

The ability to read and write was a prerequisite for a successful career in the administrative bureaucracy. The highest officials of the land were certainly literate, but, like the king, they had under them corps of professional scribes who often did the actual letter writing. At what point down the ladder of the bureaucracy an official ceased to have the assistance of a subordinate scribe is uncertain, but it is doubtful that very many officials, even at the bottom of the hierarchy, were illiterate, given the extreme emphasis placed on the acquisition of scribal skills for embarking on a career in the civil service (James 1984: chap. 5; Kemp 1989: chap. 3).

For the Old Kingdom it has been assumed that corresponding to each elite official owning a tomb in the Giza and Sakkara necropoleis, there were ten sub-elite scribes, who did not themselves possess decorated tombs but who are frequently depicted performing the scribal occupation in tombs of the elite (Baines and Eyre 1983: 66–67). The Egyptians regarded a scribal education as a national priority and an economic asset to the country. This is confirmed by the great attention devoted in the Twelfth Dynasty to recreating a scribal bureaucracy after the fragmented administration of the land during the First Intermediate Period (Posener 1956).

Despite the existence of secretaries who did the actual penning of their superiors' communications, there is no statement in any of the letters that anyone other than its author actually inscribed it. Bakir (1970: 34) refers to the Toronto ostracon mentioned above as providing evidence for the secretarial use of scribes in letter writing, but where the name of the scribe Siamon appears on this document in Letters Nos. 47 and 48, the naming of this scribe merely indicates that he copied the letters on the ostracon, not that he wrote out the original letters sent to the vizier. In the case of real official letters it is indeed difficult to determine if the author made use of a secretary or penned the letter himself. The only chance of making some headway in solving this delicate problem is when several letters happen to exist that were authored by the same person and the handwritings of each letter can be compared. This is an approach that is just in its infancy, but initial strides have been made by Janssen (1987) in examining the palaeography of some of the Late Ramesside Letters, translated in Part X. One of his conclusions is that the general Piankh did employ his scribe Kenykhnum to do the actual inscribing of several, but not all, of his letters (Nos. 301–3). Since the three letters written by the standard-bearer Maiseti (Nos. 133–35) all belong to the same hand (Allam 1987: 24), there is the possibility that he himself wrote these orders unless he had only one professional scribe in his service.

In some letters of the Ramesside period and the Twenty-first Dynasty (Bakir 1970: 14) there is reference to a letter's evidential value that requires its being preserved as testimony for use at some later date. In such cases the letter may have been penned by its author, for the handwriting of a letter writer can serve to demonstrate its authenticity, as indicated by a statement in Letter No. 318: "As soon as my letter reaches you, you shall [write] me a letter in your own handwriting that I may know that you are still alive." The sentence at the end of Letter No. 312, "Now you haven't written a letter in your handwriting to be sent [to] the general . . . so that it may serve you [as testimony]," suggests, if my restoration is correct, that letters which are to be used as evidence should preferably be in the handwriting of the author of the letter. Thus, when the general Piankh states in two of his letters (Nos. 319 and 327) that they should be kept to serve as testimony, we might suppose that they were in his own handwriting. On the other hand, it has been observed that other sorts of legal documents, such as sale records, did not rely on autograph or witness, the mere fact that such a document was written by a professional scribe being a sufficient guarantee of official cachet (Baines and Eyre 1983: 74–75).

It has been estimated, primarily on the basis of evidence from the Old Kingdom, that approximately 1 percent of the population of ancient Egypt was literate, or that one in twenty to thirty males was able to read and write (Baines and Eyre 1983: 65–72). There would, of course, have been a higher concentration of literate people in major administrative centers, while in peasant villages throughout the land the rate would have been considerably lower than 1 percent. It is generally assumed that an illiterate free person who wished to send a letter sought the professional services of a public scribe, who for a fee would draw up a letter, using the appropriate formalized greetings and invocations, and composing the body of the letter in the vernacular. "The writing of letters was undoubtedly a prime occupation for many scribes, especially those who failed to find employment in the various bureaucracies that managed the civil and religious affairs of ancient Egypt," remarks James (1984: 177). Professional scribes whose primary employer was the government, such as those at Deir el-Medina, might be expected to write private letters, sales documents, and legal instruments for illiterate clients and charge a fee for their services, although we actually possess no record of payments made to professional scribes for such moonlighting (Baines and Eyre 1983: 75). The government scribe would, of course, have had ready access to papyrus, especially to old inscribed papyrus rolls that might be easily erased and reused for letter writing.

What deserves some reconsideration, however, is the concept of the self-employed "village scribe," who made a living by inscribing documents for private clients. Although this type of public scribe functioned in the Greco-Roman period and even as late as modern Egypt, the situation may have been different in pharaonic Egypt, when legal documents were far simpler than the highly formulaic contracts of the Ptolemaic period (Baines and Eyre 1983: 74–77). The Hekanakht letters (Nos. 68–70) might be considered as exemplifying the use of a public scribe by a free person not directly involved in the bureaucracy or other institution, for on the basis of the handwriting it can be concluded that two different scribes inscribed the letters sent by him (James 1984: 167; Goedicke 1984: 120). Reviewing both the palaeographic and contextual evidence, Baer (1963: 19), however, suggests that the elderly Hekanakht himself penned his two longest letters, while his third letter, plus a fourth letter from a woman to her mother, as well as some accounts written over a span of three years, were inscribed by Hekanakht's son, Sihathor. Making use of the scribal and epistolary abilities of one's own literate son is not quite the same as paying a self-employed village scribe to do one's letter writing. As it was, Sihathor also seems to have functioned as his father's letter carrier (Baer 1963: 19; Goedicke 1984: 121).

The external address almost never indicates the place to which a letter was to be sent. In the case of private letters, such an omission, especially when the addressee was not a well-known personality, argues against the existence of a regular postal service for the transmission of private letters. Although there is one instance in which an official dispatch carrier is engaged in the transmission of a private letter, it is unlikely that such irregular use of the "diplomatic pouch" was common (James 1984: 171–72). Rather, most private letters were carried by friends, relatives, or subordinates of the writer, or anyone who happened to be journeying in the direction of the recipient. If there were no professional letter carriers to handle private correspondences, it appears rather unlikely that there were professional village scribes making a living writing letters for illiterate clients. It would seem more likely that when an illiterate person wished to have a letter written, he would seek the services of some family member or acquaintance who knew how to write. At Deir el-Medina, where the degree of literacy was higher than average, the scribes who performed such a role for illiterate inhabitants of the village, were government employees and thus not comparable to the self-employed village scribe whose existence in pharaonic times has been postulated.

Concerning the recipient's ability to read, Letter No. 330 is of some interest. Formally it is addressed to the well-known scribe of the necropolis, Butehamon. The content of the letter indicates that the communication is really for the benefit of an illiterate person named Peterpayneb. Butehamon is first asked to visually read, "look at," the letter for Peterpayneb, which was sent to Butehamon, and then take it and verbally read it out to Peterpayneb. When the recipient mentioned in the body of a letter is different from the addressee in the exterior address, we might suspect that the recipient of the communication was illiterate. Such letters are Nos. 26, 71, and 282, all intended for women, but bearing a man's name in the exterior address. Since the degree of education and literacy among women was certainly lower than among men (Baines and Eyre 1983: 81–85; Bryan 1984), it seems likely that the female recipients of these letters were illiterate and that the men were expected to read out the letter verbally for their benefit.

Although women were not generally afforded the advantages of a school education and did not compete with men for posts in the bureaucracy, there were certain positions that were genuinely female, such as priestesses, chantresses, and personnel surrounding the position of Divine Votaress of Amon during the New Kingdom. Although women did not officially compete with men, they were occasionally accorded considerable authority, especially to act on behalf of their husbands (Janssen 1986). Such letters as Nos. 24, 139, 289–91, 303, 311, 315, 319, 321, 324, 336, and 339 provide evidence for women functioning with varying degrees of authority, and certainly some of these women were literate. Occasionally there are references to a woman's writing a letter (Nos. 104, 124, 270, 282, and 297), but one must be cautious in concluding that a woman actually penned the document. Letter No. 124, if my restoration of the passage is correct, provides evidence for a female recipient reading a letter visually (the verb is "look at," the same as the one mentioned above in connection with No. 330). Regarding the women of Deir el-Medina, Janssen (1987: 167 n. 25) considers it probable that the letters on ostraca sent by women were actually inscribed by them.

With regard to the conventions and formulae employed in letter writing, letters from the Old and Middle Kingdoms generally display a greater consciousness of the relative social status existing between writer and addressee than do New Kingdom correspondences. Adopting a humble attitude toward a superior recipient, the writer may refer to himself in the salutation as "servant of the estate," while in the body of the letter he uses an expression which I, for sake of clarity, have rendered by "I, your humble servant," although the first person pronoun is not actually present in the Egyptian. The superior recipient in the older letters is referred to either as "lord," or sometimes obliquely as "your scribe," that is, the recipient's secretary, who supposedly would read out the communication to his master. The writer of the letter in such cases does not want to presume that the recipient will have to read the letter himself. A writer who is equal in status to the recipient may politely refer to himself as "your brother." Since "your scribe" and "your brother" are rather cumbersome expressions and likely to confuse the reader, I have in most instances rendered them simply by "you" and "I" respectively. By the New Kingdom such formal expressions are normally dispensed with in the body of a letter, and first and second person pronouns are used almost exclusively. In the introductory formulae of New Kingdom letters, however, the writer often continues the earlier practice of calling a superior "lord."

When inferiors write to superiors, greetings and invocations to gods on the addressee's behalf are commonly employed, but very rarely does a superior writer proffer wishes for the well-being of a subordinate, an exceptional instance being Letter No. 113. For the Old and Middle Kingdoms the formulae of invocation tend to be more rigidly phrased than in the New Kingdom, when a freer style was adopted, reflective of a more personal relationship between a person and a god. This was true particularly during the Ramesside period, which was noted for pietistic developments in religion. More detailed information on the introductory formulae used in letters is provided by James (1962: Appendix D), Bakir (1970), and Sweeney (1985: 213–30).

As mentioned above, private letters were not transmitted through any sort of organized postal system. The letters themselves indicate that they were carried either by agents, retainers, relatives, or acquaintances of the writer, or by travelers who happened to be going in the right direction (Bakir 1970: 29–31). For the transmission of official letters in the Old Kingdom, some sort of rudimentary postal system may have been developed, one in which the messenger was also empowered to represent the sender in a manner beyond that of a simple postman. At that time temples, unless exempted by royal decree, were required to provide support for these government agents who carried official letters. In the Middle Kingdom these messengers, at least on occasion, served as simple letter carriers (Letter No. 99). The large number of mud sealings and fragments of papyrus letters from the Nubian forts attest to an intensive communications system, which must have used messengers operating with some degree of regularity.

In the New Kingdom there were "dispatch carriers," who transmitted orders from high authorities, while messengers were entrusted with the delivery of normal letters. Even with the existence of some sort of state messengers, it was hardly anything at all comparable to our modern postal system. A journal of a border official has been taken as showing some sort of system for relaying official dispatches beyond the Egyptian border, but even here the official dispatches were carried not by official dispatch carriers but by retainers (James 1984: 171). Letter No. 24 lists a variety of persons, none called "messenger" or "dispatch carrier," who were involved in the transmission of letters from the Ramesside court. The letters of Ramesses IX and XI (Nos. 35 and 39) provide evidence for the transmission of royal correspondences by treasury overseers and royal cupbearers as well as a courier, who was probably mounted.

The Late Ramesside Letters, translated in Part X, are a mixture of official and personal correspondences, but there is little indication of an organized postal service. Letter No. 310 refers to messengers who regularly convey letters from Thebes to the west side of the Nile, but the communications going north and south were for the most part transmitted by retainers of the officials involved. One has the impression that the Egyptians were often less concerned with the speedy transmission of letters than with preserving confidentiality and assuring that they reach their final destination intact — this despite literary references to the speed of messengers and to the use of the horse and chariot and mounted couriers for relaying letters (Valloggia 1976: 259–60). A truly organized and regularly functioning postal service would demand more specific indication as to the location of the recipient than extant letters on the whole indicate. Were we to possess the papyrus letters that were sent between major urban centers, like Thebes, Memphis, and Heliopolis, it is entirely possible that these correspondences would illustrate more clearly the existence and functioning of a postal service more in line with that described by Valloggia (1976).

In organizing the letters for presentation in this volume I have adopted, in general, a chronological framework, but with some exceptions. By way of introducing the reader to the epistolary genre, Part I presents a translation of the Book of Kemit, the oldest didactic composition in epistolary form. Parts II and III treat letters relating to the two highest positions in the land: the king and the vizier. Within each of these sections the arrangement of the correspondences is chronological. Thereafter the parts follow in chronological sequence. In Part VII, a long literary letter from the reign of Ramesses II has been translated as an example of the sort of material used in the contemporary scribal education. Part IX is devoted to the abundant epistolary documentation from the Ramesside village of Deir el-Medina. Here the documents have been arranged topically rather than chronologically. Part XII forms a fitting conclusion to the volume, for here we witness the ancient Egyptian communicating beyond the world of the living into the realm of the dead and the gods.

In following the guidelines of this series I have attempted to let the letters speak for themselves with a minimum of footnotes. Parentheses ( ) are used

to enclose words not in the Egyptian but necessary for a proper understanding of what the Egyptian was attempting to say, or additions clarifying
a preceding word or phrase. Square brackets [ ] enclose the restorations of
text in a lacuna or words inadvertently omitted by the scribe. A sequence of
three dots . . . serves to indicate the presence of text defying translation,
while within brackets these same dots are used where no attempt has been
made to restore words that have been lost. Italics are employed to give a
general idea of what stood in a lacuna or are used to indicate Egyptian words
left untranslated. The abbreviation "l.p.h." is a device commonly employed
by Egyptologists to render "May he/she live, be prosperous, and healthy,"
following personal designations or personalized institutions such as "palace."

In Egyptian, rather complex constructions lead to what has, perhaps
somewhat erroneously, been termed "confusion of pronouns." Often this is
a matter of the logic of the ancient Egyptian language, which does not always
correspond to that of English. In such cases, I have generally adjusted the
person of the pronoun to correspond to English usage.

Many of the letters included in this volume have been previously translated, and obviously the labor of predecessors has greatly facilitated my task.
By consulting the "Sources" section that follows the whole body of translations, the reader will be able to locate previous editions and translations of
the individual letters. In order to keep the "Sources" and "Bibliography" of
manageable size, however, it has not been possible for me to include articles
which contain translations of individual passages that occur in the letters. In
particular, I owe a great debt of gratitude to my graduate students, with
whom over the years I have been privileged to read many of the documents
presented in this volume.

For the second printing of this volume a number of minor changes that do
not involve repagination have been made. The author is much indebted to
John R. Huddlestun for his constructive comments in this regard.

Translations

I

The Book of Kemit

Introduction

Compiled in the late Eleventh Dynasty, the Book of Kemit, meaning "summation" or "completion," was a compendium intended for the education of the Egyptian scribe. It comprises three main sections: epistolary greetings, a narrative that concludes with a letter, and phraseology drawn from the realm of the ideal biography. The individual texts that were incorporated in this school book were probably older than the date of compilation. In particular, components of the epistolary formulae are already attested in the Sixth Dynasty (Posener-Kriéger 1976: 2:454-55). This frequently copied text is preserved on a New Kingdom writing board and on nearly a hundred ostraca. The translation is based on the pioneering reconstitution of the whole text by Posener (1951: pls. 1-21) and consideration of previous translations by Kaplony (1974) and by Barta (1978). The "Mistress of Bubastis" mentioned in the text is the cat goddess Bastet, whose pleasant feline disposition contrasts with that of the ferocious lioness goddess Sakhmet. In this didactic composition the term "son" is tantamount to "pupil."

1. The Book of Kemit
(Early Middle Kingdom)

It is a servant who addresses his lord, whom he wishes to live, be prosperous and healthy throughout all eternity, as I, your humble servant, desire. May you be justified before the Souls of Heliopolis and before all the gods. May they grant to you that you live, and may they do everything good for you each day, as I, your humble servant, desire.

Your condition is that of one who lives innumerable times. May Montu, lord of the Theban nome, help you, as I, your humble servant, desire. May Ptah, South-of-his-Wall, gladden you with living fully, a ripe old age, and a passing on to blessedness, and may your standing be good with the *Ka* of Montu, lord of the Theban nome, as I, your humble servant, desire. In very good peace!

Now as for these writings upon which your personal agent has set me, I will do your pleasure so that you will be happier than the Mistress of

15

Bubastis. As for what might make me glad, it is that Au be allowed to return. When I last saw him in his third year (of training), he was salved with oliban of Punt and perfumes of God's Land and garbed in a kilt of blue linen.[1] When as a cadet he visited a dancing-girl, she said, "Go, Au, and see to your wife. How bitterly she weeps for you! Because of your (catching) fish by night and your (snaring) fowl by day, she is constantly weeping for you."

(Au's letter to his wife): Come north that I may relate to you these words of my comrades and their companions. When they met me to the south of the city, my heart was happy in a faraway place[2] with (my) head upon (my) knees like an orphan at the edge of a strange city. I have come here from my beloved's city and have passed by the great city gate after having met my father on the day of my(?) feast (birthday?) while my mother had gone off to the Sycamore Shrine.

I am one beloved of his father, praised of his mother, and beloved of his brothers and sisters. I never perturbed my father, nor did I show disregard to my mother. I repeat what my instructor said so as to master temperament. I am one who is eminently quiet, who controls his temper, being tight-lipped and devoid of vociferousness, namely, this scribe that I am, who is valuable to his lord and most expert in his calling.

Pray, open up your papyrus scrolls and become a son who is educated in texts profitable from the start, as my father educated me in texts profitable even before him, so that he checked himself from wrongdoing(?). I found that this favored one that I am was impelled ahead as a consequence of my wisdom and my perspicacity. It is the servant who must remain with the drudge woman, so become a son who is educated in texts. As for the scribe in whatever position he has at the Residence, he can never become miserable in it.

Thus it finally concludes successfully.

Notes

1. Variant: "a kilt of my making."
2. I.e., happy in reverie.

II

Letters to and from Royalty

Introduction

At the apex of Egyptian society stood the king, whose nature was both divine and human. Although he was primarily the earthly incarnation of the falcon-god Horus, he was also the son of the sun-god Re. Just as Re regulated the cosmic order, so the king performed the role of Re on earth in defending and maintaining the social order. The king was also the corporate personality of his subjects, and his high priestly function served to integrate human society with the divine realm. In order that the reader may discern the constants and changes in the concept of the divine kingship during the course of pharaonic history, this section provides a chronologically ordered selection of correspondence involving the king either as writer or recipient.

A letter written by the king was called a "decree," the same term also used for more formal royal edicts. A number of royal letters have been preserved as hieroglyphic inscriptions on stone, being copies of letters originally written on papyrus in the cursive hieratic script. In some cases, particularly when the content of the king's letter had broad implications, the document, being a decree, was recorded on stone for public display (Nos. 7, 13, and 15). But also quite personal letters from the king to loyal high officials might be inscribed on the walls of a tomb chapel (Nos. 2–6) or on steles (Nos. 10 and 16) to indicate to the reader the position of honor that the recipient had with the king. Two royal letters, one from the Hyksos king Apophis to the ruler of Kush (No. 14) and the other, purportedly from the Hittite king Muwatallis to Ramesses II (No. 20), were incorporated in the framework of historical texts that served to laud the power of the Egyptian king. In a similar vein are the king's letter and the response to it (Nos. 8 and 9) that were inserted as literary compositions in the Story of Sinuhe, a pseudo-autobiographical work designed to elevate the king's position after a period when the institution of divine kingship had been called into question. The other royal letters that have been preserved on papyrus (Nos. 11, 12, 35, and 39) can be considered genuine letters, with the exception of the letter from Papyrus Anastasi IV (No. 32), which is a student's copy of what might possibly have been a real royal reprimand.

Letters to the Egyptian king have not survived in great abundance, for no royal archives have been found in Egypt except for the Amarna letters, written in Akkadian on clay tablets. New translations of these diplomatic correspondences from Tell el-Amarna have been made by Moran (1992). With the exception of the selection from

17

Papyrus Anastasi II (No. 31), which is a model letter of adulation to the pharaoh that is translated to illustrate aspects of the divine kingship, the remaining letters to the Egyptian king (Nos. 17–19, 21, 33, and 34) can be regarded as copies of genuine letters.

Included in this section is a group of nine letters (Nos. 22–30) involving members of the royal family and its entourage at the Ramesside capital of Pi-Ramessu. Since the letter of Ramesses IX to the high priest Ramessesnakht (No. 35) was from a find that included ancillary correspondences (Nos. 36–38), the whole of this collection has been translated. This letter of Ramesses IX to the high priest of Amon is an important document in illustrating the relationship between two major figures of the period. The peremptory tone of the king's letter suggests that the growing power of the Amon priesthood at the end of the New Kingdom may not have constituted as great a threat to the throne as has often been maintained. A similar imperious quality is evident in Ramesses XI's letter to the viceroy of Kush Panehsy (No. 39), written at the very end of the New Kingdom. Indeed the Old and Middle Kingdom royal letters betray a kinder, gentler king than do the latest royal letters.

There has been no comprehensive treatment of the royal letters from ancient Egypt. For details the reader is referred to "Sources."

The King to His Vizier

2. Sakkara Mastaba of Rashepses
(Dynasty 5: Djedkare-Izezi)

Royal decree to the chief justice and vizier, the overseer of scribes of royal documents, Rashepses:

My Majesty has read at court this very fine letter that you sent on this fine day of very truly gratifying Izezi with what he very truly likes. It was more desirable to My Majesty than anything else to read this letter of yours, for you surely know how to express what My Majesty likes above all else, and your diction is surely more pleasing to me than anything else. My Majesty knows full well that you desire to say everything that My Majesty likes.

O Rashepses, I say to you innumerable times as follows: O you who are beloved of your lord and praised of your lord, who are a favorite of your lord and who are privy to your lord's secrets, it is because Re has given you to me that I know full well that he must love me. As truly as Izezi lives forever, you should express immediately any wish of yours in a letter from you today so that My Majesty might have it fulfilled immediately.

3. Giza Mastaba of Senedjemib
(Dynasty 5: Djedkare-Izezi)

Royal decree to the chief justice and vizier, the overseer of all works of the king and overseer of scribes of royal documents, Senedjemib:

My Majesty has reviewed this ground plan which you sent to be considered at court for the (pool?) area of the broad court(?)¹ belonging to the jubilee palace of "Lotus-of-Izezi." Now you say unto My Majesty that you have made it to a [length] of 1,000 cubits (523 meters) and to a [width] of 440 + cubits (230 + meters) in accordance with what was commanded to you at court. How well you surely know how to express what Izezi likes above all else. It is indeed for Izezi's delight that the god has produced you.

My Majesty knows that you are more skillful than any overseer of works who has ever been in this entire land. I am doing on your behalf something far greater than I ever did for [you]. You have indeed achieved distinction(?) innumerable times, so [you] shall serve as overseer of all works of the king. O Senedjemib Senior, it is with me that I want you to be, for you know full well that I love you.

Year of the Six[teenth(?)] Count, fourth month of the third season, day 28.

4. Giza Mastaba of Senedjemib
(Dynasty 5: Djedkare-Izezi)

Royal decree to the chief justice and vizier, the overseer of scribes of royal documents and overseer of all works of the king, Senedjemib:

My Majesty has read this letter of yours which you wrote in order to inform My Majesty of everything that you have done in the drafting of the inscriptional(?) decoration for the Sacred Marriage Chapel of Izezi, which is in the (lake?) area of the palace. Isn't it truly so that I am gratified thereby? It is not a case of saying something merely by way of gratifying Izezi. May My Majesty be informed immediately of the truth of the matter. Will it in fact get accomplished?

You are one who says what Izezi likes better than any functionary who has ever been in this land. Since My Majesty knows full well that every ship is on an even keel, I know in what way you are surely very useful to me. [Really] pleasing to me is the diction of the overseer of all works of the king. It very truly is to Izezi's gratification. If only [you] might come to [me! But] it means that you are working at this very assiduously. You have acted innumerable times so that [My Majesty] should love you, and you know full well that I love you.

5. Giza Mastaba of Senedjemib
(Dynasty 5: Djedkare-Izezi)

[Consideration has been given to the substance of this letter of yours which you directed to the king] at the palace in order to inform My Majesty that a command of the king was delivered to you regarding [. . . Now you say] unto My Majesty that you are going to make the lake in accordance with what was said at court [. . .] without you. And you say that you are going to [. . .] the jubilee. My Majesty has very much liked hearing these words of yours [. . .] beside you. The *Ka* of Izezi did not appoint you for just any sort of thing in your(?) [. . . You are one] for whom My Majesty [will do] anything which is made known [to] My Majesty because the overseer of all works of the king is immediately mentioned whenever I inspect a project at court, for you are [. . .] that whereof My Majesty commands them to give to him while under the king according as I retire(?) in order to [read] each letter [which arrives from you] every day. It is because Re has given you to me that I know full well that he must love me.

=========== **The King to an Expedition Leader** ===========

6. *Aswan Tomb of Harkhuf*
(Dynasty 6: Pepi II)

Royal decree to the sole companion, lector priest, and commander of Nubian auxiliaries Harkhuf:

Consideration has been given to the substance of this letter of yours which you directed to the king at the palace to let it be known that you have come back down safely from Iam[2] along with the expeditionary force which is with you. You mentioned in this letter of yours that you have brought back all sorts of great and fine gifts which Hathor, lady of Imaau, has given to the *Ka* of the King of Upper and Lower Egypt, Neferkare (Pepi II), may he live forever and ever.

You mentioned in this letter of yours that you have brought back a dwarf of the god's dances from the land of the horizon-dwellers, one like the dwarf which the god's seal-bearer Werdjededkhnum brought back from Punt in the reign of Izezi. You mentioned unto My Majesty that one like him has never been brought back by anyone else who had previously traveled through Iam.

How well indeed you know how to do what your lord loves and praises! If you continue day and night being concerned with doing what your lord loves, praises, and commands, His Majesty will fulfill your many worthy aspirations so as to benefit the son of your son forever, so that all people will say whenever they hear of what My Majesty has done for you, "Is it like that which was done for the sole companion Harkhuf as he was coming back down from Iam, because of the vigilance he displayed in order to do what his lord loves, praises, and commands?"

Come sailing north to the Residence at once! Cast off, bringing back with you this dwarf whom you have brought from the land of the horizon-dwellers, alive, prospering and healthy, for the god's dances in order to amuse and delight the King of Upper and Lower Egypt, Neferkare, may he live forever.

When he goes with you aboard the ship, assign able men so as to be round about him on both sides of the ship lest he fall into the water. When [he] sleeps at night, also assign able men so as to sleep round about him in his tent. Inspect ten times during the night, for My Majesty wishes to see this dwarf more than the products of Sinai or Punt. If you arrive at the Residence with this dwarf still alive, prospering and healthy in your charge, My Majesty will do for you something greater than was done for the god's seal-bearer Werdjededkhnum in the reign of Izezi, reflecting My Majesty's yearning to see this dwarf.

Orders have been delivered to each chief of a new town and to each companion and overseer of priests to command that provisions be exacted from the charge of each: from every estate of the department of supplies and from every temple respectively. No exemption has been made therein.

Sealed by the king personally in Year 2, third month of the first season, day 15.

The King to His Vizier and Governor in Upper Egpyt

7. Coptos Decree M
(Dynasty 8: Neferkauhor)

Royal decree to the god's father, beloved of the god, the city prefect, chief justice and vizier, governor of Upper Egypt, overseer of prophets and stolist of [Min, Shemai] regarding your son, the count and overseer of prophets Idi.

He is hereby count, seal-bearer of the king, governor of Upper Egypt, and overseer of prophets from the south in the first nome of Upper Egypt to the north in the seventh nome of Upper Egypt. It is under his authority that the counts, seal-bearers of the king, sole companions, overseers of prophets, overlords, estate chiefs, and potentates(?) who are there shall function. My Majesty has commanded that he serve as magistrate, that he act exemplarily in these nomes in accordance with your command, and that he be your spokesman. No one shall have a legal claim upon this.

My Majesty has informed you of these nomes, [each] nome named individually: To-sety, Wetjeset-Hor, Nekhen, Waset, Bawy, Iker, and Bat.

It is [in complete harmony] that he shall act in conjunction [with you. The sole companion Iniotef, son of Hemi], has been sent [regarding this].

[Sealed in] the king's own [presence in the second month of the second season, day 20].

=========== The King and a Self-Exiled Retainer in Asia ===========

8. *Sinuhe B, 178-99*
(Dynasty 12: Senwosret I)

Horus, living in birth; the Two Ladies, living in birth; the King of Upper and Lower Egypt, Kheperkare; the Son of Re, Senwosret I, may he live forever and ever. Royal decree to the retainer Sinuhe:

Now this decree of the king is brought to you to inform you that it was through your own heart's decision that you traveled around foreign countries, leaving Kedem for Retenu, and that one country kept handing you over to the next country. What have you done for action to be taken against you? You did not blaspheme so that your speech should be reproved, nor did you speak out against the counsel of the magistrates so that your utterances should be opposed. This notion, it took over your senses. It was not in my mind against you. This heaven of yours (the queen) that is in the palace still endures and prospers today as in her former state in the kingship of the land, and her children are in the palace apartments. You shall accumulate riches that they give you and shall live off their bounty.

Return to Egypt and visit the Residence in which you grew up. You shall kiss the ground at the Great Double Portals and join with the courtiers, for today it is that you have started growing old and lost virility. Ponder the day of burial and the passing into a blessed state.

A night will be appointed for you with balsam oils and bandages from the arms of Tayet. A funeral procession will be made for you on the day of interment, with the mummy case being of gold and its head of lapis lazuli, with the sky³ above you as you lie on the funeral sledge, and with oxen hauling you as chanters precede you. The dance of the Muu will be performed for you at the entrance of your tomb. The menu of offerings will be invoked for you, and sacrifice will be made at your offering slab, your (tomb's) pillars being constructed of limestone amid those of the royal children.

You shall not die abroad! Asiatics shall not inter you! You shall not be placed in a sheep's skin when your grave enclosure is made. All this is too much for one who has roamed the earth. Be concerned for your corpse and come back!

9. *Sinuhe B, 204-38*
(Dynasty 12: Senwosret I)

Copy of the acknowledgment of this decree:

It is the palace servant Sinuhe who says: In very good peace! This flight which I, your humble servant, undertook without comprehension is understood by your *Ka*, O Perfect God, Lord of the Two Lands, beloved of Re and favored of Montu, lord of the Theban nome, and also Amon, lord of the Thrones of the Two Lands, Sobek-Re, lord of Sumenu, Horus, Hathor, Atum and his ennead, Sopdu-Neferbau-Semseru, the eastern Horus, the Lady of Imet—may she enfold your head, the magistrates that are upon the flood-waters, Min-Horus residing in desert lands, Wereret, lady of Punt, Nut, Haroeris-Re, and all gods of Egypt and the Islands of the Sea. May they give life and dominion to your nose[4] and endue you with their bounty. May they give you everlastingness without end and eternity without bounds. May fear of you be bruited abroad in lowland and highlands, for you have subdued what the solar disk encircles. Such is the prayer of this your humble servant on behalf of his lord, who has preserved him from the West.

The lord of perception, who comprehends the commonality, has perceived in the majesty of the palace, that I, your humble servant, was too afraid to mention it. It is like something too great to repeat. He is a great god, the peer of Re, in understanding the mind of one who has voluntarily served him. I, your humble servant, am in the care of one who takes thought for me, while I am placed under your guidance. Your Majesty is the conquering Horus, and your arms are victorious over all lands.

Now may Your Majesty command that there be brought to you the Meki chief from Kedem, the mountain chiefs from out of Keshu, and the Menus chief from the lands of the Fenkhu. They are rulers with renowned names who grew up in love of you. I will not mention Retenu, which belongs to you the same as your dogs.

This flight, which I, your humble servant, undertook, I did not anticipate. It was not in my mind. I did not devise it. I do not know who removed me from my place. It was after the manner of a dream, as when a Delta man sees himself in Elephantine or a marsh-man in Nubia. I did not become afraid, nor was I pursued. I did not hear a word of censure, nor was my name heard in the mouth of a herald. But it was those shudderings of my body as my legs kept scurrying and my heart kept impelling me, for the god who ordained this flight kept drawing me on.

I am not overly(?) presumptuous. Should a man be afraid to know his homeland when Re has instilled respect for you throughout the land and dread of you in every foreign country? Whether I am at the Residence or in this place, it is you who overspreads this horizon. The sun rises at your pleasure, while water is in the river to be drunk as you desire, and air is in the sky to be breathed as you bid. I, your humble servant, shall bequeath to my brood that I, your humble servant, have begotten in this place.[5]

I, your humble servant, have been sent for. Your Majesty can do as he pleases! People live by the breath that you give. May Re, Horus, and Hathor love this august nose of yours, O you whom Montu, lord of the Theban nome, wishes to live forever.

The King to His Chief Treasurer

10. *Berlin Stele 1204*
(Dynasty 12: Senwosret III)

Live Horus, divine in manifestation; the Two Ladies, divine in birth; Horus of Gold, who has become manifest; the King of Upper and Lower Egypt, Khakaure, the Son of Re, Senwosret (III), given life like Re forever. Royal decree to the hereditary noble, count, seal-bearer of the king, sole companion, overseer of the two houses of gold and overseer of the two houses of silver, the chief treasurer Ikhernofret, a possessor of honor:

My Majesty has commanded to have you sail upstream to Abydos of the Thinite nome in order to make a monument for my father Osiris, Foremost of Westerners, that is, to refurbish his mysterious cult image with the electrum which he (Osiris) caused My Majesty to bring back from Nubia in victory and in triumph.

Now it is in the proper way of doing things in benefiting(?) my father Osiris that you will do this since My Majesty sends you, trusting in your doing everything to justify My Majesty's confidence, because it is a fact that you profited from My Majesty's tutelage when as My Majesty's foster son, a sole pupil of my palace, you grew up. My Majesty appointed you as a companion when you were a young man of twenty-six years of age. Because I discerned that you were one of excellent behavior and of keen tongue, who had issued from the womb already wise, My Majesty did this.

And now My Majesty is sending you to do this, for My Majesty has perceived that there is not anyone who should do it except you. Go now and return after you have done according to all that My Majesty has commanded.

The King to His Vizier

11. *P. Brooklyn 35.1446, insert B*
(Dynasty 13: Khendjer?)

[Year 5], third month of the second season, day 20 + . [Copy of] a royal decree that was brought to the office of the [reporter] of the Southern City (Thebes).

Royal decree [to the] city [prefect], vizier, and overseer of the six great law-courts, Ankhu:

Now this decree of the king is brought to you to inform you that the elder of the portal Ibiyau, son of Remenyankh, has made petition saying, "May a warrant be put in writing, drawn up in the pavilion of the king's servant [. . .] against the assistant accountant of prisoners, Pay, who has been making illicit use of the fugitive Sankhu, in having him (Pay) brought to the Residence in order that he may be interrogated about the misappropriation he has committed," so he said.

Now it (the petition) has been granted. Have him brought in custody(?) to the Residence so that you may then take action against him.

Now the King, l.p.h., is prosperous [and flourishing].

12. P. Brooklyn 35.1446, insert C
(Dynasty 13: Khendjer?)

Year 6, third month of the second season, day 3. [Copy of] a second [royal decree] that was brought to the office of the reporter of the Southern City (Thebes).

Royal decree to the [city] prefect, vizier, and overseer of the six great lawcourts, Ankhu:

Now [this decree of] the king is brought [to you to] inform you that the seal-bearer of the Lower Egyptian king and overseer of fields of the Southern City, [Haankhef], son of Ibiyau, has made petition saying, "Some cultivators(?) are in [my] domain engaged in transporting(?) by seizure people of my home to Iatsekhtiu. Let there be given to me from the office of Provider of Laborers some household dependents of my lord(?) by having them given over to me to be household dependents," so he said.

Now it (the petition) has been granted for action to be taken. Now that orders have been given to the warden of the palace(?) that is in the Residence, you shall have a directive issued [to] the wardens of the palace(?) that is in the Southern City so that you may then take action against him.

Now the King, l.p.h., is prosperous and flourishing. May your wish be accordingly!

══════════ The King to Officials in Coptos ══════════

13. Cairo Stele 30770
(Dynasty 17: Nubkheperre Iniotef)

Year 3, third month of the second season, day 25, under the Majesty of the King of Upper and Lower Egypt, Nubkheperre, the Son of Re, Iniotef, given life like Re forever. Royal decree to the seal-bearer of the Lower Egyptian king and mayor of Coptos, Minemhat, to the "king's son" (an honorific title) and commander of Coptos, Kinen, to the seal-bearer of the Lower Egyptian king, stolist of Min and temple scribe, Neferhotep Senior, and to the entire army of Coptos, and all the priestly staff of the temple:

Now this decree is brought to you to inform you that My Majesty, l.p.h., has sent the scribe of the God's Treasury of Amon Siamon and the elder of the portal Amenusera to conduct an investigation into the temple of Min because the priestly staff of the temple of my father Min has approached My Majesty, l.p.h., saying, "An evil situation has developed in this temple in that a sacred relic has been stolen by the one to be deprived of his name, Teti, son of Minhotep." Have him expelled from the temple of my father Min and have him stripped of his temple rank from son to son and heir to heir, he being cast upon the ground and his food stipend, his title deed, and his meat taken away. His name shall not be remembered in this temple as is done to one like him who has rebelled against a sacred relic of his god. His inscriptions shall be removed from the temple of Min and from the treasury as well as from each papyrus roll.

As for any king or any potentate who will pardon him, he shall not assume the White Crown nor wear the Red Crown. He shall not sit upon the Horus-throne of the living, nor shall the Two Ladies be gracious to him as one whom they love.

As for any commander or any mayor who will petition the Lord, l.p.h., to pardon him while he is still alive, his people, his property, and his land-holdings shall be assigned to the divine offering of my father Min, lord of Coptos, and not anyone of his family or of the relatives of his father and mother shall be allowed to be inducted into this rank, but this rank should be conferred on the seal-bearer of the Lower Egyptian king and overseer of a work-center, Minemhat, and its food stipend, its title deed, and its meat given to him, it (the rank) being confirmed in his possession in writing in the temple of my father Min, lord of Coptos, from son to son and heir to heir.

================= **The Hyksos King to the Kushite Ruler** =================

14. *Second Kamose Stele, lines 20-24)*
(Dynasties 15/17: Apophis and Kamose)

Aawoserre, the Son of Re, Apophis greets my son, the ruler of Kush. Why did you accede as ruler without informing me? Do you see what Egypt has done against me? The ruler who is in it, Kamose the Mighty, given life,[6] is assailing me upon my soil—although I did not attack him—the very same way he did against you. It is in order to torment these two lands that he picks them out. Both my land and yours he has ravaged. Come north! Don't blanch(?)! Since he is occupied with me here, there is no one who can be opposed to you in this Egypt. Since I won't let him go until you arrive, we can then divide up the towns of this Egypt, and [both] our [lands] will be happy in joy.

=============== **The King to His Viceroy of Kush** ===============

15. *Cairo Stele 34006*
(Dynasty 18: Thutmose I)

Royal decree to the viceroy and overseer of southern lands, Turoi:

Now this decree of the king is brought to you to inform you that My Majesty, l.p.h., has acceded as King of Upper and Lower Egypt to the Horus-throne of the living, there never to be his like again, and that my titulary has been formulated as "Horus, Mighty Bull, beloved of Maat; the Two Ladies, crowned with the royal serpent, great in strength; Horus of Gold, well supplied with years, causing hearts to live; the King of Upper and Lower Egypt, Aakheperkare, the Son of Re, Thutmose (I), may he live forever and ever."

So you shall have divine offerings presented to the gods of Elephantine in the province of the Head of the South in doing what is praiseworthy on behalf of the life, prosperity, and health of the King of Upper and Lower Egypt Aakheperre, given life, and you shall have the oath established in the name of My Majesty, l.p.h., born to the king's mother, Senisoneb, may she be healthy.

It is a missive to inform you of this, that the king's house is prosperous and flourishing.

[It was recorded in] Year 1, third month of the second season, day 21, the day of the festival of the royal accession.

16. *BMFA Stele 25.632*
(Dynasty 18: Amenhotep II)

Year 23, fourth month of the first season, day 1: the day of the festival of the king's accession. Copy of the decree which His Majesty prepared with his own two hands to [the viceroy Usersatet while His Majesty was in ...⁷ in] the private apartment of Pharaoh, l.p.h., sitting drinking and making holiday.

[Now there is brought to you this decree of the king, who is great] with the sword's stroke, with a mighty [arm], and valiant with his forearm, who has subdued [northerners and overthrown southerners] wherever they are so that there is no longer an opponent in any land. You have taken up residence [in Nubia(?)], a brave who made captures in all foreign countries and a chariot-warrior who fought on behalf of His Majesty, Amenhotep (II), [who has ...] Naharin and set the fate of Pakhaty. O you [possessor of a] woman from Babylon, a maidservant from Byblos, a young maiden from Alalakh and an old woman from Arapkha, the people of Takhsy (in Syria) are all of no account. Of what use are they anyway?

A further communication to the viceroy: Don't be at all lenient with Nubians! Beware of their people and their sorcerers! Keep an eye on that servant of nobodies whom you brought to be appointed as an official because he is not an official whom you would recommend to His Majesty unless it is to let it (the proverb) be heard, "For want of a battle-ax of electrum, hafted(?) with bronze, one sturdy quarterstaff exists in the waterplace and the other exists in the acacia spring(?)." Don't listen to their words! Don't take a report of theirs seriously!

The King from the Steward of Memphis

17. P. Gurob I.1 and I.2
(Dynasty 18: Amenhotep IV)

The servant of the estate Apy communicates to Horus, [Mighty] Bull with lofty plumes; the Two Ladies, great of kingship in Karnak; Horus of Gold, who has put on the crowns in Southern Heliopolis (Thebes); the King of Upper and Lower Egypt, living on Maat, [the Lord of the Two Lands], Neferkheperure; the Son of Re, living on Maat, Amenhotep (IV), the god-who-rules-Thebes, great in his life-span, may he live forever and ever.

May [Ptah with the] benign countenance aid you, he who created your beauty, your true father, from whom you issued to be ruler of the circuit of the sun. May [he] stretch out his [arms] and bring back [for] you southerners prostrate [before] you, while lands [are filled with] terror. May he place them all beneath your sandals while you are Sole Lord, the likeness of Re. [As long] as he keeps shining in the sky, you shall possess eternity and perpetuity with life and years of peace.

[This is] a communication [to the] Lord, l.p.h., to let One (the king) know that the temple of your father Ptah, South-of-his-Wall, lord of Ankhtowy, is prosperous and flourishing, that the palace of Pharaoh, l.p.h., is in good order, that the palace establishments of Pharaoh, l.p.h., are in good order, and that the quarter of Pharaoh, l.p.h., is in good order and secure. The offerings for all the gods and goddesses who are on the soil of Memphis [have been] issued in full, and not any part thereof is held back in arrears, being fit to be offered, pure, acceptable, approved, and selected on behalf of the life, prosperity, and health of the King of Upper and Lower Egypt, living on Maat, the Lord of the Two Lands, Neferkheperure-waenre; the Son of Re, living on Maat, Amenhotep (IV), the god-who-rules-Thebes, great in his life-span, may he live forever and ever.

It is a communication concerning this. Year 5, third month of the second season, day 19.

Address: Pharaoh, l.p.h., the lord, from the steward of Memphis Apy.

===== **The King from the Two Necropolis Scribes** =====

18. *O. Cairo 25676*
(Dynasty 19: Ramesses II)

[A communication] to Pharaoh, l.p.h., our good lord, the [...], the son of Pre-Harakhti, [from] the two necropolis scribes: In life, prosperity and health! This is a missive to inform [Pharaoh, l.p.h.], our good lord.

A further communication with (the wish for) millions of jubilees, a good [...] Tatenen(?), to the effect that Amon-Re, King [of the Gods, Mut], Khonsu, Ptah the Great, South-of-his-Wall, and the gods, those of heaven and those of [earth], have broken the first portal of the august tomb of Pharaoh, [l.p.h., our good] lord, in Year 2, second month of the second season, day 13, using the silver spike and the golden [spike] of King Usermare-setepenre (Ramesses II).⁸ [*End lost*].

===== **The King from His Viceroy of Kush** =====

19. *Kuban Stele, lines 31-36*
(Dynasty 19: Ramesses II)

There arrived one with a letter from the viceroy of vile Kush saying: [...]. O Sovereign, [my] lord, everything [has been carried out in accordance with] what Your Majesty said with your own mouth. When the waters issued from it (the well) at twelve cubits (6.28 meters), four cubits (2.1 meters) were they in depth. [...] in it [...] it outside after the manner of a god in satisfying himself with the love of you. Never had [the like] been done [since the time of the god]. [...] great [...]. The land of Akuyta shouted in great joy. Those who were far away [... at] seeing the well which the ruler has [made]. The water which is in the underworld obeys him. He has drawn forth water from the mountain [...] last year [...] was drawn [...], so said the viceroy in sending a message.

===== **To Pharaoh from the Hittite King** =====

20. *Kadesh Poem 300-320*
(Dynasty 19: Ramesses II)

Thereupon he (Muwatallis) sent his messenger with a letter in his hand bearing the great name of My Majesty, sending greetings to the majesty of the palace, l.p.h., of Re-Harakhti, Mighty Bull, beloved of Maat, the sovereign who protects his army and is energetic with his strong arm, a bulwark for his soldiers on the day of battle; the King of Upper and Lower Egypt, Usermare-setepenre; the Son of Re, the lion, possessor of strength, Ramesses (II), given life forever:

I, your humble servant, speak so as to let it be understood that you are the Son of Re who has issued from his body. He has given you all lands united together. As for the land of Egypt and the land of Khatti, they are yours; and your servants, they are under your feet. Pre, your august father, has given them to you. Do not overwhelm us, for your power is great and your strength weighs heavily upon the land of Khatti. Is it proper for you to keep on slaying your servants with your face savage among them, showing no mercy? Now you spent yesterday slaying myriads, and today you have come back and left no heirs. Do not be harsh in your dealings, O victorious king! Peace is more profitable than warfare. Give us breath!

The King from the Chief Treasurer

21. O. Berlin 12337
(Dynasty 19: Ramesses II)

The royal scribe and chief treasurer Suty communicates to Pharaoh, l.p.h.: In life, prosperity and health! This is a missive [to inform] my good lord, l.p.h., of his goodly plans within the Place of Truth [for] his crew with regard to their annual wages in the following amounts:

31,270 *gay*-bowls of bread
22,763 kyllestis-loaves
250 sacks of lubya-beans by the bushel
[. . .] of *genen*-fruit
132 sacks of assorted *sety*-fruit by the bushel
32,700 assorted fish
100 *beg*-fish of Upper Egypt(?)
43,150 tilapia fish
50 sacks of *tepy*-fish of the Canal of Abu(?)
60 vats of jerked meat
[. . .] calves
33 assorted cattle
18 flanks of red meat
200 loin-cuts of red meat
10 handfuls of entrails
[. . .]
63 intestines(?)

On behalf of (?) one greatly favored, lastingly favored, happy [in] the favor of the king(?) [. . .] of Upper and Lower Egypt, greatly loved in the palace, l.p.h., [. . .] of the Lord of the Two Lands, the royal scribe, city prefect and vizier of Upper and Lower Egypt, Khay, [. . .] the prince, count, and [seal-bearer] of the Lower Egyptian king, beloved [*End lost*].

Princes and Those about Them

22. *P. Leiden I, 368*
Dynasty 19: Ramesses II)

The overseer of cattle Sul communicates to his lord, the *setem*-priest of Ptah, Prince Khaemwase: In life, prosperity and health! This is a missive to inform my lord that I am carrying out properly and efficiently every assignment that has been charged to me.

A further communication to my lord: [. . .] collect(?) [. . .] a great(?) [. . .] in the Estate of Ptah along with the harvest for my lord that is under my authority. Moreover, my lord told me after I had returned, "Have a search made for those retainers of Prince Iotefamon who are in the region of Heracleopolis and have them name their partners, and let the shield-bearer Neferher be charged to bring them back." I reached the region of Heracleopolis and met the Generalissimo's[9] retainer Piay and Prince Iotefamon's retainer as they were bringing six of those people who had been in the jail of the treasury overseer's son. They passed by heading southward, picking up the others.

I am writing to inform my lord that a message should be sent advising me whether they should be brought back while they are still under the supervision of these men. And also, should these retainers be interrogated in Memphis and it be ascertained whether it was Merenptah, the General's son, who [gave the orders] to bring them back since my lord had told him to send out some men to round them up?

23. *P. Leiden I, 367*
(Dynasty 19: Ramesses II)

The servant Meryiotef communicates to his lord, Prince Ramesses-Maatptah: In life, prosperity and health! This is a missive to inform you. I am calling upon all the gods of Pi-Ramessu-miamon, l.p.h., the great *Ka* of Pre-Harakhti, to keep you healthy, to keep you alive, and to keep you in the favor of Ptah, your good lord.

A further communication to my lord: Now such is my luck; in short, I find no letter from you. What's the use of my sending you this string of letters when you aren't answering me a one of them? Farewell!

Address: To Prince Maatptah.

24. P. Leiden I, 366
(Dynasty 19: Ramesses II)

The servant Meryiotef greets the chantress of Amon Ernute: In life, prosperity and health and in the favor of Amon-Re, King of the Gods! I am calling upon Pre-Harakhti in his rising and in his setting, upon Amon of Ramesses-miamon, l.p.h. , upon Ptah of Ramesses-miamon, l.p.h., and (upon) all the gods and goddesses of Pi-Ramessu-miamon, l.p.h., the great Ka of Pre-Harakhti, to keep you healthy, to keep you alive, to keep you prosperous, and to let me see you in health and fill my embrace with you. And further:

I have taken note of all matters about which you wrote me. I am all right. I am alive today, but I don't know my condition tomorrow.

Now with regard to the statement I made that you should write certifying the conformity of the imprint of my seal, you [replied], "See, it is from the very start that I shall write by way of certifying." Why have I trusted in you since you have not been sending me the answers to my letters which I've sent to you? To inform you of them: one by the hand of Prince Ramesses's scribe Huy, one by the hand of the shield-bearer Pensakhmet, one by the hand of Tabes's retainer Usy, and one by the hand of that retainer of (?) Maatptah. The letter which I sent to (Prince) Maatptah was transmitted, but no replies to them have yet been returned. You shall write about your condition immediately, for I'm concerned about you. Farewell!

Address: To the chantress [of Amon Ernute].

25. P. Leiden I, 365
(Dynasty 19: Ramesses II)

[The servant] Meryiotef greets the [servant] Rudefneheh: In life, prosperity and health and in the favor of Amon-Re, King of the Gods! I am calling upon all the gods of Pi-Ramessu-miamon, l.p.h., to keep you healthy, to keep you alive, and to keep you prosperous. And further:

As for what you wrote to the servant Mermaat saying, "Ask the man,[10] 'What is your condition?'" is Mermaat your servant, and I your personal agent? The man is all right.

And as for what you wrote concerning the three girls, they are all right. If only everyone were like them! They set out, and they have returned to you. They are no longer here with us.

A further communication to the chantress of Amon Nubem[. . .]y and to the chantress of Amon Saupatjau as well: How are you? I am calling upon all the gods of Pi-Ramessu-miamon, l.p.h., to keep you healthy, to keep you alive, and to keep you prosperous.

Further, I'm all right. I'm alive today. What does your failing to answer me my letter mean? Are you prospering, or might you die? Farewell!

Address: To the servant Rudefneheh.

26. P. Leiden I, 364
(Dynasty 19: Ramesses II)

The servant Mermaat greets the chantress of Amon Hathor: In life, prosperity and health and in the favor of Amon-Re, King of the Gods! I am calling upon Ptah the Great, South-of-his-Wall, lord of Ankh[towy], upon Pre-Harakhti in his rising and in his setting, and (upon) all the gods and goddesses of Pi-Ramessu-miamon, l.p.h., the great Ka of Pre-Harakhti, to keep you healthy and to keep you alive. And further:

I'm all right today, but I don't know my condition tomorrow. Please write me about your condition through whatever retainer is coming here from you.

A further matter for the servant Rudefneheh as well. How are you? I am calling upon all the gods of Pi-Ramessu-miamon, l.p.h., to keep you healthy.

Address: The servant Mermaat to the servant Rudefneheh.

27. P. Leiden I, 362
(Dynasty 19: Ramesses II)

The singer Pentawere and the singer Paukhed communicate [to their mistress], the Princess Isisnofre: In life, prosperity and health! This is a missive to inform you. I (sic) am calling upon all the gods and goddesses of Pi-Ramessu-miamon, l.p.h., to keep you healthy, to keep you [prosperous], to keep you alive, and to keep you in the favor of Ptah, your god. And further:

We are alive today, but we don't know our condition [tomorrow]. May Ptah bring us back and we see you in good shape(?), for we are exceedingly anxious.

28. P. Leiden I, 360
(Dynasty 19: Ramesses II)

The servant Mersuiotef communicates to his mistress, the chantress of Isis, Tel: In life, prosperity and health and in the favor of Amon-Re, King of the Gods! I am calling upon Pre-Harakhti, upon Amon of Ramesses-miamon, l.p.h., upon Ptah of Ramesses-miamon, l.p.h., upon Seth, great in virility, of

Ramesses-miamon, l.p.h., and upon all the gods and goddesses of Pi-Ramessu-miamon, the great *Ka* of Pre-Harakhti, to keep you healthy, to keep you alive, to keep you prosperous, and to keep you in the favor of Isis, your mistress, and let me see you in health. And further:

The General is all right; his people are all right; and his children are all right. Don't worry about them. We are all right today, but I don't know our condition for the morrow. Farewell!

Address: The servant Mersuiotef to his mistress, the noble lady, Tel.

29. *P. Leiden I, 363*
(Dynasty 19: Ramesses II)

The servant Mersuiotef greets the servant Sebtyemptah: In life, prosperity and health and (in) the favor of Ptah every day! I am calling upon the gods of Pi-Ramessu-miamon, l.p.h., to keep you healthy and to keep you alive. And further:

We are alive today, but we don't know our condition tomorrow. Moreover, please write me about your condition, for I'm concerned about you. Farewell!

Address: The servant Mersuiotef to the servant Sebtyemptah.

30. *P. Leiden I, 361*
(Dynasty 19: Ramesses II)

The servant Shemsenptah greets the servant Petersuemhab: In life, prosperity and health and in the favor of Ptah every day! I am calling upon Ptah and all the gods and goddesses of Pi-Ramessu-miamon, l.p.h., to keep you healthy, to keep you alive, and let me see you in health and fill my embrace with you. And further:

I have taken note of the fact that you wrote inquiring after my welfare. I'm all right. It is Pre who shall inquire after your welfare. And write me about your condition and your health because I'm concerned about you.

It is good if you take notice.

═══════════════ Adulation of the King ═══════════════

31. *P. Anastasi II, 5,6-6,4*
(Dynasty 19: Merenptah)

In life, prosperity and health! This is a missive to inform One (the king) at the Palace, l.p.h., "Beloved-of-Maat," the two horizons in which Re is: Turn your face to me, you shining sun who illumines the Two Lands with your beauty, you solar disk of humankind, who has banished darkness from Egypt. You are similar in nature to your father, Re who rises in the sky. Your rays penetrate the cavern; no place is devoid of your beauty. While you are at rest in your palace, you are told the condition of each land. You learn about the affairs of all lands, for you possess millions of ears. Your eyes are more radiant than the stars of the sky. You can see better than the solar disk. If one speaks—even if the utterance is in a cavern—it descends into your ears. If something is done—even if it is concealed—your eyes see it. O Baenre-miamon (Merenptah), gracious lord, who creates breath.

A Royal Reprimand

32. P. Anastasi IV, 10,8-11,8
(Dynasty 19: Seti II)

This royal decree is brought to you to say: What concern do you have with the Tjukten-Libyans of the Oasis Land that you should send out this scribe of yours to take them off their reconnaissance patrols? If meanwhile neither Pre nor Ptah is going to let anything be heard to counter these rumors that are being heard, and this mayor writes that you have removed the Tjukten who are engaged in reconnoitering, where will you go? Whose house will you be off to? So he (the mayor) will come down upon your head like a mound of sand, and you will be taken away and put there to be a Tjukten for punishment.

The same for the other very great offense that you have now committed in that you let Pharaoh, l.p.h., come to make an excursion to Heliopolis without having sent weapons of the armory in readiness to back up your lord. Why is it that you must do things so apathetically when you should not have let him make the journey? Isn't it so that you have put yourself in the position of other treasury overseers who meddled with a Tjukten of the Oasis so as to take him off his reconnaissance patrol? Are you an exception?

As soon as the dispatch from Pharaoh, l.p.h., reaches you, you shall write a letter to this scribe of yours whom you sent off to the Oasis Land, saying, "Beware of meddling with the Tjukten even to remove just a single one of them, or it will be held against you as a capital offense." And you shall put your letter in the hand of a retainer of yours and send him with the courier very quickly.

The King from His Vizier

33. O. Cairo JE 72467
(Dynasty 19: Seti II)

To the ruler, l.p.h., of(?) [. . .], the possessor of dread, great in renown, who subdues the rebel and makes him desist at his bidding, Userkheperure-miamon, l.p.h.; the Son of Re, Seti (II), l.p.h., [from] his lord's servant, the fan-bearer on the king's right, the city prefect and vizier Hori. This is a missive to inform my lord.

A further communication to my lord to the effect that the Place of Pharaoh, l.p.h., my lord, l.p.h., is well supplied. It is [in] excellent [order. *End lost*].

The King from a Lady in Charge of the Harem

34. P. Gurob III.1, rt.
(Dynasty 19: Seti II)

[*Beginning lost*] Amon [. . .] which I have made, for they are exactly like those which had been made for Pre. I shall have myself boasted about because of them and not let fault be found with me. It is advantageous that my Lord, l.p.h., has had people sent to me to be taught and instructed how to perform this important occupation (of weaving). It is fortunate that my Lord has found someone fit to do that the like of which had not been done for Pre, because those who are here are senior apprentices. It is only such people as are like those people whom my Lord, l.p.h., sent who are capable of functioning and who are capable of receiving my personal instruction, since they are foreigners like those who used to be brought to us in the time of Usermare-setepenre, l.p.h., (Ramesses II), the Great God, your good (grand)-father, and who would tell us, "We were quite a number in the households of the officials," and who would receive instruction and so be able to perform whatever was told them.

This is a missive for One's (the king's) information. Year 2, third month of the first season, day 20.

The King to the High Priest
of Amon and Related Letters

35. P. Cairo B
(Dynasty 20: Ramesses IX)

[Horus, Mighty Bull], appearing in Thebes; the Two Ladies, powerful of falchion, [causing the Two Lands to live; Horus of Gold, rich in years like] Tatenen, [beloved of] Mut, the Sovereign, l.p.h., great in kingship, who has subdued the Nine Bows; the King of Upper and Lower Egypt, [Lord] of the Two Lands, Neferkare-setepenre, l.p.h.; the Son of Re, lord of diadems like Amon, Ramesses (IX), l.p.h., beloved of all the gods.

A royal decree to the high priest of Amon-Re, King of the Gods, Ramesses-nakht, to the following effect:

This royal decree is brought to you to say that I wrote to you through the overseer of Pharaoh's treasury and royal cupbearer Amenhotep, saying, "Send doubly good galena suitable for Pharaoh's eye-paint to the place where One (the king) is," and you sent through him 15 *deben* of galena. When it was given to the physicians of the Bureau of Pharaoh's Physicians at the Residence to be processed, it was discovered to be such weak galena that there was nothing in it suitable for the eye-paint for Pharaoh's use. It was but a single *deben* of galena that was found in it! So it has been returned to you. As soon as this dispatch from Pharaoh, l.p.h., your lord, reaches you, you shall take back this galena which has been returned to you and send 100 *deben* of quadruply good galena suitable to be eye paint for Pharaoh, l.p.h., your lord, to the place where One (the king) is, very quickly.

See, I have written to provide you with authorization. This is a missive to let you know that the Palace is safe and sound. Year 2, first month of the third season, day 19.

Delivered in Year 2, second month of the third season, day 13, by the hand of the chief courier Hori.[11]

36. P. Cairo E
(Dynasty 20: Ramesses IX)

[It is the vizier Neferronpe(?)] who addresses the scribe and chief physician Tjel [of] the Temple of Amon and the retainer Iheby as follows:

I sent you forth to furnish this doubly good galena in an ivory tusk, for Pharaoh, l.p.h., my lord, has said, "Have him send it again." As soon as my letter reaches you, you shall set out at once in order to furnish this galena for Pharaoh, l.p.h., and have it brought at once. Now I have written a letter to the steward of Amon and prophet of the Temple of Khnum(?), Hori, regarding this. The god's father priest Wenennofer of the Temple of Amon shall outfit you to deliver these other things also. Look, be careful and take heed! Get yourselves going!

37. P. Cairo A
(Dynasty 20: Ramesses IX)

[*Beginning lost,* and that I may] see you when you have returned alive and healthy, and that I [may fill my eyes] with the sight of you. Now see, daily I am taking the time calling [upon Min, lord of] Coptos, to give you prosperity every day. And further:

The vizier has come south. Now I am your brother, and [I have never been in need] of products of the desert ever since I became scribe of the fortress [through what] I did so as to make me confident enough on a day like this to say, "My superior will come, and so you shall have deliveries made," so I said. Don't let me be treated as a foolish person when I am at the Residence, for I am one of you.

As soon as my letter reaches you, you shall procure for me some galena from whatever district and supply me with [very good] galena and some tusks(?), some cardamom and acacia wood — these are but a few supplies from the desert that you/we know about. Then shall Amon-Re, King of the Gods, your good lord, who daily spends time serving as a pilot for you, give to you. Don't be neglectful of this commission of mine about which I've written you, for I am your brother, but you [. . .]. Farewell!

38. P. Cairo C-D
(Dynasty 20: Ramesses IX)

It is the high priest of Amon-Re, King of the Gods, Ramessesnakht who addresses the feather-wearing Nubian Anytun, the feather-wearing Nubian Senet, the feather-wearing Nubian Tarbedidi, and the bow-carrying Nubians of the land of Akuyta: In life, prosperity and health and in the favor of Amon-Re, King of the Gods, every day! And further:

I have learned that you have set out as an escort troop along with the members of the gold-washing teams of the Estate of Amon-Re, King of the Gods, who are under my authority and (with those of) any other administration. The energetic arm of Pharaoh, l.p.h., my lord, has cast to the ground all those Beduin enemies of Muked who dwell in Kehkeh on the shore of the Red Sea, it being Amon-Re, King of the Gods, this great god, lord of every land, who went along with you to lend you his support. Rejoice accordingly because of the many good things which Amon-Re, King of the Gods, has done for Pharaoh, l.p.h., his son, in casting to the ground those Beduin enemies who used to come to attack the land of Egypt. May Amon-Re, King of the Gods, favor you, may Montu favor you, and may the *Ka* of Pharaoh, l.p.h., favor you now that you have removed those Beduin enemies who used to come to attack the land of Egypt and have taken them captive. Henceforth you shall do likewise!

I have dispatched this policeman and sent him to you with a list of such supplies as I am regularly furnishing so as to have them brought to you. As soon as my letter reaches you, you shall station yourselves there in the gold-working settlement until these supplies, which I have sent to you under the supervision of this scribe and personal retainer of mine, reach you. And also you are to give your personal attention to those members of this gold-washing team of the Estate of Amon who are under my authority, to have them bring this gold belonging to Amon-Re, King of the Gods, your lord, and to prevent those Beduin from attacking them (the gold-washers). And also you must not come in order to create disturbance in the land of Egypt.

As for what you may be in need of, you shall write me so that I may send it on to you. And you are to be good servants of Amon-Re, King of the Gods, and of Pharaoh, l.p.h., your lord, and see to this.

List of the supplies which are destined for the feather-wearing Nubians and Nubians of the land of Akuyta who went as an escort troop against those Beduin enemies of Muked to cause the energetic arm of Pharaoh, l.p.h., to cast them to the ground:

25 kilts of thin cloth
25 tunics of smooth cloth
25 bronze canteens
25 copper knives
5 copper axes bound at the haft
1,000 good loaves of normal kyllestis-bread
100 triangular cakes of kyllestis-bread
50 assorted small cattle
5 pack-donkeys
1 bushel of condiments
1 bushel of caraway seed.

The King to His Viceroy of Kush

39. P. Turin 1896
(Dynasty 20: Ramesses XI)

[Horus, Mighty Bull, beloved of Re; the Two Ladies, powerful of falchion], vanquishing myriads; Horus of Gold, great in strength, causing the Two Lands to live; the Sovereign, l.p.h., taking pleasure in Maat and pacifying the Two Lands, Menmare-setepenptah, l.p.h.; the Son of Re, lord of diadems, Ramesses (XI), the god-who-rules-Heliopolis, l.p.h.

A royal decree to the viceroy of Kush, royal scribe of the army, overseer of granaries, and leader of Pharaoh's troops, Panehsy, to the following effect.

This royal decree is brought to you to say that I have dispatched Yenes, this majordomo and cupbearer of Pharaoh, l.p.h. He has been sent with those commissions from Pharaoh, l.p.h., his lord, which he has set out to execute in the Southern Region. As soon as this dispatch from Pharaoh, l.p.h., reaches you, you shall cooperate with him to have him carry out the commissions from Pharaoh, l.p.h., his lord, with which he has gone forth. And you shall see to this carrying-stand of this great goddess and finish it up and load it on board a boat and send it under his supervision to the place where One (the king) is.

And you shall send carnelian, red jasper, crystal, corundum, and very many flowers of saffron and flowers of lapis lazuli blue to the place where One (the king) is in order to keep the craftsmen supplied with them. Don't be neglectful of this commission which I have sent to you. See, I have written to instruct you.

This is a missive to let you know that the Palace is safe and sound. Year 17, fourth month of the first season, day 25.

Notes

1. The reading of the signs for "broad court" is uncertain, and a possible alternative is "House of Gold," an expression designating a sculptor's workshop where sacred statues were made.

2. Located in the Sudan.

3. I.e., the baldachin over the mummy.

4. The symbols of life and dominion were presented to the king's nostrils to be inhaled and thus absorbed into his person.

5. I.e., the children born to Sinuhe by his Asiatic wife.

6. Kamose was the last king of the native Theban Dynasty 17 and opposed the Hyksos Apophis. The words, "the Mighty, given life," were surely absent from the original letter.

7. Either Perunefer, the northern royal residence, near Memphis, or possibly the Southern City (Thebes).

8. The reference here is to the initiation of work on Ramesses II's tomb in the Valley of the Kings.

9. This person, subsequently in the letter referred to as the "General," might be Ramesses II himself; see Janssen 1960: 46–47.

10. "The man" here and in the next line could also be a personal name, Prome.

11. This letter took twenty-four days to reach Thebes from the king's Delta residence, hardly a case of "posthaste special delivery."

III

Letters to and from the Vizier

Introduction

Next to the king the most powerful figure in the land was the vizier, who controlled the administrative bureaucracy and functioned as head of the judiciary. His executive responsibilities were manifold, and the onerousness of the office of vizier, described as being "bitter," demanded an individual of extraordinary wisdom and knowledge to maintain the efficient operation of a diversity of governmental agencies including the treasury, royal and public works, agriculture, riverine transport, and the army and navy. Much of the vizier's time was spent hearing without partiality the petitions of citizens. Two Old Kingdom viziers, Ptahhotep and Kagemni's father, are credited with the authorship of two wisdom texts; and of an Eighteenth Dynasty vizier Rekhmire it is said, "There is nothing that the god has shut away from him. There is nothing that he is ignorant of in heaven, on earth, or in any hidden place of the underworld" (Sethe 1906: 1071).

As prime minister, the vizier was in close contact with the king, for whom he served as a "mouth(piece) that brings contentment in the whole land," and he was "the great curtain of the entire land and great screen sheltering His Majesty, l.p.h., one according to whose every command things are carried out and regarding all whose projects no one is idle" (No. 52). Articulating and executing the king's will, the vizier also served as a sort of filter deciding which matters were of sufficient importance to bring to the king's attention.

Letters written by the king to the vizier (Nos. 2-5, 7, 11, and 12) have been translated in Part II above. Although several of these royal letters refer to the king's receiving pleasing letters from the vizier, only one partially preserved letter from the vizier to the king has actually survived (No. 33, also translated in Part II).

The extant letters from the vizier to subordinates include three administrative orders from the Twelfth Dynasty vizier Iniotefoker dealing with the outfitting of ships at a dockyard in the Thinite nome and the delivery of food supplies to the Residence (Nos. 41-43), three Ramesside letters (Nos. 51, 53, and 59) dealing with the wages and provisioning of the Deir el-Medina crew of tomb decorators and work on the royal tombs in the Valley of the Kings, and No. 61 from the reign of Ramesses XI concerned with contingents of Medjay-police and Meshwesh-Libyans in the Delta. Letter No. 36, translated in Part II, was probably a vizier's order to supply galena for Ramesses IX's personal use. Since letters from viziers to subordinates are

41

executive orders, they are devoid of any greetings and are generally imperious in tone, but unlike royal letters they are not described as decrees.

More numerous are letters sent by subordinates to the vizier. With the exception of the Sixth Dynasty letter No. 40, all relate to affairs of the Ramesside Deir el-Medina community. No. 40 is striking because of the total absence of any felicitations and the blunt manner in which the writer complains to his superior. The Ramesside letters to the vizier are more polite, but not obsequious, usually employing a set formula of communication in which the vizier is referred to as the writer's lord, and the greeting is limited to a terse wish, "In life, prosperity and health!" In several letters (Nos. 47, 48, and 56) the writer mentions that he is calling on various deities. However, the principal object of these invocations is the well-being of Pharaoh and only secondarily the vizier's continuance in Pharaoh's favor. Despite the vizier's exalted status, his underlings do not reveal themselves as overly cowed by his authority and often boldly express their grievances.

In the following letters the term "Construction Site" refers to the royal tomb of the reigning pharaoh that was being excavated in the Valley of the Kings, while the expressions "Place of Pharaoh" and "Great Place (of Pharaoh)" both designate the general area of the royal necropolis in western Thebes that was guarded by watchposts. "The Village" was the workmen's settlement of Deir el-Medina, located in the Theban necropolis.

A Protest to the Vizier

40. P. Cairo JE 49623
(Dynasty 6)

[Year] 11, first month of the third season, day 23. It is the commander of (work) troops who says:

The chief justice and vizier's letter has been delivered to me, your humble servant, so as to bring the detachment of crewmen of the Tura quarries to get clothing in his presence at the Western Enclosure.[1] However, I, your humble servant, am protesting against the necessity of out-of-the-way locations since you[2] are going to come anyway to Tura with the barge, whereas, I, your humble servant, have to spend six days at the Residence with this detachment before it gets clothing. That is what obstructs the work in my, your humble servant's, charge, since it is one day only that needs be wasted for this detachment to get clothing. I, your humble servant, speak that you may be informed.

=========== Orders from the Vizier ===========

41. P. Reisner II, Section D
(Dynasty 12: Senwosret I)

Year 17, second month of the first season, day 7.

It is the city prefect, vizier, and overseer of the six great lawcourts, Iniotefoker, who commands the steward(s): Montuser's son Montuser, Rudjahau's son [Sobekankh], Hedjenenu's son Iniotef, Djebas's son Dedu's son Dedu, Iy's son Anhurhotep, Nakhti's son Ankeku, and Iniotef's son Senankhu:

[. . .]. Procure gear(?) for yourselves from whatever equipment there is. It is fully outfitted that each one of you shall be at his quay. It is I who have written about the cargo, and now it is each one of [you] who should take the oar-blades and boards(?) in his own boat without letting any fall into [. . .], and supply(?) the . . . -(items) about which I wrote to you to be selected from all the choicest of your store(?). You shall act so that the vizier's scribe Nakht finds your stores(?) of . . . -(items) at the riverbank since I have sent him to load them. And muster for me thirty men for the crew of the boat of each one of you from whatever able-bodied men there are.

Delivered by the dog-keeper Mesu's son Iniotef of(?) the crew of Siagerteb(?).

42. P. Reisner II, Section E
(Dynasty 12: Senwosret I)

Year 17, second month of the first season, day 8.

It is the city prefect, vizier, and overseer of the six great lawcourts, Iniotefoker, who commands the stewards of the palace administration who are in the Thinite nome:

You must get yourselves readied and outfit(?) yourselves in accordance with all that I have ordered you, and let there be sent downstream to the Residence 150(?) *hekat*-measures of wheat, a double(?) *hekat*-measure of malted barley, and 10,000 *ter*-loaves from each one of you, since I shall reckon them at the Residence. To furnish this wheat in the form of new wheat is something to be attained(?). You shall act so that it is readied. And supply a slave-girl of the labor establishment who is able-bodied [. . .] of each one of you with(?) him.

Delivered by the dog-keeper Montuhotep's son Montuhotep and Iniotef's son Sonbef of(?) the crew of Siagerteb(?).

43. P. Reisner II, Section G
(Dynasty 12: Senwosret I)

It is the city prefect, vizier, and overseer of the six great lawcourts, Iniotefoker, who commands the stewards of the palace administration who are in the Thinite nome:

As for whoever [of you] is dry-docked(?) at a dockyard workshop and whose carpenters have been requisitioned, let him write me about his carpenters who have been requisitioned that I might then have them returned to him. Moreover, as for the stewards who [may] take the boats belonging to the gateway of the palace, here is the list [thereof]: The steward Montuser's son Montuser, the steward Rudjahau's son Sobekankhu, Hedjenenu's son Iniotef, Djebas's son Dedu's son Dedu, Iy's son Anhurhotep, Nakhti's son Ankeku, Iniotef's son Senankhu.

See, [. . .] this fleet of yours lest [. . .] see the [. . .] white(washed?) timber [. . .] the fleet in festivity. As for the shipwrights, each one [. . .] with white(washed?) timber from which one's eyes must be shielded(?)[3] [. . .] by filling the quota of *sekheru*-planks and planing the post [. . .] in the presence of the shipwrights, each one. Now send your scribes to receive for you the white(wash?) [. . .] that is coming by the boats.

══════════ Reports to the Vizier ══════════

44. O. Gardiner 13
(Dynasty 19: Ramesses II)

The [chief?] scribe [Inu]shefenu communicates to [his lord], the fan-[bearer] on the king's right, the city prefect and vizier Paser: In life, prosperity and health! This is a missive to inform my lord.

A further communication to my lord to the effect that I have delivered the necropolis wages in full in perfect order. There are not any arrears therein. The outside administrators received them and took them to the necropolis community. But see, I spent four full months en route having no one else with me in the boat except for one of my two boys. (*A certain individual*), who had been sent on this mission, recruited them to be servicemen, while I myself stayed with the elder since there was no one else. I wrote the administrators asking them to send me men to bring me south, but they failed to [send me] any men. And so I wrote the authorities of Hutnesu [. . .], and they sent me four laborers, who brought me south.

45. O. Toronto A 11, vs. 13-25+12-23
(Dynasty 19: Ramesses II)

The scribe Nebre communicates to his lord, the fan-bearer on the king's right, the overseer of the crew in the Place of Truth, the chief treasurer, the overseer of priests of all the gods of Upper Egypt, the city prefect and vizier, who administers justice, Paser: In life, prosperity and health! This is a missive to inform my [lord].

The Village of Pharaoh, l.p.h., that is under my lord's authority is in excellent order, and every watchpost that is in its vicinity is secure. As for the servants of Pharaoh, l.p.h., who are in it, they are being given their wages that have been granted them [by my lord. I am] calling upon Amon, Ptah, and Pre [. . . that] Pharaoh, l.p.h., [our good lord, l.p.h.], may be preserved in health, and [. . .] to give it to you here eternally while [my lord continues to be] in [his] favor [every day].

A further communication to my lord to the effect that my lord's estate is providing for them. It is a large consumption(?). To inform my lord of the [. . .] that are there.

46. O. Gardiner 71
(Dynasty 19: Ramesses II)

The scribe Mose communicates to his lord, the fan-bearer on the [king's] right, the city prefect and vizier Paser [. . .]:

[I am] carrying out very properly every assignment that my lord has given. I won't let my [lord] find fault with me. [. . .]. The overseer of the granaries Kherue[f] was sent out to inspect the stalls of Pharaoh's palace establishment, [and he] summoned us beside the portal of Pharaoh, l.p.h., saying, "Have the [. . .] made ready." [. . .] their fatted cattle. Their needs have been met(?) by rounding(?) them up like [. . .] necropolis [. . .], and someone sealed [End lost].

47. O. Toronto A 11, rt. 1-11
(Dynasty 19: Ramesses II)

The servant [. . . communicates to] his lord, [the city] prefect [and vizier Khay: In life, prosperity and health! This is a missive to inform my lord that] the Village [of Pharaoh, l.p.h., that is under my lord's authority is in excellent order and the] servants of Pharaoh, l.p.h., [who are in it are prospering(?). The wages] which my lord has given them are in proper order. [I] am calling [upon] Amon-Re, King of the Gods, upon Mut, [. . . A]mon, and upon Khonsu in Thebes, who initiates(?) the new moon, lord of heaven, [. . .], Horus-Neferhotep, [to keep] Pharaoh, l.p.h., your good lord, l.p.h., [healthy] and to let him achieve the duration of the mountains, the sky, and the water, being [in] the house of his father Re, lord of eternity and ruler of everlastingness, while my lord continues to be in his favor every [day].

A further communication [to] my lord: May my [lord] please give his personal attention to the crew and give them their wa[ges].

(Copied) by the scribe Siamon.

48. O. Toronto A 11, rt. 12-30
(Dynasty 19: Ramesses II)

The chief of police Mininuy communicates to [his] lord, the city prefect and vizier Khay: In life, prosperity and health! This is a missive to inform my lord.

A further communication [to] my lord to the effect that the Great Place of Pharaoh, l.p.h., that is [under] my lord's authority is in excellent order, and the watchposts in [its] vicinity are safe and sound. The yearly wages have been delivered; they are in excellent order, comprising (fire)wood, vegetables, fish, and new [pottery]. I am calling upon Amon, Ptah, Pre, and all the gods of the Place of Truth to keep Pharaoh, l.p.h., my good lord, healthy and to keep my lord in his favor daily.

A further communication to my lord to the effect that I have been my lord's veteran servant since Year 7 of King Djeserkheperu[re] (Haremhab). I ran ahead of Pharaoh's horses, held the reins(?) for him, and yoked up for him. I made report to him, and he called upon my name in the presence of the Council of the Thirty. Not any fault was found in me.

I served as policeman of the West of Thebes, guarding the watchposts of his Great Place. I was appointed chief of police, being handsomely rewarded on account of the goodness of [my] conduct.

Now look, the chief of police Nakhtsobeki has been letting the Great Place of Pharaoh, l.p.h., in which I am (employed), go to ruin(?). [I am informing] my lord of his failings(?). He has been beating my policemen in conducting investigations(?). "You are an old man, and I am young," so he says to me. "Put the place in order for me. You are a . . . ," so he says to me. He appropriated my fields in the countryside. He appropriated two planted with vegetables, which belong to my lord as the vizier's share. He gave them to the chief of police Monturekh and gave the rest [to] the high priest of Montu. He appropriated my grain while it was stowed in the countryside. This is a missive to inform my lord.

The draftsman Sia[mon].

49. O. Toronto A 11, vs. 1-13
(Dynasty 19: Ramesses II)

The workman in the Place of Truth Anhurkhau communicates to his lord, the fan-bearer [on the king's] right, the overseer of the crew in the Place of

Truth, the city prefect and vizier, who administers justice, Khay: In life, prosperity and health! This is a missive to inform my lord.

A further communication to my [lord] to the effect that we have been working [in] the places (the royal tombs) which my lord said must be decorated in proper order, but there are [no more] pigments at our disposal(?). May my lord [let] me carry out his good purposes and [have] a message sent that Pharaoh, l.p.h., may be informed. And have a dispatch sent to the majordomo of Ne, to the high priest of Amon and the second prophet (of Amon), to the mayor of Ne, and to the administrators who are managing in the treasury of Pharaoh, l.p.h., in order to supply us with whatever we require.

List for my lord's information: yellow ochre, gum, orpiment, realgar, red ochre, blue frit, green frit, fresh tallow for lighting and old clothes for wicks. And so I shall carry out [each] assignment that my [lord] has given.

50. O. Cairo 25832
(Dynasty 19: Ramesses II)

The necropolis scribe [Kenhi]khopeshef communicates [to] his [lord], the fan-bearer on the king's right, the city prefect and vizier Khay: In life, prosperity and health! This is a missive to inform my lord.

A further communication to my lord to the effect that the Place of Pharaoh, l.p.h., which [. . . is in excellent order], and the watchposts are calm. [No harm has befallen] them. [. . . are] delivering the necropolis wages [. . .], each [one] of them. I [am . . .] the Construction Site [. . .] the vizier properly [. . .] excess of work(?) [. . .].

[From the necropolis scribe] Meryre and [the necropolis] scribe Penta[were], saying further: What's the point of our telling you to send gypsum to the Construction Site of Pharaoh, l.p.h.? You haven't been about to send any for seven whole months. [. . .] send us gypsum. Now [we are] mentioning it [. . .] hear. What's the point of [. . .]? [The Construction Site(?) of] Pharaoh, l.p.h., is in need of gypsum. [As soon as our] letter reaches you, send [us] gypsum very quickly right now. [. . .] Good is my [End lost].

Orders from the Vizier

51. O. DM 114
(Dynasty 19: Ramesses II)

It is the fan-bearer on the king's right, royal scribe, the city prefect and vizier Khay who addresses the foreman Nebnefer to the effect that this letter is brought to you to say:

Please be very attentive in properly carrying out every assignment of the Great Place of Pharaoh, l.p.h., in which you are (employed). Don't let fault be found with you! And you are to inquire about the crew's wages which derive from the treasury of Pharaoh, l.p.h. Don't let any part of them be withheld in arrears because the administrators of the necropolis have written to me about your wages, which derive from the treasury of Pharaoh, l.p.h., saying, "Let them be issued to them."

Now I shall be traveling downstream to the place where One (the king) is, and I shall inform Pharaoh, l.p.h., of your needs. Now I shall be sending the chief scribe Paser on business to Ne. As soon as he comes to you at the Gateway of the Necropolis, you shall come to meet him there and send him back to us with word about your condition.[4]

A Report to the Vizier

52. P. Chester Beatty III, vs. 4-5
(Dynasty 19: Merenptah)

The scribe Kenhikhopeshef of the Great Necropolis of Baenre-miamon; the Son of Re, Merenptah-hetephimaat, in the Estate of Amon communicates to his lord, the fan-bearer [on] the king's right, the city prefect and vizier of Upper and Lower Egypt, Panehsy: In life, prosperity and health! This is a missive to inform my lord.

A further communication to my lord to the effect that the Great Place of Pharaoh, l.p.h., that is [under] my lord's authority is in good order, and the watchposts are calm. No harm has befallen them. And we are working quite assiduously in the Great Place of Pharaoh, l.p.h. Since it is with good and excellent work that we are building, the will of Pharaoh, l.p.h., our good lord, is being carried out. May Pharaoh, l.p.h., our lord, pass his lifetime as lord of every land and exercise the kingship which Pre, his father, exercised as king, being ruler of all that the solar disk encircles, while the true scribe of the king, his beloved, the fan-bearer on the king's right, who is the mouth-(piece) that brings contentment in the whole land, the principal favorite of His Majesty, l.p.h., the great curtain of the entire land and great screen sheltering His Majesty, l.p.h., one according to whose every command things are carried out and regarding all whose projects no one is idle, the city prefect and vizier Panehsy continues to be in his (Pharaoh's) favor every day.

A further communication to my lord to the effect that we are not being supplied with spikes and gypsum. The workmen of Pharaoh, l.p.h., have finished off the remainder(?) of spikes that were in their hands. May my lord mention this as well to the overseer of the treasury of Pharaoh, l.p.h., and may he write to the deputy of the treasury of Pharaoh, l.p.h., Piay so he may supply spikes and baskets. And may he write to the two deputies of works to have them meet our requirements for gypsum, and may he write to the two necropolis scribes to have us supplied with tools. And may he write [to] the scribes to have them issue our rations because the chief [of scribes] of the offering table Pay has been here until today, and we are being disregarded so as to prevent our voices from being heard owing to the fact that Pharaoh, l.p.h., our good lord, is now so far from us, and One (the king) did not [. . .] fight [. . .].

Send [. . .] kilts of good quality smooth cloth, one shawl of good quality smooth cloth, [. . .], loincloths of good quality smooth cloth, [. . .] clews of yarn, [. . .], and five baskets from the citizeness Heret, your sister, [. . .], and he [. . .] one small bronze double-edged knife for the native of the necropolis community [. . .].

Now as soon as the boat sets sail, I will bring you your articles of joinery. [. . . I have taken note of] the fact that you mentioned the small bed which was in the course of fabrication [. . . ordering] to have it completed, and so I gave it to a colleague of mine. [*Remainder fragmentary.*]

Orders from the Vizier

53. O. Michaelides 66, rt.
(Dynasty 19: Merenptah)

[It is the fan-bearer on the king's right, the city] prefect [and vizier *name lost*] who addresses the foreman Neferhotep and the [necropolis] scribe [Amenemope(?)]. This [letter is brought to you] to say, "Attend to the Great Place of Pharaoh, l.p.h., in which you are (employed) [and receive] the wages of [the crew . . .] for him daily." [And] further:

The scribe [. . .] has dispatched [. . .] regarding(?) this scribe [. . .] waiting there with you as scribe of the necropolis and of the outside service personnel. As soon as he reaches you, you shall give him your attention and pick up the orders he will be issuing.

Reports to the Vizier

54. O. Cairo 25831
(late Dynasty 19–early Dynasty 20)

The necropolis guardian [*name lost*] communicates to his lord, the [fan]-bearer [on the king's right, the city prefect and vizier] Hori: In life, prosperity and health! This is a missive to inform [my lord] that you, the vizier, had me take an oath not to [mistreat(?)] those people among whom I am (employed), as you said. Now look, [. . .] are working for Pharaoh, l.p.h., as well, all according to written instructions of [. . .] to the effect that a certain widow's daughter left in Year 1, second month of the first season, day 20, and she [. . .] that(?) Pharaoh, l.p.h., gave regarding the captains [. . .] together with the guardian. She reached the watchpost [. . .]. May my [lord] send his administrators [to] hear her deposition.

55. O. Nash 11 = O. BM 65933
(Dynasty 20: Ramesses III)

The fan-bearer [on the king's right, the city prefect and vizier To]. The foreman Hay [and the foreman Khonsu] communicate to their [lord: In life, prosperity and health! This is a missive to inform] our lord.

A further communication to our lord to the effect that we are working at the Construction Site, on which you, the vizier, commissioned us, and we are in no way slackening. Our lord will boast of us when he comes to cause Amon to appear in procession in his [feast].

Moreover, we have caused(?) the statue of [. . .], which he said to have made, to be made, so that one statue of Pharaoh, l.p.h., [is . . .], while a second statue of [. . .] is counterbalanced [with] the statue of Pharaoh, l.p.h., itself. We caused it to stand in the presence of Hathor, the goodly mother of Pharaoh, l.p.h.

Send us copper (money) for the wicks.

56. O. Oriental Institute 16991
(Dynasty 20: Ramesses III)

The fan-bearer on the king's right, the city prefect and vizier To. The scribe Neferhotep communicates to his lord: In life, prosperity and health! This is a missive to inform my lord.

A further communication to my lord to the effect that I am calling upon Amon-Re, King of the Gods, Mut and Khonsu, upon Pre-Harakhti, upon Amon of Menset, upon Nofretari of Menset, upon Amon of the Thrones of the Two Lands, upon Amon of the Beautiful Encounter, upon Ptah of Ramesses-miamon, upon Ptah of the Place of Beauty (Valley of the Queens) to the south of the Village, upon Hathor, mistress of the West, to its north, and upon Amenophis, who takes his seat in the vicinity of the West Side, to keep Pharaoh, l.p.h., my good lord, healthy and to let him celebrate millions of jubilees as great ruler of every land forever and ever while you continue to be in his favor every day.

A further communication to my lord to the effect that I am working on the princes' tombs which my lord commanded to be made, I am working very properly and very excellently with good work and with excellent work.

Let not my lord worry about them, since I am working very assiduously and am in no way slackening.

A further communication to my lord to the effect that we are exceedingly impoverished. All supplies for us that derive from the treasury, that derive from the granary, and that derive from the storehouse have been allowed to run out. A load of excavated(?) stone isn't light! Six *oipe*-measures of grain have been taken away from us besides only to be given to us as six *oipe*-measures of dirt.

May my lord provide us with a means for staying alive, since we are already starving. We are no longer living if nothing whatsoever is given to us.

57. O. BM 50734+O. Gardiner 99+O. Cairo 25673
(Dynasty 20: Ramesses III or later)

The deputy of the crew Amenkhau communicates to his lord: In life, prosperity and health! This is a missive to inform my lord that my lord forced me into being an opposing party to his administrators when he wrote to us at the Gateway—ineptitude was displayed—saying, "What's the meaning of these [matters]? I, the vizier, have asked for an explanation from him (Amenkhau) at the Gateway." "You shall answer him," so they kept urging me on account of their reprehensible actions.

The third month of the first season, day 6, was spent with invectives being heaped upon the *wab*-priest of Maat, saying, "You sent a letter to where my lord is, which should not have been sent." Let my lord seek out the person who fabricated those lies which should not have been told.

See, I am informing him (my lord) of every [. . .] who went up [. . .] his companions, and they kept him detained in the Village—to inform you of his name: the slave-boy Usermarenakht—after his companions had been fetched. They have been made to look at the great statues at night, having no captains, no deputy, and no controllers to go before them.

58. O. Gardiner 59
(Dynasty 20: Ramesses IV)

[. . . to the vizier] Neferronpe: In life, prosperity and health! This is a missive to inform my lord.

A further communication to my [lord] to the effect that we are working very properly at the great Construction Site of Pharaoh, l.p.h., with good work in a construction for eternity. And we don't ask for anything.

To let my lord know that as regards the (fire)wood, the vegetables, [the *neheh*]-oil, fish, our(?) clothing, our(?) tallow and rations, [my] lord himself has provided for us a means of subsistence.

===== **Orders from the Vizier** =====

59. P. DM 28
(Dynasty 20: Ramesses IV–IX)

It is the fan-bearer on the king's right, the city prefect and vizier Nefer-ronpe [who addresses] the necropolis [administrators], the foreman Nekhemmut and the foreman [Anhurkhau(?) to the effect that] this letter is brought to you to say:

Give your personal attention to carry out the assignments [of the Place of Pharaoh, l.p.h.], in which you are (employed). Don't let yourselves be found fault with. And [further:

I submitted] your memoranda regarding your wages before Pharaoh, l.p.h., [and he] decided to give them all. See, [. . .] the first (supplies) have been placed in the boat of the divine standards of the House of [. . .], being handed over to the scribe of the temples Djeba and the *wab*-priest Ka[. . .] for you in a document bearing the imprint of my seal. As soon as they [reach you, you shall] receive them and give each man his due. See, [I shall] send you the other things which I shall be receiving. [You are to write] me about each memorandum regarding the Place of Pharaoh, l.p.h., [in which] you are (employed). I shall send you your drawings[5] [now that] they have been decided upon. I shall send them to you at once. [You shall] improve your-selves and energize yourselves in your [occupation], so that I may boast of you and you may spend many a day [. . .]. Now see, I opened up the Con-struction Site for you. Don't be remiss on your part. Let them(?) be done, the high deeds which you shall carry out. Now I have decided upon the [draw-ings which] you mentioned. I shall send them to you at once [. . .] all [the] memoranda. Please take note of them.

Address: The fan-bearer on the king's right, the city prefect and vizier to [the necropolis] administrators. [Delivered in Year . . . , month . . . of the . . . season], day 18, by the hand of the vizier's scribe Djeba.

===== **Report to the Vizier on a Transaction** =====

60. P. DM 13
(Dynasty 20: Ramesses IX)

[The fan-bearer] on the king's right, the city prefect and vizier Nebmare-nakht. [The carpenter of the Lord of the Two Lands] Maanakhtef com-municates to his lord: [In life, prosperity and health! This is a missive] to inform my lord.

[. . .] copper with(?) a donkey, [. . .] thirty garlands, [. . .] one goat(?) valued at five *deben*, six *khar*-measures of emmer valued at twenty-four *deben;* again [. . .] *oipe*-measure [. . .], three *hin*-measures of *neheh*-oil valued at three(?) *deben, ibu*-fruit, [. . .], gum . . . valued at one *deben*.

===================== Orders from the Vizier =====================

61. P. Louvre 3169
(Dynasty 20: Ramesses XI)

It is the vizier of the land who addresses [. . .]:

As soon as the captain of police Ser[montu reaches you, you shall] return at once with him and (with) all men of the Medjay-police contingents that are with you in the town of Perhebit (in the northern Delta). And don't let a single man of them linger. (But) it is only after you have properly ascertained the state of the Meshwesh-Libyans so that you can return that I will call them (the Medjay-police) up according to their name-list, which I have in my possession in writing. Don't be remiss on your part either! Pay heed, pay heed! Please take note of this.

Notes

1. I.e., the Djoser pyramid complex, which served as the administrative center of the Sakkara necropolis in the latter half of the Old Kingdom.
2. Here and in the final sentence of the letter the recipient is obliquely referred to by a title meaning "archivist," but the sense is "you."
3. Perhaps an allusion to the brightness of the wood.
4. Or, "and [have] him write to us about your condition."
5. Probably the preliminary sketches of scenes for the decoration of the royal tomb.

IV

Letters from the Old
and Early Middle Kingdoms

Introduction

Considering the remoteness in time of the Pyramid Age, it is not surprising that so few papyrus letters have survived from the Old Kingdom. Letters Nos. 62 and 63 are the oldest such documents. Both derive from the funerary temple of Neferirkare-Kakai at Abusir during the reign of Djedkare-Izezi of the Fifth Dynasty, several of whose own letters have been translated in Part II (Nos. 2–5). The Sixth Dynasty letters are of diverse origin. Nos. 64 and 66 were found at Sakkara, while No. 65 is believed to have come from the island of Elephantine, the source of an archive of Old Kingdom papyri that includes No. 67, dealing with the crimes of a crooked count. The Nubian troops mentioned in this letter, which can be dated to the Eighth Dynasty (Edel 1970: 117), were possibly serving as Egyptian mercenaries, a role they were to play during the troubled First Intermediate Period that followed the collapse of the Old Kingdom.

The divided administration of Egypt during the First Intermediate Period ended when the Theban king Mentuhotep II defeated the Heracleopolitan dynasty to the north and reunified the country. The remaining letters in Part IV were written during the period immediately following the death of Mentuhotep II before intensive measures were undertaken in the Twelfth Dynasty to reconstitute a scribal bureaucracy loyal to the king. All the letters translated here probably came from Thebes and are the products of somewhat unsophisticated scribes of the provincial south. With the exception of the fragmentary letter No. 74, the correspondences of the early Middle Kingdom have been edited by James (1962).

The most important of these documents are the Hekanakht correspondences (Nos. 68–71), two of which are among the longest letters surviving from ancient Egypt. Also translated and discussed by Baer (1963) and more recently by Goedicke (1984), these letters, three of which (Nos. 68–70) were written by the gentleman farmer Hekanakht, throw considerable light on the subject of private ownership and rental of land. Shrewd in his business dealings, Hekanakht appears as a miserly individual. Considering the number of people he had in his household, it was more profitable for him to rent than to purchase land for cultivation, and thus he accumulated fluid capital reserves which he could ultimately use for his burial expenses. Being himself a mortuary priest in the Theban necropolis, Hekanakht was fully aware of the cost of a decent burial, which was, in the long run, more important to an Egyptian than social status in this life.

In the Hekanakht letters there are references to a woman, whose designation I have translated by "(new?) wife," though translated as "concubine" by James and Baer and as "bride" by Goedicke. Since there is no reference to any other woman who might be identified as Hekanakht's primary wife, it does not appear that he was one of those very rare commoners practicing polygamy in ancient Egypt. With Ward (1986: 65–69) I believe that the term used to identify this woman conveys her legal status as a second wife, taken after the death of the first spouse. The existence of food shortages mentioned in letter No. 69 reflects a situation resulting from low inundations, which also marked the First Intermediate Period.

Several of the early Middle Kingdom letters employ epistolary formulae similar to those found in the Book of Kemit, translated in Part I. Letters Nos. 70, 72, and 73 include Arsaphes, lord of Heracleopolis, among the gods that are invoked. Since Heracleopolis had been the seat of the royal house that the Theban kings had previously opposed and defeated, it may seem strange that the deity of a former enemy was so easily accepted by the Thebans. However, Theban recognition of the religious creativity and cultural superiority of the Heracleopolitans is indicated by the presence of Heracleopolitan mortuary texts in tombs at Thebes. Thebans also brought artists from the north to impart a higher degree of sophistication to the provincial style that had characterized the Theban Eleventh Dynasty.

=========================== Private Affairs ===========================

62. *P. Berlin 11301*
(Dynasty 5: Djedkare-Izezi)

[*Beginning lost.* May you be justified with Ptah, South-of-his-Wall, with the Foremost] of the Tjenenet-sanctuary, with the august Djed-pillar, and with all the gods. May they keep you alive and do for you everything good every day and also everything [you] desire. [. . .] which you [caused] to be issued to the place where [I] am because [I] complained so much [that although] I had caused you to be satisfied when I supplied the foodstuffs, I myself never got any. I am like [. . .] in the register of those adjudged. Isn't it owing to

the magistrates of the portico of the lawcourt that I have returned? Isn't it
[. . .] that I have returned from there?

As Re, Hathor, and all the gods desire that King Izezi should live forever
and ever, I am lodging a complaint through the commissioners concerning
a case of collecting a transport-fare [. . .]. It was owing to the kindness of
Ankhnebef that I gained access to it. Let not [. . .] say [. . .].

The youths who are designated cadets of the temple are persevering [. . .],
for it is the wish of the inspector of priests Ipi [. . .] from the Tura quarries.
It is you who shall remember this [which I/you have said].

63. P. BM 10735
(Dynasty 5: Djedkare-Izezi)

The second month of the third season, day 1[6]. The scribe of a boat phyle,
Horemsai.

The scribe of a boat phyle [. . .]. He said to [. . .] you forage(?) [. . .] in
giving you payment [. . .] which you did against the household of the
tenant landholder Djef [. . .]. I don't have much fear of you [. . .], but I will
make him give you an ox [. . .]. There is no one who is reckoning [. . .].

[. . .] the secretary and inspector of [. . . . As truly as Re], Hathor, and
all the gods [love] King Izezi in(?) [. . .] every magistrate dispatched(?) to the
place [. . .] to you [. . .] in order to give you foodstuffs [. . .]. You used
to place for yourself your declaration in the hand of the commissioners. The
second month of the third season, day 16: there is sent to you [. . .].

Servants

64. P. Cairo CG 58043
(Dynasty 6: Pepi I)

[Year after the . . . count], third month of the first season, day 5. [It is . . .
who addresses . . . Meh]u(?).

[. . .] your personal [agent]. What's the meaning of your staying at home?
This Mehu has returned to the place where I, your humble servant, am. Shall
misfortune come [upon] me, your humble servant, and this fellow maidservant of mine? I swear by the eyes of Mereri, my lord, that this maidservant
of Mereri is surely elated whenever she sees her lord's agent. Mehu, however,
has set forth his legal commitment to support her [in] this letter which I had
him bring to me.

On the other hand, it is some honey and ished-fruit (Balanites aegyptiaca)
that are the requirements of the family [of] my fellow servant, the palace
attendant Irenakhty. I mentioned his case to your personal agent just so that

he could be reinstated as scribe of a phyle of the Sacred Marriage Chapel of Nefersahor (King Pepi I). He was dismissed therefrom because of what had been omitted from the assignment order of your personal agent. Won't Mereri, my lord, make the mistress of the maidservant of (your) estate pleased by hearing my plea regarding this fellow servant of mine?

Come help me, come help me, as quickly as you, my lord, can!

=== **Farming** ===

65. P. Turin CG 54002
(Dynasty 6: Pepi II)

[Year . . . , . . . month of the . . . season], day 3.
[It is . . . who addresses the . . . of Me]mi:

[. . .] cultivated for(?) [. . .]. He told me that you caused ten *hekat*-measures of emmer seed to be sown in the Hieraconpolite nome . . . , which this Memi cultivated alongside the companion and overseer of priests [. . . in] the town of Imiotru (Rizeiqat) under the supervision of the sole companion Shemai after the sole companion Senkau had come to this nome. [He employed(?)] me within the farm, planting the dry land [with] one man's allotment of emmer seed and his allotment of Upper Egyptian barley, whereas your claim is false in [. . .] that I should make litigation. Come to the landing place(?) of the farm. [My?] agent [is sent] by way of informing you how evil are the transgression and insolence of those with false claims. Were I in fact to hold you under guard for the magistrates, I would be acting according to your disfavor.

=== **Work on a Pyramid Complex** ===

66. P. Cairo JE 52001
(Dynasty 6: Merenre or Pepi II)

[*Beginning lost*] the pyramid complex "Merenre Gleams and Is Beautiful," being made excellently [. . .] of stone. It is in accordance with the order [that was given] to me that I passed this year in the pyramid complex "Merenre Gleams and Is Beautiful," which is flourishing indeed.

Address(?): [The Director of those relating to the property(?) of the] granary of the Residence and lector priest Pepyankhu.

═══════════════ A Crooked Count ═══════════════

67. P. Berlin 8869
(Dynasty 8)

The count, seal-bearer of the Lower Egyptian king, sole companion, and chancellor of the god, Iruremtju to the sole companion and lector priest, Sobekhotpi's son Khnumhotpi's son, the commander of troops, Merrenakht:

I have given my considered [attention] to the account of the business concerning which you sent the sole companion and steward Hotep in order that I not do anything you dislike. If the purpose of your writing to me is that you might expose the robbery that has been committed against me, well and good! But if the purpose of your doing this is to break up the fighting because of your seeing two foreign countries [. . .] me(?) [. . .] united, then I shall see whether you like the count, seal-bearer of the Lower Egyptian king, [sole companion], and overseer of scribes of the crews Sabni more than me.

It is, however, better to desire righteousness than prolonged crookedness. Consequently this is an occasion for attending to every violation on the part of this count, for he is not one who is living off his own possessions. Inasmuch as you and I are in agreement that this count should not brush aside the robbery he has committed, you vouched for me in the Court of Horus (the king).

Moreover, the sole companion and steward Hotep has seen that I am not taking a stand against the troops of the lands of Medja and Wawat (in Nubia) in order that I [not] do what you dislike.

Address: Iruremtju to the count, sole companion, and overseer of priests, Re.[1]

═══════════════ Concerns of a Gentleman Farmer ═══════════════

68. P. Hekanakht No. 1
(Dynasty 11: Sankhkare Mentuhotep)

Communication by the mortuary priest Hekanakht to Merisu:

As for whatever gets soaked by the inundation in our farmland, it is you who should cultivate it with attention on the part of all my people including yourself since I am holding you responsible for this. Be very assiduous in cultivating! Take great care that the seed of my grain be preserved and all my property be preserved since I am holding you responsible for this. Take great care of all my property!

You must get Hety's son Nakht and Sinebniut to go down to the town of Perhaa and cultivate for [us] 20(?) arouras of land on lease. It is with the cloth—which has been woven where you are—that they shall secure its lease. If, however, they have gotten a good value in exchange for the emmer which is in Perhaa, they shall apply it there also so that you no longer need be concerned with the cloth about which I had said, "Weave it! After it has been evaluated in the village of Nebeseyet, they should take it and rent farmland for what it (the cloth) is worth." Besides, if it is convenient for you to cultivate 20 arouras of land there, cultivate them! You should locate suitable farmland—10 arouras of land to be in emmer and 10 arouras of land to be in northern barley—in [good] farmland [of the region of Khe]pesheyet. Don't settle on just anybody's land! You should ask of Hau Junior. If you can't locate any with him, then you are to go before Herunefer. He it is who can put you onto some irrigated land of Khepesheyet.

Now when I came south to where you are, you reckoned for me the rent of 13 arouras of land in northern barley alone. Beware lest you misappropriate even a *khar*-measure of northern barley therefrom as one might if sowing with his own northern barley, because you have already made the rent thereof unpleasant for me, being in northern barley alone and its seed. Moreover, as for one sowing with northern barley—in this case 65 *khar*-measures of northern barley from 13 arouras of land is equivalent to 5 *khar*-measures of northern barley from one aroura of land—now this isn't a mediocre squeeze (i.e. , net yield) since the normal yield of 10 arouras of land is 100 *khar*-measures of northern barley. Beware lest you be presumptuous with even a *hekat*-measure thereof of northern barley since this isn't a year for an individual to be remiss with regard to his master, his father, or his brother.

Now regarding all that Hety's son Nakht shall do for me in Perhaa, since I haven't allotted him a food allowance in excess of that for one month, which is one *khar*-measure of northern barley, I will allot yet an additional (allowance) amounting to 5 *hekat*-measures of northern barley for his dependents at the very beginning of the month. If you overstep this, I will hold it against you as a misappropriation. Now regarding what I've just told you saying, "Give him one *khar*-measure of northern barley for the month," it is only 8 *hekat*-measures of northern barley that you should give him for the month. Take great care!

Now what's the idea of sending Sihathor to me with the old parched northern barley which was in Djedisut (Memphis) without my being given the 10 *khar*-measures of northern barley in good fresh northern barley? Are you therefore happily consuming good northern barley while I am stuck aground, and, moreover, the boat is moored at your wharf while you are behaving in all manner of evil?[2] If you sent me old northern barley so as to stock up on the fresh northern barley, what am I to say?—"How good that is!" If you don't allot me a single (*hekat*-measure) of northern barley from the fresh northern barley, I will never allot such (an amount) to you.

Now I've been told that Snefru is [. . .]. Take great care of him! Give him a food allowance! And greet Snefru—in Khentykhe's words, "a thousand times and a million times." Take great care and write to me!

Now if my land gets soaked by the inundation, he should cultivate together with you and Anup—with attention on your part and on the part of Sihathor. Take great care of him! Right after cultivating you should send him on to me. Have him bring me three *khar*-measures of wheat along with what you can spare in the way of northern barley—but only in excess of your food allowance until you reach harvest time. Don't be unmindful of anything about which I've written you, for this is a year when a man should act in his master's best interest.

Now regarding all aspects(?) of my farm and all aspects(?) of my parcel of land on the *maawy*-canal, it was in flax that I had sowed them. Don't let anybody go down (settle?) upon it. Now as for whoever may have words with(?) you, you should proceed against him(?) [. . .]. Moreover, northern barley is what you should sow this parcel of land with. Don't sow emmer there. If, however, it ends up being a high Nile, it is with emmer that you should sow it.

Take great care of Anup and Snefru! You shall either die with them or live with them. Take great care, for there is no one more important than he in the house, including yourself. Don't be unmindful of this.

Moreover, you must turn the housemaid Senen out of my house—take great care!—on whatever day Sihathor reaches you (with this letter), for if she spends one more day in my house, I will take action! It is you who are responsible for letting her mistreat my new(?) wife. Now why should I make it miserable for you? What can she do to you, you five boys?

And greet my mother Ipi a thousand times and a million times! And greet Hetepe and all the household including Nofre. Now what's the idea of mistreating my new(?) wife? You are much too full of yourself! Are you associated with me as a partner? If you would desist, how good that would be!

And send an account of what should be collected from the produce of Perhaa. Take great care! Don't be unmindful!

Address: What the mortuary priest Hekanakht sends to his household of Nebeseyet.

69. P. Hekanakht No. 2
(Dynasty 11: Sankhkare Mentuhotep)

It is a son who speaks to his mother, namely, the mortuary priest Hekanakht to his mother Ipi and to Hetepe: How are you both? Are you alive, prospering, and healthy? In the favor of Montu, lord of the Theban nome!

And to the entire household: How are you? Are you alive, prospering, and healthy? Don't worry about me, for I'm healthy and alive. Now you are the case of the one who ate until he was sated having gotten so hungry that his eyes had become glassy white. Whereas the whole land has died off, [you] haven't hungered; for when I came south to where you are, I fixed your food allowance in good measure. Isn't the Nile inundation very [low]? Since [our] food allowance has been fixed for us according to the nature of the Nile inundation, bear patiently, each of you, for I have succeeded so far among you in keeping you alive.

Record of food rations for the household:

Ipi and her maidservant	8 *hekat*- measures
Hetepe and her maidservant	8 *hekat*- measures
Hety's son Nakht and his dependents	8 *hekat*- measures
Merisu and his dependents	8 *hekat*- measures
Sihathor	8 *hekat*- measures
Sinebniut	7 *hekat*- measures
Anup	4 *hekat*- measures
Snefru	4 *hekat*- measures
Siinut	4 *hekat*- measures
My's daughter Hetepe	5 *hekat*- measures
Nofre	3.5 *hekat*- measures
Sitwere	2 *hekat*- measures

Total: 6 (text: 7) *khar*-measures, 9.5 *hekat*-measures (of barley).

(Note): It is from his northern barley that rations should be meted out to Sinebniut; and until he leaves for Perhaa, they (the rations) should be at his disposal.

Lest you be angry about this, look here, the entire household is just like [my] children, and I'm responsible for everything so that it should be said, "To be half alive is better than dying outright." Now it is only real hunger that should be termed hunger since they have started eating people here,[3] and none are given such rations anywhere else. Until I come back home to you, you should comport yourselves with stout hearts, for I shall be spending the third season here.

Communication by the mortuary priest Hekanakht to Merisu and to Hety's son Nakht, who is subordinate: Only as long as my people keep on working shall you give them these rations. Take great care! Hoe every field of mine, keep sieving (the seed grain), and hack with your noses in the work! Now if they are assiduous, you shall be thanked so that I will not have to make it miserable for you. On the first day of the month of Khentykhetyperty one shall start distributing the rations about which I have written for the new first day of the month.

Don't be unmindful then of the 10 arouras of land which are in the neighborhood and which were given to Ip Junior's son Khentykhe and hoe them. Be very assiduous since you are consuming my food.

Now as for any chattel belonging to Anup which is in your possession, give it back to him! As for what is lost, reimburse him for it. Don't make me write you about this again since I've already written you about this twice.

Now if, as you say, Snefru wants to be in charge of the bulls, you should put him in charge of them. He neither wants to be with you plowing, going up and down, nor does he want to come here to be with me. Whatever else he may want, it is with what he wants that you should make him happy.

Now as for whoever of the women or men may reject these rations, he should come to me here to be with me just to live as I live.

Now when I came to where you are, didn't I warn you not to keep a companion of Hetepe's from her, be it her hairdresser or her domestic? Take great care of her! If only you would persevere in everything accordingly. But since, as you say, you don't want her around, you should have Iutenhab (Hekanakht's new wife?) brought to me.

As this man lives for me—it's Ip I'm referring to—whoever shall make any sexual advance against my new(?) wife, he is against me and I against him. Since this is my new(?) wife and it is known how a man's new(?) wife should be helped, so as for whoever shall help her, it's the same as helping me. Would even one of you be patient if his wife has been denounced to him? So should I be patient! How can I remain with you in the same community if you won't respect my new(?) wife for my sake?

Now I have sent to you by Sihathor 24 copper *debens* for the renting of land. Have then 20 arouras of land cultivated for us on lease in Perhaa next to Hau Junior's (paying) in copper, in clothing, in northern barley, or [in] any[thing] else, but only if you shall have gotten a good value there for oil or for whatever else. Take great care! Be very assiduous and be vigilant, [since] you are on good irrigated land of the region of Khepesheyet.

Address: What the mortuary priest Hekanakht sends to his household of the village of Nebeseyet.

70. P. Hekanakht No. 3
(Dynasty 11: Sankhkare Mentuhotep)

It is the servant of the estate, the mortuary priest Hekanakht who addresses [the overseer of Lower Egypt Herunefer]: Your condition is like that of one who lives innumerable times! May Arsaphes, lord of Heracleopolis, and all the gods who are [in heaven and earth] help you, and may Ptah, South-of-his-Wall, gladden you with living fully and a [ripe] old age. May your standing be good with the *Ka* of Arsaphes, lord of Heracleopolis.

I, your humble servant, speak to inform you, l.p.h., that I have sent Hety's son Nakht and Sinebniut concerning the northern barley and emmer which are there where you are. What you, l.p.h., are to do then is to have it collected without allowing any of it to get mixed up, according to all your good offices, if you please. Now after collecting it, it should be put in your, l.p.h., house even until I come for it. See now, I have caused them to bring the *oipe*-measure with which it should be measured. It is mended with black hide.

Now 15 *khar*-measures of emmer are in the village of Huthaa with Neneksu and 13.5 *khar*-measures of northern barley are with Ipi Junior in the village of Iusobeku. As for what is in the village of Sepatmat with Nehri's son Ipi, it is 20 *khar*-measures of emmer, and with his brother Desher, it is 3 *khar*-measures—a total of 38 *khar*-measures of emmer and 13.5 *khar*-measures of northern barley.

Now as for him who might give me the equivalent in oil, it is either for 2 *khar*-measures of northern barley or for 3 *khar*-measures of emmer that he should give me one *hebnet*-measure (of oil), although I would rather be paid my property (dues) in the form of northern barley.

And let there be no neglect regarding Nakht, that is, regarding anything about which he may come to you since it is he who is looking after all my property.

Address: The overseer of Lower Egypt Herunefer.

======= A Daughter to Her Mother =======

71. *P. Hekanakht No. 4*
(Dynasty 11: Sankhkare Mentuhotep)

[It is a daughter who] addresses her mother; it is Sitnebsekhtu who addresses Sitneb[sekhtu]: A thousand cola in greeting you with life, prosperity, and health! May you [prosper] happily. May Hathor gladden you for my sake. Don't be concerned about me since I am well. Now as for whatever is brought to [*personal name*] by way of reminder, the like thereof is brought to you.

And greet Gereg with life, prosperity, and health. Now I have sent Si[hathor(?)] to look in on you. Don't let Gereg be neglectful regarding [what I told] him. And greet the entire household with life, prosperity, and health.

Forwarding(?) address: Gereg.

======= Fowl =======

72. *P. Meketre*
(late Dynasty 11)

It is the servant of the estate, the god's father priest(?) Uhem, who speaks: Your condition is like that of one who lives innumerable times! May Arsaphes, lord of Heracleopolis, help you as I desire. May Ptah, South-of-his-Wall, gladden you with living fully and a [ripe old] age. May your standing be good with the *Ka* of Arsaphes, lord of Heracleopolis, and may all the gods provide you with a million years in life, prosperity, and health, as I, your humble servant, desire.

I speak to inform the lord, l.p.h., that my subordinate, the god's father priest(?) Iam(?) has come in order that he might fetch 2 geese, which are *serut*-geese, 100 ducks(?), and 100 dressed geese.

And [I] communicate with the lord, l.p.h., about having a message sent to the scribe(?) [. . .] Senmeri about giving me that strong(?) water.[4]

=========== **Cloth and the Sale of a House** ===========

73. P. Cairo 91061
(late Dynasty 11)

It is the servant of the estate, the scribe Nakht, who addresses the scribe Aau: Your condition is like that of one who lives innumerable times! May Arsaphes help you and Ptah, South-of-his-Wall, gladden you with life. May your standing be good with the *Ka* of Arsaphes, lord of Heracleopolis(?).

I, your [humble] servant, [speak] to inform you, l.p.h., that I, your humble servant, have sent this letter to learn about every favorable circumstance of yours, l.p.h. Now as for the *men*-cloth, it is set up (on the loom). Now as for the bolt of cloth, it is woven; and in fact, I have sent you the bolt of cloth. Now as for your house, it has been sold to the *wab*-priest Nakht including its doors and all its accessories.

Now that I have sent you seven rings of *pat*-cakes,[5] it is in accordance with a holiday mood that you should attune your heart. What's the idea of sending a reminder without writing about relevant details? Now Tjennu is bringing ten jugs of strong ale (?) so that your personality might experience well-being.

Address: What the scribe Nakht sends to the scribe Aau.

=========== **Building Stones** ===========

74. P. Haun. No. 1
(late Dynasty 11)

[*Beginning lost.* Your condition is like that of] one who lives innumerable times! May Montu, [lord of the Theban nome], help you. [May Ptah, South-of-his-Wall, gladden] you with living fully [and with a ripe old age].

[. . .] me, your brother (colleague?) there, [. . .] to learn about every favorable circumstance of yours, l.p.h., [. . .] in having the stones delivered from [. . .] the two paving blocks which he brought from [. . .] have them delivered without letting him delay there [. . .]. This is a communication to you, l.p.h. It is good if [you] take note.

=========== **Household Provisions** ===========

75. P. BM 10549
(late Dynasty 11–early Dynasty 12)

Communication by the general Nehsi [to the . . .] Kay:

How are you? Are you alive, prospering, and healthy? Your condition is [like that of one who lives] innumerable [times]! May Montu, lord of the Theban nome, and all the gods [help] you and provide you with a million years in [life, prosperity], and health [starting from today], as I desire.

Now what's the meaning of Senet's writing me that no provisions have been delivered to her [although I in fact did send . . . khar-measures of barley] to my household and ten khar-measures of barley to you? It was Kay's (i.e., your) daughter[. . .]senet and Kay's (i.e., your) son Nefer-the-Scribe who fetched it with the barge [that I had put at] their [disposal(?)]. So you should fetch it again since it must be fetched in full(?).

Moreover, what's the idea of [letting] yourself be turned away from your own daughter? It is through [. . .]'s failure to hand over the southern barley [to] my [house]hold that you will have succeeded in killing her. Now I for one have discerned the character of my stepmother. Is it by killing off my household that you are pursuing your wife's wish? Now that word is sent to me that there are no provisions there, can I remain confident that I have given provisions to my household? The barge shall be sent back as soon as it has reached me.

Address: [. . .] Kay.

=========== **Sundry Matters** ===========

76. P. BM 10567
(late Dynasty 11–early Dynasty 12)

From the servant of the estate Sankhuire:

Your condition is like that of one who lives [innumerable times! May . . . help you], and may Ptah [South-of-his-Wall, gladden you with living fully and a ripe old age]. May your standing be good [with the Ka of . . .], Sobek, Horus, Hathor, lady of [. . . , and all the gods] that are in heaven and that are in earth. May they let the lord, l.p.h., spend a million years [in life, prosperity, and health, starting from today] as I, your humble servant, desire. I, your humble servant, say:

[This is] a communication [to the lord, l.p.h., to] the effect that all business affairs of the lord, l.p.h., are prosperous and flourishing, so flourishing that there is nothing whatever about which the lord, l.p.h., need be concerned.

This is a communication to the lord, l.p.h., [to the effect that I, your humble servant, have] sent this letter to learn about all favorable circumstances of the lord, [l.p.h.].

This is a communication to the lord, l.p.h., about having a message sent [to me, your humble servant], about every good disposition of the lord, l.p.h., and about the well-being [and prosperity of the lord, l.p.h.].

This is a communication [to the lord, l.p.h., about sending] me a response to this letter through whoever may be coming.

[This is a communication] to the lord, l.p.h., about the fact that the children did not find [. . .] and about the fact that the south and north are in the charge of the scribes of the field districts(?)[6] [. . .] here.

It is good if the lord, l.p.h., takes note, while he is healthy and alive.

Address: The lord, l.p.h., the count Montusu, l.p.h., [from the . . . Sankh]ui[re].

================= Ship's Gear =================

77. Writing Board MMA 28.9.4
(early Middle Kingdom)

It is the servant of the estate Sekhsekh's son Inetsu who addresses the lord, l.p.h., Sekhsekh's son Penhensu: It is in order to learn about every favorable circumstance of the lord, l.p.h., that I, your humble servant, have sent this letter. In the favor of Montu, lord of the Theban nome, of Amon, lord of the Thrones of the Two Lands, of Sobek, of Horus, of Hathor, and of all the gods! It is as I, your humble servant, desire that they shall let the lord, l.p.h., spend millions of years in life, prosperity, and health, starting from today.

I, your humble servant, have said: This is a communication to the lord, l.p.h., about sending me a (rudder) post of pine wood, a steering oar of juniper, and a rudder-rest(?) of ebony for the poop(?) of your humble servant's sea-going galley. Moreover, it is indeed your humble servant's poop(?). It is good if the lord, l.p.h., takes note.

Notes

1. Taking "Re" as a hypocoristic form of the name Merrenakht.
2. Perhaps a metaphor meaning, "While you are holding all the cards, you (can) do all sorts of evil," according to Goldwasser (1981).
3. Possibly hyperbole rather than genuine cannibalism.
4. Possibly meaning "thick" or "hard" water.
5. A method of stringing cakes together.
6. Or possibly reading "master of servants Kis."

V

Later Middle Kingdom Letters

Introduction

The fruits of the campaign undertaken in the Twelfth Dynasty to train more scribes through an intensive educational program are evident in the documents presented in Part V. The scribes of the later Middle Kingdom reveal a confident maturity in their calligraphy. Being more cursive and employing more ligatures than heretofore, the hieratic script of this period presents considerable difficulties of decipherment that have resulted in long delays in the publication of papyri, particularly those in the Berlin collection, catalogued by Kaplony-Heckel (1971) and currently being prepared for publication by Ulrich Luft.

A series of brief model letters (No. 78), all inscribed on a single papyrus from Kahun, are translated initially to illustrate the standardization of epistolary formulae. Nos. 79–83, written in the reign of Amenemhat III, are actually copies of a series of dispatches sent from the Semna fortress in Nubia. These letters, admirably edited by Smither (1945), were inscribed in the form of a report on a papyrus discovered in a tomb in the vicinity of the Ramesseum in western Thebes. At the Nubian forts of Uronarti and Buhen were uncovered many small fragments of original letters and their mud sealings, attesting to massive communications among the Nubian fortresses and the central administration during the Twelfth and Thirteenth Dynasties (James 1984: 164; Smith 1976: chaps. 3 and 5). The remainder of the letters in Part V are from the valley temple and pyramid town, called anciently "Content is Senwosret" and modernly "Kahun." These were associated with the pyramid of Senwosret II at El-Lahun, which is located just off the Bahr Yusef channel of the Nile as it turns westward toward the Fayum lake, the Birket Karun.

The documents fall into two main groups: the Berlin papyri (Nos. 84–95) and the Kahun papyri (Nos. 78, 97–110). The Berlin letters, published initially by Borchardt (1899) and Scharff (1924) and retranslated here, form only a portion of a much larger corpus of still unpublished documents (Kaplony-Heckel 1971) which were discovered in a rubbish heap associated with the valley temple. They deal largely with temple affairs. The Kahun letters, discoverd by William Flinders Petrie in his excavations of the pyramid town that immediately adjoined the valley temple, were published by Griffith (1898), who early in the history of Egyptology displayed extraordinary skill in deciphering the difficult hieratic hands. These documents are generally somewhat later than the Berlin papyri (Luft 1982; Matzker 1986) and are broader in the range of their content. Letter No. 96 subsequently appeared on the market at Medinet el-Fayum and obviously comes from the same general area as the Berlin and Kahun papyri.

The pyramid town of Kahun initially housed the workers engaged in building the pyramid of Senwosret II during this king's lifetime. None of the letters dates as early as this phase of the town's occupation, but all derive from the period when the town functioned as the settlement for a sizable population of some three thousand priests, officials, and workers whose primary function was to maintain the funerary cult of Senwosret II and members of his family. The town of Kahun, which is the largest settlement surviving from the Middle Kingdom, displays in its careful planning something of the bureaucratic mentality of the period. Basically there were two types of houses: the large residences of the bureaucrats, including that of the governing mayor, and the more numerous small houses for the non-elite, who were dependent on the large residences for the redistribution of rations. In reality the population, which included Asiatics, was more diversified than the strict planning of the town indicates (Kemp 1989: 149–57). Apart from the neighboring mortuary temple, a temple to the god Sopdu, lord of the East, was constructed in the town itself to serve the religious needs of the townsfolk. David (1986) has provided an excellent overview of this community based on Petrie's excavations, the written documents, and artifacts from Kahun that are now in the Manchester Museum.

=============== Brief Model Letters ===============

78. P. Kahun III.2
(Dynasty 12: Amenemhat IV)

[It is the servant of the estate *name lost* who addresses *name lost*, l.p.h.: In the favor of] the King of Upper and Lower Egypt Maakherure (Amenemhat IV) and all the gods as I, your humble servant, desire! This is a communication to the lord, l.p.h., about sending ten geese for me, your humble servant. It is good if the lord, l.p.h., takes note.

It is the servant of the estate Djashe who addresses Renisoneb, l.p.h.: In the favor of Sokar in the town of Tepsedjemu as I, your humble servant, desire! This is a communication to the lord, l.p.h., about sending me raisins for me, your humble servant. It is good if the lord, l.p.h., takes note, if he pleases.

It is the servant of the estate Wehemmesut who addresses Hekaib, l.p.h.: This is a communication to the lord, l.p.h., about sending raisins for me, your humble servant. It is good if the lord, l.p.h., takes note, if he pleases.

so that there is nothing whatever that the lord, l.p.h., needs be concerned about except to remain healthy and alive. In the favor of Anubis, lord of the town of Shenaut, as I, your humble servant, desire! This is a communication about sending the boat loaded with produce of northern barley for me, your humble servant. It is good if you take note.

It is the servant of the estate Iuferankh who addresses Iufersep, l.p.h.: In the favor of the King of Upper and Lower Egypt Sehetepibre (Amenemhat I), the deceased, as I, your humble servant, desire! This is a communication to the lord, l.p.h., about sending me [the boat] loaded with [. . .].

It is the servant of the estate Ankhtify who addresses Soneb, l.p.h.: [In the] favor of the King of Upper and Lower Egypt Khakheper[re] the deceased and all the gods as I, your humble servant, desire! This is a communication to the lord, l.p.h., [about] sending me natron [. . .].

It is the servant of the estate Nehyu [who addresses] Senebtify, l.p.h.: In [the favor of] Sakhmet and She[sme]tet(?) as I, your humble servant, desire! This is a communication to the lord, [l.p.h., about] sending raisins for me, your humble servant.

It is the servant of the estate Ser who addresses [personal name], l.p.h.: In the favor of Sobek, lord of the town of Silsila, as I, your humble servant, desire! This is a communication to the lord, l.p.h., about sending some roasted grain for me, your humble servant. It is good if you take note.

It is the servant of the estate Horwerre who addresses Iatib, l.p.h.: In the favor of Hathor, [lady of] Byblos, as I, your humble servant, desire! This is a communication to the lord, l.p.h., about sending ten sacks (of grain) for me, your humble servant. It is good if you take note.

It is the servant of the estate Inpuherkhenet who addresses the dean of the temple, Re, l.p.h. In the favor of Sobek, lord of the "Great City" (Crocodilopolis), as I, your humble servant, desire! This is a communication to the lord, l.p.h., about sending some milk(?) for me, your humble servant. It is good if you take note.

=========== Nubian Affairs: The Semna Dispatches ===========

79. P. BM 10752, rt. 1
(Dynasty 12: Amenemhat III)

[Beginning lost] wrote [. . .] the troop(?) [. . .] found that his(?) [. . .] had done it [. . .]. Then in the fourth month of [the second season, day . . .] sent food down to him [. . .]. He wrote to me, your humble servant, about this [. . .], and I, your humble servant, wrote [. . .] the track which I, your humble servant, traveled(?) in [Year 3, fourth month of the second season, day] 7, [at] evening time. Then [. . .] informed him. [They] reported [to me, your humble servant], saying, "We found that [X-number of] Nubian [women had departed following] after two donkeys [. . .]." These Nubian women [. . . the fortress] "Powerful is Khakaure (Senwosret III), the deceased" (West Semna Fort). [X-number of] Nubians [arrived in Year] 3, fourth month of the second season, day 7, at [evening] time in order to do some bartering. What [they] had brought was bartered [. . .] the bartering thereof. They sailed south to the place they had come from after they had been given bread and beer as customarily(?) in Year 3, fourth month of the second season, day 8, at time of morning.

It is a communication about this. All business affairs of the King's Establishment are prosperous and flourishing, and all business affairs of the lord, l.p.h., are prosperous and flourishing. It is good if the lord, l.p.h., takes note.

(Postscript): Six other Nubians arrived at the fortress "Powerful is Khakaure, the deceased" (West Semna fort), in order to do some bartering according to this . . . in the fourth month of the second season, day 8. What they had brought was bartered. They sailed south on the same day to the place they had come from.

80. P. BM 10752, rt. 2-3
(Dynasty 12: Amenemhat III)

Another dispatch brought to him, being the one brought from the dispute overseer Sobekwer, who is in Iken (Mirgissa fort), as one fortress sends a communication to another fortress.

It is a communication to you, l.p.h., to the effect that the two warriors and seventy(?) Medjay-people who had departed following that track in the fourth month of the second season, day 4, returned to report to me on the same day at evening time, bringing three Medjay-men, and four male and female infants(?), saying, "We found them on the south of the desert margin beneath the inscription of the summer season, and also three women(?)," so they said. I then questioned these Medjay-people, asking, "From where have you come?" They then replied, "It's from the well of the region of Ibhayet (southeast of the Second Cataract) that we have come."

[. . .] the [. . . in] the fourth month of the second season, [day . . .] came to report [to . . .]. He said concerning [. . .], "I departed upon the [track . . .] explained(?) [. . .] the [. . .] brought him [. . .] the frontier patrol. Then I returned [. . . ," so he said]. I sent word about them to the fortresses that lie north.

[All business affairs of the King's] Establishment, l.p.h., are prosperous and flourishing, and all business affairs of yours, [l.p.h., are prosperous and flourishing]. It is good if you, l.p.h., take note.

81. P. BM 10752, rt. 3-4
(Dynasty 12: Amenemhat III)

Another dispatch brought to him from the retainer Ameny, who is in the fortress "Repeller of the Medjay" (Faras fort?), as one fortress sends a communication to another fortress.

It is a communication to the lord, l.p.h., to the effect that the warrior of the city of Hieraconpolis, Senu's son Heru's son Renoker, and the warrior of the city of Tjebu, Rensi's son Senwosret's son Senwosret, came to report to me, your humble servant, in Year 3, fourth month of the second season, day 2, at breakfast time on business of the soldier, Khusobek's son Mentuhotep's son Khusobek . . . , who is substituting for the marine of the Ruler's Crew in the troop of Meha (near Abu Simbel), saying, "The frontier patrol that set out to patrol the desert margin extending near(?) the fortress 'Repeller of the Medjay' in Year 3, third month of the second season, last day, has returned to report to me saying, 'We found the track of thirty-two men and three donkeys, that they had trod [. . .],' [. . .] the frontier patrol [. . .] my places," so [he] said. [. . .] command to(?) the troop [. . .] on the desert margin. I, your humble servant, have written [about this to . . . , as one fortress sends a communication to another] fortress.

It is a communication [about] this. [All business affairs of the King's Establishment], l.p.h., are prosperous [and flourishing].

82. P. BM 10752, rt. 4
(Dynasty 12: Amenemhat III)

Copy of a document brought to him, being the one brought from the fortress [of] Elephantine, as one fortress sends a communication to another fortress.

A communication to you, if you please, to the effect that two Medjay-men, three Medjay-women, and two infants(?) came down from the desert hills in Year 3, third month of the second season, day 27. They said, "It is in order to serve the Palace, l. p. h., that we have come." They were questioned about the state of the desert, and they replied, "We haven't heard of anything except that the desert population is starving to death," so they said. Then I, your humble servant, had them dismissed to their desert hills on the same day. One of these Medjay-women then said, "If only I might be given my Medjay-man in this(?). . . ." Then that Medjay-man [said], "It is only one who has presented(?) himself who can barter."

83. P. BM 10752, rt. 5
(Dynasty 12: Amenemhat III)

[It is a communication to] the lord, l.p.h., to the effect that the chief(?) of [. . .] reported [. . .] in [Year 3, fourth month of] the second season, day 8, at time [of] morning, saying, "[. . .] is going to see me. I found [. . .]."

It is a communication about this. All business affairs of the King's Establishment, [l.p.h., are prosperous and flourishing], and all business affairs of the lord, l.p.h., are prosperous and flourishing. It is good if [the lord, l.p.h.], takes note.

A response to this dispatch has been made in the dispatch sent to him about (X-number of) Nubians who arrived at the fortress "Powerful is Khakaure, the deceased," (Semna West fort) in the fourth month of the second season, day 7, at evening time and who were sent back to the place they had come from in the fourth month of the second season, day 8, at time of morning.

The Heliacal Rising of Sothis

84. *P. Berlin 10012, 18-21*
(Dynasty 12: Senwosret III)

It is the mayor and dean of the temple Nubkhaure who addresses the chief lector priest Pepyhotep:

I am speaking in order for you to know that it is on the sixteenth day of the fourth month of the second season that the heliacal rising of Sothis (Sirius) will occur. May the attention of the priestly corps of the mortuary temple "Powerful is Senwosret (II), the deceased," of Anubis who is upon his mountain, and of Sobek be directed thereto. And have this letter entered into the journal of the temple.

Temple Personnel

85. *P. Berlin 10003A II, 16-19*
(Dynasty 12: Senwosret III)

Report of the first phyle of the priestly corps of this temple which is entering upon the monthly duties. What they said was:

All your business affairs are safe and sound. With everything belonging to the temple being safe and sound, we have received all property of the temple from the fourth phyle of the priestly corps of this temple which is retiring from the monthly duties. The temple is flourishing in very good order.

Hides for Sandals

86. *P. Berlin 10050, 1-5*
(Dynasty 12: Senwosret III)

Copy of a [communication(?)] from the pyramid town "Content is Senwosret (II), the deceased," which the sandal-maker Werniptah, son of Sankhptah, brought:

Send an oxhide or a goatskin! You shall give it, but only to the sandal-maker Werniptah. And record it in writing that an oxhide has been given to this sandal-maker.

87. P. Berlin 10014
(Dynasty 12: Amenemhat III)

Year 4, fourth month of the third season, day 13. Send an oxhide which is of good quality since it must serve its due purpose. Now I have sent the sandal-maker Hetepi for it, so please give it to him.

Address: The temple scribe Horemsaf.

Corvée Labor

88. P. Berlin 10023A
(Dynasty 12: Amenemhat III)

It is the mayor and dean of the temple Senwosret who addresses the temple scribe Horemsaf.

I am speaking to inform you that the temple doorkeeper, Senet's son Ameny, approached me saying, "I was seized as a substitute for my son, the porter of the temple there, [by] my district officers who said that he is in deficit for the corvée force," so he said. Now his son has met his labor obligations for me(?). If [. . .].

Address: The temple scribe Horemsaf. Year 11, first month of the [. . . season, day . . .]. Delivered by the porter of the temple [. . .].

Letters about Deliveries and
Drafts of Their Replies

89. P. Berlin 10023B
(Dynasty 12: Amenemhat III)

It is the servant of the estate Horemsaf who speaks:

[This is] a communication [to the lord, l.p.h.], to the effect that all business affairs of the lord, l.p.h., are prosperous and flourishing wherever they are. [This is] a communication to the lord, l.p.h., about sending [wine, . . .], earth almonds, and grain for the divine offerings. And a communication to the effect that the [remainder of (?)] the contributions for the procession (of the divine bark) have not been brought [by] Sibastet. And a communication about sending fowl for this evening's divine offerings. And a [communication] to the effect that I, your humble servant, have sent two hearth fans [. . .] of the august chamber (i.e., sanctuary) of the temple to replace them anew. It is a communication about this.

[This is] a communication [to] the lord, l.p.h. It is good if the lord, l.p.h., takes note.

Address: The temple scribe Horemsaf.

(*Draft of Reply*):
Wine and [. . .] have been brought to you, and ground earth almonds have been brought to you. Who is he that he did not bring a cup and ink to bring [. . . ?] [. . .] bring the controller of the phyle, your superior. [. . .] it against(?) him. Two pigeons have been brought to you, and [. . .] have been brought to you.

90. P. Berlin 10016
(Dynasty 12: Amenemhat III)

It is [the servant of] the estate Horemsaf who speaks:
This is a communication to the lord, l.p.h., to the effect that the *wag*-feast will take place in Year 18, second month of the third season, day 17. [. . .]. The contribution of one long-horned bull comprises the divine offering for the *wag*-feast that should be delivered to me[1] from the pyramid town "Content is Senwosret (II), the deceased." May the lord's assets [. . .].

A communication to the effect that those twenty turtledoves have not been brought about which a message was sent saying, "I sent them to you."

A communication [to the effect that] I, your humble servant, have re-funded 114 fowl (which were) in deficit to(?) the temple employees. They had not been delivered. It is a communication concerning this.

This is a communication to the lord, l.p.h., [to the effect that] I, your humble servant, [wrote] to the overseer of the food magazine User, "Now I will give you the grain provisions and the confections for the daily offer-ings." He said that I didn't do this. It is a [communication] concerning this.

This is a communication to the lord, l.p.h. It is good if the lord, l.p.h., takes note.

Address: The lord, l.p.h., from Horemsaf. Year 18, second month of the third season, day 13. Delivered by the porter of the temple Sobekamsaf. Accomplished(?).

(*Draft of Reply*):
Now I have taken note of this. Since the steward of divine offerings Sobeknakht has written about offering (the bull) [. . . in] the mortuary temple "Powerful is Senwosret (II), the deceased," I shall send you the bull. (*Regarding the turtledoves*): The porter of the temple has not taken heed to bring

them, not even as of the second month of the third season, day 13. Now I have taken note of this.

Did you send women substitute workers? I haven't received any. Half of them have been removed from the mortuary temple "Powerful is Senwosret (II), the deceased." Please send women substitutes for them.

Field Hands

91. P. Berlin 10073
(Dynastry 12: Amenemhat III)

It is the servant of the estate Senebni [who speaks]:

[This is a communication to the lord, l.p.h.], to the effect that the mayor sent me, your humble servant, from Settlement Town to muster the labor force, having charged me, your humble servant, saying, "As for any persons whom you may find missing among them, you are to write to the steward Horemsaf about them." I, your humble servant, have sent a list of missing persons in writing to the pyramid town ["Content is] Senwosret (II), the deceased." [. . .] shall be given(?) . . . concerning them. [List of names follows.]

This is a communication to the lord, l.p.h., [. . .]. I, your humble servant, am writing in communicating about this [. . .].

Address: [The Lord, l.p.h., the steward Hor]emsaf, l.p.h.

The Cult of a Dead Man

92. P. Berlin 10031A
(Dynasty 12: Amenemhat III)

It is the prophet of Sobek, Hetepi's son Neferiu, who addresses the dean of the temple Horemsaf, l.p.h.

You are [in the favor of(?) . . .], since you brought one large bag and two hin-measures of fat. You came and ignited a torch for the deceased Senebni. May Sobek deem to reward you since you brought one swt-joint of beef, one shin of beef, one [. . .] of beef, and [X-loaves] of bread. It is good if you take note.

Address: The dean of the temple Horemsaf, l.p.h.

════════════ Temple Matters ════════════

93. P. Berlin 10037
(Dynasty 12: Amenemhat III)

It is [. . .] who addresses the steward Horemsaf.

I speak [to inform] you about that concerning which a charge was given to you as follows, "You should give [. . . in the] first month of the third season, day 10 + [. . .]." The deliveries are outstanding(?) [. . .]. I have written [. . .] so that [. . .] may furnish [. . .]. My brother, it is you [who should write to me . . .]. The musical troop is included in this total. The musical troop, those who plait ornaments(?): amount [. . .] them.

And have the beautiful girl-children of the mortuary temple "Powerful is Senwosret (II), the deceased," and of the region(?) of Ahetmer brought to stand as a jubilating crowd. Place the papyrus scrolls with name-lists in a sack(?) container after they have been given a charge concerning the amount of [. . .] unhindered [. . .] them to them [. . .] since [. . . is] waiting [. . .] at the town of El-Lahun, [. . . Ahe]tmer, and [. . . the mortuary temple "Powerful is] Senwosret (II), the deceased."

Address: The steward Horemsaf. Delivered by Sigebu from(?) the controller of the phyle User's son Senwosret.

══════════ A Subordinate in Trouble ══════════

94. P. Berlin 10025
(Dynasty 12: Amenemhat III)

It is [the servant of the estate] Imbu who speaks:

This is a communication to the lord, l.p.h., to [the effect that] all people of the lord's milieu are prosperous [and flourishing wherever they are. In the favor of the King of Upper] and Lower Egypt Khakheperre (Senwosret II), [the deceased, as] I, your humble servant, desire!

This is a communication to the lord, l.p.h., to the effect that I, your humble servant, have been told that the lord, l.p.h., was(?) issued [a directive . . .] under me, your humble servant, as a loss, and the lord, l.p.h., keeps having letters sent [to me, your humble servant], inquiring about what the mortuary priest there is doing. Is the lord, l.p.h., seeking what action is to be taken against me, your humble servant, [. . .] against me, your humble servant? Am I in trouble, O lord, l.p.h.? I am your retainer. What is [it, what is it] that he (the mortuary priest?) is going to do against me, your humble servant, before I, your humble servant, have been permitted to hear what I (text: he) have done? Don't speak in opposition to me, your humble servant(?). [I have I], your retainer, [erred(?)] by my being indifferent toward the young servant of the lord, l.p.h., who came to me? I am not(?) [. . . the young servant] of the lord, l.p.h., for he has reneged on his obligations. The magistrate will say, "He has done these things [. . .]." [I, your humble servant], will find a letter like snakes. If afterward the [magistrate] pardons me, [I, your humble servant shall] turn over an offering of goods on your holiday. You shall not quarrel [with me, your humble servant, . . . the matter] in its entirety.

Now people are saying as follows, "[. . .]." You shall begin on my account by doing something [. . . the pyramid town "Content is Senwosret (II)], the deceased." Send me an answer to this letter [. . .], and have a message sent to me, your humble servant, about the life, prosperity, and health of the lord, l.p.h. This is a communication to the lord, [l.p.h. It is good if the lord, l.p.h., takes note].

Address: The lord, l.p.h., from Imbu.

Order for Meat

95. P. Berlin 10017
(Dynasty 12: second half)

A communication to the effect that the butler of the food magazine has been sent in order to fetch offering meat of the bull for the month from the mortuary temple "Powerful is Senwosret (II), the deceased," in accordance with all that is at the disposal of the lord, l.p.h.

The mayor, l.p.h.
The controller of the phyle
The chief lector priest

May the lord, l.p.h., please send it in very good order, attending to it without allowing any arrears to accrue therein. And dispatch someone with it immediately without its being allowed to spend time there where you are. The amount thereof shall be brought in copy. This a communication regarding it.

Coming Home

96. P. El-Lahun
(Dynasty 12: Amenemhat III?)

[It is . . . who addresses . . .].
I am speaking to inform you that all your business affairs are prospering.

Now I shall reach the mortuary temple "Powerful is Senwosret (II), the deceased," [. . .]. It is(?) [. . .]. So please let me find the house put in very good shape. And write me about every matter pertaining to the health and life of the nurse Tima. Only after the house has been tidied up, shall you have me come there.

Address: The seal-bearer Neni.

=============== Farming and Food Rations ===============

97. P. Kahun VI.6
(Dynasty 12: Amenemhat III)

[It is the servant of the estate] Iyib who addresses the steward [Sehetepib], l.p.h.

[This is a communication to] the lord, l.p.h., to the effect that all [business affairs] of the lord, l.p.h., are prosperous and flourishing wherever [they are]. In the favor of Sobek the Crocodilopolite, [of Horus residing in Croco-dilo]polis, of Khentikhtai, lord of Athribis, of the King of Upper and Lower Egypt Nimare (Amenemhat III), may he live forever and ever, and of all the gods as I, your humble servant, desire!

This is a communication to the lord, [l.p.h.], to the effect that some fields were sown with seed for me, your humble servant, in the district of the pyramid town "Content is Senwosret (II), the deceased," and the province of the District of Horus. In communicating about this, I, your humble servant, am writing about having [attention] paid [to . . .] to bring them(?) food rations from the Residence [. . .] them. Then a boat will take them [. . .].

This is a communication to the lord, l.p.h., about having a message sent to me, your humble servant, about the life, prosperity, and health of the lord, l.p.h. It is a communication about this.

This is a communication to the lord, l.p.h. It is good if the lord, l.p.h., takes note.

Address: The lord, l.p.h., [the steward] Sehetepib, l.p.h., from Iyib.

=============== Attention to a Household ===============

98. P. Kahun II.2
(Dynasty 12: Amenemhat III or later)

It is the servant of the estate Neni who addresses the steward Iyib, l.p.h. This is a communication to the lord, l.p.h., to the effect that all business affairs of the lord, l. p. h., are prosperous and flourishing wherever they are. In the favor of Sopdu, lord of the East, of his ennead, and of all the gods as I, your humble servant, desire!

This is a communication to the lord, l.p.h., about having attention paid to the household of Wah in accordance with that about which I informed you inasmuch as it is you who can do whatever is necessary. You shall then acquire your well-being.

Now the dean of the temple Teti said to me, "See, I have also informed him about it," so he said. So it shall be done accordingly in order that the *Ka* of the Ruler might continue to favor you.

It is a communication concerning this. This is a communication to the lord, l.p.h. It is good if the lord, l.p.h., takes note.

Address: The lord, l.p.h., the steward Iyib, l.p.h., from Neni.

=============== **Shipping and Conscripts** ===============

99. *P. Kahun VI.4*
(Dynasty 12: Amenemhat IV)

It is the servant of the estate Irysu who addresses the chamberlain Sikaiunu, l.p.h.

[This is] a communication [to the lord, l.p.h., to the effect that] all [business affairs] of the lord, l.p.h., are prosperous and flourishing wherever they are. In the favor of [*name of a god*] and his ennead!

This is a communication to the lord, l.p.h., to the effect that I arrived at the quay of the town of Hutnebes (near Heracleopolis) in the fourth month of the third season, day 5, in the morning. I found out that you, the lord, l.p.h., had already set sail southward. The foreman Impy told me, "I gave him three conscripts." The list thereof: Renisoneb, the mat-maker; Iotef; and the Asiatic of the estate Oker. It is a missive informing you of this.

I then sent to you the foreman Henar in the boat that I found at the quay of Hutnebes, and I caused him to bring you cargo. Since this boat was sent down (launched?) by the woman Baket when it was already loaded, I couldn't have him bring you further goods. I have caused him to bring back to you this one conscript of the locality "Garden (?) of the Prince" whom you had assigned here. Renefsoneb's son Sineb has told me, "I gave him twenty *hekat*-measures of northern barley and thirty *hekat*-measures of emmer."

Amount of cargo consigned to the foreman Henar:

50 *hekat*-measures of northern barley; 20 *hekat*-measures being the balance due as Iotef's wages from the warden(?) of the gateway Sonbi.

4 floor-mats

1 mat

[X-number of] *hebnet*-measures of [. . .]

1 tube of[. . .]

What was given to be parched in addition to this:

6.33 *hekat*-measures of northern barley

A[mount of . . .]-grain allotted to the treasurer Ikaiunu and [consigned to the foreman Hen]ar, being that which he got from Renefsoneb's son Sineb:

30 *hekat*-measures of northern barley

[X-number of *hekat*-measures] of emmer(?)

And send me the retainer Soneb that he may bring me a final accounting of disbursements with respect to these conscripts. Then I shall have word(?) brought . . . there where you are in(?) [. . .] them. Now if these eleven conscripts are waiting there where you are for their remuneration, all well and good! It is you who shall write about matters in your charge, if you please, because for want of a messenger here with me, I couldn't send one to bring me back a reply with your opinion. If nothing has been brought in the way of remuneration for the eleven conscripts, you shall write to me about this, "Nothing has been brought in the way of remuneration for them," so you shall say to me about this also. It is a communication about this.

And have a message sent to me about your life, prosperity, and health. Now I have written commending you to the steward Hetu. So you shall be with him as one person. It is a communication to the lord, l.p.h., about this.

And send [to me . . .] quickly. It is a communication about this.

Now five conscripts who haul stone here from the Iaku-quarries are at your disposal(?). So you shall make your way(?).

Address: The lord, l.p.h., the chamberlain Sikaiunu, l.p.h., from Irysu. Year 2, fourth month of the third season, day 12. Delivered by Henar.

=========================== **Fishing** ===========================

100. *P. Kahun III.4*
(Dynasty 12: Amenemhat IV)

It is the servant of the estate Khemem who addresses the chamberlain [. . .].

This [is a communication] to the lord, l.p.h., to the effect that [all business affairs of] the lord, l.p.h., are prosperous and flourishing wherever [they] are. In the favor [of] Sobek, lord of Rosehwy, of the King of Upper and Lower Egypt Maakherure (Amenemhat IV), may he live forever and ever, and of all the gods as I, your humble servant, desire!

[This] is a communication [to] the lord, l.p.h., to the effect that no one is writing to me, your humble servant, about any condition [of] the lord, l.p.h., as whom[ever the lord], l.p.h., has encountered in health and [life] should do.[2] I, your humble servant, couldn't come to learn about any condition of the lord, l.p.h., owing to the fact that the boat was taken by Sehetepibre in sailing south. I, your humble servant, am alone with the sole exception of the lord's retainer Ite, who has been designated for corvée labor [. . . He] demanded a boat in order to spear ten fish for the lord, l.p.h. He then brought in 500 gutted(?) fish which he got by fishing.[3]

In communicating about this, I, your humble servant, am writing about having an accounting made by the lord, l.p.h., at the quay of Perkheny.[4] I, your humble servant, have sent Ite on account of this in order to have attention paid [to . . .] Nebirut and to cause [. . .] of Ite [. . .]. It is a communication about this.

[. . .] to the province [. . .] the deputy Senwosret and the chief steward.

This is a communication to the lord, l.p.h., [to the effect that] the business affairs of the lord, l.p.h., [are prosperous and flourishing].

Address: The lord, l.p.h., Good luck(?)! from Khemem. Year 6, first month of the second season, day 2. I, your humble servant, am told that the lord, l.p.h., is coming to the mortuary temple "Powerful is Senwosret (II), the deceased."

══════════════ **Weaving Clothes** ══════════════

101. P. Kahun III.3
(Dynasty 12: second half)

What the lady of the house Irer sends:

This is a communication to the lord, l.p.h., to the effect that all business affairs of the lord, l.p.h., are prosperous and flourishing wherever they are. In the favor of the King of Upper and Lower Egypt Khakheperre (Senwosret II), the deceased, and of all the gods as [I, your humble servant, desire]!

[It is] a communication to the lord, l.p.h., about this neglectfulness on the part of the lord, l.p.h. Are you all safe [and sound? The women weavers(?)] are left abandoned, thinking they won't get food provisions inasmuch as not any news of you has been heard. It is good if [the lord, l.p.h.] takes note.

This is a communication to the lord, l.p.h., about those slave-women who are here unable to weave clothes. Your presence [is demanded(?)] by those who work at(?) the warp-threads so as to be guided(?). I, your humble servant, couldn't come myself owing to the fact that I, your humble servant, entered the temple on the twentieth day of the month to serve as *wab*-priestess for the month(?). [So] may the lord, l.p.h., bring them (food supplies?) with him. It is a case of paying attention to that other(?) woman Heremhab when coming [for the(?)] Asiatic.[5] The lord, l.p.h., should spend some time here since [not] any clothes [have been made] while my attention is being directed to the temple, and the warp-threads are set up on the loom without its being possible to weave them.

This is a communication to the lord, l.p.h. It is good if the lord, l.p.h., takes note.

Address: The lord, l.p.h., Good luck(?)! [from the lady of the house Irer].

To a Woman about a Runaway Slave

102. P. Kahun XII.1
(Dynasty 12: after Amenemhat III)

[*Beginning lost.*] Now [I] was told [that . . .] is prospering. I'm delighted that I found the royal slave Sobekemhab, for he was in flight. I turned him over to the corvée compound for trial, and [. . .] works for me [. . .] the mortuary temple "Amenemhat (III), the deceased, lives."

[*considerable loss*] which I sent to the scribe of the fields Seryu on account of all that I had said. Now see, what's with you that you should let him die in the office of the reporter? Have someone approach him right now and say, "It is to me(?) that he is to be turned over [. . .]." Then you shall send [me] every [report(?)]. If he says good(?), let him come. [*considerable loss*].

[This is a communication that] he [may be made] to report about him.

And greet the lady of the house Kebes, [. . .], the [por]ter Nebsumenu, and the lady of the house Iku in stating that I have taken note of what you wrote about. [. . .] Send me some oil [and] send me [. . .].

Payment for Cloth

103. P. Kahun IV.4
(Dynasty 12: second half)

[It is the servant of the estate, the assistant(?) in charge of the seal, Irypersen who speaks]:

This is a communication to the lord, l.p.h., [to the effect that all business affairs of the lord], l.p.h., are prosperous and flourishing [wherever they are]. In the favor of Sobek, lord of [Ro]sehwy, of the King of Upper and Lower Egypt Khakheperre (Senwosret II), the deceased, and of all the gods, as I, your humble servant, desire!

This is a communication to the [lord], l.p.h., about having a message sent to me, your humble servant, [concerning the life, prosperity, and health of the lord], l.p.h., because I, your humble servant, am happy once I have learned [that the lord], l.p.h., [is alive, prosperous, and healthy].

This is a communication to the lord, l.p.h., to the effect that the storekeeper Hori has departed sailing north to Lower Egypt so that I, your humble servant, am alone here. In communicating about this I, your humble servant, am writing about having me, your humble servant, recompensed with that bit of green frit[6] about which the lord, l.p.h., promised, "I myself shall have it prepared for you after the bolts of cloth have been woven." It is a communication about this.

Now the scribe in charge of the seal, Nehty, has sailed north together with the mayor [Sonb]u. The mayor didn't let me depart [. . .] the letters which are [. . .] me [. . .]. You [didn't] bring me the yellow ochre(?) for it when you came to escort Nebusen. Now it is being said that the crucial time is advancing and has drawn near(?). Now as for the bolt of cloth that is due from me, I am not setting it up on the loom, because the green frit is still wanting. It is a communication about this.

And greet the lady of the house Sittepihu with life, prosperity, and health, and also the steward Khemu, the lady of the house Bebu, the chief washerman Sidjehuti, and the lady [of the house] Sonbi. It is a [communica]tion about this.

This is a [communication] to the lord, l.p.h. [It is good if the lord, l.p.h., takes note].

Address: The lord, l.p.h., from the assistant(?) in charge of the seal, Irypersen.

===== **To a Woman about a Thief** =====

104. P. Kahun XV.1
(Dynasty 12: second half)

What Pepu sends to the lady of the house Sobekhotep, l.p.h. A thousand cola in greeting you! In the favor of Hathor, lady of the town of Atfih!

As for what you wrote about [regarding what] the reporter did to this thief, see, that is what was authorized(?). Now what is being done at the Residence is extremely painful. Has it ever been commanded that a thief be tried by anybody except a dispute overseer? A dispute overseer, however, cannot try a thief unless he is apprehended.

Now if one deems to mention this in the presence of the king's servant, he shall fill him in with further details(?)[7] so that there is no one who will suffer(?) on account of him.

As for the saying that I am spending all my time weeping about it—a dead person(?) cannot return—after I went out from . . . , if I(?) am going to be found fit, I won't be found fit now(?) [. . .].

Address: What Pepu sends to the lady of the house Sobekhotep, l.p.h.

===== A Letter and a Sarcastic Reply =====

105. P. Kahun VI.8
(Dynasty 12: second half)

A communication to the effect that I, your humble servant, have been told that the lord, l.p.h., reached the mortuary temple "Powerful is Senwosret (II), the deceased," in the fourth month of the third season, day 10. How bad it is that you arrived safe and sound!

(*Reply*): It is only all manner of evil that you utter. In the favor of Sobek, lord of Rosehwy, who shall put you into the caldron, and in the favor of his *Ka!* May action be taken for the benefit of the dean of the temple of Heket, Pepi, against you so as to be lasting and enduring forever and ever. It is bad if you take note. A plague upon you!

(*Postscript*): Come that I may see you. See, we will have a bad time.

===== Laborers =====

106. P. Kahun I.7
(Dynasty 12: second half)

It is the servant of the estate Iyemiatib who speaks:

This is a communication to the lord, l.p.h., to the effect that all business affairs of the lord, l.p.h., are prosperous and flourishing wherever they are. In the favor of Atum, lord of Heliopolis, and his ennead, of Re-Harakhti-Sopdu, lord of the East, and his ennead, of your local god who loves you daily starting from today, and of all the gods as I, your humble servant, [desire]!

This is a communication to the lord, l.p.h., [about] having a message sent to me, your humble servant, concerning [the life, prosperity, and health] of the lord, l.p.h., because I, your humble servant, am happy once I have learned that the lord, l.p.h., is alive, prosperous, and healthy.

[This] is a communication to the lord, l.p.h., to the effect that I, your humble servant, have carried out whatever the lord, l.p.h., has commanded in that concerning which a charge was given to me, your humble servant, by bringing the forty(?) people in accordance with the charge lest the lord, l.p.h., say that I am unresponsive to what he told me.

When I, your humble servant, come for the corvée force in the second(?) month of the first season, it shall return with me, your humble servant, right [away] because tomorrow is here (i.e., time is short). And I, your humble servant, [. . .]. It is a communication about this.

And greet the children of the entire household!

This is a communication to the lord, l.p.h. It is good if the lord, l.p.h., takes note.

Address: The lord, l.p.h., the dean of the temple, Ptahpuwah, l.p.h., from Iyemiatib. First month of the first season, day 15. Delivered by the seal-bearer(?) Neni.

=============== **Educating a Royal Slave** ===============

107. *P. Kahun VIII.1*
(Dynasty 12: second half)

It is the servant of the estate Kemny who speaks:

[This is] a communication [to the lord, l.p.h.], to the effect that [all] business affairs [of the lord, l.p.h.], are prosperous and flourishing [wherever they are. In] the favor of Sobek the Crocodilopolite [and] his ennead, of Sobek, lord of Rosehwy, and his ennead, of the King of Upper and Lower Egypt Khakheperre (Senwosret II), the deceased, and of all the gods as I, your humble [servant], desire!

[This is] a communication [to] the lord, l.p.h., about having attention paid to your royal slave Wadjhau in making him learn to write without being allowed to run away, in accordance with every good office that you, the lord, l.p.h., exercise, if you please, and about having attention paid to your household in accordance with every good office that you, the lord, exercise, if you please, because it is you, the lord, l.p.h., who can do whatever is necessary in turning(?) to me, your humble servant.

A communication to the effect that I, your humble servant, shall send the goods of the treasury with(?) Kheper[. . . (?)] when he comes southward since Soneb was already met as he was being sent coming southward after he had brought the nets in. It is a communication about this.

This is a communication to the lord, l.p.h. It is good if the lord, l.p.h. takes note.

Address: The lord, l.p.h., the steward Yey, l.p.h., from Kemny.

=============== **Sundry Matters** ===============

108. *P. Kahun LVII.1*
(Dynasty 12: second half)

It is the servant of the estate Panetyni who speaks:

This is a communication to the lord, l.p.h., to the effect that all business affairs of the lord, l.p.h., are prosperous and flourishing wherever they [are].

This is a [communication] to the lord, l.p.h., to the effect that [. . .] the clothes and bread that were in the charge of Pa[. . .] have been consigned to Iotef. The amount thereof: one strip of cloth, one . . . -cloth, one . . . -cloth, and twenty . . . -cloths, being what I, your humble servant, withdrew(?), sealed with the seal of your humble servant.

One . . . for the nurse Yeye.

One watermelon(?), of which he said, "It is for my household."

It is a communication about this.

This is a communication to the lord, l.p.h., to the effect that [. . . sent(?)] a copy of the memorandum to the [. . .] of my lord, the scribe Senbebu, saying, "[. . .] these memoranda that are upon it." It is good [if you send] a reply to me, your humble servant.

[. . .] Take hold. take hold(?)! Look, please, the one who prepared my mother for burial has departed from me. See, he excels(?) Montu at binding exceedingly. It is a communication about this.

This is a communication to the lord, l.p.h. It is good if the lord, l.p.h., takes note.

Address: The lord, l.p.h., from [. . .].

================================ Food Supplies ================================

109. P. Kahun III.6
(Dynasty 12: second half)

It is a brother (colleague?) who addresses a brother (colleague?), who addresses Ankhtify:

May Arsaphes, lord of Heracleopolis, do your will for you! You shall send me *haget*-fish(?), a handful of onions, and . . . for me, your brother here. It is good if you take note.

Address: To Ankhtify from Sonbu.

110. P. Kahun VI.9
(Dynasty 12: second half)

This is a communication to the lord, l.p.h., to the effect that the lord, l.p.h., is sailing south [. . .], which had been done for me, your humble servant, without my knowing it. I, your humble servant, am writing about [this?] on the day for food rations just like any retainer of the lord, l.p.h., to whom a communication is sent.

Notes

1. Following the suggestion of Mr. Andrew Baumann.

2. Or possibly, "to prepare for the homecoming of [the lord], l.p.h., in health and [life]."

3. Or, "He caught 500 *redet*-fish and brought them in as catch."

4. Or possibly, "about having them assessed against the port of Perkheny by the lord, l.p.h."

5. Or, "to your [wife(?)], Heremhab, upon returning [like(?)] an Asiatic," perhaps a bit of sarcasm, alluding to Sinuhe B 265.

6. Used as pigment and in the manufacture of glaze.

7. Or, "he shall compensate him with other things."

VI

Eighteenth Dynasty Letters

Introduction

It is remarkable that so few letters of the Eighteenth Dynasty are extant, for during this period, when the Egyptian empire was established abroad and reached its zenith, there were extensive building activities in the Theban area. One would have expected the epistolary documentation to be more copious than it actually is, if only by comparison with the abundance of letters from the Ramesside community of Deir el-Medina. With the exception of the letters from Tell el-Amarna (Nos. 123–27), all the examples of correspondence in this section have either been discovered or can be presumed to have been found in the Theban necropolis. The first two documents, Nos. 111 and 112, are from excavations in the area of Hatshepsut's funerary temple at Deir el-Bahri in western Thebes. The Senenmut who is casually named in No. 112 is without a doubt the influential steward of Queen Hatshepsut and possessor of a tomb excavated in the area in front of her temple. Also involved in the building of Hatshepsut's temple was the scribe Ahmose, the recipient of several letters (Nos. 113–16) and author of No. 117. These papyrus letters were probably found in western Thebes, where Ahmose served as the deputy of the overseer of works Peniaty.

Sennofer, the mayor of Thebes and the author of letter No. 118, possessed a tomb in the Theban necropolis, noted for its beautifully decorated burial chamber. His letter was never sent, for it reached the Berlin Museum with its mud sealing still intact.

Although Letters Nos. 119 and 120 were acquired in the Theban area, the latter perhaps from Medinet Habu, Letters Nos. 121 and 122 were discovered in excavations at the workers' settlement of Deir el-Medina and represent two of the very few hieratic documents from the Eighteenth Dynasty phase of the town's occupation (Valbelle 1985: 21–22).

The two papyrus letters from a tomb at Tell el-Amarna (Nos. 123 and 124), though fragmentary, are especially important. They provide the earliest occurrence of epistolary formulae that were subsequently used in letters of the Ramesside period, and they supply evidence regarding a commoner's ability to call directly upon the Aton without the intermediation of the Pharaoh Akhenaton. Akhenaton has frequently been considered to be the only one with direct access to the Aton, the solar disk whose cult this king pursued with monotheistic fervor. The two brief letters on ostraca (Nos. 126 and 127) were discovered in the city of Akhetaton.

Letter No. 128, inscribed on a bowl, bears a certain similarity to the letters to the dead, translated in Part XII, but the request made to the recipient that he should write to a certain woman Tey suggests that he was still very much alive (Gunn 1930: 154).

============ **Personnel Problems** ============

111. *P. Deir el-Bahri 2*
(Dynasty 18: Hatshepsut)

Tit communicates to his lord Djehuty, l.p.h. In the favor of Amon-Re! This is a missive to inform my lord of a matter regarding Ptahsokar, inasmuch as it is you who interfered with him in connection with the personnel of Heliopolis. Confer with the reporter Geregmennefer, and then both of you send a letter about him to the Chief of Seers (the high priest of Re in Heliopolis).

Address: Tit to his lord Djehuty.

============ **Problem with an Old Man** ============

112. *O. Deir el-Bahri 7*
(Dynasty 18: Hatshepsut)

[*Personal name* greets] the scribe of the high priest of Amon-Re, King of the Gods. In the favor of Amon! [It is a communication to] you about the one whom you gave to me. See, he is an old man and is causing a bit of trouble for his [son(?)], Senenmut's stone-cutter, nowadays. [. . .] twenty blows.

============ **Letters to the Scribe Ahmose** ============

113. *P. BM 10102*
(Dynasty 18: Hatshepsut)

The mayor Mentuhotep greets the scribe Ahmose, Peniaty's man: In life, prosperity and health and in the favor of Amon-Re, King of the Gods, of Atum, lord of Heliopolis, of Re-Harakhti, of Thoth, lord of sacred writings, of [Seshat], mistress of script, and of your august god who loves you! May they give you favor, love, and proficiency wherever you may be.

A further matter: When the wall has attained a height of six cubits, you shall have the matting and beams of the storerooms and of the rear of the house installed. Now as for the doors of the storerooms, let them measure five cubits in their height; and as for the doors of the living room, let them measure six cubits in their height. And tell the builder Amenmose that he should do it just so and expedite the building of the house with great care. How good it is that my brother should be with you! It is you I am pre-occupied with.

A further matter: I shall send you the height[1] of the house and its width as well.

A further matter: Let some of the mats be saved and given to Benia.

A further matter: Let payment for the site of the house be given to its owner. Have him put in a good mood, mind you, lest he dispute with me when I return.

Address: The mayor Mentuhotep to the scribe Ahmose, Peniaty's man.

114. P. BM 10103
(Dynasty 18: Hatshepsut)

Hori greets his [lord] Ahmose: In life, prosperity and health and in the favor of Amon-Re, King of the Gods, of Ptah South-of-his-Wall, of Thoth, lord of sacred writings, and of the gods and goddesses who are in Karnak! May they give you favor, love, and proficiency wherever you may be. And further:

How are you? Are you all right? See, I'm all right.

Address: Hori to the scribe Ahmose, Peniaty's man, his lord.

115. P. BM 10107
(Dynasty 18: Hatshepsut)

Ptahu greets the scribe Ahmose: In life and prosperity and in the favor of Amon-Re!

This is a missive to inform you about the case of the maidservant who is in the charge of the mayor Tetimose. The master of slaves Abuy was sent to him to say, "Come, you shall litigate with him (Ptahu)." But he refused to be legally answerable for Mini because of what the overseer of fieldworkers Ramose had said. Look, as for this maidservant, she is a maidservant belonging to the mayor Mini, the sailor, whereas he (Mini?) does not give heed to me so as to litigate with me in the court of magistrates.

Address: Ptahu to the scribe Ahmose.

116. P. Louvre 3230a
(Dynasty 18: Hatshepsut)

Teti greets his beloved brother (colleague?) and fond friend, the scribe Ahmose: In life, prosperity and health and in the favor of Amon-Re, King of the Gods, your august god who loves [you], of Thoth, lord of sacred writings, and of Ptah the Great, South-of-his-Wall, lord of Ankhtowi! May they give you favor, love, and proficiency in everyone's presence. And further:

How are you? Are you all right? Now it is very much my desire to look upon you.

A further matter: I sowed much barley for you, and now it has grown [for] you into [. . .] your(?) barley which is in a corner of arable land along with your flax. It is [. . .] very much. And I won't let you be lacking in anything with regard to any of my obligations while I'm alive.

A further matter: Set your mind to finishing(?) [my(?)] house which is on the riverbank. Have it made properly like every successful enterprise of yours. Just as soon as I arrive, you shall have me come to enter into it. And let [. . .].

================ **Letter from the Scribe Ahmose** ================

117. *P. Louvre 3230b*
(Dynasty 18: Hatshepsut)

Addressed by Ahmose, Peniaty's (man), to his lord, the chief treasurer Tey:

Why is it that the maidservant who was with me has been taken away so as to be given to someone else? Am I not your servant obeying your orders both night and day? Let payment for her be accepted for her to be with me because she is only a child and unable to work. Or let my lord command that I be made to bear her work load just like any maidservant of my lord because her mother writes me saying, "It was you who allowed my daughter to be taken away although she was there in your charge. However, it is only because she is a daughter to you that I haven't complained to my lord," so she says by way of complaint.

======= **Instructions from the Mayor of Thebes Sennofer** =======

118. *P. Berlin 10463*
(Dynasty 18: Amenhotep II)

It is the mayor of the Southern City (Thebes) Sennofer who addresses the cultivator Baki, the son of Keysen:

This letter is brought to you by way of saying that I shall come to you after One (the king and his entourage?) has moored at the town of Hu-Sekhem within three days. Don't let me find fault with you regarding your post. Don't keep it from being in proper order, but pick for me many plants, lotus blossoms, and flowers to be made into bouquets(?) that will be fit for presentation. And also cut 5,000 boards and 200 planks(?) so that the boat which will come bringing me may pick them up since you haven't cut any wood this year. Mind you, you shall not be remiss. If you are prevented from cutting (wood), you shall turn to the mayor of Hu (i.e., Hu–Sekhem), User. See, there are the herdsmen of the town of Qus and the herdsmen of the cattle that are under my authority; requisition them for yourself to cut wood along with the workers who are already with you. And also order the herdsmen to have them furnish freshly jugged milk to await me on my arrival. Mind you, you shall not be remiss since I know that you are lethargic and enjoy eating while lying down.

Address: The mayor of the Southern City Sennofer to the cultivator Baki.

================ **Stonemasons** ================

119. O. Berlin 10614
(Dynasty 18)

Addressed by Kenamon to Hormose:
The eight stonemasons have finished with these. Write me about the other one that you desire so that I might have it/him brought to you. Do this! Send me payment for them.

============ **Complaint about a Woman** ============

120. O. Colin Campbell 21+O. Berlin 10616
(Dynasty 18)

It is the *wab*-priest Userhat who addresses his (text: my) sister Resti:
I have noticed the woman Iupy's indifference toward me in the midst of my adherents. Why has this chaff been given to me? Must I fetch for myself from [my own] house even though I have(?) no magazine? But [it is you who should] advise her properly so that she might be able to help you [in] whatever you [may do], for I have taken good care (of her). No accusation [has been] brought (against me?) as conclusive(?). Every time [I] enter to serve as *wab*-priest, I must go to fetch for myself [. . .] in order to have them become like my adherents.

Mind you, reprimand her! Don't let her be indifferent in the midst of my adherents.

Unloading a Boat

121. O. Cairo 25664
(Dynasty 18)

Amenemhat to Senu: Have the boat belonging to Nebiry unloaded.

Offerings

122. O. Cairo 25667
(Dynasty 18)

You are to tell the scribe Amenemone [. . .] to send me the statue. Give [. . .] the summary of apportionment. Now as for the divine offerings, hand them over to the *wab*-priest who is in Djeseret (Hatshepsut's Deir el-Bahri temple) and to the one who is in Akhset (Mentuhotep II's Deir el-Bahri temple), while the builder's workman should remain at the work.

Letters from Akhenaton's Capital at Amarna

123. P. Robert Mond 1
(Dynasty 18: Akhenaton)

The unguent preparator of the house of Princess [Meritaton], Ramose, greets his brother, the treasury scribe Meh: In life, prosperity and health and in the favor of the living Aton every day! And [further]:

How are you? Are you all right? I'm all right. Now here am I calling upon the Aton, l.p.h., in the city of Akhetaton, l.p.h., to keep [you] healthy each day and to keep you in the favor of [. . . the(?) . . . Meritaton]. I am [carrying on my] occupation in the house [of the mistress . . .].

A further matter: What's the meaning of your failing to write me about [all your state of health, for it is my desire to learn of your condition] each and every day. Now see, you know that [I am exceedingly concerned about you. Please tell (*feminine personal name*) what] you [have done] for Towy and [tell] her to send the woman [. . . that] he wrote me about [. . .], and you shall grant me that which [I am requesting(?)], look, or I shall appeal to the magistrates, and I promise that she shall have recourse to whom[ever] she should have recourse. [. . .] the house of the mistress, for I have no woman here with me to [. . .] for you. Keep silent about me and decide with her(?) [. . .].

Now if she gives heed to you so as to come, take her and go down(?)

[. . . bread], beer, and whatever else she may request just as(?) [. . . . If she] says, "I won't give heed to you," write to me right away [. . .] appeal to the magistrates, because to do or not to do is(?) [. . .]. "May the Aton [provide] me with guidance," so I said. And so he (the Aton) has provided [me with guidance. . . .] servants whom he [asked for]. The Aton-servant A[. . .] shall bring them/her [. . .] whom [I am] asking for, and you shall bring him and have him assent(?) to [. . .] that he may stay with me at the house of Meritaton [. . . until] you return.

Address: His brother, the treasury scribe Meh.

124. P. Robert Mond 2
(Dynasty 18: Akhenaton)

The unguent preparator of the house of Princess Meritaton, Ramose, greets his sister, the lady of the house Sherire: [In life, prosperity and health and in the] favor [of the] living Aton every day! And further:

How [are you? Are you all right?] I'm all right. Now here am I [calling upon the] Aton, l.p.h., to keep [you] healthy each and every [day], when he sets and when he rises, [and to . . .] knowledge of the Aton, l.p.h.

A further matter: What's the meaning of your failing to write me about all your state of health through whoever happens to come here [from you, for] you know that I am exceedingly concerned about you? Am I being too pushy (about this)?[2] If you have committed a million [faults], have I [not] forgotten them just as I forget my own which are in me? For my heart [. . .] at sending [. . . in(?)] the service of Meritaton. It has been a period of four(?) years now that no letter has reached [me] here from you. Now as for the letter, you/I shall [. . . say to(?)] Pamen, "Is [it] my daughter who told you not to write to him lest he take her away from [. . . ?" . . .] people(?), and he [. . .] his belittling me, for I had acted against her will. Did not [. . .] against me secretly? And you shall find me someone and send him to me, since the administrator of [. . .] them(?).

A further matter: As for . . . the footmen of my brother, you found [. . .] a way with you when you/I come returning from the country. [I] told you to write to the [. . . , but he(?)] didn't respond to them.

A further matter: When my letter reaches you and you read [it, you shall proceed] to return right away because I am concerned about you. Don't delay because [. . .] Aton [. . .] everyone who is friendly (?) [. . .] the Aton-[servant(?)] of the house of Princess Meritaton [. . .] against(?) me. Keep watch over the things that are in your possession because you can't comprehend how I live without a woman [here with me]. I can't find a person to have [him] bring her(?) [to me].

A further communication [to] Nebnefer(?): [If it is *personal name*] who said to you [. . .], it hasn't been done for me. And [you] shall write me about whatever I am to say. [When my] letter arrives there, you shall denounce him to the magistrates, and I will surely have recourse to whomever I should have recourse to. Now as for [. . . Pen]huybin.

A further matter: If it is my daughter who said to you, "Don't proceed [. . . to] return," don't listen to her.

A further communication to Towy: I say, "How are you? [Are you] all right?" Now here am I saying to the Aton, l.p.h., "Good cheer! Good cheer!" See, [I'm] all right. I have been provided with guidance.

A further communication to his brother Sehen[. . .]: The same.

A further [communication to the administrator(?)] Huy: The same.

A further communication to Weri: It is only because [no one(?)] came of those who are yours like those people who did come that I have not written to [. . .].

Address: The unguent preparator of the house of Meritaton, Ramose, to his sister, the lady of the house Sheri[re].

125. *O. Amarna 1*
(Dynasty 18: Akhenaton)

[*Personal name*] to the scribe Ramose:
Please give ten *deben* to Piay and give fifty [handfuls of rushes to . . .]. They have been [complaining] to me ever since I stood there myself with you [in court(?) and said], "Give fifty handfuls of rushes to the carpenter," so I said to you, and you told the guardian who was watching over the rushes to give them to him.

126. *O. Amarna 2*
(Dynasty 18: Akhenaton)

The scribe May of the city of Assiut to the scribe Meh:
Write! Please issue gypsum for the House of Sehetep-Aton, l.p.h., and the House of Nebmare (Amenhotep III), l.p.h.

127. *O. Amarna 3*
(Dynasty 18: Akhenaton)

Please open the magazine and issue seven bundles(?).

═══ Family Matters ═══

128. *Moscow Bowl 3917*
(late Dynasty 18)

The scribe Neb to his lord, the *wab*-priest Khenememuskhet:

This is a missive to inform my lord. Please have the woman Tit brought to you and reprimand her, asking whether it isn't so that Tit's share really belongs to me. What's the use of my speaking any further since I acted as an impatient man in divorcing (her as) my wife because of the food rations(?) and her share.

A further matter: Please may my lord write to the woman Tey saying that if she approaches me, I will strike her. Then you shall be able to do all that you(?) mentioned to me(?).

A further matter: Isn't it so that if you cease your kindness toward me, I shall do the same?

Notes

1. Or possibly, "length," rather than "height"; see O. Cairo 25581, rt. 2 and 4 (Černý 1930–35)

2. Perhaps literally, "As for being aggressive, is it what it (my heart) is doing exceedingly?"

VII

Papyrus Anastasi I:
A Satirical Letter

Introduction

The manuscript containing the most complete version of this lengthy epistle is Papyrus Anastasi I, written in a Lower Egyptian hand that is datable to the second half of the Nineteenth Dynasty. The provenience of the papyrus is unknown, but it is probably from the vicinity of Memphis, perhaps the nearby Sakkara necropolis. Although the composition was certainly intended for pedagogical purposes, it is by no means certain that Papyrus Anastasi I was a schoolboy's copy. In view of the cost of a roll of papyrus, it may instead be the product of a more advanced scribe, prepared for the use of younger students who would more than likely have made their trial copies on ostraca (James 1984: 144). Indeed, some eighty ostraca containing portions of this didactic letter derive from Deir el-Medina. There were apparently two recensions of the Satirical Letter, a northern one and a southern one, the former being closer to the original composition, which was probably written at the Delta capital of Pi-Ramessu in the first years of the reign of Ramesses II.

The author of this literary text in epistolary form was a certain Hori, who was both a scribe and a squire attached to the royal stables. In the Anastasi I version the recipient is entitled "command-writing scribe of the victorious army" but is not further identified by name, whereas the Theban recension further specifies that the recipient was a "scribe of recruits of the Two Lands, Amenemope, son of the steward Mose." Although in my translation I have supplemented the Anastasi I text with the titles and name of the recipient from the Theban recension, it is quite possible that the original version intentionally failed to name a specific recipient in order to make the audience of the work as broad as possible. Elsewhere in the text the recipient is designated by an expression which I have translated "What's-your-name?," something equivalent to an indefinite "So-and-so." It is possible that this vague designation of a recipient was reinterpreted as the proper name Mepu, a hypocoristic form of Amenemope, which was then secondarily inserted as the name of the recipient in the writer's greetings (Fischer-Elfert 1986: 283–86). At any rate, the author's intention was to have his work broadly disseminated in the schools, and in this he seems to have succeeded, as witness the many documents bearing portions of the text.

There is much that is touched upon in this epistle: proper greetings with wishes for this life and the next, the rhetoric of composition, interpretation of aphorisms in wisdom literature, application of mathematics to engineering problems and the calculation of supplies for an army, and the geography of western Asia. The writer not only evinces stylistic superiority but also is a master of a vocabulary that includes many Semitic loanwords, whose interpretation is often difficult.

One is impressed by the geographical awareness of the writer as he guides the reader through those portions of Syro-Palestine that were under Egyptian hegemony at the beginning of Ramesses II's reign. There is some paralleling with Asiatic localities named in earlier war-reliefs of Seti I at Karnak. With the Battle of Kadesh in Ramesses II's Year 5 and the Hittite Treaty in Year 21, there was an Egyptian withdrawal from Syria, but the Egyptian presence in Palestine continued to be felt even more strongly than in the preceding dynasty.

Although this composition was used in schools that had no association with military training, the military aspects of the text are evident, and there is no belittling the position of a military officer who was literate. This stands in contrast to other literary texts that stress the superiority of the scribal profession as against the hardships of the common soldier's life. This treatment of the elite military class falls in line with the militaristic tone of the first part of the Nineteenth Dynasty, whose kings were of military background.

The Satirical Letter can be viewed as a polemical tractate against the long-entrenched system of scribal education that laid great stress on rote memorization of lists of places, occupations, and terms for the natural world. It was no longer sufficient for the scribe simply to know the names of Asiatic localities, but he must also be acquainted with their topography and the routes connecting various places. The text employs sarcasm and irony in its attempt to improve the quality of the student's mind above the level of mere regurgitation of memorized facts.

For many years the basic edition of the Satirical Letter was that of Gardiner (1911), but since then a host of new documents providing illuminating parallels has come to light, chiefly ostraca from Deir el-Medina but also several papyri. None, however, is nearly as complete as Papyrus Anastasi I. Making use of all the new variants that have been published since Gardiner's edition, Fischer-Elfert (1983) reedited the entire composition with all the published parallels and produced a new translation in German with extremely valuable commentary (Fischer-Elfert 1986). The translation presented here owes much to earlier renditions, but the reader should be aware especially of my dependence on the work of Fischer-Elfert—even if I have not always followed his interpretations of certain passages.

129. P. Anastasi I
(Dynasty 19: Ramesses II)

The scribe of superior intellect, with sound advice, over whose utterances there is rejoicing when they are heard, so skilled in God's Words[1] that there is nothing of which he is ignorant, who is an able champion in the occupation of Seshat (goddess of writing and accounting) and a servant of the lord of Hermopolis (Thoth) in his writing chamber; an instructor of apprentices in the bureau of archives, the first of his colleagues and foremost among his associates, a leader of his class like whom there is none; of whom an example

is made for every young man, one who has advanced through his own efforts
and whom his fingers have aggrandized; a precocious child who has attained
his maturity, versed in intellectual pursuits and astute because of them;
discreet in his character, one beloved in people's hearts and not rebuffed,
whose friendship one longs for and never gets tired of; who bestirs himself
in inscribing blank sheets of papyrus; youthful, of distinguished appearance
and pleasant demeanor, who can interpret difficult passages in past records
just as the one who wrote them, whose every utterance is so steeped in honey
that hearts are restored thereby as through a ready potion; groom of His
Majesty, l.p.h., and retainer of the lord, l.p.h., who trains the Sovereign's
steeds, who is such an energetic stable hand that even a senior man who toils
as he is outstripped; one who loosens the yoke, Hori, son of Wennofer, of
the district of Abydos, the Island of the Righteous, born of Tawosre from the
region of Bilbeis, a chantress of Bastet in God's Field.[2]

He sends greetings to his friend and esteemed colleague, the royal
command-writing scribe of the victorious army, who is of exceptional intel-
ligence and good character, versed in intellectual pursuits, whose like does
not exist in any other scribe; beloved of everybody, as beautiful to one who
observes his demeanor as is a swamp flower in the estimation of foreigners;
such a scribe in every respect that there is nothing of which he is ignorant,
whose response is sought after in order to ascertain what is best; alert,
patient, and humanitarian, rejoicing over instances of justice and eschewing
iniquity, the scribe of recruits of the Lord of the Two Lands, Amenemope,
son of the steward Mose, a possessor of reverence (i.e., deceased).

May you live, be prosperous and healthy, O esteemed colleague, being well
supplied and well established without suffering want, possessing the requirements of life in food and provisions while joy and gladness are combined in
your vicinity. May they be issued to you during your lifetime and your
gateway not be barren. May you observe the rays of the sun and be satiated
thereby. May you spend [your] lifetime [in happiness] with your gods
pleased with you without displaying anger. May your reward [be receiv]ed
after old age. May you be salved with fine quality unguents like the blessed
ones. May you enter your tomb of the necropolis and associate with the
excellent Bas. May you be judged among them and be declared righteous in
Busiris before Onnophris, being well established in Abydos in the presence
of Shu-Onouris. May you cross over to the district of Poker in the god's
retinue and traverse the divine region in the retinue of Sokar. May you join
the crew of the Neshmet-bark without being turned away.[3] May you see the
sun in the sky when it initiates the year.

May Anubis (god of embalming) unite for you your head to your bones.
May you come forth from the hidden district without being annihilated. May
you observe the solar glow in the netherworld when it passes by you. May
the primordial waters overflow in your domain, immerse your path, and
irrigate to a depth of seven cubits near your tomb. May you sit down at the

river's edge at your moment of repose and wash your face and hands. May you receive offerings, and may your nose inhale the breezes and you let your throat breathe freely. May Tayet (goddess of weaving) clothe [. . .]. May Neper (grain god) give you bread and Hathor give you beer. May you suck from the udder of Sekhayet-Hor. May fine quality unguents be opened up for you. May you enter [. . .] your [. . .], and may you place him upon his seat. May [your] *ushebti*-figure[4] be accepted [when] it [comes over] carrying sand from the east [to] the west. May you grasp [. . .] of your sycamore goddess, and she lubricate your throat. May you drive [your opponents] away. [May you be powerful in] the earth, and may you be glorified [. . .] air. May you be triumphant in the sky, a luminary [. . .]. May you descend to the slaughterhouse(?) without being annihilated. May you transform yourself into whatever you desire like the phoenix, with each form of yours being that of a god according to your [predilection].

A further matter: Your letter reached me during the hour of siesta. Your messenger found me as I was sitting beside the horses which are in my charge. Being so glad and joyful, I was all set to reply, but when I entered my stable to have a look at your letter, I discovered that it comprised neither praises nor insults. Your sentences are jumbled, this one with that one, and all your words are turned about and disconnected. Each composition of yours is fragmented by digressions(?). [. . .] bottom and top(?). Your beginning is [. . . . Your letter is mix]ed up treating improprieties and niceties and the best with [. . .]. Your statements are neither sweet nor bitter. All that issues from your mouth is [bitter almonds] and honey. You have surpassed pomegranate wine mixed with second-rate wine.

I have written to you advising you as a friend, instructing one who is senior to myself to be a proficient scribe. Now as for me, since you have expressed yourself, I must respond inasmuch as your statements are idle words. You act like one who is agitated(?) so as to alarm me, but I have not become awestricken before you knowing your character. I fancied that you would answer alone by yourself. However, your aides stand in back of you, and you have assembled many agents(?) as helpers as though you were on your way to court. Your face is wild as you stand coaxing supporters, saying, "Come along with me and assist me." You tender them gifts, each one individually, and they tell you, "Have courage, we shall prevail over him."

You stand per[turbed . . .] in their presence, and they sit deliberating, that is, the six scribes. You go with them [for a] seventh, and you assign two sections to each one so that you might finish off your letter of fourteen sections. While one composes praises and two compose insults, the next one is standing by instructing them regarding the proper arrangement. The fifth says, "Don't rush! Be patient at it with careful work." The sixth hurries off to measure the lake. He squares it off in cubits in order to have it dug. The seventh stands near at hand receiving the rations for the soldiers. Your pay schedules are so disorganized that they cannot be unraveled. Kheruef[5] plays deaf and does not listen. He swears by Ptah saying, "I won't let a seal be put on the granary," and off he goes in a huff. By what amount is the *hekat*-measure too scant when the loss is five *hin*-measures for each *oipe?*[6]

See here, you are the scribe who issues commands to the army. Men hear what you have to say, and you are not bypassed. You are expert as a scribe, and there is nothing which you are ignorant of. Yet your letter is too inferior to merit consideration. You have foolishly been deprived of your papyrus. If you had only known beforehand that it is no good, you would not have sent it but said, "As for the documents(?), they are all the time in contact(?) with my fingertips like an incantation scroll against ague on an invalid's neck. They are all the time on [my] la[p](?) and do not tire of being bound by the string of my seal."[7]

I will answer you in a similar manner in a letter that is original from the first page to the colophon, it being filled with utterances from my lips that I have composed alone by myself with no one else with me. By the *Ka* of Thoth, it is on my own that I have written without having summoned any scribe to have him assist. I shall deliver even more to you by twentyfold. I will detail for you what you have said, point by point, (in) the fourteen sections of your letter.

Keep me supplied with papyrus, and I will tell you many things and pour out to you choice words just as the Nile inundation overflows, and the flood glitters [in] the inundation season when it has attained the raised mounds, for all my words are sweet and pleasant in diction. I will not do as you when you cursed and started out against me with insults at the very onset. You did not even greet me at the beginning of your letter. Far from me be your threats! They shall not assail [me], because my god Thoth is a shield about me. By the *Ka* of Ptah, lord of Maat, I wouldn't think of repulsing them. Look here, carry out your threats! They have proved so effective! Turn each utterance of yours against whatever enemy! I will yet be buried in Abydos in my father's tomb, for I am a son of Maat in the Island of the Righteous. I will be buried among fellow men in the mountain of the Holy Land (the Abydos necropolis).

Of what does my fault consist in your opinion? Then you should reprove it. And to whom have I mentioned you with an evil mention? As if for recreation, I will write for you a composition so that it becomes diversion for everybody.

You continued by calling me a weakling lacking vigor. You have held me in contempt as a scribe and have said, "He knows nothing." I won't spend a moment in your presence for the sake of coaxing you and saying, "Be a protector for me, for someone else is tormenting me." By the decree of the Mighty Lord (the king), whose name is powerful and whose statutes are as enduring and permanent as those of Thoth, it is I who am the supporter of all my kinsfolk. Again you have said concerning me, "You shall fall," . . . but I know many persons lacking vigor, weaklings who are exhausted and have no strength, yet who have been so enriched in their homes with food and provisions that they need not express want of anything.

Come, let me describe to you the way of the scribe Roy, dubbed the firebrand of the granary. He neither budged nor stirred since his birth. Strenuous work was an abomination to him, and he never became acquainted with it. Now he rests in the West with his body intact, and dread of the Perfect God (the king) shall never overtake him.

You are more foolish than Kasa, the reckoner of cattle. But to move on, since I have already described to you his way lest you should scoff(?). Haven't you heard the name of Amenwahsu, a veteran of the treasury? He spent his lifetime as manager in the workshop next to the armory.

Come, [let me tell] you about Nakht, the one employed in the wine store. He seems ten times more glamorous to you than these others. Let me tell you about Paherypedjet, who used to live in Heliopolis. He is a veteran of the Palace, l.p.h. He is smaller than a cat but bigger than a monkey, yet he is well-off in his home having his property in his possession. It is forever(?) that you will remain there in the stable!

Have you heard the name of Kyky, the dust ball? It is unnoticed that he moves over the ground, disheveled in attire and tightly girt. If you were to see him at evening in the dark, you would think that he was a bird passing by. Put him on the scales and see how heavy he is! He will weigh for you twenty *deben,* excluding rags. If you should exhale close to him as he passes by, like a leaf of foliage he will drop down far away.

If I tell you about Wah, the one employed in the cattle stalls, you will reward me with thrice-refined gold. I swear by the lord of Hermopolis (Thoth) and Nehemawayet, saying, "You are strong-armed and will overthrow them." You should let [them] be tested, those and these. I will overwhelm them with my arms, [for none can thwa]rt my hands. O What's-your-name?, my friend, who does not know what you say, see, I will interpret your difficult passages and render them easy.

You have come provided with great secrets and have quoted to me one of Hordedef's maxims, but you do not know whether it is good or bad. Which stanza precedes it and which one follows it? You are supposed to be an expert scribe at the head of your (text: his) colleagues having the lore of every book engraved in your memory. How precious your tongue is when you speak! A single maxim issues from your mouth worth three *debens.* You cast aspersion upon me so as to frighten me. My eyes stare at what you do, and I am aghast when you say, "I am profound as a scribe regarding heaven, earth, and the underworld, even knowing the size of mountains in *deben*-weights and *hin*-measures." Granted that the library is hidden and not to be seen, and its ennead of gods is concealed far away from [your sight], tell me what you know. Then I will answer you, "Beware lest your fingers approach God's Words!" If an apprentice . . . as when [. . .] sits down to play the game of *senet.*

You have told me, "You are neither a scribe nor are you a soldier, yet on your own you have set yourself up as an authority. You are not on the register." But you yourself are a royal scribe who enrolls soldiers, and all [commands] under the sky are spread out in your presence. Go to the office of the record [keepers] that they may let you see the chest containing the rosters, taking a bouquet for Heresh that he may quickly disclose to you information about myself. You will discover my name on a papyrus scroll as a squire in the Great Stable of Sese-miamon, l.p.h.,[8] and you will find testimony in the administrative order of the stable that a food allowance is on record in my name. So I will prove to be a squire and prove to be a scribe! There is no youth of my generation who can even match me. Inquire about a man from his superior! Be off to my captains that they may report on me to you!

You continued saying to me, "A lofty forested mountain(?) lies ahead of you. Enter into such a wild mountain forest(?), which you do not know." As soon as you have entered therein ahead of me, I must come in after you. If only you had not drawn near to it, you would not have attempted it! If you should discover its interior, while I have turned back, beware of helping me extricate myself.

You have told me, "You are not a scribe, an appellative that is empty and hollow. You hold the palette illicitly without having been authorized." I am stupid [for want of] a teacher. Tell me such confounded things [so as to] be able to displace me. You have harnessed yourself against me once more again. Your utterances falsify and will not be listened to. Let your fetters be taken before the god Onouris that he may determine for us who is right lest you become angry.

A further matter: See, I have come replete with your calling so that I might inform you of your situation since you have said, "It is I who am the command-writing scribe of the troops." You have been assigned a lake to dig. Having forsaken your calling, you have come to me to inquire about the distribution of rations to the workforce and have told me, "Figure it out!" To teach you how to do it has fallen upon my shoulders.

Come, and I will tell you more than what you have said. I warn you that you will be disheartened. I will disclose to you a command from your lord, l.p.h., inasmuch as you are his royal scribe. You are dispatched from beneath the royal audience window for all sorts of splendid products when the mountains are disgorging great monuments for Horus, Lord of the Two Lands. See, it is you who are the expert scribe who is at the head of the troops.

There is to be constructed a ramp of 730 cubits in length with a width of 55 cubits, containing 120 compartments provided with rushes and beams, having a height of 60 cubits at its summit and 30 cubits at its middle, with a batter of 15 cubits, while its base is of 5 cubits. The amount of bricks required for it is asked of the commander of the workforce. The scribes are all gathered together through lack of one who knows among them. So they all put their trust in you, saying, "You are an expert scribe, my friend. Decide for us quickly. See, your name is celebrated. Let one be found in this place capable of magnifying the other thirty. Don't let it be said of you that there is anything of which you are ignorant. Answer for us the amount of bricks required for it. Look, its dimensions(?) are before you with each one of its compartments being 30 cubits long and 7 cubits wide."

O What's-your-name?, you vigilant scribe who is at the head of the work-force, with a distinguished position at the Great Double Portal and hand-some while bowing down beneath the royal audience window. A dispatch arrives from the crown prince at the district of Ka⁹ to convey good tidings to the Horus of Gold and to glorify the raging lion (the king), saying, "An obelisk has been newly made, engraved with the name of His Majesty, l.p.h., and having a shaft of 110 cubits. Its pedestal is of 10 cubits, while the perim-eter of its (the obelisk's) base measures 7 cubits on each side. It proceeds with a taper of one cubit and one digit as far as the top, and its pyramidion is one cubit in height with its point(?) being two digits." Total up their parts(?) to make them into portions so that you may assign each man who is needed to haul them and they may set out for the Red Mountain. See, they are awaited. Give fair passage to the crown prince. The sun's offspring (the prince) is near at hand. Determine for us the required number of men who shall be at his disposal.

Don't make it so that a communication has to be sent again, for the monu-ment lies ready in the quarry. Answer quickly! You should not dawdle, since it is you who are seeking them (the number of men required) for yourself. Press on! See, if you bestir yourself, I will make you glad. Previously I used to [work] like you. So let us marshal the ranks together, for my mind is shrewd and my fingers obey being skillful just where you go astray. Get on and do not weep! Your helper is right behind you. I will cause you to say, "Horus, Mighty Bull, has a royal scribe." May you commission men to make chests into which letters can be put. I would have written you secretly, but see, it is you who are seeking them (the number of men) for yourself. You have caused my fingers to be slicing away up as if at a bull in a feast at every festival of eternity(?).

You are told to empty the magazine that is loaded with sand beneath the colossus of your lord, l.p.h., which has been brought from the Red Moun-tain. It measures 30 cubits lying extended on the ground and has a width of 20 cubits. The foundation consists of ten cells filled with sand from the river-bank, while the partitions of [its] cells have a width of 12(?) cubits, and they all have a height of 50 cubits. Vents are located in their encasements(?). You are charged to ascertain what should be before (the statue). How many men will be required to remove it in six hours—although they are reliable, their will is insufficient to remove it before midday has come and you can give a break to the workforce that they may take their lunch(?)—so that the colossus may be erected in its place? It is One's (the king's) wish to see it beautiful!

O you scribe, so alert and competent that there is nothing at all of which you are ignorant, who blazes in the darkness at the head of the troops and illumines for them, you are dispatched on a mission to Djahy (Syro-Palestine) at the head of the victorious army in order to crush those rebels who are called Naarin-warriors. The host of soldiers that is under your charge comprises 1,900 men (Egyptians), 520 Sherden, 1,600 Kehek, [100] Meshwesh and 880 Nubians, a total of 5,000 all told, apart from their captains. There are brought to you bonus rations into your presence: bread, sheep and goats, and wine. The number of men is too large for you, and the foodstuff is insufficient for them: only 300 sweet loaves, 1,800 cakes, 120 assorted goats and sheep, and 30 jugs of wine. The army is so numerous that the foodstuff has been underestimated as though you had pilfered from it. You receive it in charge to be deposited in the camp. The troops are prepared and ready, so divide it quickly into portions, each man's share into his hands. The Shasu-Beduin are watching furtively. O Sṛpher yodea,[10] midday is come, and the camp is hot. One says, "It's time to move on." Don't make the troop marshaler angry. We still have a long march ahead of us. What bread do we have at all? Our night camp is far away. O What's-your-name?, what's the sense of scourging us so, when you are supposed to be an expert scribe? It is only after six(?) hours have elapsed in the day that you proceed to distribute the provisions through want of a scribe from the Ruler, l.p.h. Getting you to scourge us, that's not good! Mose[11] shall learn of it and send to do away with you.

Your letter abounds in sarcasm and is overburdened with grandiose words. See, I will requite you with such as they deserve, for you have piled them on just as you pleased. "I am a soldier-scribe," so you did retort. If there is truth in what you have said, come outside in order that you may be tested.

There is harnessed for you a span of horses, swift as a leopard, whose ears are red, and which are like a storm-wind when they burst forth. You let go of the reins and pick up the bow. We will see what your hands can achieve! I will explain to you the way of a Maher-warrior and show you what he has to do.

You have not journeyed to the land of Khatti nor have you visited the land of Upe. As for Khadum, you do [not] know its topography, nor that of Yagadiya either. What is the Simyra of Sese, l.p.h.,[12] like? In which direction from it lies the city of Aleppo? What is its river like? You have not had occasion to set out for Kadesh and Tubikhi, nor have you gone with the host of soldiers to "Spring of the Shasu-Beduin." You have not trodden the road to Magara, where the sky is dark by day. It is overgrown with junipers and oaks, and pine trees reach the sky. Lions are more abundant than leopards and bears, while it is hemmed in on all sides by Shasu-Beduin. You have not climbed Mount Shawe barefoot with your hands placed upon your legs and your chariot lashed with ropes while your horses are tugging.

O come and visit [I]birta(?). You panic [at] the prospect of climbing it after you have crossed its river for it (the climb). You experience how it feels to be a Maher-warrior with your chariot placed on your shoulder. Your aide is exhausted. When at last you quit in the evening, your whole body is crushed and battered, and your limbs are bruised. You get lost in sleep. You wake up when it is time to move on in the too-short night, being alone to harness up, for no colleague comes to (assist) another. The vagabond band has penetrated the camp, and the horses have been cut loose. The [. . .] has withdrawn by night, and your clothes have been stolen. Your groom awoke during the night and realized what he must do. He has taken what was left and has joined up with those who are wicked. He consorts with the Shasu-Beduin tribes and assumes the guise of an Asiatic. The enemy comes furtively to pillage, and they find you torpid. You awake but can find no trace of them. They have carried off your possessions. So you have become a fully outfitted Maher-warrior if you have been attentive!

I will recount to you another remote city which is called Byblos. What is it like? And its goddess?[13] Once again [you] have not set foot in it. Please inform me about Beirut, about Sidon, and Sarepta. Where is the river Litani? What is Usu (Old Tyre on the mainland) like? They speak of another city in the sea the name of which is Tyre-of-the-Harbor. Water is taken over to it in scows, and it is richer in fish than in sand.

I will mention to you another difficulty: "The Pass of the Hornets" (the Ladder of Tyre). You will say that it burns more than a (hornet's) sting. How miserable he is, a Maher-warrior! Come and put [me] on the road heading south to the region of Acco. Where does the route to Achshaph originate? Next to which city? Please inform me about the mountain of User. What is its summit like? Where does the mountain of Shechem rise? Who can conquer it? The Maher-warrior, where does he march to get to Hazor? What is its river like? Put me [on] the highway to Hamath, Dagal, and Dagal-El, the promenade of every Maher-warrior. Please instruct me about his route and let me visit Yan. If someone is traveling to Adumim, in which direction should he head? Do not falter from your teaching. Guide us to know them (the places)!

Come and I will tell you of other cities which lie above these. You have not gone to the land of Takhsy, to Kur-Marruna, Taminta, Kadesh, Dapur, Azaya, or Hermon. You have not visited Kiriath-Anab and Beth-Sopher. You are not acquainted with Adurun or Sidiputu either. You do not know the name of Khalsu, which is in the land of Upe, a bull on its frontier and the battle scene of all sorts of champions. Please instruct me about the topography of Kina, acquaint me with Rehob, and explain Bethshan and Tirek-El. As for the river Jordan, how can it be crossed? Inform me of the pass to Megiddo, which lies above it.

You are a Maher-warrior who is experienced in heroic deeds. A Maher-warrior such as yourself should be found qualified to advance at the head of an army. O Maryan-warrior, forward to shoot! See, the declivity(?) is a ravine

2,000 cubits deep, filled with boulders and small stones, so you make a detour. You pick up the bow and draw to your left that you might let the chiefs see, but their vision is perfect and weakness is discerned(?) in your hands. "You wander about like a sheep, dear Maher-soldier!" Thus you celebrate the name of every Maher-warrior, Egypt's chariot officers. Your name has become like that of Kezardy, the prince of Asher, when the bear found him in the balsam tree.

The narrow pass is dangerous, having Shasu-Beduin concealed beneath the bushes, some of whom are of four cubits or five cubits (from) their nose to foot and have fierce faces. They are unfriendly and do not take to cajolery while you are alone having no aide with you nor soldiery backing you up. You find no scout to prepare safe passage for you. You reach a decision by forging ahead ignorant of the road. Such bristling fright grips you that (the hair of) your head is ruffled. Your *Ba* lies in your hands. Your path is filled with boulders and small stones without a toe hold for passage as it is overgrown with reeds and thorns, brambles, and "wolf's-paw." The declivities lie to one side of you, and the mountain rises on the other side of you. With your chariot lying on its side, you move along swerving to and fro too afraid to pursue your horses. If they are thrown toward the abyss, your horse collar is left exposed and your harness(?) falls. You unharness the team in order to repair the horse collar in the middle of the narrow pass, but you are inexperienced in how to lash it and cannot tie it fast. The clamp(?) is left where it is, for the team is too overburdened to support it. You are disgusted and get set to trot off. The sky is now clear, but you imagine that the enemy is behind you, and trembling grips you. If only you had a hedge of shrubbery to put on the other side! The team is exhausted by the time you locate a camping spot. You have undergone a miserable experience.

You have now entered Joppa and find the meadowland verdant in its season. You force your way in because of appetite and encounter the beautiful maiden who is tending the vineyards. She allures you to herself to be a partner (in love) and surrenders to you the flesh of her bosom. You are recognized as soon as you have uttered advice.[14] So judgment is rendered against a Maher-warrior, and you must sell your tunic of fine thin linen.

Tell me how you can go to sleep each evening with only a piece of sackcloth over you. You slumber only because you are so exhausted. A poltroon(?) takes away your bow, your girdle-dagger, and your pair of quivers. Your reins have been severed in the darkness, and your team goes off picking up speed(?) over the slippery terrain as the road extends ahead of it. It smashes your chariot and makes [. . .] your leather canteens fall to the ground and are buried in the sand. They become part of the dry earth. Your aide begs for bread(?) for your mouth, "Now that I have safely arrived, you people should give a bit of food and water." But they play deaf and do not hearken. They take no notice of your accounts.

If only you could enter inside the armory with workshops surrounding

you and carpenters and leather workers in your vicinity, they would do all
that you desire. They would take care of your chariot so that it would cease
to be inoperative. Your chariot pole would be retrimmed and its supports(?)
installed. They would attach leather straps to your horse collar and . . . and
furnish your yoke. They would mount your chariot case, which has burin
engraving, [on] the frames. They would attach a pommel to your whip and
fasten a lash [to] it. You would then go quickly forth to fight on the battle-
field in order to perform heroic deeds.

O What's-your-name?, you elite scribe and Maher-warrior, who know
how to use your hands, a leader of Naarin-troops at the head of the soldiery,
I have described to you the hill countries of the northern reaches of the land
of Canaan, but you have not answered me in any way nor have you rendered
a report to me. Come, and [I] will describe [ma]ny things [to] you. Head
toward(?) the fortress of the Way[s of Horus].[15] I begin for you with the
Dwelling of Sese, l.p.h. You have not set foot in it at all. You have not eaten
fish from [its pool(?)] nor bathed in it. O that I might recall to you Husayin.
Whereabouts is its fortress? Come now to the region of Edjo of Sese, l.p.h.,
into its stronghold of Usermare, l.p.h., and [to] Seba-El and Ibesgeb. I will
describe to you the appearance of Aiyanin.[16] You are not acquainted with its
location. As for Nekhes and Heberet,[17] you have not visited them since your
birth. You Maher-warrior, where is Raphia? What is its enclosure wall like?
How many miles march is it to Gaza? Answer quickly! Render a report to
me that I may call you a Maher-warrior and boast of your name to others.
"He is a Maryan-warrior," so I shall tell them.

You have become angry over my having told you that I am versed in every
calling. My father taught me what he knew and gave instruction so many
times that I am able to hold the reins even more skillfully than you. There
is no champion who can even match me, for I am initiated in the ordinances
of Montu.[18] How slanderous is all that issues from your tongue! How feeble
your sentences are! It is wrapped up in confusion and laden with errors that
you have come to me. You split words apart in charging straight ahead and
are not loath to grope (for words). Be energetic! Forward! Hurry on! You
shall not fall! What is it like for one to be ignorant of what he has attained?
And what will the outcome of this be? I shall back off now that I have reached
the end. Submit yourself! Control your emotions with a composed mind.
Don't get in a huff, rushing because of appetite(?). I have cut short for you
the end of your letter and have answered you what you have said. Your
discourses are collected on my tongue and remain fixed on my lips, for they
are so confused when heard that no interpreter can unravel them. They are
like a Delta man's conversation with a man of Elephantine.[19]

Yet you are a scribe of the Great Double Portal who reports the affairs of
the Two Lands, so comely and handsome [to] one who observes this that you
should not say that I have made your name reek before foreigners and all.
See, I have described to you the way of a Maher-warrior and traveled

through [Re]tenu for you. I have introduced to you foreign countries at a single time with cities in their proper sequence. O that you might look them over at leisure so that you might be found able to describe them and become with us a well-traveled guide(?).

Notes

1. An expression that includes both script and sacred writings in all fields of learning.

2. The region of Bubastis in the Delta.

3. These lines refer to the annual ceremonies at Abydos in which the dead were believed to participate.

4. A small mummiform image of the deceased capable of performing agricultural labor in the beyond on his behalf.

5. A superintendent of the granary by this name is attested in the first part of Ramesses II's reign, see Letter No. 46 and Kitchen (1968-: 3:30, 147, 154).

6. Since there are four *hekat*-measures in an *oipe*, the answer is one and one-fourth *hin*.

7. Perhaps the implication of this obscure passage is that Amenemope should have kept his letter tied up without sending it.

8. The name of the stable employs the nickname of Ramesses II, Sese.

9. "Ka" was perhaps a designation of one of the branches of the Nile in the western Delta.

10. Meaning "expert scribe" in Semitic language.

11. Probably the name of a high military officer.

12. Sese is Ramesses II's nickname.

13. This goddess was Hathor.

14. Possibly advice in love-making.

15. The frontier fortress of Tjel at the head of the military road to Palestine.

16. Meaning "Two Wells."

17. Or, "As for the runnels of Heberet."

18. I.e., the art of warfare, whose patron deity was Montu.

19. Evidence for the existence of dialects in ancient Egypt.

VIII

Ramesside Letters

Introduction

In this section are letters of the Nineteenth and Twentieth Dynasties, except those relating to affairs of the workmen's village of Deir el-Medina in western Thebes. These are translated separately in Part IX. The majority of Nineteenth Dynasty correspondence, including nine letters from the reign of Ramesses II (Nos. 22–30, translated in Part II), is either from the Memphite area or deals with affairs in Lower Egypt. By contrast, the Twentieth Dynasty letters are all from Upper Egypt.

There are two respects, reflected in the letters, in which Lower Egypt differed from Upper Egypt. The broad expanses of the Delta provided excellent tracts for the grazing of livestock and afforded good opportunities for fowling and fishing. In addition, Lower Egypt was noted for specialized crops grown in its orchards, vineyards, and papyrus swamps.

The other feature that differentiated Lower Egypt from Upper Egypt during the Ramesside period was the greater proportion of the population employed in the military or in occupations associated with the royal stables. The Nineteenth Dynasty line of pharaohs, being of Lower Egyptian origin, founded a new capital, Pi-Ramessu, in the southeastern Delta. This was a vast city with a significant military component, including barracks and parade grounds for the armed forces. The concentration of the military in Lower Egypt was logical, for it was closer than the south to areas of great strategic importance: western Asia, where the Egyptian empire faced the threat of an expanding Hittite empire, and Libya, whose aggressive tribes sought to penetrate the western Delta.

Reflecting the agricultural aspects of Lower Egypt are two letters addressed to overseers of cattle (Nos. 130 and 137) and another (No. 131) concerned with a cattle census; the subject of cattle figures prominently also in No. 144. No. 141, a copy of a real letter sent from Lower Egypt to Thebes, details the diversity of agricultural occupations carried on in the Delta estate of the god Amon of Thebes, and No. 143 deals with the shipping of wool, fish, rushes, and papyrus, all products of Lower Egypt.

Illustrating the military aspects of Lower Egypt are several letters written by a standard-bearer (Nos. 133–35) and other letters sent to persons whose occupation was related directly or indirectly to the military (Nos. 138–40, and 145). No. 150 is a copy of a communication sent by a garrison scribe stationed at Gaza to his superior.

111

Other letters contain references to military personnel within the text of the communication (Nos. 130, 132, 139, 146, and 147).

With the exception of the brief letter on an ostracon from Abydos (No. 136), the Nineteenth Dynasty letters from Upper Egypt were probably all found in the area of Thebes. No. 142 is a copy of a letter sent from the southern border of Egypt to an overseer of cattle, who was presumably located at Thebes, and is concerned with the delivery of cattle from Nubia, the source of long-horned cattle that figure prominently in depictions of the Feast of Opet in the Luxor temple. No. 146 may have been sent from Memphis to the Theban area, while No. 148, inscribed on an ostracon, seems to have been a purely local communication between two priests functioning at Amenhotep III's mortuary temple in western Thebes. Rather puzzling is the provenience of No. 149, a papyrus letter from Deir el-Medina, addressed by a scribe of the offering table to an army captain, for the contents of the letter have no apparent relevance to affairs of this village.

The probable provenience of two Twentieth Dynasty letters written by the cattle overseer of the Estate of Amon-Re (Nos. 151 and 152) is Thebes, but it is not quite clear from where these letters were sent. It has been supposed that Kheriu was located in Middle Egypt. The writer's instructions have to do with the clearing of land and the cutting of wood and charcoal, which were used for fuel. No. 153, sent from Thebes to Elephantine, is a complaint about some poor quality honey the mayor of Elephantine had sent for the god Harakhti, while No. 154, from a builder at Thebes to a traveling merchant of the Temple of Amon-Re, treats the complicated case of the seizure of a slave-woman and her son. The affair of a fugitive in Upper Egypt (No. 155) mentions a consultation with the oracle of the god Seth. Although the god's response is expressed in the form of a statement, it is known that the technique for rendering oracular decisions in the New Kingdom required the petitioner to submit his petition before the god in the form of a question demanding a yes-or-no answer. The motions of a portable bark or litter of the god carried on the shoulders of lay priests was the manner in which the god indicated his decision after a manner akin to the movements made on the modern Ouija board.

Letter No. 156 was written during the last reign of the Twentieth Dynasty by the mayor of Elephantine to a superior official at Thebes named Menmarenakht. Although called "chief taxing master," he was probably the same person as the "overseer of the treasury and overseer of the granary Menmarenakht," mentioned in Letter No. 290, translated in Part X.

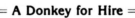

A Donkey for Hire

130. P. Cairo 58057
(Dynasty 19: Ramesses I)

The warden Dhutmose of the Estate of Menpehtyre (Ramesses I) greets the overseer of cattle of the herd Payiry . . . : In [life], prosperity and health! And further:

Please return the donkey for hire that you have in your charge through the agency of the servant Piay because it has been assigned to him for hire on the farmland of the Estate of Menpehtyre, which is on the Island of Pekha, under the authority of the soldier Mesha of the Estate of Menpehtyre. To inform you of this: one donkey is what was given to you by the soldier Tenen of the regiment "Dazzling like the Sun Disk" in the year of the Bow of Djeper.[1] He told you to give it to Dhutmose, but you didn't give it. I and the stable master Amenmose apprehended you there in Memphis saying, "Give it back!" And you said to me, "Don't take [me] to court! See, the donkey is in my charge. Is it that you sent someone to take it (for hire) and I refused to hand it over?" so you said. And you took an oath by the lord, l.p.h., saying, "I shall return it." Look here, you haven't returned it yet, and the tariff on it is being exacted from me year after year even though it remains in your charge.

===== The Cattle Levy =====

131. P. Cairo 58058
(Dynasty 19: Ramesses I–Seti I)

It is the scribe Mesha who addresses the servant Piay:

When my [letter] reaches [you, you shall] inspect the contribution of cattle of the estate that are in the charge of the slave Lulu and press(?) him very hard. And you shall look into the status of Pabak, who follows him, since I've heard that he has departed from him and no longer has cattle in his charge.

Now look, they have come to take the cattle census. Pay attention carefully and take heed! It is only when the cattle of the contribution are made ready that you should let the [. . .] proceed [to] return.

===== Treatment of a Visitor =====

132. P. Northumberland 1
(Dynasty 19: Ramesses I–Seti I)

The scribe Meh greets the scribe Yey Junior: In life, prosperity and health and in the favor of Amon-Re, King of the Gods! And further:

What is your condition? How are you? What is your condition? Are you all right? I'm all right. Now I am calling upon Amon, Ptah, Pre-Harakhti, and all gods of the Temple of Thoth to keep you healthy, to keep you alive, to keep you in the favor of Ptah, your good lord, to let you undertake things and have them succeed, and to let you be rewarded for whatever you have achieved.

A further matter: Please give your personal attention to the chariot officer Merymose. See, I've sent Merymose to the mayor to say, "Seek out those two boats which Pharaoh, l.p.h., assigned to him and have them sought for him wherever they may be." And also give your personal attention to Merymose while he is there with you. Don't let him be treated after the manner you dealt with me when I was there in Memphis and you kept half rations in your possession to be converted into money.

A further communication, being the words of the chantress of Amon Isisnofre: How are you? I very much long to see you, with my eyes as big as Memphis since I'm hungry for the sight of you! But here am I calling upon Thoth and all gods of the Temple of Thoth to keep you healthy, to keep you alive, and to let you be rewarded for whatever you have achieved.

A further matter: Please give your personal attention to Merymose and give heed to the assignment about which the general has written you. And write to him in your name and write to me all about your state of health. Farewell!

A further communication, being the words of the scribe Meh: Please have Merymose bring me a roll of papyrus as well as some very good ink, and don't send any bad. And also write to me all about your state of health. Farewell!

Address: The scribe Meh to the scribe Yey Junior.

=============== **Orders from a Standard-Bearer** ===============

133. P. Cairo 58053
(Dynasty 19: Seti I)

It is the standard-bearer Maiseti who addresses the garrison captains who are in the Northern Region:

I have learned that you have been interfering with the god's personnel in Tell el-Balamun who are under the authority of the royal scribe Iuny. What's the meaning of your acting this way? By Amon and by the Ruler, [l.p.h.], if I learn that you have further interfered with the god's personnel who are in your vicinity, see, I shall severely reprimand you, if that's what you want, for the officials of Pharaoh, l.p.h., are severely reprimanding me personally.

Please carry out your assignment properly. Don't be remiss concerning the orders which I entrusted to you. As regards all this that is in the orders, don't ignore it but procure for us men who have been dismissed from this and no longer constitute a squad. And don't create a commotion in the place which is sublime, but come that you may return.

When this letter reaches you, you shall prevent service for the god there from remaining inactive, or you will go to jail. Please take note of this.

Address: It is the standard-bearer Maiseti who addresses the squad leaders who are in the Northern Region.

134. P. Cairo 58054
(Dynasty 19: Seti I)

It is the standard-bearer Maiseti who addresses the soldier Hat:

What is the reason for your apprehending the laborers(?)[2] who are [...]? Did I tell you to apprehend them? Aren't the (arrest) orders which I gave to you in your hand spelled out in writing? It is these only whom I told you to apprehend. Is it [in order to] have me humiliated that you have proceeded to do wrong with respect to the laborers(?) [who are ...]? Now when this letter reaches you, you shall investigate this which you have done and put matters aright. Take heed of me! Don't keep a hold on the laborers(?) any longer!

A further matter: Please round up the soldiers [of the army who] are in the villages that are in your vicinity. Mind you, if you let any soldiers of the army tarry in the villages that are in your vicinity, be careful! Keep them occupied with the steeds of the stable masters of the villages until I reach Memphis.

A further matter: Don't let a one of the orders that I submitted to you in writing be obstructed.

A further matter: Please procure especially fine men who will perform well, for [...] has brought to [...] his(?) colleagues, [and you shall] procure [fine] workmen.

A further matter: Please fetch the gravid(?) sow which Neby will give you and tend it. [That] is what should be done for it/them. And don't let those belonging to Neby be mistreated.

[A further matter: Don't] let any soldiers of the army tarry in your northern districts(?).

A further matter: As for all those marked with a seal who might escape following the roundup, seize hold of them very securely! You shall render them serviceable, for the grooms have branded [...] Let your(?) attention be directed toward (obtaining) especially fine men. [Give heed(?)] to your orders which I submitted to you and procure an especially fine crew.

Address: The standard-bearer Maiseti to the soldier Hat of the squadron "The Bull[3] is in Nubia."

135. P. Cairo 58055
(Dynasty 19: Seti I)

The standard-bearer Maiseti to the chief of impressment Hat:

[I] have sent you this letter to say: As for my having told you to mobilize in the near future, look to yourself carefully! You should not mobilize your prison there until a message has been sent [to] you since if one is coming to fetch the men of the prison who are on the island, a message will be sent to you saying, "Come with them," and you shall be attentive in bringing up your reserves. Don't make it that a single one who is in your charge has to be asked for. Mind you, take heed! Seek for yourself a day of life, or you will die under my hand.

A further matter: Please have another very good rope made for us since the one which we had has been stolen. Have another made to replace it. Please take note of this.

Address: The standard-bearer Maiseti to the chief of impressment Hat of the Island of Debu.

A Shipment

136. O. Osireion 2
(Dynasty 19: Seti I)

Regarding what Panefer told me saying, "Whenever you finish unloading, you shall return with the wood inasmuch as the [. . .] are not being delivered," [shall I] return after having delivered it or not?

Inquiries about Well-Being

137. P. Leningrad 1117
(Dynasty 19: Ramesses II)

The scribe and lector priest Wernemty(?) communicates to his lord, the overseer of cattle Su(?)[4] of the Temple of Ptah: In life, prosperity and health! This is a missive to inform you. I am calling upon all the gods of Pi-Ramessu-miamon, l.p.h., to keep you healthy daily and to keep you in the favor of Pharaoh, l.p.h., your good lord, daily.

A further matter: Please write me about your condition and also about the condition of men and property(?) because I'm concerned about them.

A further matter to the effect that I'm alive today, but I don't know about my condition hereafter. Farewell!

138. P. Leningrad 1118
(Dynasty 19: Ramesses II)

The scribe and lector priest Wernemty(?) greets the master chariot-maker Huy: In life, prosperity and health and in the favor of Amon-Re, King of the Gods! I am calling upon all the gods who are in the vicinity of Pi-Ramessu-miamon, l.p.h., to keep you healthy, to keep you alive, and to let me see you in health and fill my embrace with you.

A further matter: Please write me about your condition and that of your people, for I'm concerned about them.

A further matter to the effect that I'm alive today, but I don't know about my condition hereafter.

A further communication to the chantress of Amon Naia: What is your condition? How are you?

A further matter: The papyrus scrolls are here(?).

============ A Ship and Money Owed ============

139. P. Cairo 58056
(Dynasty 19: Ramesses II)

The [title lost] of Ptah [name lost] greets his brother (colleague?) the standard-bearer Akhpe: In life, prosperity and health and in the favor of [god's name lost]! [I] am calling upon Ptah the Great, South-of-his-Wall, lord of Ankhtowy, upon his ennead, upon Sakhmet the Great, beloved [of Ptah, and upon] all [gods] and goddesses of Hikuptah to keep you healthy, to keep you alive, and to let me see you in health and fill my embrace with you. And further:

I noticed two ships of yours here in Memphis and was told that it was you who had sent them, whereas when you had set out from here during the mobilization of the army, you told me, "Keep silent, don't speak. I'll send you the ship upon my arrival." Please write to the soldier Pasanesu to hand the ship over to me in order that I might put [it] to use, for it is now the day for the use of it. Then shall Ptah keep you healthy!

But if you are unwilling to hand over the ship, write to your wife that she should give me the eighty deben of copper or the eighty khar-measures of emmer which you promised to give three years⁵ ago. Don't let my payment be wanting any longer this year so that I remain without the emmer while the copper is absent.

Now when you write to the soldier Pasanesu, send him your letter, it being direct and to the point. Farewell!

Address: The [title lost] of Ptah [name lost] to the standard-bearer Akhpe.

===== **A Retainer and a Money Document** =====

140. *P. Cairo 58059*
(Dynasty 19: Ramesses II)

The *wab*-priest Nebiemon greets the stable master of the Residence, Neferabu: In life, prosperity and health and in the favor of Amon-Re, King of the Gods! And further:

Every day I am calling upon the gods and goddesses who are in the Temple of Ramesses II, l.p.h., who has put the Two Lands in order, to keep you healthy and to keep you in the favor of Pharaoh, l.p.h., your good lord, l.p.h.

A further matter: By the time that I succeeded in arriving here from you the day before yesterday, the retainer had already set out on his errands to this side of the locality of Perbener. It was late in the evening that he reached me. He will wash his clothes today, and I shall be attentive and return with him.

Moreover, the superior assigned me a stone-hewer from among those who are under his supervision, but those who are [rounding up(?)] the deserters apprehended him the day before yesterday. I shall dispatch this boy of mine with a letter to the superior about this so as to inform him. If you have made [the . . .] which you promised, send it, and I will surely have it transmitted to him.

Moreover, as for the promissory note which you had me negotiate, it is no longer here since the time when it was in Huy's hands and I negotiated it. Have it returned to me, and I will surely have it transmitted.[6]

===== **The Estate of Amon in the Delta** =====

141. *O. Gardiner 86*
(Dynasty 19: Ramesses II)

The royal scribe and overseer of the treasury [of Pharaoh(?)], Panehsy, who is in the Northern Region, [greets the prophet] of Amon in the Southern City (Thebes), Hori: In life, prosperity and health!

This is a missive to inform you of the [status(?)] of the Estate of Amon that is under my authority here in the Northern Region extending from the Portal [of . . . and reaching the] extremities of the Delta on the three branches of the Nile, namely the Great River, [the Western River], and the Waters of Avaris, including the occupations(?) of all personnel of the Estate of Amon, comprising [cultivators], comprising herders of all sorts of animals that are in the countryside belonging to the Temple of Amon in the Southern City (Thebes), namely [. . .], cattle herders, goatherds, shepherds, swineherds, donkey herders, mule(?) herders, and bird wardens, and comprising fishermen, fowlers, vintners, salt workers, natron workers, papyrus gatherers, [. . .], who are in the marshes cutting stalks(?), rope makers, and mat makers(?).

[When I] obtained their list of names with each one included among them: men, [wives], and their children, for their list of names had been [in the office] of the Estate of (Queen) Tiye, may she live, in the Estate of Amon, Bakpy(?), I [. . .], and I assessed them for taxes and found [. . .] people [. . .] in Year 24, first month of the third season, day 21, under the Majesty of the King of Upper and Lower Egypt [Ramesses II]. To inform the prophet Hori of them, with each person according to his occupation(?). The summary [. . .]:

Cultivators: 8,760 men, each one of them producing 200 khar-measures of barley by the bushel.

Cattle herders: [X-number of] men, with cattle, the herd of each one of them containing 500 cattle.

Goatherds: 13,080 men, [each one of them having X-number of goats].

Bird [wardens]: 22,530 men, each one of them having 34,230 birds.

Fishermen: [X-number of men, the delivery of each one of] them being equivalent to three deben of silver for this year.

The donkey herders: 3,920 men, [each one of them having] 2,870 [donkeys].

The mule(?) herders: 13,227 men, each one of them having 551 (beasts).

Men [. . . . Here is the] way I've dealt with them. To wit: I took men from among them and had [them] build a large granary for the labor-camp(?) of Memphis, embracing ten arouras (about seven acres) [with] grain-bins in it on its four sides, totalling 160 grain-bins. [Besides, I have brought in] goods for the treasury: an abundance of silver, gold, copper, clothing, [Remainder lost].

========= **Preparations for the Feast of Opet** =========

142. O. Gardiner 362
(Dynasty 19: Ramesses II)

The scribe Ramose communicates to his [lord], the royal scribe and overseer of cattle Hatia: [In life, prosperity and health! This is a missive to inform] my [lord.

A further communication to] my lord to the effect that the Feast of Opet has approached to within [X-number of days] from today, but the fleet(?) of the Estate of Amon has not come to us from(?) [. . .] for the Feast of Opet as well as the cattle to be introduced for the offerings to all the gods, and also the goods [. . . . May] my lord [carry out] his good plans in order that

Pharaoh's demand(?) may be executed, saying, "Let every scow of the fleet(?) of the Estate of Amon [be loaded]," and saying, "Attention! Load fifty barges at the [. . .] goods for the Feast of Opet as well as his/its cattle," because the due date elapsed yesterday while [. . . . Now] look, his/its crewmen(?) who were before [me] loaded ten today. They have departed.

Now look, the fan-bearer on the king's right, the viceroy of Kush, and overseer of southern lands Paser [has sent a letter to me] at the fortress of Bigga to the following effect: This [letter is brought to you] by way of saying, "As soon as my letter [reaches] you, you shall muster the men of the dockyard together with [. . . , and have] twenty barges [outfitted] at the dockyard." Now look, [I] have loaded for you [the . . . which I have sent] to you. Send your scribe to meet up with [them. I have sent a] letter to the mayor of Elephantine, Nebseny, saying, "[. . .] the surpluses as well as whatever you are lacking in [. . .]. Now the granary is under your control." As for the one whose prow is filled with goods, [he shall] not [. . .]. It is because I am exceedingly impoverished that I have written to you, for a troublemaker [. . . took away the men of the] dockyard whom I used to have here with me hewing and [*Remainder lost*].

Riverine Commerce

143. *P. Anastasi VIII*
(Dynasty 19: Ramesses II)

It is the scribe Ramose who addresses the scribe Dhutemhab to the effect that this letter is brought to you saying:

What are you doing there still? The fortress commander has sent a letter saying, "You shall bring 46(?) silver bars as cargo with fish and wool[7] so that I may distribute them to the ship captains. 600 bricks of pile and 760(?) silver *deben*'s-worth [of] fish are the amount that you owe this year. It is fitting to have you consign them as cargo on one single day."

Moreover, I've heard that the crewman of the cargo ship Any, son of Piay, of the town of Aperel, belonging to the great statue of Ramesses II, "Re of Rulers," has died along with his children. Is this correct [or] incorrect? What has the fortress commander done with the cargo of the estate? As regards the wool belonging to the god which lies in the dockyard of [Pi]-Ramessu-miamon, l.p.h., on the bank of the Waters of Pre (the Pelusaic branch of the Nile), to whom was it consigned as cargo? Didn't the scribe Pa[ser] proceed to have it consigned as cargo? What has been done with it? Make an investigation into it in records at the disposition of the agents who assign cargoes and also investigate his (the god's) fishermen's output. To whom was it consigned(?)? Now his ship captain [approached me saying], "Proceed to have these two men of ours put on board since they have in their charge as cargo such a vast amount of silver now that their fellow crewmen are dead. Now see, [. . .]. Aren't they now looking [. . . ? . . .] sailor(?) consigned [. . . as] cargo for the god this year.

Moreover, the scribe Dhutemhab (the addressee?) wrote me saying, "I had the fifty [. . .] made ready [in accordance with] all that you wrote about, but the boat hasn't arrived in order to be loaded with [. . .]." This is [an obstruction] of work which men were charged with. Dispatch the boat of the fisherman Serdy immediately and send it to meet the retainer Huy, bringing the gear for this new boat since we are going to start traveling: And you shall send [me] pine timbers from the scribe Dhutemhab (the addressee?). Take great pains with them. The [shipwrights] have to wait for them [to] finish up this boat. And you shall finish carrying out precisely every assignment of yours [from] last year and return [to me] in Memphis. I shall be staying there from the eighth to the tenth of the second month of the first season, and then we shall depart for Pi-Ramessu-miamon, l.p.h., that is, if we are still alive.

You will take leave of the crewman of the cargo ship Pashed and the crewman of the cargo ship Iner only when they are fully supplied with cargo to your complete satisfaction with regard to what they shall be able to take aboard in the way of fish. Don't assign them the scribe Paser's cargo this year until they have constructed a boat for themselves since we told them to construct one this year and to get cargo for themselves. See, I will cause men to be readied for them as a crew, and I shall compensate them in full.

A further matter: You have salved yourself bald(?); you have salved yourself well. Is it true that you sent the cattle ferry which used to carry the wool with the sailor Seti in it, so that it was kept empty as far as Heliopolis while the six men were in it as a crew? Is it true? You are a sensible person now. Is it proper to keep silent to you about this neglectfulness that you displayed? Are there no rushes in the papyrus swamp? Is there no output? Take heed of me if you fail to load this boat lest it should be sent empty. Or at least it should be loaded with loaves of this kyllestis-bread of the area of the Great River. Please(?) write about its status in proper order, because its sailor said when I brought him to be beaten, "I told the scribe Dhutemhab (the addressee?) to put freight aboard the boat. The servant Suemperamon told me to load it with rushes, but Dhutemhab said to me, 'I won't give you any. It is the fishing boats which should get loaded.'"

As for the barge which goes to the town of Usermare-setepenre, l.p.h., carrying the wool each year, it will not arrive in your presence laden with produce of papyrus plants apart from the boats of the fishermen. What, I ask, is the size of them, namely, the boats of the fishermen? Can you rely on them? I won't forgive you for this gross act of defaulting that you have committed except by carrying out the multitude of assignments which I told you to carry out in this establishing [. . .] such a precedent thereby(?). If only you had not abandoned proper behavior so that you might set an example for whoever happens to be sent! Otherwise would you have dared to send this extra large boat empty with only its crew in it? On the contrary, it is loading it with straw of(?) a great [. . .] that you have done. You cannot find another boat to load like this one in. . . .

A further matter: Write reporting on all that you have done in conjunction with whomever you had at your disposal and also the day date set for your departure to return — through the agency of the retainer Iia, you having written a letter to be put in his hand at the time you dispatch him. Please take note of this. The first month of the first season, day 27.

Address: The scribe Ramose to the scribe Dhutemhab.

Agricultural Matters

144. P. Anastasi IX
(Dynasty 19: Ramesses II)

The scribe Hori communicates to his lord, the scribe Ramose: In life, prosperity and health! This is a missive to inform my lord. A further communication to my lord to the effect that I have taken note of the controversies about which you wrote to me. Although what you have said is true, they are merely some precepts for life from a man's father to his son that you wrote concerning them and not capital charges.

Further: I sent a message to bring the cattle in order to thresh the barley, they being in the charge of their assistant herdsman. Now regarding that lot of cattle which they mentioned to you, they belong with their offspring that follow after them. And regarding the cattle, they are in the charge of their herdsman wherever they are; they are not in the charge of a retainer of mine.

Now as for your writing me saying, "You aren't perceptive(?)," was it not two months ago, before you had even demanded the cattle, that I brought them? When the threshing of the barley was finished, I sent a message to summon their herdsman saying, "Come and take them away," before you had even written to me.

Now regarding your remark about the *shay*-pot and the curd, "Of what use are they to me?" I would like to have them. Can't I even seek nourishment for myself? Not so? Look, it is in order to have me kill my own cattle that the boy has [. . .] cattle [. . .]. We're in your service in the eyes of many a scribe. Put the men under someone else's authority so that I may be kept safe unto my own self from their hands. Every day my lord lives only because all that I snared(?) in the way of cattle is in the charge of the herdsman of cattle Ria. [. . .] slaughter(?) [. . .] many [. . .] bulls and cows. He took away my eighteen head of cattle. See, he has gone to get backers(?). Since my witnesses are ready at hand, may I be judged with [him] in your presence that you might realize that what I've said is true.

Now regarding [my(?) . . .] lead [. . .] yoke-oxen. Now look here, it is you who accepted the cattle for slaughter, and it is you who ordered [. . .]. Aren't you my superior, and aren't you the herdsman of the beasts? Now(?) regarding all personnel [of] (the cult of) "Re of Rulers," [. . .] herd [. . .] under their supervision there. [. . .] to deliver(?) [. . .] god [. . .], it being [for] the god, but you did not do this for me. If [he makes for] me the [. . .] against me [. . .], how will [I] be able to live and how will I bring some vegetables to my lord? Now look, your [. . .] example(?) [. . .] in the presence of their lord. [. . .] my standing up to(?) [. . .].

Moreover, as for my [. . .] on account of it [. . .], my good qualities and my bad qualities are placed before you. [. . .] the people of the Northern Region [. . .] in the Southern Region, although one is [. . .] every [. . .]. Now it is one who is in your position who can stand up to them. And you shall not [. . .].

[A further communi]cation to my lord: [. . .] cattle in the charge of the herdsman of cattle Bakenamon, and they set about doing it. [. . .] with(?) them, after I had caused it/her to go bearing a load(?). [. . .] them to the Estate of Usermare-setepenre (Ramesses II), l.p.h., to await my arrival. As soon as [I] return, I shall [. . .] them to await me, for I have been told that one is [. . .]. And I went to the chief of police Ka[sa] to have him withdraw some grain. As for [. . .] Thoth, I went [. . .].

Send me a message by the hand of this boy whom I've sent. If only(?) [. . .]. May my lord [. . .].

This is a missive to inform my [lord], in the first month of the first season, day 12(?).

Address: [Lost].

================== **To a Charioteer** ==================

145. P. Leiden I, 349, vs.
(Dynasty 19: Ramesses II)

Horus, Mighty Bull, beloved of Maat, [lord of jubilees] like [his father Ptah-Ta]tenen; the Two Ladies, [protecting Egypt and sub]duing [foreign] lands, the Re who has fashioned the gods and set the Two Lands in order; Horus of Gold, rich in years and great in victories; the King of Upper and Lower Egypt, Usermare-setepenre, l.p.h., the son of Re, Ramesses II, l.p.h., given life forever and ever like Re.

The scribe Kenyamon communicates to his lord, the charioteer Huy of the stable of Ramesses II, l.p.h.: In life, prosperity and health! This is a missive to inform my lord, l.p.h. A further communication [to] my lord to the effect that I have taken note of my [lord's] message to me saying, "Attend [to] the people who are [under] my supervision." I won't let my lord find fault [with me].

A further matter: My lord's horses are in very good shape, for I am giving them grain daily.

A further matter: [I] have taken note of my lord's message to me saying, "Give grain rations [to] the soldiers and the Apiru-(laborers) who are drawing (water from) the well of Pre of Ramesses II, l.p.h., south of Memphis. Farewell!

Various Matters

146. P. Turin 1977
(early Dynasty 19)

[*Beginning lost*]. And further:

I have taken note of the message you sent regarding the matter of the policeman Nakhtseti. The policeman Nakhtseti is in the labor service, being beaten with the rod just like any enemy of Pre. If Amon lets me live long enough to return south, I shall bring him back, and I shall side with you and ascertain what ought to be done with him, and it shall be done.

Now as for what you wrote about your mother, stating that she has died, you said, "Let the stipend that used to be issued to her be given to my sister who has been a widow here for several years till now," so you said. Do thus, give it to her until (I) return and ascertain whatever ought to be done, and I will do it for her.

Now your brother, the stable master, is standing here in the court concerning this case of his servants. I will cause him to be judged.

Now it is good that you wrote me saying, "I'm in good shape, and the crew is in good shape." Please write me about your condition and the condition of the crew. Please take note of this.

Slaves and Agricultural Labor

147. P. Bologna 1086
(Dynasty 19: Merenptah–Seti II)

The scribe of the offering table Bakenamon to the prophet of the Temple of Thoth Ramose.

The scribe of the offering table Bakenamon greets his father, the prophet

Ramose of the Temple of Thoth, Content-of-Heart, in Memphis: In life, prosperity and health and in the favor of Amon-Re, King of the Gods! I am calling upon Pre-Harakhti in his rising and in his setting, upon Amon, Pre and Ptah of Ramesses II, l.p.h., and upon all the gods of Pi-Ramessu-miamon, l.p.h., the great *Ka* of Pre-Harakhti, to give you health, to give you life, to give you prosperity, and to let me see you in health and fill my embrace with you.

A further matter: I have taken note of the message you wrote inquiring after my welfare. It is Pre and Ptah who will inquire after your welfare. I didn't know that my boy would reach you since it was to the town of Sekhempehty that I had sent him. Otherwise I would have sent you a letter by his hand. Moreover, don't cease writing to me regularly that I may learn about your condition.

Further, I investigated the matter of the Syrian of the Temple of Thoth about whom you had written me, and I discovered that he was assigned to be a cultivator of the Temple of Thoth under your authority in Year 3, second month of the third season, day 10, from among the slaves of the ships' cargoes that the superintendent of fortresses had brought back. To inform you of his identity: the Syrian Nekedy, son of Serertja whose mother is Kedy, of the land of Aradus, a slave of the ship's cargo belonging to this temple in the ship captain Kel's boat, whose certificate reads, "It is the captain of heralds of the soldiers of the garrison of Pharaoh, l.p.h., Khaemope who received him in charge in order to have him conscripted." I went to the captain of heralds of the soldiers of the garrison of Pharaoh, l.p.h., Khaemope. He disclaimed responsibility for him with me; he told me in short, "It is the vizier Merysakhmet who received him in charge in order to have him con-scripted." I went to the vizier Merysakhmet, and he and his scribes disclaimed responsibility, saying, "We never even saw him." I am after the captain of assault officers daily, saying, "Produce the Syrian cultivator of the Temple of Thoth whom you received in charge that he may be taken to his prophet." I am now contending with him in the great court.

Moreover, I have taken note of the matter of the sacred standard of Thoth, about which you wrote me. It has not been brought to me straightaway, even though I had arranged for it to proceed in procession. But don't worry about it, although it is better if you send it to me so that I may have it proceed in procession.

Moreover, don't worry about the seed-order. I examined it, and I found that three men and one boy, totaling four persons, produce 700 *khar*-measures (of grain). I spoke with the chief record keepers of the granary and told them, "Take the three cultivators of the god to serve this year." And they answered me, "We will do so, look, we will do so. We shall heed your request," so they said to me. I am staying in their presence until they have caused the registration documents to go out to the fields and you find out about everything which I shall have done for you, because it is only one man, producing 200 *khar*-measures (of grain) that they have determined for me to carry it out, leaving at your disposal two men and one boy, producing 500 *khar*-measures (of grain).

Now regarding this Syrian cultivator who was assigned to you, he was assigned to you during the summer months. As long as he survives, his summer shall be charged against you.

Temple Offerings and Agricultural Matters

148. O. BM 5627
(Dynasty 19)

It is Minmose, the *wab*-priest of Ptah-Sokar in the Temple of Nebmare (the mortuary temple of Amenhotep III) on the West of Thebes, who addresses the *wab*-priest of Sakhmet, Sobekhotep, son of Oamon:

Please be attentive in observing the festivals of the gods and also in making their divine [offerings in] the chapel of each god who resides within the Temple of Nebmare, given [life, presenting(?)] them to the one of his sunlight, namely, Amon who is in his solar disk, to Nefertum-Horus the Exultant, to Sakhmet the Great, who is in this temple, to Wepwawet of Upper Egypt and to Wepwawet of Lower Egypt, the gods of(?) Amon-Kamutef, and to every god and every goddess. Please make their offerings. Don't ignore what I've said. Be mindful of the gods whom you are serving [that they may give] you life.

A further communication: Please send a message as well to your cultivator who is in the fields as one having control over grain, and tell him of the harvest assessment in barley and emmer which is [due] the granary. Don't let the granary be lacking in barley or emmer, for it is upon its granary that a house stands firm. And you shall attend [to] the cattle stable. Attention, be mindful! Please have them (the cattle) properly cared for. Don't turn your back! It is good if you take note.

Field Hands

149. P. DM 33
(Dynasty 19)

The scribe of the offering table Paherypedje communicates to the captain of a contingent(?) of the army and captain of [. . .]: In life, prosperity and health and in the favor of Amon-Re, King of the Gods, your good lord who [looks] after you! And further:

You sent me word(?) [. . .] gone back on(?) [. . . to] fetch those men who were in the fields because of the matters to be investigated, and I came to fetch them. As soon as this letter reaches you, you shall have them procure a man for me in very short order(?). I will spend five days here and then return to carry out the task that you mentioned to me. Send the boy back in the fourth month of the third season, day 25, for I must continue reporting to you regularly.

════ Pharaoh's Asiatic Towns and the Cult of Anath ════

150. *O. Michaelides 85*
(Dynasty 19)

The garrison scribe Ipuy [communicates to his lord, the standard-bearer of] the garrison Bakenamon: In life, prosperity and health! This is a missive [to inform my lord] that the towns of Pharaoh, l.p.h., which are situated in each district are prosperous [and that the servants] of Pharaoh, l.p.h., who are in them are prospering and in health, calling upon [all the gods and] all the goddesses who are in the region of the land of Khor (Syro-Palestine) [to keep] Pharaoh, l.p.h., my lord, l.p.h., [healthy], with every land cast down beneath his sandals, [while] my lord (Bakenamon) [continues to be] in his (Pharaoh's) favor.

A further communication to my [lord: The offerings that you sent for] the festival of Anath of Gaza have all [arrived], and I received your(?) [. . .] for the goddess. A scout [   ] the ship [captain] Kar [. . .]. See, the [*Remainder lost*].

════ Agricultural Matters ════

151. *P. Mallet III–IV*
(Dynasty 20: Ramesses IV)

It is the cattle overseer Bakenkhons of the Estate of Amon-Re, King of the Gods, who addresses the policeman Maiseti, the policeman Setemhab, the administrator Paukhed [of] the sacred palanquin of King Userkhare-setepenre-miamon (Setnakht), l.p.h., the cultivator Paiuten, the cultivator Usekhnemtet, and each herdsman of the altar of Amon who is in the district of Kheriu:

As soon as the servant Amenemwia comes to you, you shall set out with him and perform corvée labor for me on the farmlands to which he will take you to be cleared since it is off of them that you will be living. Don't you proceed to return a complaint! Now look, when Amon-Re, King of the

Gods, brought forth the floodwaters for Pharaoh, l.p.h., his son, see, I came to pick out him who should go to perform corvée labor for me and to pick out him who should not go. Don't you proceed to take an opposing stand when this retainer of mine reaches you in the course of tomorrow, or you will be put in the wrong.

See, I've written to provide you with testimony. You are to preserve my letter in order that it may serve you as evidence at some later date.

Fuel

152. P. Mallet V-VI
(Dynasty 20: Ramesses IV)

The cattle overseer Bakenkhons of the altar of Amon-Re, King of the Gods, greets the offering table scribe Iryaa of the magazine of deliveries: In life, prosperity and health and in the favor of Amon-Re, King of the Gods! Every day I am calling upon Pre-Harakhti when he rises and sets to keep you healthy, to keep you alive, and to keep you vigorous. And further:

The overseer of the treasury Khaemtore passed by me in the district of Kheriu, and I was given a letter and told, "Furnish these 1,000 sticks of wood and 50 bags of charcoal in accordance with what I told you; I have no wood in store except my annual assessment." Now the overseer of Pharaoh's treasury returned bringing in his hand a copy of the order for the 1,000 sticks of wood and 50 bags of charcoal. So I had the 1,000 sticks of wood and 50 bags of charcoal cut and deposited them on the quay of the district of Kheriu. Then I had another 700 sticks of wood and another 50 bags of charcoal cut and deposited them on the quay of Permeten to await you, they being additional.

Now as I was traveling southward, I learned that you had sailed north, so I dispatched this retainer of mine, sending him to [you(?)] with a load. Now I have told him to look after you and to give you a bundle of vegetables. As soon as he reaches you, you yourself shall attend to him and prevent my people from being interfered with, for such is my desire. Don't make me quarrel with you. Now see, I've sent you a copy of the order.

Honey and Wood

153. P. Louvre E. 27151
(Dynasty 20: Ramesses III-V)

The [title lost] of the chapel of Harakhti, Khay, greets [the mayor] of Elephantine Montuhi[khopeshef: In life, prosperity] and health and in the favor of Amon-Re, King of the Gods! I am calling upon Amon-Re-Harakhti when he rises and sets, and upon Harakhti and his ennead to keep you healthy, to keep you alive, and to keep you in the favor of Harakhti, your lord who looks after you. And further:

I opened the jar of honey which you had procured for the god and proceeded to draw out ten *hin*-measures of honey from it for the divine offering, but I found that it was all full of lumps of (congealed) ointment. So I resealed it and sent it back south to you. If it is someone else who gave it to you, let him inspect it. And you shall see whether you might locate a good (jar of honey) and send it on to me. Then shall Pre keep you healthy. But if there isn't any, you shall send the *menet*-jar of incense by the hand of the *wab*-priest Netjermose until you can locate some honey.

And you shall send me the timbers of seasoned sycamore wood. Then shall Amon keep you healthy, and Harakhti shall let you achieve a long lifetime. May you fare well in the presence of Harakhti!

Address: The [*title lost*] of the chapel of Harakhti, Khay, to the mayor [of Elephantine] Montuhi[khopeshef].

=========== **A Slave-Woman and Her Son** ===========

154. *P. Bankes I*
(late Dynasty 20)

The builder Wenenamon of the Temple of Amon-Re, King of the Gods, greets the merchant Amenkhau of the Temple of Amon-Re, King of the Gods: In life, prosperity and health and in the favor of Amon-Re, King of the Gods! Every day I am calling upon Amon, Mut, and Khonsu to keep you alive, to keep you healthy, and to invigorate you. And further:

Before you left here from Ne, I had entrusted to you the slave-woman Tentuendjede and the slave Gemiamon, her son, and you had given them to the fisherman Pamershenuty and the retainer Hori, who told you while I was present, "It was by stealth that this woman was gotten." So they said to you, but you replied, "That's wrong! It was from the master of serfs Ikhterpay that I bought this woman," so you told them, "and I gave full payment for her." And they told you, "We shall corroborate this with the man who sold [her] to you," so they said to you. And I went with you before the commander of foreign Tuhir-troops Iuhepy, your superior, who told me, "Leave the maidservant be! She has been entrusted to the merchant Amenkhau," so he said. I had confidence in you and entrusted you with this maidservant up until today.

Now look, you sent the scribe Efnamon to me with the message, "It is just like those many others who were carried off that your maidservant has been carried off." So you said in writing to me, although you know that it was while I was inside the walled enclosure of (the Temple of) Mut that some came and took my maidservant away, [persuading(?)] people saying, "She is our sister," so they were saying regarding her. So you deal with her affair while you are there.

As soon as my letter reaches you, you shall deal with the affair of this maidservant [and go to(?)] those people who removed her, and if they prevail over you, you will realize that she is a conscriptable servant, it being the master of serfs who conscripted her. You will make him give you (as replacement) a satisfactory maidservant who has a son at her bosom just like the two of them, and you will bring them south when you return. See, I've written in order to provide you with authorization.

Now you know the many good things that I've done for you. Don't forget them and disobey me, or your misdemeanors will get the better of you.

Address: The builder Wenenamon of the Temple of Amon to the merchant Amenkhau of the Temple of Amon.

========= A Fugitive =========

155. P. Valençay No. 2
(Dynasty 20: Ramesses IX)

[To name lost, the title lost of] Amon from the stable master Pahen and the chief of police Sahnufe. [This is a missive] to inform our lord.

A further communication to our lord to the effect that every single day we are [calling upon names of deities] and upon all the [gods] of heaven and earth to give you life, prosperity and health, a long lifetime, and a ripe old age. [And further]:

[We have taken note of all matters] about which you have written us. As for what you wrote regarding the matter of this [. . . , saying], "Search for him!" as you said in writing to us, the retainers came. They [. . .]. We have stopped to visit Hathor, lady of Dendera, your mistress, [. . .], as we sail northward pursuing the mission you wrote us about. We have [not] delayed at all. Now we sent men to Setsankh, [the prophet of Seth, lord of] the town of Sheneset, and we submitted the matter before [the god who said, "He is to the] south of you and will be found," so he (the god) said. We shall [. . .]. We shall not be remiss either if he attacks(?) us.

========= Unjustified Tax Demands =========

156. P. Valençay No. 1
(Dynasty 20: Ramesses XI)

May Amon [favor] Menmarenakht! The mayor of Elephantine Meron sends a communication: In life, prosperity and health and in the favor of Amon-Re, King of the Gods! [And further]:

Every single day [I am calling] upon [Amon-Re]-Harakhti when he rises and sets and upon Khnum, Satis, Anukis and all the gods of Elephantine to keep the chief taxing master healthy, to give him life, prosperity and health, a long lifetime and a good ripe old age, and to give him favors in the presence of Amon-Re, King of the Gods, his good lord, and in the presence of Pharaoh, l.p.h., his good lord.

The scribe Patjauemdiamon of the House of the Votaress of Amon has come. He arrived in Elephantine in order to demand that grain which has been specified for the House of the Votaress of Amon, and he said to me, "Hand over 100 *khar*-measures of barley," so he said to me even though there are no field holdings yielding such an amount. He said to me, "It is because of a holding of *khanto*-land of the *gezira* of Ombi (Kom Ombo) that they are being demanded of you," so I was told, although I had cultivated no holding of *khanto*-land on the *gezira* of Ombi. By Amon and by the Ruler, l.p.h., if it be ascertained that I have cultivated a holding of *khanto*-land on the *gezira* of Ombi, it is from me that this barley shall be exacted. It is merely a holding of some free tenants, who pay gold into Pharaoh's treasury, that those free tenants have cultivated, they regularly handing its gold over to Pharaoh's treasury, whereas I had nothing to do with a holding there.

And I was told about the matter of another holding in the vicinity of Edfu which had not been irrigated, for it was a mere four arouras of land that had been irrigated on it and upon which I had put one man and one yoke of oxen who cultivated the scrap of land which they found usable in it. Now when harvest time came, 40 *khar*-measures of barley were brought to me from it, and I kept them secure, never even touching a single *oipe*-measure thereof. But I handed them over to the scribe Patjauemdiamon, they being just 40 *khar*-measures. And I swore regarding them with a firm oath, saying, "I have not touched a single *oipe*-measure or a single half-*oipe*-measure thereof."

I am writing to inform the chief taxing-master.

Notes

1. An obscure expression, perhaps referring to a military engagement in Asia, used here to designate a year.

2. Or possibly, "attendants" or "detainees," but certainly not "patrolmen" in this context.

3. "The Bull" is an epithet of the king.

4. Perhaps a hypocoristic form of the name Sul (Suner) rather than the less-suitable reading of the name as Yey.

5. Equivalent to two years by our reckoning.

6. For alternative suggestions regarding this difficult passage, see Vernus 1985: 159–60.

7. Or possibly, "You shall sell 46(?) silver bars for cargo in (the form of) fish and wool."

IX

Letters of the Ramesside Community of Deir El-Medina

Introduction

The village of Deir el-Medina was situated some distance from the flood plain at the base of the desert escarpment on the west side of Thebes. Founded in the early Eighteenth Dynasty, when royal tombs were first excavated in the famous Valley of the Kings, Deir el-Medina served as the settlement for those engaged in the preparation of these tombs as well as tombs of queens and princes in the Valley of the Queens. While there is considerable archaeological evidence pertaining to the Eighteenth Dynasty occupation of Deir el-Medina, it is only with the Nineteenth Dynasty that information about the town's inhabitants is vastly supplemented by ostraca and papyri. Indeed, much of what we know today of the phase of the Egyptian language known as Late Egyptian derives from the abundance of Ramesside documents from the village of Deir el-Medina and its environs.

The Ramesside village numbered about 400 inhabitants, including men, women, and children. As employees of the government, the villagers were supplied by the central administration. Many letters to and from the vizier (Nos. 44–45, 47–60, translated in Part III) relate to the affairs of Deir el-Medina, and the king was kept abreast of the villagers' work and wages (Nos. 18, 21, 33, translated in Part II).

The work crew normally comprised sixty men and was divided into two sides, each headed by a foreman, assisted by a deputy. The two foremen, who usually had risen through the ranks, directed the work in the royal tomb but also represented the crew in relation to higher authorities, particularly the vizier. Also associated with the crew were two or three administrative scribes, called "scribes of the necropolis," who kept detailed records pertaining to the progress of the work, the distribution of rations, and such matters as absenteeisms. As administrators, the scribes were responsible not to the foremen but directly to the vizier.

With a literacy rate perhaps as high as 5 percent, Deir el-Medina was probably one of the more literate communities in ancient Egypt (Baines and Eyre 1983: 86–91). We know that the village possessed a school, and scores of schoolboy exercises have survived on ostraca. The job of laying out the hieroglyphic inscriptions and scenes depicting the netherworld was performed by outline draftsmen in the royal tombs, but these draftsmen had also been trained to write the cursive hieratic script. In

132

writing letters such a draftsman might call himself "scribe," not as a formal title but simply as an indication of his ability to write. According to Janssen (1987: 167 n. 25), there were literate women in Deir el-Medina, who were able to write their own letters.

Because artisans of the village were engaged in work on tomb projects requiring utmost secrecy, their movement beyond the confines of the necropolis was generally restricted. There were watchposts and a major gateway that maintained the security of the area in which they lived and worked. Seeing to the safety of the royal tombs were policemen, who did not themselves reside in the village and thus had more frequent contact with the world outside Deir el-Medina. Because of the trust placed in the policemen, they frequently served as letter carriers. Most of the Deir el-Medina correspondence was inscribed on ostraca and hand-carried over relatively short distances in western Thebes. While working in the Valley of the Kings, the crew was absent from the village for nine days, spending nights in huts atop the *gebel*. Thus arose the occasion for sending communications back to the village. Other letters, often requests for items not readily available in the desert town, were directed to people living in the fertile valley, where goods could be obtained at marketplaces along the river or canals. One letter on an ostracon, No. 170, was discovered at Abydos, 105 miles from Deir el-Medina.

While many of the deities of the Theban area are mentioned in these letters, of particular importance to the Deir el-Medina community were the deified King Amenophis I and his mother Queen Nofretari. The oracle of Amenophis functioned regularly during processional feasts occurring every tenth day and on special festivals held in honor of this deceased king. At Deir el-Medina there was also a sanctuary to the goddess Hathor, and the goddess of the western peak at Thebes Mereseger figured prominently in the lives of the workmen. Priestly duties were carried out by the workmen themselves in this tightly knit community.

Many of the letters from Deir el-Medina have been translated into German by Allam (1973a). There are a number of books that provide comprehensive treatment of the Deir el-Medina village community. Among the more readable accounts are those by Bierbrier (1982) and Romer (1984), while the indispensable works by Černý (1973), Valbelle (1985), and Ventura (1986) are more scholarly in their treatment.

========= **Work on the Royal Tomb** =========

157. O. Cairo 25756
(Dynasty 19: Ramesses II)

The two foremen and the scribe of the necropolis com[municate to [*name lost, the title lost* of the Temple of] King Usermare-setepenre, l.p.h., (Ramesses II's mortuary temple) in the Estate of Amon on the West of Thebes: In [life, prosperity and health]!

[A further] communication to our lord to the effect that the Construction Site[1] is [in need of (?)] candles. Now we are not [neglecting any of] our lord's [commissions]. Send us [*X-number*] of *deben* of [old] clothes (for the making of candle wicks). [. . .] is coming in life, prosperity and health. [*End lost*].

158. P. Ashmolean 1958.112
(mid-Dynasty 20)

The draftsman Hormin to his father, the scribe [of the necropolis] Hori: In life, prosperity and health and in the favor of Amon-Re, King of the Gods! To wit:

I am calling upon Amon-Re, King of the Gods, Mut, Khonsu, and the ennead of Karnak to keep you healthy, to keep you alive, and to give you wealth, health, and joy. And further:

As soon as my letter reaches you, you shall send the man who will go to receive the grain and the donkey. See, the priest of Hathor has written me, saying, "Come and receive them!" And also send a message to protest to the captains that they should promote this servant of yours so that he may assist me with the drawing—I'm alone, for my brother is ill. The men of the right side have carved in relief one chamber more than the left side—and he will eat his/my rations with me.

Now a commission of Pharaoh, l.p.h., like this one can go straight ahead if men are doubled for it. When I mentioned this [to] the high priest, the captains said to me, "We will bring him up. It isn't the priest's responsibility," so they said. Send [. . .] you. As for all that my mouth spoke, I shall double it, and more(?).

159. O. DM 437
(Dynasty 20)

As for the remark you made, "It has been a full month till now since gypsum was brought to me," and that this is why you have come back down (from the Valley of the Kings) [to] work, see, I'm sending you some. Don't quarrel with me! Then shall Ptah let you get (gypsum). You won't have to wait at all to get any. Now look, I have assigned those men to[day].

=========== **Wages and Supplies for the Crew** ===========

160. O. Berlin 11238
(Dynasty 19: Ramesses II)

[The mayor] of the West of Ne (Thebes) Ramose communicates to the foremen of the crew, namely, [to] the foreman Nebnefer and to the foreman Kaha and the entire crew as well. To wit:

Now the city prefect and vizier Paser has written me saying, "Please have the wages delivered to the necropolis crew comprising vegetables, fish, firewood, pottery, small cattle, and milk. Don't let anything thereof remain outstanding. [Don't] make me treat any part of their wages as balance due. Be to it and pay heed!"

161. *O. DM 360*
(Dynasty 20: Ramesses III)

Send me the balance due of (fire)wood for the left side (of the crew) starting from Year 22, fourth month of the first season, day 20, until Year 23, third month of the first season, day 10.[2]

162. *P. Turin 1978/208*
(Dynasty 20)

[*Beginning lost*] grain. Look, I will give you 100 *khar*-measures of grain from my house. Send your scribes and your men to pick them up and see if there are old documents of the necropolis in your possession apropos of the wages of the necropolis community which are brought downstream in the boats of officials or which are put aboard them to be brought south. Search for them in the place where you are. "Indeed, it is not we who regularly transport them," so say the officials.

======= Administrative Matters =======

163. *O. DM 429*
(Dynasty 20: Ramesses IV–V)

The scribe Hormin greets the scribe Amenmose: In life, prosperity and health and in the favor of Amon-Re, King of the Gods, your good lord, who remembers you every day! May Thoth and Nehemawayet be with you, and you be satisfied with praises(?) from the Lord of the Two Lands, while you are Hathor's scribe of truth. To wit:

It is your gods who keep your person safe throughout every day, you royal scribe, skilled in your calling and perspicacious. Please give me what I am seeking from you now. It's a piddling. Have a list of the items [sent to] the vizier Neferronpe. In short, [. . .] ask advice.

164. *P. DM 29*
(Dynasty 20: Ramesses IV–IX)

[To] the three captains of the guarded necropolis on the West of Thebes: In life, prosperity and health and in the favor of Amon-Re, King of the Gods! To wit:

I am calling upon Amon, Amenophis, [l.p.h.], and Nofretari, l.p.h., of Menset, your mistress, to keep you healthy, to [keep you prosperous, and to give you] favor in the presence of Pharaoh, l.p.h., our good lord, [. . .]. And further:

I have put the dispatch in the hands of the vizier, our superior, [. . .] since I came from you until now. [. . . , and] he said to me, "May the Ka of Amon, your(?) [good lord], favor you! [. . .]. May he keep him calm en route to the place where One (i.e., the king) is [. . .] boast of all that you have done." Farewell!

[A further matter] to the foreman Nekhemmut: In life, prosperity and health to be with you every day, and in the favor of your god, [god's name], Lord of the Two Lands(?), every day! And further:

I told the vizier the matter which you had mentioned to me, and he became exceedingly pleased. He told me what he had to tell me [. . .], and I am telling it to you. I am writing to inform you(?). Farewell!

I have returned to you your surplus of papyrus (as writing material), but without having added(?) to it.

165. P. Turin 1981
(Dynasty 20)

To the captains of the necropolis [. . .], we being three members of the crew, [who] have not [. . .] anybody except [. . .]. We are calling upon the gods of Pharaoh, l.p.h., to give [you . . .] and our people of the Village many favors [in the presence of] Pharaoh, l.p.h., your lord. And further:

As for all matters about which you [wrote us], they have been submitted before Pharaoh, l.p.h., our good lord. What's the meaning of your telling the vizier that you won't [. . .] if you are denying all words that you spoke in the presence of the vizier, our lord? [. . .]. They have [not] listened to(?) our words [. . .] of ours. Don't let [. . .]. And assign work [. . .] make another(?). Farewell!

Address: The captains of the necropolis.

166. O. DM 227
(Dynasty 20)

Give heed to me to make the proclamation on your part(?). Then shall Amon keep you healthy. The vizier will be departing immediately.

=================== **A Slow Worker** ===================

167. O. DM 328
(Dynasty 19: Ramesses II)

Addressed by the scribe Pabaki to his father, the draftsman Maaninakhtef:
I have heeded what you told me, "Let Ib work with you." Now look, he
spends all day bringing the jug of water, there being no other task charged
to him, each and every day. He hasn't heeded your admonition to ask of him,
"What have you accomplished today?" See, the sun has set, and he is still far
off [with] the jug of water.

=================== **Donkey Problems** ===================

168. O. Berlin 12398
(Dynasty 19: Ramesses II)

Addressed by Khabekhene to his brother (colleague?), the deputy Bennakhtef: In life, prosperity and health and in the favor of Amon-Re, King of
the Gods, your good lord! And further:
What means your telling me in speaking falsely about the donkeys,
"They have become of no use to you," and your telling [me], "The she-ass
is ill owing to the *shabuti*,"[3] when I asked you if its illness commenced during
the decade (a ten-day period)? Now look here, you shall bring it back loaded
up [for] all your people, for surely its affliction has mitigated(?).
Now I have supplied you with the gourds(?): 31 bunches, delivered 18,
remainder due 13. Write me about the matter of the rushes with the instructions you will be giving. Moreover, bring the *shabuti* back and also a piece
of wood for part(?) of a *shabuti*.
Tell the scribe Amenhotep to inquire about the chest which he told me to
buy, and send the stone for my father's offering table. [*End broken*].

169. P. Turin 1976
(Dynasty 20: Ramesses IX)

[*Title and name lost* to the scribe of the] guarded [necropolis]: In life,
prosperity and health and in the favor of Amon-Re, King of the Gods! Every
day I am calling upon the "Sovereign,"[4] Amon, Mut, and Khonsu to keep you
healthy, to keep you alive, to keep you vigorous, and to let you spend a long
lifetime and achieve a ripe old age forever unto eternity. And further:
The officials of Ne (Thebes) sent over two apparitors, and they seized
possession of the she-ass that you had given me, but I prevailed over them

and retrieved it. I have sent it back to you through the agency of the scribe Scramon.

Now look here, I noticed a fine donkey in their charge. Pick out the good one and acquire it since its face is up to size. You are not to pick a quarrel, although it is for your own peace of mind that you should act. Select the good one and treat it well [with] proper treatment.

See, it was in Year 6, third month of the third season, day 25, that I returned to you your she-ass, and it was along with the other items which I was engaged in procuring that I sent to you the *khar*-measure of grain. Farewell!

An Inventory and House Sitting

170. O. Cairo 25670
(Dynasty 19)

To inform you of the items left behind by me in the Village: three *khar*-measures of barley, one and a half *khar*-measures of emmer, twenty-six bundles of papyrus, two beds, a clothes hamper(?), two couches for a man, two folding stools, one chest, one inlaid(?) box, a stool, two griddle-stones, one box(?), two footstools, two folding stools of wood, one basket of lubya-beans (amounting to) three *oipe*-measures, twelve bricks of natron, two pieces of *iker*-furniture, one door, two *seterti*-pieces of sawn wood, two offering tablets(?), one small offering tablet(?), one mortar, and two *medjay*-containers. They are what are with Pashed and the woman Sheritre, all recorded.

A further matter for Sheritre: Please let Amenemwia dwell in my house so that he may keep an eye on it. Please write me about your condition.

Cult Matters

171. O. Brussels E. 6781
(Dynasty 19: Ramesses II)

Addressed by the draftsman Nebre to his brother (colleague?), the draftsman Preem[hab]: In life, prosperity and health and in the favor of Amon-Re, King of the Gods, your good lord!

Please [may you have] a concern for Amenophis, [l].p.h., and cause there to be prepared for him [. . .] date-brew of (the type of the land of) Kode, it being in a *menet*-jar, and writings(?) [. . .] before him. And cause this portion(?) of flour to be made [. . .] into *pat*-cakes and fetch this basket [and fill(?) it] with herbs and vegetables [. . .] for Amenophis in the [. . .], day 27, as well as these two bowls of lubya-beans.

172. O. DM 127
(Dynasty 19: Ramesses II)

To the following effect: I sent to you by the hand of the policeman Pasaro two cakes baked at the ratio of ten per *oipe*-measure of grain, five *deben* of incense, and again five *deben* of incense on the day of the offering which you made for Amon during the Feast of the Valley. They aren't handing over anything which you happen to be sending me.

173. O. DM 551
(Dynasty 19)

What was brought to you by the hand of the laundryman Ka: one large loaf. Send me a goatskin as well as some paint and some incense. And send us leaf-mats and garlands [on] day 18, because they are going to pour libations on day 19.

174. O. DM 124
(Dynasty 20: Ramesses III)

Addressed by the scribe Neferhotep to the deputy of the crew Hay: Come that you may receive offering bread for Hathor(?).
A further matter: As for the words you told me in your chapel courtyard, this is a reminder of your not speaking with me truthfully. As for the man you mentioned, I am not with my side (of the crew), for mine has been discharged, [. . .] so I should not come to receive offering bread [for] Hathor(?). [*End broken*].

175. O. DM 246
(Dynasty 20: Ramesses III?)

Please send this back to me right away today. Pay heed, pay heed!
A depiction of Montu seated on a throne and a depiction of the scribe Pentawere kissing the ground before him in adoration of him—(to be) in outline drawing.

176. O. DM 248
(Dynasty 20: Ramesses III–VI)

The scribe Amennakht, likewise. The *hin*-measure of wine that I promised you is in the chapel courtyard of Amenophis, l.p.h., our lord.

177. O. Gardiner 5
(Dynasty 20: Ramesses IV–V)

To the guardian Khay:

As soon as my letter reaches you, you shall spend money and buy an ox for Mereseger. But you shall not look for a bull(?), nor shall you look for a goat, dog, pig, or other animal. You are one whose mouth is fearsome(?). As for the jar of fat, it belongs to the [goddess(?)]. You have consumed plenty of fat. You have consumed the one (jar) belonging to me, a chief administrator of the [. . .]. If you speak out again, I will come down to watch on you and keep you in check from(?) [. . .]. What are you doing there in this sacred town, you man of [. . .]? I went as far as your town to meet you.

178. P. DM 3
(mid-Dynasty 20)

The workman Hay greets the scribe Imisiba: In life, prosperity and health and in the favor of Amon-Re, King of the Gods! To wit: I am [calling] upon Pre-Harakhti to keep you healthy, to keep you alive, and to keep you in the favor of Amon, your lord. To the following effect:

I am engaged in making the bed. It will be beautiful! Send the ebony so that it may not be delayed and also the webbing material.

Now see, I am going to offer to Sobek, your lord. Send a pair of garments [for] your servants. As soon as I celebrate the feast, I will send them back to you. And you are to send me some pigments and also a [. . .] King(?) A[menophis . . .]. Farewell!

179. P. DM 15
(mid-Dynasty 20)

The carpenter Khonsu to his mother, the citizeness Nofretkha: In life, prosperity and health! And further:

I swore that I wouldn't eat a haunch or tripe either, but see, I have eaten them. I won't do it again. Tell the god by whom I swore to have mercy.

180. O. Cairo 25752
(Dynasty 20?)

Now don't say, "I shall do singing." I won't let you do singing. It is Pasen who has been assigned to do(?) the singing for Mereseger.

181. O. DM 129
(Dynasties 19–20)

The god's father priest Sheri communicates to his father. To wit:

I am calling upon Amon-Re, King of the Gods, Mut, Khonsu, and all gods and goddesses of Thebes, upon Mereseger, mistress of the West, and upon every god and every goddess whom I visit daily in the necropolis to give you health, to give you life, and to give you a long lifetime and a ripe old age, while [you] continue [. . .] forever and ever.

As soon as my letter reaches [you . . .], you shall send me the wooden door which the scribe of the necropolis [*name lost*] decorated for you in order that it may become a stele here with me bearing your name in the [. . .] door with(?) the scribe Sheri.

182. O. DM 251
(Dynasties 19–20)

Please manufacture for me a *Weret*-demon[5] because the one which you manufactured for me has been stolen, and thus it may work a manifestation of Seth against me.

183. O. Leipzig 11
(Dynasties 19–20)

[*Beginning lost*] "My manifestation shall be against your son," so says the deity to me. Please be attentive and propitiate her, and then she will forgive you.

A further matter: Please be attentive and fetch a bit of incense as well as a [. . .] for [*End lost*].

══════════════════ **Fortunetelling** ══════════════════

184. O. Letellier
(Dynasty 19: second half)

Kenhikhopeshef addresses the woman Inerwau:

What means your failing to go to the woman diviner on account of the two infants who died while in your charge? Inquire of the woman diviner about the death of the two infants, whether it was their fate or their destiny. And you shall inquire about them for me and get a view of my own life and their mother's life. As for whatever god shall be [mentioned] to you afterwards(?), you shall write me concerning his identity. You [will be rendering ser]vice for one who knows her occupation(?).

================================= Illness =================================

185. O. Berlin 11247
(Dynasty 19: Ramesses II)

Addressed by the draftsman Pay to his son, the draftsman Pre[emhab]:
Don't turn your back on me, for I'm not well. Don't be sparing in tears for me because I am in this [darkness (i.e., blindness) and] my lord Amon [has turned] his back on me.

May you bring me a bit of honey for my eyes as well as ochre that has been freshly molded (into sticks) and genuine galena. [. . .]. Be to it! Be to it! Am I not your father? Now I am incapacitated. I am searching for my eyesight, but it no longer exists.

186. O. UCL No. 3
(Dynasty 19: Ramesses II)

It is the controller of Selket (the charmer of scorpions) Amenmose [who addresses . . .] and the temple scribe and god's father priest Piay of the Temple of the King of Upper and Lower Egypt Usermare-setepenre, l.p.h., (Ramesses II's mortuary temple) in the Estate of Amon [on] the West of Thebes:
The god's father priest is ill. As soon as my letter reaches [you, you] shall send him an ear of grain(?),[6] a jar of syrup, and one of festival date-brew(?). Farewell!

187. O. DM 581
(Dynasty 19: Ramesses II)

Addressed by the draftsman Khay to the drafts[man *name lost*]: In life, prosperity and health and in the favor of Amon-Re, King of the Gods, your [good] lord, daily!
See, I am calling upon [. . .] and all the gods of Karnak to keep you healthy, to keep you alive, and to keep you in the favor of Amon-[Re], King [of the Gods], and of the King of Upper and Lower Egypt, the Lord of the Two Lands, Usermare-setepenre (Ramesses II), l.p.h., your good lord, that you may persevere in the service of Ne (Thebes). Please be attentive and get me some ink as well as a few rush brushes and some papyrus very promptly.

A further communication to Meryre, son(?) of Meh: In the favor of Thoeris (goddess of fecundity), your mistress! I'm still bedridden. [. . .] me to eat [. . . to]day. I have neither fish nor vegetables at hand, and there is no gardener [. . . to] bring me some [*End broken*].

188. O. Wente
(late Dynasty 19–early Dynasty 20)

To the police captain Montumose:
What's the point of my sending that *hin*-measure of oil to the marketplace? Search for a goat for my wife who is ill and take possession of it. I'm not aware that I have been removed from the necropolis community!

=== **A Death** ===

189. O. DM 126
(Dynasty 19: Ramesses II)

The scribe Piay and the native of the necropolis community Mehy to the foreman Neferhotep and the workman Pennebu: In life, prosperity and health! And further:
What mean the things that you are saying, "As for all people who happen to die, it is they concerning whom you have been wont to go and make inquiry. Is your man an exception?" This man died in the house of Horemhab, who sent me word saying, "Hormose is dead." I went with Mehy, [and we] had a look. We took charge of him and had [him] brought up [to you], saying, "You shall take proper care of him."
We are attempting to raise the matter with you while making [the inventory], which you will find itemized. [If you] determine that he was killed, [. . .] matters which are not [*End lost*].

=== **Tight Rations** ===

190. O. Cairo 25644
(Dynasty 19: Seti II)

[The scribe(?)] Neferhotep greets(?) [*a female relative of*] Ptahshed:
I have taken note of every matter. A woman Heretjer(?) is with me binding up vegetables. She is a sister(?) of Neb[. . .], a man of the necropolis community, the one who was here in the West during the Feast of the Valley,

Amon's festival, when they failed to send you a container(?) of coiled technique.

What sort of a girl(?) do you have with you? Does she have requirements in food at all times? Please stop the people who are there from starving to death now that I have sent one *oipe*-measure of barley and one *oipe*-measure of emmer, even though(?) the slave-women consume grain [like] water(?) daily [at] her house when I am there doling out for you(?).

Further, I sent her a basket and a mat by the hand of the policeman Khonsemhab [in] the third month of the third season, day 23, after you had asked him, "Where are the containers(?) of coiled technique?" "O(?) workman Ptahshed, may you come to me," so you(?) shall tell him. Request this of him, or(?) I shall request it myself(?). Farewell!

===== **Laundry** =====

191. O. DM 314
(Dynasty 19: Ramesses II)

To the scribe Amenemope:

As for the eight (households) you've dealt with, give over(?) four households. Has the laundryman washed or not? It was only [six(?)] households that Pharaoh, l.p.h., assigned to him. Now see, he has been assigned six households as two days' work, making three households per day. But see, [the householders(?) are] saying to [him], "[. . .] and be to it(?)," so they keep telling him.

You shall send a message concerning them to the [. . .] and cause [the laundry]man [to wash(?)] for Bakenmut. What you've done is fine. See, (I) have exa[mined . . .] in their presence. As for Nakhtsobek, I found no natron[7] in his possession although you had given him [some]. It is a [. . .] it on his account that you've done. As soon as you ascertain the [reason for] delay, they shall procure natron for the(?) clothes.

Now you are not decrying(?) this failure to supply natron even though Pharaoh, l.p.h., had allotted natron to you. Or hasn't he allotted any yet so as to alleviate your need? Now you know one side (of the issue).

===== **Property** =====

192. O. Berlin 11239
(Dynasty 19: Ramesses II)

In life, prosperity and health and in the favor of Amon-Re every day! And further:

Mark the words I told you regarding the copper that was removed from Sementowy. See, the coppersmiths of the *setem*-priest came and said, "As for this copper, it belongs to the *setem*-priest; it does not belong to the necropolis. Send the copper back to the *setem*-priest," so they said. And they brought some more copper and said, "Have it weighed out from this." Don't listen to them. Have the copper they weighed out brought back, so you shall tell them.

Now as soon as it is brought to you, you shall take possession of it along with the other (copper) to pay for his (Sementowy's?) many debts. See to it, if you might have some of it sent.

193. O. DM 558
(Dynasty 19: Ramesses II)

The draftsman Nebre to the draftsman Nakhtamon:

Please give your personal attention and take [the draftsman(?)] Nakhy to court and claim my pair of [. . .] and my [. . .] from him. He said, "I will bring you four *besy*-items [for] the one," and he said, "I will bring you the other [for the] *depy*-jars and dishes," but he failed to bring them. Please give your personal attention and go with the policeman Pasur [and] give him a grain basket and collect your price (for it) in pottery(?). Be to it! Be to it! Don't ignore my assignment. Be very prompt!

(Written) in the presence of the doorkeeper Sur.

194. O. Gardiner 67
(Dynasty 19: Ramesses II)

Hormose to Pennebu:

When I was working in the granary of the Temple of Maat, I became bedridden. The native of the necropolis community Reia, who is an apparitor of the court, confiscated an undergarment(?) of six cubits, which was not worn through, and he must also have confiscated one *khar*-measure of emmer and four temple baskets of coiled technique.

195. O. DM 289
(Dynasty 19: Siptah)

I inform you of the property that was stolen [from] the house of Ipuy: one mat, fifty pieces of wood veneer, one pair of men's sandals, one *deben* of incense, three necklaces, and three signet rings.

196. O. BM 5631, rt.
(Dynasty 19)

[*Beginning lost*] "[. . .] in Hikuptah (Memphis) [. . .] reached me," so you said. [. . . . You made for] him good plans, and all that you said was heeded. And you caused there to be released [. . .] and said to me, "You should go to our house and enter a stall, being the one where the two boxes are standing next to the pigsty. [Look] opposite those two millstones, and you will find those two pits with the copper tools lying within them."

I did accordingly while I myself was with the [. . .]: 500 copper spikes, 30 large copper hoes, 50 large copper chisels, 60 large copper spikes for splitting stone, 25 copper adzes, 30 copper double-edged knives, and 40 [copper . . .]. And I discovered a jar of Coptos ware, which was capped with gypsum and sealed with two seal impressions and which was inscribed [with a list of what was] in it: 10 *deben*-weights of silver, 2 *mine*-weights of gold, 7 heart amulets, 7 chains(?) of gold, and 20 gold signet rings. And Mose said to me, "Let the jar be opened, [and we shall divide] the items that are in it between the two of us, for no one knows of it, and you shall not inform your father about it." But I replied to him, "In no way! [I will not break the] seal," so I told him.

A further matter: Now when I withdrew the copper objects belonging to Pharaoh, l.p.h., saying, "I shall take them to the overseer of the treasury of Pharaoh, l.p.h., and [cause the] servants [to be released]," the deputy officer of the northern quarter came and apprehended me. And he said to me, "You discovered some [. . .] which were registered(?) in the house of the master of works and were issued to the necropolis. Have them handed over so that I may take them to Pharaoh, l.p.h., namely, the things that were discovered and you appropriated. [But I] replied to him, "In no way! They are the tools of work which used to be under my grandfather's supervision. One came to look for them, but they couldn't be found. So our twelve servants were taken away in place of them. My father appealed to Pharaoh, l.p.h., and he had me set free, for I am a native of the necropolis community, who is enlisted at the place where they are. I shall take them (the copper objects) to the overseer of the treasury of Pharaoh, l.p.h., and our servants, whom they [seized], shall be set free," so I said to him. And he [caused] it to be accomplished.

===================== **Family** =====================

197. O. Černý 3 + O. Cambridge 1
(Dynasty 19: Ramesses II)

The scribe Turo greets his mother, the chantress of Amon [*name lost*]: In life, prosperity and health and in the favor of Amon-Re, King of the Gods! And further:

How are you? Further, I am [calling upon] Amon, Mut, Khonsu, and all the gods of Southern Heliopolis (Thebes) and upon Pre when he rises [each(?)] day to keep you healthy, to keep you in the favor of the (deified) Western Promontory, the mistress, and to let [me see you] healthy each and every day. And further:

I am being sent as far as the east [side to the(?)] vizier in order to collect dues of(?) his agents who are in the fields. And [. . .] as last year's balance due. Now there is no loincloth for my rear, for my loincloth has been taken away. [. . .] apportioned(?) to the granary of Pharaoh, l.p.h. Please give your personal attention and have me provided that I may cause(?) [. . .]. Don't make me walk helpless, or you will be [made] helpless, because [. . .]

Now as soon as I return from the errand, I will deliver his goods in grain [. . .]. Don't listen to what Wadjmose has said, or you may have to serve as a member [of the crew]! (*Accounts follow*).

198. O. DM 560
(Dynasty 19: Ramesses II)

Addressed by the woman Wel to the scribe Huynefer: In life, prosperity and health and in the favor of Amon-Re, King of the Gods.

See, every day I am calling upon every god and every goddess who is in the district of the West to keep you healthy, to keep you alive, and to keep you in the favor of Pharaoh, l.p.h., your good lord. And further:

Please be considerate toward your brother. Don't forsake him!

A further communication to Neferkhay: Ditto greetings. Be considerate toward Khay, your brother. Don't forsake him!

199. O Petrie 61
(mid-Dynasty 19)

The workman Horemwia, he addresses the citizeness Tanetdjesere, his daughter:

You are my good daughter. If the workman Baki throws you out of the house, I will take action! As for the house, it is what belongs to(?) Pharaoh, l.p.h., but you may dwell in the anteroom to my storehouse because it is I who built it. Nobody in the world shall throw you out of there.

200. O. Prague 1826
(Dynasty 19)

Addressed by Takhentyshepse to her sister Iye: In life, prosperity and health! And further:

I shall send you the barley, and you shall have it ground for me and add emmer to it. And you shall make me bread with it, for I have been quarreling with Merymaat (my husband). "I will divorce you," he keeps saying when he quarrels with me on account of my mother in questioning the amount of barley required for bread. "Now your mother does nothing for you," he keeps telling me and says, "Although you have brothers and sisters, they don't take care of you," he keeps telling me in arguing with me daily, "Now look, this is what you have done to me ever since I've lived here, whereas all people furnish bread, beer, and fish daily [to] their (family) members. In short, should you say anything, you will have to go back down to the Black Land."[8] It is good if you take note.

201. O. DM 270
(early Dynasty 20)

I have written to you. It's none of my wife's business.

Adultery

202. O. DM 439
(Dynasty 20)

Really, it was not in order that you might become blind to your wife that I took you aside and said, "You should see the things that you've done [on behalf of (?)] your wife." You rebuffed me only to become deaf (i.e., indifferent) to this crime, which is Montu's abomination. See, I will make you aware of those adulterous acts that your [wife] has committed at your expense.

(*Response to the preceding*):
But she isn't my wife! Were she my wife, she would cease uttering her words (charges?) and get out leaving the door open.

Personal Relations

203. O. Leipzig 12
(Dynasty 19: Ramesses II)

Addressed by the scribe Huy to Neferronpe:
What's the meaning of your dealing with me like a magpie among the doves? As soon as the light of dawn, I will make for myself a dovecot(?), for you are [behaving] exactly the same way. As soon as you find out [*End lost*].

204. O. DM 303
(mid-Dynasty 19)

The draftsman Prehotep communicates to his superior, the scribe of the Place of Truth Kenhikhopeshef: In life, prosperity and health!

What's the meaning of this negative attitude that you are adopting toward me? I'm like a donkey to you. If there is work, bring the donkey! And if there is fodder, bring the ox! If there is beer, you never ask for me. Only if there is work (to be done), will you ask for me.

Upon my head, if I am a man who is bad in (his) behavior with beer, don't ask for me. It is good for you to take notice in the Estate of Amon-Re, King of the Gods, l.p.h.

(*Postscript*): I am a man who is lacking beer [in] his house. I am seeking [to] fill my stomach by my writing to you.

205. O. DM 326
(Dynasty 19: second half)

In life, prosperity and health and in the favor of Amon-Re, King of the Gods! And further:

What have I done for you to write me such(?) bitter matters as you write me about and for you to write me saying, "What have I done for you to write me saying, 'Send me bread daily!'" whereas I never wrote you saying, "Send me bread [daily]!"? It was only when I was ill that I wrote you saying, "Send me bread from the office of [. . .] in Coptos," and you sent me a sack(?) of [. . .], one by the hand of Pasur and another by the hand of Bakmut, son of Huy. [. . .] these bitter matters. What have I done that you should [write such a letter]? I am [exceedingly distressed] because of this.

206. O. Berlin 10627
(Dynasty 20: Ramesses III–IV)

To the scribe Nekhemmut: In life, prosperity and health and in the favor of your august god, Amon-Re, King of the Gods, your good lord, every day! And further:

What's the meaning of your getting into such a bad mood as you are in that nobody's speech can enter your ears as a consequence of your inflated ego? You are not a man since you are unable to make your wives pregnant like your fellowmen.[9]

A further matter: You abound in being exceedingly stingy. You give no one anything. As for him who has no children, he adopts an orphan instead [to] bring him up. It is his responsibility to pour water onto your hands as one's own eldest son.

207. *O. Leipzig 5*
(Dynasty 20: Ramesses III–V)

Statement by the assistant Amenmose greeting the scribe Hay: In life and health and in the favor of Amon-Re, King of the Gods, your good lord, every day! And further:

Daily I am calling upon Amenophis, l.p.h., the lord of the Village, to keep you healthy, to keep [you] alive, and to let you achieve the longevity of the mountains of the West.

208. *O. DM 128*
(Dynasty 20: Ramesses III–VI)

The scribe Hay greets his brother (colleague?), the scribe Userhat: In life, prosperity and health and [in] the favor of [Amon-Re], King of the Gods. To wit:

I am calling upon Amon, Mut, and Khonsu and [all] the gods of Thebes to keep you healthy, to keep [you] alive, [. . .] and let me fill [my] embrace [with you. [. . . , and I] am calling upon Pre-Harakhti [. . .] to keep you healthy.

A further matter: Please write [me about your condition through who]ever happens to come here from you, for [it is my desire to learn about your [welfare. *End broken*].

209. *P. DM 4*
(Dynasty 20: Ramesses V)

[The scribe] Nakhtsobek to the workman Amennakht: In life, prosperity and health and in the favor of Amon-Re, King of the Gods! Every day I am calling upon Amon, Mut, Khonsu, and all gods of Thebes and every god and goddess who resides [in] the West of Ne (Thebes) to give you life, to give you health, and to give you a long [lifetime] and a ripe old age, while you continue in the favor of Amenophis, the lord of the Village, your good lord who looks after you. And further:

What's up? What have I done against you? Am I not your old table companion?[10] Has the time come when you must turn your [back(?)]? What shall I do? Please write me of the wrong that I've done against you through the policeman Bes. And if you refuse to write me either good or bad, this day is really bad! I won't request anything else of you. A person is delighted when he is together with his old table companion. While certain new [things] are good to have, an old companion is better.

As soon as my letter reaches you, [you] shall send word about your condition through the policeman Bes. Inform me of the situation today. Don't make me be told not to enter your house and not to make [my] way within the walls and to flee [from] the Village. And don't [turn a deaf ear(?)] to me. I am going to enter the house and leave therefrom. I must have access [to this] abode of mine. May Amon be before you! If [he] lives, I shall (also) live. When I die, may Amon still be before you (text: him)! Farewell!

210. *P. DM 5*
(Dynasty 20: Ramesses V)

To wit: Every day I am calling upon all the gods of heaven and earth to give you life and health. And further:

What's with you? Please communicate to me the nature of your thoughts that I may penetrate them. Indeed, ever since I was a child even until today, when with you, I cannot fathom your nature. Can a person be happy if he mentions something to his companion twice and he (the companion) fails to take note of it as is the case of the *hin*-measure of unguent which I requested of you and which you promised me you would send to me but didn't even bother about?

Write me about your condition instead of the unguent. May Amon be before you! You will find benefit therein. It's not fair the way you have regularly mistreated me.

A further matter: Soak some bread and send it to me(?) straightaway! Farewell!

211. *P. DM 6*
(Dynasty 20: Ramesses V)

To wit: Every day I am calling upon Ptah of [. . . and upon Sokar], who resides in the Shetyet-sanctuary, the Sun of the day, to give you life, health, a [long] lifetime and a ripe old age, while you continue being a brother to me forever and I(?) a grown-up orphan with you. [And further]:

[Pay heed to] my communication to you yesterday saying, "Send a *hin*-measure of un[guent] to [your] lady table companion," for see, she has come, and you shall not let her be in [need]. If you are broke, can't you sell your clothes and send that about which I've written you? As soon as my letter reaches you, you shall send the unguent about which I've written you. See to it carefully.! Don't keep the man waiting while you [. . .] run off for her to the Village.

Now look, I've gotten hold of her. I didn't let her know that I had written you that she was here since it was in order to consult (the oracle of) Nofretari about a dream she had seen that she came. And you shall not act the way you have regularly acted. It is I who am regularly writing you but you never write me. [Fare]well!

212. O. Michaelides 79
(mid-Dynasty 20)

The draftsman of the guarded necropolis Hormin greets the scribe Maanakhtef.

I am calling upon Amon-Re, King of the Gods, to keep you healthy, to keep you alive, and to let you achieve a long lifetime and a ripe old age, while you continue being a great sandal-maker unto eternity, possessing fine leather and large glistening hides [. . .] anew(?) for you, and possessing [. . .] many goods. Won't you let me be dismissed? Farewell!

Disputes

213. O. Petrie 92
(Dynasty 19)

Beginning from the third month of the second season, day 21, until the fourth month of the second season, day 13, there were(?) four days (when there was) [a deficiency] in what was brought to me in the way of *bit*-loaves, for they were unleavened(?) in their preparation. To inform you what was brought [to me]: four large *bit*-loaves and eleven small ones.

Since I last wrote until today, I have been disputing [with] the man. He told me, "I will take it for myself to the Field (i.e., the work area in the Valley of the Kings)," so he said to me. Yet again I have been disputing with him, and he told me, "I will leave it [for] the children," so he said to [me].

214. O. Leipzig 16
(Dynasty 19)

To Kha[em]wia: In life, prosperity and health!

Look here, I have had a dispute with Amenemone [over] the cow. He says thus [. . .], "What shall I do [with] this other one that is in my charge? For you gave me the other one," so he says, "but you didn't give me a basket or a foot-mat(?)," so he says, "or an under-mat(?) either." What mean the things that you are doing that you should give the [gum(?)]-water to Hat and send him [to] claim the cow? Don't I know where the cow is? It was in order to hear what you had to say that I didn't go [to] fetch it.

215. P. DM 7, vs.
(Dynasty 20: Ramesses IX?)

It is a complaint about(?) our seeing our man denigrating me on the way. If you have done nothing for me after the manner(?) of all my brothers, I must not count among those for whom you have celebrated a feast. Although you go on denigrating my reputation in the presence of the people in the Village in which I am, it (the Village) keeps silent. I didn't bring you wood(?) [. . .]. He [ordered(?)] me to remove them all, but it was not there that I removed them. It was to your house that I came [in order to re]move them, and I found your [. . .] outside. Now(?) don't contest those which I have removed. Be a pilot for me while I remove them.

216. *O. Gardiner 32*
(Dynasties 19–20)

To wit: I have learned from Kenna that my superior says thus: "Come! When he reaches you, you shall give him ten very hard blows as he deserves(?)."

===================== **Consumer Needs and Transactions** =====================

217. *O. DM 440*
(Dynasty 19: Ramesses II)

To the scribe Ramose: May he favor you, namely, Amon-Re, King of the Gods, your good lord, l.p.h. And further:
I reached the overseer of the treasury, and he told his deputy who is there in the treasury of Ne (Thebes), "Give this (person) ten *menet*-jars of *neheh*-oil," so he said.

218. *O. Černý 19*
(Dynasty 19: Ramesses II)

Addressed by the draftsman Pay to his son, the draftsman Preemhab:
Please make arrangements to procure the two faience heart amulets about which I told you, "I will pay their owner whatever he may demand for the price of them." And you shall make arrangements to procure this fresh incense which I mentioned to you in order to varnish the coffin of your mother.[11] I will pay its owner for it.
And you shall be attentive to take this rag of a kilt and this rag of a loincloth in order to rework the kilt into a red sash and the loincloth into an apron. Don't ignore anything I've told you. Be to it!

219. O. DM 587
(Dynasty 19: Ramesses II)

Addressed by Paser to the woman Tutuia:

What's the meaning of your words, your reproach of me? You sent (me) a message when your mother was still alive, and I came and gave you a skirt. And I gave the [. . .], saying, "Take disposition of them," and they [became] yours. You brought three bundles of vegetables, and I [said], "From where (do they come)?" And you answered me, "[I] didn't get them from my mother Sita[mon]."

I returned again after your mother died, and I gave you a *tekhbes*-basket with the request to buy a goat with it, but you said to me, "One *tekhbes*-basket is insufficient." And I said to you, "Add a bundle of vegetables to it and buy the goat." You said to me, "[I] did add it (to enable the purchase)." But now you write saying, "I have bought for you an idle(?) (available?) goat, whose price is one *tekhbes*-basket and vegetables plus another *tekhbes*-basket to enable its purchase(?). I have bought it."[12]

Now see, I gave to you [*some item*], saying, "Buy oil with it. Use it. Don't use the bundle of vegetables. Buy oil with it. Now I am your good brother who looks after you, my sister(?)."

220. O. DM 446
(Dynasty 19: Ramesses II)

Ameke to his mother Hemenetjer: In life, prosperity and health! And further:

What's this awful behavior that is being displayed? For when I had brought leather sandals to this soldier, taking them with me to acquire a few cucumbers, he simply handed back those sandals of his, saying, "Hold on to them for me." Now by Ptah, he is sailing north tonight. Have the sandals brought immediately! Don't [oppose] me in any way! [. . .] my two hands after [. . .] brought [. . .]. Send me a container(?) and a *tekhbes*-basket. A (whole) town can be thankful if you get going(?) since he is sailing north to the royal jubilee.

221. O. DM 317
(Dynasty 19: Ramesses II)

Addressed by the scribe Nebnetjeru to the scribe Ramose: In life, prosperity and health! And further:

Now I am calling upon Amon, Ptah, and Min to keep you healthy, to keep [you] alive, and to keep [you in] the favor of Pharaoh, l.p.h., my good lord. Please be attentive and fetch me some(?) ink because [my] superior has told [me] the good (ink) has deteriorated.

Addressed by the scribe Nebnetjeru [to] his father, the scribe Pay:
What's the use of my trying to manage affairs? [. . .] which I said because
I did [*End lost*].

222. *O. DM 119*
(Dynasty 19: Ramesses II)

Addressed by Nebnetjeru to his mother T[aysen]nofre:
Send me some loaves as well as whatever else you may have on hand very
promptly! Then shall Amon give to you that you may continue being in favor
fully satisfied(?).

223. *O. Gardiner 125*
(Dynasty 19: Ramesses II)

To the scribe Huy:
Please tell Khaemtore, "You must send me your pitcher, the adze, the
double-edged knife, and two awls."

224. *O. DM 322*
(Dynasty 19: Ramesses II)

Said by Minhotep in greeting his father Neb[. . .]: In life, prosperity and
health and in the favor of Amon-Re, King of the Gods, your good lord, daily!
And further:
[Please give] your personal attention and send me a *hin*-measure (of oil)
daily as the waters flowing north, [so that I might] find [, ,] that was given
to me. I shall buy for you the *hin*-measure of *neheh*-oil to be consumed [. . .],
and when you pay for the *menet*-jar, you shall send me some hides and some
bread by the hand of the policeman [Huy]. And also send me the *hin*-measure
[*End broken*].

225. *O. Cairo 25679, vs.*
(Dynasty 19: Ramesses II)

Amen[em]hat says: Look after me daily with bread, beer, meat, and baked
goods.

226. *O. DM 681*
(Dynasty 19: Ramesses II?)

The scribe Khay greets his brother (colleague?) Pahy: In life, prosperity and
health! And [further]:
Please fetch the grain basket and give the sack(?) to Iniuhe and Penanket.
And give the hamper to Pa[nakht]. And send the grain basket and send the

two *denit*-baskets after you have supplied us with wood—so [you] shall tell Hor.

227. O. DM 116
(Dynasty 19: Ramesses II)

Addressed by the woman Nebeton to Pennebu: In life, prosperity and health! And further:

A woman took the wool(?) from me, [and she] told me, "Give me a free-woman's [. . .] in addition to it, and I will give you these five copper *deben*-pieces," so she said to me. See whether or not you might find a way to supply it. Will you mention it as well to Mehy and also to Paherypedje or not? And will you write me about the instructions you will give or not, so I can [send] your younger brother up with a bowl?

228. O. DM 117
(Dynasty 19: Ramesses II)

Addressed by the woman Nebhimaat [to her] sister Nebeton: [In life, prosperity and health]! And further:

Please be attentive and supply me with the tunic. Go and pick the vegetables, for they are now due from you.

229. O. DM 125
(Dynasty 19: Ramesses II)

A further communication to the woman Henutudjebu:

Please give your personal attention and procure a tunic for me (a woman) in exchange for the bracelet and have it furnished to me [in] ten days.

230. O. DM 324
(Dynasty 19: Ramesses II)

Ankhau to his daughter Nubemshas: In life, prosperity and health! And further:

No bread is being sent down to the marketplace as daytime requirements to allow me to take any to the boys. Send me five loaves each ten-day period, [and I shall] give to the boys from them because I can give them daily only what I've got on hand.

A further matter: Please have them furnish one *inehty*-basket of kyllestis-bread as well as one of vegetables because a message has been sent to me saying, "Bring the boat to be loaded in order that [they] may be brought downstream to me." Please have them furnish that which is . . . there(?) so that I may send them [out after the] bad people.

231. O. DM 304
(Dynasty 19: Ramesses II)

Addressed by Horemhab to Amenemwia: In life, prosperity and health! And further:

As for the grain basket which you made, it is of coarse coiling, and five (extra) coils(?) are upon it in excess of the five *hin*-measures. Have [a replacement for it] made which is of fine material and which holds [the proper amount].

232. O. DM 132
(Dynasty 19: Ramesses II)

Addressed by Isis to her sister Nubemnu: In life, prosperity and health! And further:

Please give your personal attention and weave for me that shawl very promptly before Amenophis, l.p.h., comes (in procession) because I am really naked. Make one [for] my backside(?) because I am naked. [*End broken*].

233. O. Staring [Brussels]
(Dynasty 19: Ramesses II)

Addressed by the draftsman Ipu to his brother, [the draftsman Pre]emhab:

What have I done that you have failed to bring [the goods for] Amon? If I have taken anything from you, write me about it that I may restore it to you. And you shall bring me my goods or have someone else bring them to me. Be considerate and bring me [the . . .] which I told you to give to my [. . .]. And you shall bring the grain that you have on hand. Don't be a bad fellow, for I'm your brother. Don't turn your back on us, for we are distressed. When you bring the ox, I'll give you a loincloth.

234. P. Cairo from DM
(Dynasty 19: Ramesses II)

Addressed by the draftsman Khay to his brother (i.e., uncle) Preemhab: Bring me a fledgling and also some sycamore figs.

235. O. DM 321
(Dynasty 19: Ramesses II)

To Amenemwia: In life, prosperity and health! And further:

What means this bad mood in which you are regarding my sending you a few skins with the request to make them into a sack and to get on with them? Now look, I've sent you an *oipe*-measure of colonquinthus fruit. Let me find the sack finished in ten days, wide enough to hold three *khar*-measures.

Now I'm off to the tribunal of the temple(?), so you shall have a satchel supplied for those sandals of mine. Let me find it serviceable.

I sent you sixty cakes. Were they delivered [to] you when six offering loaves and five [. . .] dishes were brought?

236. O. DM 118
(Dynasty 19: Ramesses II)

Addressed by Dhutmose to Prehotep: In life, prosperity and health! And further:

As for the goat that I acquired for twenty (pigeons), please give your personal attention and buy twenty-five pigeons with it. Don't say, "It's part of those (other) items," but seize hold of it (the goat) and have them bought for me very quickly and very promptly. Now when you buy, he (the seller of pigeons) shall cause what you demand to be brought to you.

237. O. Petrie 65
(Dynasty 19: first half)

Addressed by the draftsman Baki to his brother (colleague?), the draftsman Mehy:

Bring me a bird straightaway!

238. O. Berlin 10664
(Dynasty 19: Ramesses II)

[Ra]mose to the god's father priest Amenhotep [of the Temple] of the King of Upper and Lower Egypt, Usermare-setepenre, l.p.h., (Ramesses II's mortuary temple) in the Estate of Amon on the West of Thebes:

Every day I am calling upon Mereseger, mistress of the West, to keep you healthy, to keep you [alive], to let you achieve a long lifetime and a ripe old age, and to let you [carry on] the office of your father and let [your] children succeed you after a hundred myriad years while you continue in the favor of Amon of United-with-Thebes (the Amon of Ramesses II's mortuary temple), your good lord. [And] further:

What's the good of my writing to the keepers(?) [. . .], saying, "Send a basket(?)." [. . .]. Send me a goat [. . .], and I shall [. . .]. Please cause there to be made [*End lost*].

239. O. DM 562
(mid-Dynasty 19)

Addressed by Khor to Minmose:

What means your taking away the pair of sandals and your taking away my [. . .] and your failing to bring the [. . .] which I mentioned to you? Please give your personal attention and bring a [. . .] and also the jug filled with milk, and whatever else you may have on hand. Don't leave me in the lurch while I'm [in] this sorry plight in which I am. It is good if you take note.

240. O. Petrie 82
(mid-Dynasty 19)

What is for Penbuy: one *oipe*-measure of [. . .] emmer and two bundles of vegetables. As regards the (surplus?) amount, it belongs to Sul. As regards these two *oipe*-measures of grain, I shall [apply them] toward the (cost of) the kilt. Send the fabrics(?) which you have set aside, because with regard to the one which you could not locate, I find it complete.

241. O. DM 605
(Dynasty 19: second half)

To Baki: Please give your personal attention and ferment(?) one *oipe*-measure of grain with dates and bring it [straightaway(?)].

242. O. Turin 57081
(Dynasty 19: second half)

[Addressed by] the foreman Paneb to the scribe Pentawere:

[In the favor of] Amon-Re, King of the Gods, your good lord, every day! [And further]:

[Send] me a full ass-load of wood at once! [. . .]. Then he (Amon) shall keep you alive, and he shall keep you in the favor of [Pharaoh(?), your] good [lord], daily, and he shall keep you in the favor of [. . .] it to you in the fourth month of the second season, day 16.

243. O. Michaelides 87
(Dynasty 19: Siptah)

I went [to] Pashed, who said, "There are some of the goods which Prehotep brought." As soon as he gives (me) mine which he has, I shall give him also his which I have.

244. O. DM 228
(Dynasty 19: Siptah)

Addressed by the scribe Burekhtuinuf to the scribe Renakht: [In life, prosperity and health and in the favor of] Amon-Re, King of the Gods!

Every day I am calling upon Amon, Mut, Khonsu, Amenophis, l.p.h., the lord of the Village, and all gods and goddesses of Thebes, your good lords, who keep your body sound, to give you health and life. And further:

As soon as my letter reaches you, you shall immediately send me your pair of *khentyet*[13] so that I might carry the dirt away therewith. Then shall Ptah(?), your lord, give to you. And don't send a response (objection?) back to me since I'm in a hurry to carry away the dirt which I have here in the house.

245. O. DM 554
(Dynasty 19)

What's the meaning of your refusing to go to the policeman Nebmehy and buy for me those six beams which he has in his possession? Although I mentioned this to you ten days ago, you didn't go. Now he told me, "I did tell him this myself. Is it proper that I should tell him on behalf of some other third party?" It is not proper, what you've done. Besides I gave you an old pair of sandals with the further request to buy a beam for me with them, but you wouldn't buy it for me.

A further matter: It was found that the shabby loincloth had been given to the laundryman Nakhtamon on day 9.

A further matter: As for the fish which you sent us along with twelve *peypenu*-loaves(?), it was only thirteen fish that were delivered to us. Five of them had been removed. Demand them from the one whom you sent up with them.

246. O. DM 563
(Dynasty 19)

[Regarding] what you [wrote] saying, "Buy for me the ox which [I] picked out [as suitable]. Can I buy an ox from someone here?" Don't let your heart stand still (give up hope?). I shall buy an ox for you and also the things you mentioned. Regarding what you wrote saying, "Hand it over," take it off my hands. Send the boat of the fisherman Metun [*End broken*].

247. O. DM 644
(Dynasty 19)

To Amenemone and to An:

Send the sieve with five *peypenen*-loaves(?). Make an amphora for me. By Ptah, I am unable to make an amphora like those of Amennakht.

248. O. Michaelides 60, rt. 1–3
(Dynasty 19)

Addressed by the scribe Huy to his father, the scribe Baki:
Send me a goat and a duck as well.

249. O. DM 131
(Dynasty 19)

To Pennesettowy:
I inform you of all that you sent me: five ass-loads of dried grass, four of
dung, and two of straw. What was given to you: two *hin*-measures of oil and
one pair of sandals. What was given to you in order to bring me the palm
fronds: five baskets and five sieves. You brought two, and you took three.

I shall weave two kilts; I shall stitch one tunic; and I shall stitch the pair
of sleeves [in exchange for] two baskets and two sieves.

To pay for the vegetables that you brought me: six loaves of bread and six
jars of beer.

250. O. DM 359
(Dynasty 19)

Have a cow purchased for me with this jar of *neheh*-oil.

251. O. DM 550
(Dynasty 19)

[To *name lost:* In life, prosperity] and health and in the favor of Amon-Re,
King of the Gods, your [good lord! I am calling upon Amon-Re], King of
the Gods, and his ennead to give [you . . .] and a long [lifetime]. And further:

What means your [taking] the fat back down to the marketplace? [. . .].
A message has been sent to you about its(?) [. . .] as well. Please send me
the [. . .] straightaway, for I'm in need of it. [As for the] palm leaves, I'll
bring them to you.

252. O. Gardiner 110
(Dynasty 19?)

To the woman Isis:
May Huy be happy(?)! Please be attentive and give me some of your
remainder(?)[14] As regards Piay, you shall furnish some beer promptly and
give me some ointment for the back of his head. [. . .] *neheh*-oil.

253. O. DM 626
(Dynasty 19?)

[*Beginning lost*] by the hand of the water carrier Pabaki. . . . ; he brought me the underpants(?) in the first month of the third season, day 29, and (?) half rations in one (delivery). Now(?) he is a good fellow whom you found fit to send to me in order that he might take what I am giving to you, for my hand has been removed from service(?). It's all right, although this is in writing because I'm concerned about it. Don't mention it. Keep silent!

254. O. DM 608
(late Dynasty 19?)

It is Pentawere, the son of Tun, who brought them up. He was caused to bring you half rations and was given a dry kyllestis-loaf for himself. Did he bring you the half rations or not?

255. O. DM 121
(Dynasty 20: Ramesses III)

The scribe Neferhotep to the chantress of Amon Hathor:
As soon as my letter reaches you, you shall send me some lubya-beans since you know that I am up and about but my bread is not agreeable enough to me by itself to deserve recognition, even when there was a basket-full. Indeed I have started counting lubya-beans(?).

256. O. Berlin 12630
(Dynasty 20: Ramesses III–IV)

Statement by the workman Mose to the citizeness [. . .] to the following effect:
The scribe Amennakht, your husband, took a coffin from me saying, "I shall give the calf in exchange for it," but he hasn't given it until this day. I mentioned this to Paakhet, who replied, "Give me a bed in addition to it, and I will bring you the calf when it is mature." And I gave him the bed. Neither the coffin nor the bed is yet here to this day. If you are going to give the ox, send it on; but if there is no ox, return the bed and the coffin.

257. O. DM 420
(Dynasty 20: Ramesses III–IV)

Addressed by Nekhemmut to Hemnetes:
Send me a coarse basket straightaway! And tell Nesamon to send the mat and tell Kenymin to send the box.

258. O. Vienna NB 9
(Dynasty 20: Ramesses III–IV)

To Meryre: Now really! Please go to Seti and fetch the goat (which came) from Taanach (in Palestine). But if he doesn't give it to you, you shall bring me his underpants(?).

259. O. DM 336
(Dynasty 20: Ramesses III–V)

The scribe Amenmose to the scribe Amennakht. To wit:
[. . .] seventy-nine faience(?) [ushebti-figures . . .] them next to the hut. Send someone to pick them up(?) at once. See, I'm concerned.

260. O. DM 115
(Dynasty 20: Ramesses IV)

Addressed by the wab-priest Nekhemmut to his brother Kenhikhopeshef:
See, I've sent you the pair of papyrus sandal soles, they being very fine. As soon as my letter reaches you, you shall send two hin-measures of sesame at once and send the flour for making the loaves that you mentioned as well as whatever you are going to send me in order to procure the meat and the maziktu-jug. Don't keep [me] waiting here, [but] remember that I am to come to you with them before the god has appeared in procession in the first month of the third season, day 14.
Addressed by the wab-priest Kynebi to the workman Kenymin:
Send a hin measure of juniper oil for the first(?) feast of the god. And write me about what has been done. Please take note.

261. O. DM 361
(Dynasty 20: Ramesses IV–V)

Give (it) to me on the said day so that I may take it [upon] giving the purchase price for it," so says the son of Pahemnetjer.

262. P. DM 31
(Dynasty 20)

[To . . . of] the necropolis:
As soon as my letter reaches you, you shall procure the footwear: [. . .], one pair of men's leather enveloping sandals, one pair of a wab-priest's leather sandals, [one pair of] leather sandals, [. . .], and one (pair) of men's leather enveloping sandals. He said, "I shall buy them(?) for him from the sandal-maker [. . .]." [. . .] sent me a (pair) of leather sandal soles, [and I] sent them

to him. He did not [give] anything for them. He sent [. . .] enveloping [sandals]. Nothing was given to me for them. Sandals [. . .], and [he] sent me his leather sandals. [*End lost*].

263. O. DM 123
(Dynasty 20)

Write me what you are going to demand since the boy is unable to tell (me). Didn't I write you about it: a fine mat of dried grass as well as a fine mat of cord?

264. O. Turin 57093
(Dynasty 20)

Send me the (completed) assignment very promptly! Then shall Amon, Ptah, and Pre keep you healthy, for I am calling upon them (text: him) to keep you healthy daily. Carry out for me my assignment very promptly.

[. . .] know. You don't know [. . .] is wrangling with me. Now see, you know the nature of my superior, for he hasn't yet given me/us (any). He hasn't yet given clothing for my backside.

265. O. DM 122
(Dynasties 19–20)

Send me two *hin*-measures of fat, two *hin*-measures of incense, and two *hin*-measures of honey.

266. O. DM 668
(Dynasties 19–20)

Send me a pair of sandals and a satchel.

267. O. DM 692
(Dynasties 19–20)

It is bad money which has crossed the sea.[15] It shall revert to its owner. Give back my loincloth!

268. O. Černý 18
(Dynasties 19–20)

Send me some date-brew as well as the basket and the sieve.

269. *O. Gardiner 34*
(Dynasties 19–20)

[*Beginning lost*] him. Let there be given to me a millstone and a wooden coffin. Pay attention! Carry out my assignment and mention this to Beri as well.

======= **Writing Materials and Documents** =======

270. *O. Petrie 62*
(Dynasty 19)

Get you (woman) to the magazine of Nefery and fetch the papyri which are there along with the small scribal palette and send them on to me. And open up(?) the little chest which lies in the sitting room(?) of the Gateway and fetch the texts [. . .] and attach them to a writing board [of gesso(?)] together with some [. . .] and send me some accounts of [. . .].

And you shall write me about your condition, about the condition of the woman Tadjeddjepiti, and about the condition of Basa and the lesser folk.

271. *O. DM 348*
(Dynasty 19)

Send the document to the *wab*-priest Pahemnetjer. See [to it].

272. *O. DM 603*
(Dynasty 20: Ramesses III)

Addressed by the scribe Kensety to his brother (colleague?) Amenemope: In life, prosperity and health and in the favor of Amon-Re, Lord of the Thrones of the Two Lands, your good lord! And further:

Please give your personal attention and procure [for me some] ink as well as a handful of rush brushes with which I might fill up my scribal palette on the day of Thoth. Now look, it is to [. . .] that I shall mention this as well.

273. *O. Berlin 10628*
(Dynasty 20: Ramesses III)

To the scribe Neferhotep: In life, prosperity and health and in the favor of your august god, Amon-Re, King of the Gods, who keeps you safe every day! And further:

If you haven't written on the papyrus, send it on to me. I'm in a hurry for it since I've found this text in this man's possession. Otherwise, write me about what you want to do. Fare you well in the presence of Amon!

274. O. Berlin 10630
(Dynasty 20: Ramesses III)

To the scribe Neferhotep: In life, prosperity and health and in the favor of your august god, Amon-Re, King of the Gods, who keeps you safe every day! And [further]:

Please send me the text so that I might finish it off in turn(?). See, I'm taking up for myself the pleasure of accounting. Then shall Ptah let you achieve a long lifetime and a ripe old age with you as a father to me forever without my ever being orphaned from you, so that it (my age) may not be halved. Fare you well in the presence of Amon!

275. O. DM 438
(Dynasty 20: Ramesses IV)

It is the scribe Piay who addresses the scribe Amenmose saying:
A third one is for you.[16] I'm ready, see, I'm ready, I'm ready! Get your chapter and come.

276. O. DM 419
(mid-Dynasty 20)

The scribe of the necropolis Hori: In life, prosperity and health and in the favor of your august god, Amon-Re, King of the Gods, your good lord, every day! Please write me how you want to deal with the drawing.

277. O. DM 366
(Dynasty 20)

The scribe User: Please manufacture my scribal palette and send [it on to me].

278. O. DM 590
(Dynasties 19–20)

Bring me a compendium.

===== **A Carpenter's Correspondence**[17] =====

279. O. DM 418
(Dynasty 20: Ramesses V)

The carpenter Maanakhtef greets the carpenter Kenhikhopeshef: In life, prosperity and health and in the favor of Amon-Re, King of the Gods! To wit:

I have reached Hu (Hu-Sekhem). Both Amenmose and Pahemnetjer as well have taken very good care of me in the way of bread, beer, ointment, and clothing. As soon as my letter reaches you, you shall send me a wooden door as well as a cubit stick. Then shall Amon give to you. Farewell!

280. P. DM 11
(Dynasty 20: Ramesses V)

The scribe Maanakhtef greets the scribe Amennakht: In life, prosperity and health and in the favor [of] Pre-Harakhti! To wit:

Here am I calling upon Meres[eger, mistress of the] West, and all the gods of [Thebes] to look after you while you [. . .]. What means your being so foolish as to send the [. . .] house of Hay? I'm not afraid of [. . .] Syrian of the West [after] the manner of someone who hears [. . .] father [at] this place [where] you are, that you may give a bed to [. . .] in Ne (Thebes), and(?) this chair. You shall [send] him to fetch them from [. . .] Syrian woman this time. As soon as the letter [reaches you, you shall go to] this place where [the] three Syrians are [. . . , and you shall have] them brought to me. . . .

281. O. Vienna NB 3
(mid-Dynasty 20)

The scribe Hormin to the scribe Maanakhtef:
Take notice of the gum oils which are there in your possession lest you should say anything. See, [I have] sent [to] you [. . .] sety-fruit(?) [End lost].

282. P. DM 18
(Dynasty 20: Ramesses IX)

The scribe Amenmose of the Temple of Hathor, mistress of Hu-Sekhem, greets [the *title lost* of] Mereseger, [. . . *(feminine name)*]ses: In life, prosperity and health and in the favor of Amon-Re, King of the Gods! Every day [I] am calling upon Hathor, mistress of Hu-Sekhem, and [her] ennead, [and all the] gods [. . . to keep] you healthy, to keep you alive, to keep you [prosperous], and to give [you] a long lifetime and a ripe old age unto eternity. And further:

What's the meaning of your failing to write me about your health? What have I done against you? As soon as my letter [reaches you at the place] where you are, you shall cause this piece of *maset*-furniture and this little bed to be finished up. As soon as Nakhtmin arrives, you shall send them on.

Address: The scribe Amenmose of the Temple of Hathor, mistress of Hu, to the chief carpenter of the Lord of the Two Lands Maa[nakhtef].[18]

283. P. DM 8, rt.
(Dynasty 20: Ramesses IX)

Now as for what you wrote regarding the matter of the piece of *maset*-furniture, [I] will not tell you [. . . to] outfit your house with (articles of) carpentry. As for what I am w[riting] about, that it is not ready and that your companions are not all there, you don't [. . .]. And you shall send it, that I may know whether you have need (thereof) just as [that] little [bed] with which I already told you you should be concerned.

As soon as my letter [reaches the place] where you are, you shall have the little bed and the piece of *maset*-furniture finished up and [have] Nakhtmin [return] right away, bringing both of them. Don't proceed [to . . . the] piece of *maset*-furniture or abandon the bed so that he may bring you what has accrued to you(?). [. . .]. It is already twenty days ago since I wrote you. And you shall write [*End broken*].

284. P. DM 8, vs.
(Dynasty 20: Ramesses IX)

The scribe Amenmose of the Temple of Hathor, mistress of Hu, greets his brother, the [chief] carpenter of [the Lord of] the Two Lands Maanakhtef: In life, prosperity and health and in the favor of Amon-Re, [King of the Gods! May he give you life, prosperity and health], a long lifetime and a ripe old age, health, life, and delight to your heart and [let me see you invi]gorated and thriving in joy unto eternity every day. And further:

[The policeman] Bes has reached me. After he met me, we went [*Letter unfinished*].

285. P. DM 9
(Dynasty 20: Ramesses IX)

The chief carpenter of the Lord of the Two Lands Maanakhtef to the vizier's scribe Amenmose. To wit:

It is my wish to learn about your condition a thousand times a day [because of] the fact that you haven't come this year. Now I am decorating the inner coffin and the lid. The incense which you brought has run out a long time ago(?). Please send incense, ruddle, and wax so that I may prepare varnish. As soon as Onakht [*Letter unfinished*].

286. P. DM 10
(Dynasty 20: Ramesses IX)

The chief carpenter of the Lord of the Two Lands Maanakhtef greets the scribe Amenmose [of the Temple of Hathor], mistress of Hu-Sekhem: In life, prosperity and health and in the favor of your au[gust] god Harakhti! [I am calling upon Amon-Re], King of the Gods, Mut, Khonsu, and upon Mere-seger [. . .] to keep [you] alive, to keep [you] vigorous, and [. . .] you [. . . , the] first [. . .] is finished [. . .]. I shall send it on to you. See, [. . .]. Now see, I am about to castrate your [calf . . . because the time for] castrating has now come for it in [. . .] as work [. . .].

[As soon as my letter reaches] you, you shall procure for me a quarter of an *oipe*-measure of grapes as well as [. . .] for them and also some *ibu*-fruit in(?) an *oipe*-measure of grain [. . . , and] you shall send them on to me.

Report concerning the chantress of Amon-Re, [King of] the Gods. To wit: The great god is demanding a calf from me [. . .] my wish. Now you are the father [...] a small calf in the [. . . Baken]mut(?) today. [...] the [great] god [. . .]. [As for what] you have done, it is your failing to come to [. . .] exceedingly bad barley. So [it] is not being sent on [to] you. Send [. . .]. See, I have sent you [*X-number* of *hin*-measures of] *neheh*-oil and two *hin*-measures of [*End broken*].

287. P. DM 12
(Dynasty 20: Ramesses IX)

[*Title and name lost*] greets the carpenter of the Lord of the Two Lands Maanakhtef: [In life, prosperity and health and in the favor] of Amon-Re, King of the Gods! I am calling upon Pre-Harakhti when he rises [and when he sets] and upon all gods and goddesses [. . .] to keep you healthy, to keep you alive, and to let [. . .]. And further:

I have dispatched those people of mine. I have sent them to the place [where you are]. [*Long break*] your children and your descen[dants. . . . As for] the message you [sent] saying, "I am working on your commissions," [. . .] look at me. May Ptah keep me alive and you see [me . . .]. And as for the message you sent about the matter [of . . .], I shall [*End lost*].

Address: [. . . to the carpen]ter of the Lord of the Two Lands Maanakhtef.

Notes

1. The royal tomb under construction in the Valley of the Kings.
2. A period of nearly eleven months.
3. The word as written must designate a wooden implement that has caused the donkey some discomfort. A similarly spelled word does mean "baton" or "cudgel," but hardly "forage," as suggested by Allam (1981: 11-12), whose reading "house of forage" later on in the text is dubious.
4. Probably a designation of the god Sobek.
5. Or possibly, "a Thoeris-statuette," as suggested by Borghouts (1982b: 16).
6. Possibly a "grain-bride," a small sickle-shaped bundle of ears of grain that served as a sort of fetish; see Seeber 1979.
7. Natron was used like soap.
8. The Black Land refers to the flood plain of the Nile valley, whereas the town of Deir el-Medina was situated in the desert.
9. Since polygamy was very rarely practiced among commoners in ancient Egypt, the plural "wives" in this passage probably refers to wives the addressee may have had in successive marriages rather than simultaneously.
10. Literally, "eating companion."
11. For incense used in the preparation of varnish, see Letter No. 285.
12. Or an imperative, "Fetch it!"
13. Perhaps a carrying pole with a pair of buckets suspended at either end.
14. Or possibly a vulgar expression, "give me a bit of your behind."
15. The meaning of this expression remains obscure.
16. Or possibly an imperative, "Finish up!"
17. See also Letter No. 60 from the carpenter Maanakhtef to the vizier Nebmarenakht.
18. While the body of the letter is addressed to a woman, the addressee in the address is a man, who presumably was to read out or forward the letter to the woman.

X

Late Ramesside Letters

Introduction

Because of Deir el-Medina's vulnerability to attacks by marauding bands of Libyans, the community of tomb builders moved to the fortified enclosure of Ramesses III's mortuary temple at Medinet Habu during the first decade of Ramesses XI's reign. Known simply as "The Temple," Medinet Habu served as an administrative center for western Thebes during the Twentieth Dynasty. The two principal correspondents in these Late Ramesside Letters are the necropolis scribe Dhutmose (nicknamed Tjaroy with variants Tjuroy, Tjararoy, and Tjertja) and his son Butehamon, the ruins of whose house are still visible behind the temple of Medinet Habu.

The first decade and a half of Ramesses XI's reign was characterized by turmoil in the Theban area that involved a temporary suppression of Amenhotep, the high priest of Amon, and the attempt to restore order using Nubian troops under the viceroy of Kush Panehsy, the recipient of Letter No. 39, written by Ramesses XI in Year 17. The undisciplined Nubian troops, however, created such disruption in the Theban area that Thebans came to regard Panehsy as an enemy by Year 19 of Ramesses XI, when a ten-year period known as the Renaissance commenced, coinciding with the last decade of Ramesses XI's reign. This Renaissance era was marked by the emergence of military control at Thebes. During the first six years of the Renaissance a military commander named Herihor functioned as high priest of Amon and even assumed the trappings of kingship on a very local scale, notably at the Temple of Khonsu at Karnak. It is highly probable that Herihor was a commander of Libyan mercenary troops, who were descendants of Libyan prisoners of war settled by Ramesses III in colonies in the Delta and Middle Egypt. Upon Herihor's death the major figure at Thebes was the general Piankh, who also assumed the Theban pontificate but not the kingship. He too was probably of Libyan extraction. While Ramesses XI was still officially pharaoh, Piankh and his predominantly Libyan troops were acting quite independently in Upper Egypt. In particular, they opposed the former viceroy of Kush Panehsy in Nubia. One has the impression that the viceroy and his Nubian troops were loyalists, for the remarks made by his opponent Piankh in Letter No. 301 are quite disparaging of the pharaoh, Ramesses XI.

Letters Nos. 288 and 289 were written by Dhutmose while he was traveling outside the Theban area collecting taxes in grain to support the crew of workmen in Ramesses XI's Year 12. Letters Nos. 290–94 date to around Year 2 of the Renaissance. In

171

No. 291 there is reference to payment for weapons, perhaps to be used against Panehsy and his Nubian troops. The bulk of the remaining Late Ramesside Letters can be grouped on a geographical basis.

To the first group belong Nos. 295-97, written when Dhutmose was on a journey north of Thebes in Year 6 of the Renaissance. A second group comprises Nos. 298-307, written when Dhutmose was at home in western Thebes. Of these letters, Nos. 300-6 were written by the general Piankh, and No. 307 by his singer Pentahures at a time when preparations were being made for military action in Nubia against Panehsy in Year 10 of the Renaissance. Eventually Dhutmose himself went south to assist in the Nubian war, and this phase is reflected in a third group of letters, Nos. 308-24, written when Dhutmose was in Elephantine and in Nubia. There are a number of letters, Nos. 325-30, which are difficult to place more precisely in the Renaissance era. The recently published letter No. 331, while not directly involving Dhutmose, seems to belong to the same period. A more detailed chronology of these correspondences will be found in Wente 1967: 1-17.

With the exception of Nos. 330 and 331, all the Late Ramesside Letters were published in hieroglyphic transcription by Černý (1939b) and translated by Wente (1967). For sake of convenience the letters edited by Černý are indicated by *LRL* and the number given in Černý's volume instead of the papyrus. My earlier translations have been revised in the light of contributions to the study of Late Egyptian by Groll (1970 and 1974), Černý and Groll (1984), Frandsen (1974), and Satzinger (1976).

Early Letters from Dhutmose

288. *LRL No. 47*
(Dynasty 20: Year 12 of Ramesses XI)

[*Beginning broken*]. Every day [I am calling upon . . . Seth], the Ombite, who is in front of the Universal Lord, the great god of the primal occassion, to give you life, prosperity and health and very many favors in the presence of Amon-Re, King of the Gods, [your lord]. And further:

Really, what's the use of speaking to you if you don't listen and remain idle [in] this commission from Pharaoh, l.p.h., your good lord, in which you are engaged. Now it is a single creeper that can choke a thousand trees;[1] but see, it is you who can disentangle them. As for the men who are dwelling there confined, give [. . .] them as well. If no work exists, there can be no employment for the men. Now I told you to dispatch Nessobek, your scribe, and to have him go with the doorkeeper and guardian Dhutmose and the scribe Efnamon and have the grain fetched, but you didn't obey me.

The fishermen came to the place where the people of the necropolis were, saying, "We've been waiting around until today," and saying, "We are confined in your charge." Now they had thought to break through when the sky was low in elevation (misty?), saying, "You took our people initially so that you might exact work. See, you have taken the people again so that you might exact work. We shall spend today here and return to where the vizier is tomorrow," so they said.

See, you don't listen to me. May Amon be before you! Even if your commissions are too many for you, you won't be able to walk out on this commission from Pharaoh, l.p.h. Dispatch your scribe together with Efn[amon], the necropolis scribe, and the doorkeeper Dhutmose or the doorkeeper Khonsmose. Have them go to fetch the grain lest the people grow hungry and become idle in the commission from Pharaoh, l.p.h., and cast any blame upon you.

See, I've written to provide you with testimony through the watchman Wenamon.

289. *LRL No. 46*
(Dynasty 20: Year 12 of Ramesses XI)

[*Beginning lost*]. Every single day I am calling upon Amon-Re-Harakhti when he rises and sets to give you life, prosperity and health, a long lifetime, a good ripe old age, and very many favors in the presence of Amon, your lord. To wit:

I've heard that you are angry and that you have caused me to be maligned(?) through slander on account of that joke which I told the chief taxing master in that letter, although it was Henuttowy who had urged me to tell some jokes to the chief taxing master in my letter. You are the case of the wife blind in one eye who had been living in the house of a man for twenty years; and when he found another woman, he said to her, "I shall divorce you because you are blind in one eye, so it is said." And she answered him, "Is this what you have just discovered during these twenty years that I've spent in your house?" Such am I, and such is my joking with you.

Now if you say, "Quit this!" and I were a mere freeman, Nesamon would ridicule me, and I'd have to put up with it. But should I put up with it from him now while I am an official? It is no high official who puts up with ridicule from just anybody, (not) even from his elder brother. Are you being fair with me? If I mention your name again, sure enough, you will pick a quarrel. Look here, it was when I was in the household that you were born. Please repeat any disparaging remarks that I might have made about you in your father's presence. Don't you know the nature of my heart, that it is concerned about you, that my desire is to have your *Ba* remembered for your sake daily?

Even if you should be vizier, I wouldn't go aboard your ships, sure enough besides. Don't let yourself display weakness because of the fact that Efnamon, your elder brother, has cast blame upon those things you've done. No fault shall be found behind my back in any matters, sure enough. Farewell!

========= **Letters of the Early Renaissance Period** =========

290. *LRL No. 37*
(Dynasty 20: Year 2 of Renaissance)

The chantress of Amon-Re, King of the Gods, Henuttowy, to the necropolis scribe Nesamenope: In life, prosperity and health and in the favor of Amon-Re, King of the Gods! Every single day I am calling upon Amon-Re-Harakhti when he rises and sets, Mut, Khonsu, and all gods of Thebes to give you life, prosperity and health, a long lifetime, a good ripe old age, and very many favors in the presence of Amon-Re, King of the Gods, your good lord who has been looking after you.

I've taken note of all matters you wrote me about. As for the mention you made of the matter of those 162.5 *khar*-measures of emmer about which you said, "Let the scribe Pentahunakht go and receive them together with the captains, but they should not draw them out by means of a large *oipe*-measure," as you said, your letter reached the place where the vizier is, and he dispatched the scribe Saroy together with the measurer. He caused them to come bringing an *oipe*-measure that was one *hin*-measure greater than the granary's *oipe*-measure. I went myself and caused the grain to be received while I was there. It amounted to 146.75 *khar*-measures by this *oipe*-measure. This native of the necropolis and the fisherman said, "It is 150 *khar*-measures of grain that we measured out for you with the *oipe*-measure of the granary of the Estate of Amon," so they said. I checked out the *oipe*-measure and told them, "I'm satisfied with the check. I shall find the grain wherever it is," so I said to them.

You wrote me saying, "Receive the 80 *khar*-measures of grain from this transport boat of the fisherman Iotnefer," so you said [in] writing. I went [to] receive them and found only 72.5 *khar*-measures with him. I asked him, "What's the meaning of only 72.5 *khar*-measures of grain," so I asked him, "whereas it is 80 *khar*-measures that are stated in his letter?" The men replied, "It is three completely full withdrawals that we have measured out for ourselves, each having 2.5 *khar*-measures, thus netting 72.5 *khar*-measures of grain," so they replied. I maintained my silence thinking that until you return, Amon, United with Eternity, will have done every sort of bad thing to me.

Attend to the grain of his, which you caused to be brought in, since there is no longer even a *khar*-measure of grain for his divine offerings. It is I who have given 30 *khar*-measures of emmer for his [divine offer]ings beginning [from Year] 2, second month of the first season, [day] 27, until the third month of the first season, day 2, from the grain which is stored under my supervision [. . .] for the divine offerings.

Now Amon, United with Eternity, has caused the grain to be put in a chest and has caused a seal to be affixed to it. See, you shall join up with Paseny, and you two shall consult with the overseer of granaries concerning the grain for Amon, United with Eternity, because he (Amon) hasn't got even one *oipe*-measure's worth for his divine offerings today. You mustn't abandon him, either of you two.

Now don't worry about your father. I've heard that his condition is very good. The steward of Amon and *wab*-priest Nespamedushepses has written me saying, "Don't worry about him. He is all right; he is in health. No harm has befallen him."

Now Preunemef has contended in court with your father in the presence of Pharaoh, l.p.h. One (the king) has caused your father to be justified against him; and One (the king) has charged the officials to make the examination of his men in order to give them back to him. Thus Pharaoh, l.p.h., has said, "Give him men as is fitting."

Now the *wab*-priest of the Temple of Mut Paunesh has written that Pharaoh, l.p.h., has dispatched your father, after Pharaoh, l.p.h., his lord, had done for him every sort of good thing, although the officials did not leave [anything] good for him [in] the boat which I sent to him loaded [with] salt and every entire share(?) of the Northern Region after Tjema had sent a scow carrying him and his dues(?), but not having left anything good for him. [Now] he told me, "It was after he departed with the overseer of the treasury and overseer of granaries Menmarenakht and the scribe of the offering table Hori that I returned from there."

"Now the general of the place 'Beloved of Thoth' (a military establishment) has been sent," so they say, "in order to take men to the Temple of Millions of Years (Medinet Habu), which is under the authority of the *setem*-priest and majordomo, to hand over the oil(?)," so they say, "and One (the king) has given the office of prophet of the goddess Nebetuu to the god's father priest Nesamenope, whom Pharaoh, l.p.h., has clothed with a tunic as is fitting," so they say.

As soon as my letter reaches [the place] where [you are], you shall [. . .] Amon [. . .] and send someone to me very quickly, since the vizier has written me saying, "Cause [. . .]." They have [prepared(?)] rations for them, they going [. . .] dispatched your letter [*End lost*].

291. *LRL No. 36*
(Dynasty 20: Year 2 of Renaissance)

The scribe of the [great and noble Necropolis of] Millions of Years of Pharaoh on the West of Thebes Nesamenope to the chantress of Amon-Re, King of the Gods, Mutenope: In life, prosperity and health and in the favor of Amon-Re, King of the Gods! Every day I am calling upon Amon-Harakhti when he rises and sets and upon every god and every goddess by whom I pass to keep you alive, to keep you healthy, and to cause [you] to be invigorated. And further:

The deputy of the Temple (of Medinet Habu) Nessobek has sent a message to the place where the prophet of Montu, lord of Armant, is saying, "Let me be given an aroura of land in Peniufneri next to the house of the god's father priest of Montu Ahauaa, and I will have it farmed in fruit." He said, "I shall give it. Send someone to receive it." As soon as my letter reaches you, you shall dispatch Sobeksankh to the place where the prophet of Montu is, and he shall receive from him this aroura of land, it being [to] the north of the house of Ahau[aa], the god's father priest of Montu, that he shall receive (it) from him. And you shall give him ten *hin*-measures of fruit and have him go with Sekhayeniot, and they shall plant it with fruit before the flood has soaked it. By the time the floodwaters enter onto it, it must be planted.

And you are to tell Sobeksankh, "Spend these five days together with Sekhayeniot in cutting wood for the chief taxing master and proceed to finish with clearing in this land which is in your charge. When there is no longer any brush(?) upon it, you shall have me (Nesamenope) return from the south land (Nubia)," so you shall say to them. And you shall write Penhapi saying, "Have the calf milk-fed until I (Nesamenope) come and take it to its owner."

And you are to have the tin which I have in my charge taken to Onery and receive this other from the treasury scribe Nesamon, and he shall give it to him too. And you are to tell the laborer Ahautinefer, "Give me a *deben* of tin." As soon as he gives it to you, I will compensate Onery with a *deben* and five *kite* of tin for the job of the fifteen pieces of weaponry that I told him to make. And you shall tell him, "It is only after you have finished with them that you shall succeed in having me (Nesamenope) return from the south land (Nubia)," so you shall tell him. Farewell!

Address: The necropolis scribe Nesamenope to the chantress of Amon Mutenope.

292. LRL No. 12
(Dynasty 20: Year 2 of Renaissance)

The deputy of the Estate of Amon-Re, King of the Gods, Hori [from] the necropolis scribe Tjaroy and the army scribe Pentahunakht [of] the Temple of King Usermare-miamon, l.p.h., (Ramesses III's mortuary temple) in the Estate of Amon: In life, prosperity and health and in the favor of Amon-Re, King of the Gods! Every single day we are calling upon Amon, Pre, Ptah, and every god and every goddess who rest here to give you life, prosperity and health, a long lifetime and a ripe old age, and to give you very many favors in the presence of Amon-Re, King of the Gods, this one who has been looking after you. And further:

We have heard that you have returned and have reached the port of Ne (Thebes). May Amon receive you with a good reception and do for you every sort of good. Now we are dwelling here in the Temple (of Medinet Habu), and you know how we are living inside and out. Now the natives of the necropolis have gone. They are dwelling in Ne (Thebes), while I am dwelling here alone with the army scribe Pentahunakht. Please have the necropolis personnel who are there in Ne (Thebes) assembled and have them brought back to me to this (west) side (of the river). List of them for you: Pennesti-towy, Neferamon, Horimose, Wenamon, Panakhtenope son of Panebaku, Amenhotep, and Kadjadja, a total of seven men. Place them under the super-vision of the scribe Butehamon. Have them brought back in all haste, and don't let them linger at all—together with Pakhor and Audjar, a total of nine men.

And write us about what you have heard to cause our hearts to be elated. Now don't let a youth whom you might send to stay here with us indulge in plotting like Hereferniutef or any other also like him—one doesn't yet know of an arrival of the Meshwesh (Libyans) here—who might speak with him. You know that as for whoever happens to come, it is to this wall that he turns his face before being handed over. Is it to the pilot here that you will give further payment?

Address: The deputy of the Estate of Amon-Re, King of the Gods, Hori, [from] the scribe Tjaroy and the army scribe Pentahunakht.

293. *LRL No. 27*
(Dynasty 20: early Renaissance)

The scribe of the treasury of the Temple of Amon-Re, King of the Gods, Painefernefer to the [necropolis] scribe Tjaroy: In life, prosperity and health and in the favor of Amon Re, King of the Gods! Every day I am calling upon Amon-Re, King of the Gods, Mut, Khonsu, and all gods of Thebes to give you life, prosperity and health, a long lifetime, a good ripe old age, and very many favors in the presence of Amon-Re, King of the Gods, your good lord. And further:

When the prophet of Sobek left here to go to the countryside, you had already reached an agreement with him concerning the matter of Kassu. Now see, I have heard that you have come and have taken him (Kassu). As soon as my letter reaches you, you shall release this man until the prophet of Sobek returns. Indeed, it was only after he had provided for his household that he left here. Now this [prophet of Sobek] is a brother of mine. I shall write to him, and he shall come to take up his case with you. Yield(?)! Don't create difficulty against this man apropos of me until he comes to take up his case with you.

Address: The scribe of the treasury of the Temple of Amon Painefernefer to the scribe Tjaroy.

294. LRL No. 26
(Dynasty 20: early Renaissance)

The steward, mayor of Ne (Thebes) and captain of the troops [. . .]atref [to] the necropolis scribe Tjaroy: In life, prosperity and health and in the favor of Amon-Re, King [of the Gods, your lord], every day! And further:

I've taken note of all matters you wrote me about. [As for your saying], "I caused this workman to say [. . .] although his words are correct," so you said, haven't you heard [the] adage: "Right is one who has spoken in private"? If your superior has returned [. . . , don't let] him depart from you. You shall have this man brought from the(?) [. . .] passes by and bring my retainer with you [. . .]. If I find that this workman was right [with regard to] his having beaten my retainer, I shall give to him [. . .] on account of them. But if I determine that my [retainer] is right [. . .] beating him violently, I shall let you see what I shall do [to him . . .] him. Indeed, the man [. . .] has been abandoning(?) work, while he is in mourning [. . .], and the harvest has been left to spoil.

Address: The mayor of Ne (Thebes) and majordomo to the [necropolis] scribe Tjaroy.

Dhutmose in Middle Egypt

295. LRL No. 1
(Dynasty 20: Year 6 of Renaissance)

The scribe of the great and noble necropolis Dhutmose [to] the foreman Bak[en]mut and the foreman Amenhotep, the prophet Amen[. . .], the guardian Kadere, Pentaumte, Paby, Heramenpenaf, Pakhor, and all the necropolis workmen. I am calling upon Arsaphes, lord of Heracleopolis, Thoth, lord of Hermopolis, and every god and [every] goddess by whom I pass to give you life, prosperity and health, a long lifetime, and a good ripe old age, and to give you favor in the presence of gods and people. How are you? How are your people? Indeed I'm alive today; tomorrow is in God's hands. It is I who long to see you and to hear about your condition daily. What's the point of my sending you these many letters whereas you haven't sent even one? What have I done against you? Even if I were to have committed innumerable wrongs, can't one good deed make them forgotten? For I am one who is well-disposed to you; I am not one who is ill-disposed to you.

Please call upon Amon of the Thrones of the Two Lands and Mereseger to bring me back alive [from] the wilds of Namekhay and give your personal attention to Butehamon, Shedemdua, her little children, and the people who are in the fields to prevent another from doing wrong to them.

A further communication to the citizeness Tanedjeme, Nene, Henutaa, Irymut, Isis, Baketmut, Kerinefer, Tanedjeme, Tasepa, the barge man, and all the people: Please call upon Amon to bring me back, for I have been ill since I arrived north and am not in my normal state. Don't set your minds to anything else. As soon as my letter reaches you, you shall go to the forecourt of Amon of the Thrones of the Two Lands, taking the little children along with you and coax him and tell him to keep me safe.

Address: The necropolis scribe Tjaroy to the [necropolis] scribe Butehamon.

296. LRL No. 14
(Dynasty 20: Year 6 of Renaissance)

The scribe of the great and noble necropolis Dhutmose from the prophet of Amenophis, l.p.h., Amenhotep: In life, prosperity and health and in the favor of Amon-Re, King of the Gods, Mut, Khonsu, and all gods of Thebes! Every single day I am calling upon Amon-Re-Harakhti when he rises and sets, upon Amon of the Thrones of the Two Lands, upon Amenophis, l.p.h., and Nofretari, l.p.h., and upon Amon, United with Eternity, and his ennead to give you life, prosperity and health, a long lifetime, a ripe old age, and very many favors in the presence of Amon-Re, King of the Gods, and in the presence of the general, your lord. And may Amon of the Thrones of the Two Lands bring you back safe and we fill our embrace with you. And further:

I've taken note of all matters you wrote me about. As for what you said, "Give your personal attention to the scribe Butehamon, to the chantress of Amon-Re, King of the Gods, Shedemdua and the children," so you said, they are all right. Don't worry about them. They are alive today; tomorrow is in God's hands. It is you whom we long to see.

I am calling upon Amon-Re, King of the Gods, to give you favor in the presence of the general, your lord, and may Amon bring you back safe and I fill my embrace with you unharmed, danger removed(?), Amon of the Thrones of the Two Lands having rescued [you]. You are his servant. I am submitting your (case) before (the oracle of) Amenophis, l.p.h., whenever he appears in procession. "I will protect him (text: you); I will bring him (text: you) back safe. He (text: you) shall fill his (text: your) eyes with the forecourt of mine," so he keeps responding. I am writing to let you know. Farewell!

(*Postscript*): And don't cease writing me about your condition through whatever people may come south so that our hearts may be elated.

A further matter for the necropolis scribe Tjararoy: Don't worry about Hemesheri's girl. She's in good health. No harm has befallen her.

297. LRL No. 5
(Dynasty 20: Year 6 of Renaissance)

The scribe of the great and noble necropolis Dhutmose to the scribe Butehamon and the chantress of Amon Shedemdua: In life, prosperity and health and in the favor of Amon-Re, King of the Gods! Every single day I am calling upon Amon-Re-Harakhti, Arsaphes, the great god, Thoth, lord of Hermopolis, and every god and every goddess by whom I pass to give you life, prosperity and health, a long lifetime, and a good ripe old age. And [further]:

I've taken note of all matters you wrote me about through the retainer Nesamon, namely, what you stated regarding the matter of the vessels of smaragdus² and two flagons which you said you are having finished up, as well as the matter of the donkeys which you said you gave to the wab-priest Tjaumehi[em]hab in order to carry in the grain, as you said. It's all right, this which you have done. If he has finished carrying in the grain, you shall receive it enregistered in full and enter it into its granary. And you shall turn them (the donkeys) over to the police captain Sermontu in order to carry in his grain which is in the fields, excluding any of that which is stowed in the settlements, for it is only that which is scattered about in the fields that you should have brought in, while that which is in the magazines should be retained where it is. As soon as this floodwater rises, you shall receive in charge this transport boat which I sent to you and give it to the fishermen and the policemen. And they shall bring in the balance of it (the grain); and you shall receive it fully enregistered, the scribe Pentahunakht, son of Sobek-nakht, being with you, for he shall supervise for you, and you shall enter it. And you shall receive this transport boat, its oars, its mast, and the fittings(?) and take care of it, for you will find it useful to carry out your assignments with it, along with the wood and the charcoal to have them transported. And you shall enter [them] into their proper place, along with the wood which [the] men [will] cut; and you shall take [it] to my house. Indeed you have a full day ahead of you!

And you are to look after the little children and take care of them properly in the same way as this daughter of Hemesheri, her mother and her nurse. And you shall look after their need. And you shall attend to the soldiers and watch over them closely. And you shall give your personal attention to the men who are in the country and make them perform their field labors properly. And you shall not let the young boys who are in school cease studying. And you shall look after the people who are in my house and give them clothing. Don't let them go naked! And you shall claim back the three garments which Pakhor has in his possession. And you shall look after these three riparian plots of ours and have the trees which are on their mounds pruned in the same way as the holding which Nesmontu used to cultivate.

And you shall prune its trees beginning from the district of Pre as far as the well of the district.

And you shall see this daughter of Khonsmose and have her write a letter and send it to me. And you shall not let Hemesheri and Shedemdua nor their little children be lacking in anything.

And you shall tell Tapeses that I met Paturaa at the Northern Promontory (El-Hiba). And you shall write to me the house in which you found the covering(?), and you shall write me whether you have handed Hori's grain over to him. And you shall have this courtyard³ finished up, protected with stone patchwork. And you shall look after the yoke of oxen which are in the charge of the herdsman Nesamon, son of Djahy, and hand them over to Paydegesh.

And you shall take water to Amon of the Thrones of the Two Lands and tell him to keep [me] safe. And you shall not neglect [. . .] Paykamen, my brother. Don't neglect them [. . .] on the day I return. And you shall tell Amon to remove this illness which is in me.

═══════════════ **Dhutmose in Western Thebes** ═══════════════

298. LRL No. 23
(Dynasty 20: Year 7 of Renaissance)

The second prophet of Amon-Re, King of the Gods, Hekanefer to the scribe of the great and noble Necropolis of Millions of Years Tjertja: In life, prosperity and health and in the favor of Amon-Re, King of the Gods! Every single day I am calling upon every god and every goddess by whom I pass to give you life, prosperity and health, a long lifetime, a ripe old age, and very many favors in the presence of Amon-Re, King of the Gods, your lord.

As soon as my letter reaches you, you shall call upon Amon-Re, King of the Gods, Mut, Khonsu, Amon, United with Eternity, and all gods of Thebes to rescue me and bring me back to Ne (Thebes) alive and I fill my embrace with you. And you shall not cease writing me about your condition. Farewell!

A further communication to the scribe of the great and noble Necropolis of Millions of Years Tjertja [from] the general's servant Penhershefy: In life, prosperity and health and in the favor of Amon-Re, King of the Gods! Every single day I am calling upon Amon-Re-Harakhti when he rises and sets daily and every god and every goddess by whom I pass to give you life, prosperity and health, a long lifetime, a ripe old age, and very many favors in the presence of Amon-Re, King of the Gods, your lord who has been looking after you.

As soon as my letter reaches you, you shall call upon Amon to bring me back. And don't cease writing me about your condition. Farewell!

Address: The second prophet of Amon-Re, King of the Gods, Hekanefer, to the necropolis scribe Tjertja.

299. LRL No. 24
(Dynasty 20: Year 7 of Renaissance)

The second prophet of Amon-Re, King of the Gods, Hekanefer, to the scribe of the great and noble Necropolis Tjuroy: In life, prosperity and health and in the favor of Amon-Re, King of the Gods! [And further]:

Every day [I am calling upon] Amon-Re-Harakhti when he rises and sets daily and every god and every goddess by whom I pass to give you life, prosperity and health, a long lifetime, a ripe old age, and many favors in the presence of Amon-Re, King of the Gods, your lord, and let me see you when I have returned alive and fill my embrace with you. And further:

As soon as my letter reaches you, you shall not cease writing me about your condition through whoever may come northward. And you shall call upon Amon-Re, King of the Gods, to bring me back.

The scribe of the great and noble necropolis of Millions of Years Tjuroy from the second prophet of Amon's servant Penhershefy: In life, prosperity and health and in the favor of Amon-Re, King of the Gods! Every single day I am calling upon Amon-Pre-Harakhti when he rises and sets daily and every god and every goddess by whom I pass to keep you alive, to keep you healthy and to keep you in the favor of gods and people. To wit:

Hemesheri is alive; she is in life, [prosperity and health]. Don't worry about her. It is you whom she longs to see and whose condition she wishes to hear about [daily]. As soon as my letter reaches you, you shall call upon Amon-Re, King of the Gods, to bring me back alive. And don't cease writing me about your condition through whoever may come. Farewell!

Address: The second prophet of Amon-Re, King of the Gods, Hekanefer, to the scribe of the great and noble necropolis Tjuroy.

300. LRL No. 20
(Dynasty 20: Year 10 of Renaissance)

The general of Pharaoh, l.p.[h., to] the scribe Tjaroy. Quote:

As soon as my letter reaches you, you shall send some old clothes in the form of many strips. . . . And don't let them go to waste(?), for they shall be made into bandages with which to wrap up men.[4] You know about this expedition which I am going to make. Send them on to me quickly! Don't let them delay either on your part. Please take note of this.

Address: [The gen]eral [. . .].

301. LRL No. 21
(Dynasty 20: Year 10 of Renaissance)

The general of Pharaoh, l.p.h., to the necropolis scribe Tjaroy. Quote:
I've taken note of all matters you wrote me about. As for the mention you made of this matter of these two policemen saying, "They spoke these charges," join up with Nodjme and Payshuuben as well, and they shall send word and have these two policemen brought to this (my) house and get to the bottom of their charges in short order. If they determine that they are true, you shall put them [in] two baskets and they shall be thrown [into] the water by night—but don't let anybody in the land find out!

A further matter: As for Pharaoh, l.p.h., how will he ever reach this land (Nubia)? And as for Pharaoh, l.p.h., whose superior is he after all? Moreover, these three full months, although I have sent a barge, you haven't sent me a *deben* of gold or a *deben* of silver either. That's all right. Don't worry about what he(?) has done.

As soon as my letter reaches you, you shall supply a *deben* of gold or a *deben* of silver and send it to me by barge.

Address: The general's agent Payshuuben from the general's scribe Ken[y]khnum.

302. LRL No. 34
(Dynasty 20: Year 10 of Renaissance)

The general of Pharaoh, l.p.h., to the agent Payshuuben. Quote:
I've taken note of all matters you wrote about. As for the mention you made of this matter of these two policemen saying, "They spoke these charges," join up with Nodjme and the scribe Tjaroy as well and send word and have these two policemen brought to my house and get to the bottom of their charges in short order and kill [them] and throw them [into] the water by night—but don't let anybody in this land find out about them!

303. LRL No. 35
(Dynasty 20: Year 10 of Renaissance)

The general of Pharaoh, l.p.h., to the principal of the harem of Amon-Re, King of the Gods, the noble lady Nodjme: In life, prosperity and health and in the favor of Amon-Re, King of the Gods! To wit:
Every single day I am calling upon every god and every goddess by whom I pass to keep you alive, to keep you healthy, and to let me see [you] when I return and fill my eyes [with] the sight of [you].

I've taken note of all matters you wrote me about. As for the mention you made of this matter which you said these two policemen had said, join up with Payshuuben and Tjaroy, this scribe, and have these two policemen brought to my house and get to the bottom of their charges in short order and have [them] killed and have them thrown [into] the water by night.

And write me about your condition. Farewell!

Address: The principal of the harem of Amon-Re, King of the Gods, the noble lady Nodjme from the general's scribe Kenykhnum.

304. LRL No. 18
(Dynasty 20: Year 10 of Renaissance)

The general of Pharaoh, l.p.h., to the scribe Tjararoy. Quote:

I've taken note of all matters you wrote me about. As for what you wrote saying, "I have accomplished every assignment and all commissions of my lord which were charged to me. I do not slacken," so you said, it's all right, what you have done. Henceforth you shall do thus. As soon as my letter reaches you, you shall accomplish every assignment and every commission of mine which are charged to you and carry them out. Don't let me find fault with you. Please take note of this.

Address: The general of Pharaoh, l.p.h., to the necropolis scribe Tjaroy.

305. LRL No. 19
(Dynasty 20: Year 10 of Renaissance)

The general of Pharaoh, l.p.h., to the necropolis scribe Tjaroy. Quote:

What is the matter with the [. . .]-people of the necropolis who used to give bread-rations [to] the Meshwesh (Libyans) nearby(?) that you don't let them give them bread-rations now? As soon as my letter reaches you, you shall see the one who used to give bread-rations to the Meshwesh (Libyans) nearby(?) and entrust them (the rations) to Akhmenu to let him withdraw bread-rations for the Meshwesh (Libyans) from them. Please take note of this.

Address: The general of Pharaoh, l.p.h., to the scribe Tjaroy.

306. LRL No. 22
(Dynasty 20: Year 10 of Renaissance)

The general of Pharaoh, l.p.h., to the scribe of the great(?) necropolis Tjaroy. Quote:

I've taken note of all matters you wrote me about. As for what you wrote saying, "I have placed the papyrus scrolls in the presence of (the oracle of) this great god in order that he may decide upon them with a favorable decision," so you said, it's all right, your having written (thus). As soon as [my] letter reaches you, you shall join up with Pentahunakht, this scribe, regarding the affair of this Akhmenu. As for what he will tell you to do, you are to assemble men for it and do it. As for what you wrote saying, "Let a job be given to this coppersmith," I have written to the scribe Pentahunakht to have him give [it] to him.

Address: The general of Pharaoh, l.p.h., to the necropolis scribe Tjaroy.

307. *LRL No. 17*
(Dynasty 20: Year 10 of Renaissance)

The general's singer Pentahures to the scribe of the great and noble necropolis Dhutmose, the songstress Hemesheri and the chantress of Amon Shedemdua: In life, prosperity and health and in the favor of Amon-Re, King of the Gods! Every day I am calling upon Amon-Re-Harakhti when he rises and sets and every god and every goddess by whom I pass to keep you alive, to keep you alive (*sic*), to keep you safe, to keep you healthy, and to let us return alive and I fill my embrace with you. And further:

I'm all right today; tomorrow is in God's hands. Call upon Amon, United with Eternity, and every god of my village to keep me safe with my lord. And write through the retainers of my lord who come that my heart may be elated.

Address: The singer Pentahures to the scribe of the great and noble necropolis Dhutmose.

Dhutmose Journeys South of Thebes to Nubia

308. *LRL No. 4*
(Dynasty 20: Year 10 of Renaissance)

The necropolis scribe Dhutmose to the scribe Butehamon and the chantress of Amon Shed[emdua]: In life, prosperity and health and in the favor of Amon-Re, King of the Gods! Every day I am calling upon the gods of the land to give you [life, prosperity and health, a] long [lifetime], and a good ripe old age, to give you many favors and to let [me] return [and fill my em]brace with you. And further:

I have reached my superior. Really, it was only when they encountered me in the midst of Edfu that I found out he had sent a *tesem*-boat to pick me up. I met him at the town of Elephantine, and he told me, saying, "Another time you won't have to come," so he said to me. He gave me bread and beer as previously and said to me, "May Montu favor [you]." Now we are moored at Elephantine, and he keeps saying, "I shall go up (to Nubia) to attack Panehsy at the place where he is," so he keeps saying.

Please call upon Amon of the Thrones of the Two Lands, my lord, to bring me back safe and give your personal attention to the little children of Hemesheri and Shedemdua and [give] some oil to let the little(?) children consume it. Don't let them be in need. And give your personal attention to this daughter of Khonsmose; don't neglect her either. But don't worry about me. My superior has done everything good for me. And you are to attend to the soldiers. Don't let them run off, nor let them grow hungry.

A further communication to the workman Amenhotep, Heramenpenaf, Paby, Pentaumte, Sedjaa, Shedsuamon, Irymut, Isis, Bakamon, Ikhtay, and the head of the ergastulum Penpawenher, to wit:

Please call upon Amon and the gods of the Temple (of Medinet Habu) to bring me back alive from the next war.

The scribe Ken[y]khnum to the scribe Butehamon and Amenpanefer: Every single day I am calling upon Amon to give you life, prosperity and health. And further:

Tell Amenpanefer to write a letter. Need I mention for you to engage(?) the man to receive it from him?

A further matter for the scribe Butehamon and Heramenpenaf: [End lost].

309. LRL No. 3
(Dynasty 20: Year 10 of Renaissance)

[The scribe of the great and noble Necropolis] of Millions of Years of Pharaoh, l.p.h., [Dhutmose] to the necropolis scribe Butehamon [. . .]. Every day [I am calling upon] Amon-Re-Harakhti when he rises and sets [. . . to give] you life, prosperity and health and to give you favor in the presence of gods and people. [. . . the fourth month of the second] season, day 13. I reached my superior at [. . .]. He took me in charge and did everything good for me. He [said to me, " . . . . If you hadn't] come, I would have put up a fuss with you; but good [. . . that you found] goodness in your heart and have come." He said to me, "You shall [. . .]." [. . . bread] and beer daily. He took me to my [. . .] great because of an offense in the presence of my superior.

[. . .] me safe. Moreover, do not neglect [ta]king water to his forecourt and pray to him to rescue me. Moreover, do not [ne]glect any commission of mine which is in the fields, namely, to sow the grain and (to see) to the planting for me of the vegetables as well. And you are to give your personal attention to Shedemdua and her little children and to Hemesheri and her little daughter as well. Don't proceed [to do] wrong against them, or I will hold it against you as a great offense. It is on a day like this that a man is tested.

Now regarding the matter of the two *kite* of gold which [I] told [you] to put into the socle(?), you failed to put them there. Indeed I returned to [. . .], but I didn't find them. This which you have done is not good.

You are to give your personal attention [to . . .] and look after her distress, and [. . .] write her a letter and tell her, "Don't [. . .] them [to] the fowlers in the town of Edfu [. . .]," [so you] shall say to her. And you are to send me a letter through the one who [. . .] her little daughter and Hemesheri as well [. . . Shed]emdua and her little children, [. . .], Tainedjeme, Paadjadja the younger, and everybody [. . .]. Every single day [I am calling upon every god and every goddess by] whom [I pass] to give you life, prosperity and health. And further:

[. . .]. I am alive. Don't worry about me. [. . .]. They suffer no deprivation. Don't cease [. . .] the bread-rations which I had. And write about the matter of [. . . by] his hand.

310. LRL No. 8
(Dynasty 20: Year 10 of Renaissance)

The scribe [of] the great and noble Necropolis [of] Millions of Years [of] Pharaoh l.p.h., Dhutmose [from] the necropolis scribe Buteh[amon]: In life, prosperity and health and in the favor of Amon-Re, King of the Gods! Every single day I am calling upon Amon-Re, King of the Gods, Mut, [Khonsu], and all gods of Thebes, upon Pre-Harakhti in his rising and in his setting, upon Amon of the [Thrones] of the Two Lands, Foremost of Karnak, upon Amon-Userhat and his ennead, and upon every god and every goddess whom I visit daily to give you life, prosperity and health and very many favors in the presence of the general, your lord. And may Amon bring you back safe and I fill my eyes with the sight of you, and you fill your eyes with Amon of the Throne[s] of the Two Lands, your protector and great shield, to whom you bend your back; and may your brethren and your wards see you having returned alive, prospering and heathy and fill their embrace with you. And further:

As for what you wrote saying, "Don't be neglectful of any affair of mine or any commissions which are in the fields, to sow the grain and to [plant] the vegetables as well," so you said, I have caused [. . .]. As for the vegetables, they are planted; and as for the grain, I do not walk away therefrom.

"And you are to give your personal attention to the chantress of Amon Shed[em]dua and her little children and to Hemesheri and her little daughter," so you said. I will do, I will do whatever I might be able to do for them. Indeed they are alive [today; to]morrow is in God's hands. It is you whom they long to see.

Now regarding the mention you made to me of the matter of the woman in Ne (Thebes), saying, "Don't show neglect to her [like] the chief brewer Khonspatjau, who was someone who showed neglect to his own sister," I, for my part, will do whatever you shall say. Don't worry about them.

Now regarding what you wrote me about the matter of this Red Crown amulet, "Have you got it? Or has it gotten lost?" so you asked. It has not gotten lost. I've got it.

Now as for your saying, "Don't neglect writing me about your condition," what might happen to us while you remain alive? It is you who should write us about your condition. Indeed the (official) messengers are [coming] from you daily, going back and forth. They are the (official) messengers who come [to] this side (of the river) from Ne (Thebes), while I am [on] this (side). It is others who have to receive the letters [on] this side and send them on to me. Don't cease writing me about your condition. Farewell!

A further communication to Heramenpenaf, Amenpanefer, Amenopenakht, and the general's [singer] Pen[tahures]: In life, prosperity and health and in the favor of Amon-Re, King of the Gods! I am calling upon Amon-Re, King of the Gods, Mut, Khonsu, and all gods of Thebes to give you life, prosperity and health and very many favors in the presence of gods and people, and to let [me find] you alive, prospering and healthy and fill [my] embrace with you. It is you who are the concern that is on my mind. I am writing to let you know that your people are alive, prospering and healthy [. . .]. Do [not] worry about them.

A further matter for Heramenpenaf and Amenpanefer. Don't neglect the scribe Tjaroy. We know that he is a sick man who has never made such an expedition(?) [as this one. *End broken*].

Address: The scribe of the great and noble Necropolis of Millions of Years of Pharaoh, l.p.h., Dhutmose from the necropolis scribe Butehamon.
(*Note at top of recto*):
My receipt of the 17 spears which the guardian Karoy sent south. Your payment has been received and weighed out for their coppersmith. 8 large spears, each one 2 *deben*, amounting to 16 *deben*. 9 small spears, each one 1.5 *deben*, amounting to 13.5 *deben*. Total: 17 spears amounting to 29.5 *deben*.

311. LRL No. 2
(Dynasty 20: Year 10 of Renaissance)

The necropolis scribe Dhutmose to the [necropolis] scribe Buteh[amon and the chantress of Amon Shedemdua]: In life, prosperity and health and in the favor of Amon-Re, King of the Gods, residing in Elephantine! [I am calling upon Amon-Re, King of the Gods, and the gods] of the hills in which I am to let [me be brought back . . .] and fill my embrace with you while I am alive. To wit:

[. . .] in the fourth month of the second season, day 21, with my superior [. . .] safe as well. No harm has befallen them. There [is no . . .]. I left him in Elephantine in the company of Herere to cause [. . .].

How are you? How are Hemesheri, her little girl, the scribe [. . .], the scribe Amenhotep, Takamene the younger, Shedsumut, and the people who [. . . ? What means] your spending up until today without having sent [me one (letter)? Write] me about your condition, whether good or bad, through the men who will come [. . .], and they shall give it (the letter) to the scribe Kenykhnum. He will send it up to me [(in Nubia) . . . with] the men who come up from Elephantine. Indeed the [. . .] do not [. . .], and your letter shall cause my heart to be elated [over] the words [. . .] first (?). And do not be neglectful of them and send [. . .] to this girl of Hemesheri.

Moreover, [don't neglect taking water to Amon of the Thrones of the] Two Lands and call upon him to bring me back [from] the wilds, the place where I am, for [I do not] sleep either night or day, being so anxious about you. Moreover, [don't neglect taking water to] Amon, United with Eternity, and ask him, "Will you bring him back safe?" Moreover, [don't neglect sending] me a letter. Moreover, don't show neglect to your commissions [. . .].

A further communication to the workman Amenhotep, Bakeamon, Henutaa, [. . .]: Every single day [I am calling upon] Horus of Kuban to give you life, prosperity and health. Please call upon Amon [. . .], Amon of the Beautiful Encounter, and Mereseger to bring me back alive and I fill [my] embrace [with you in the fore]court of Amon of the Thrones of the Two Lands.

And you are not to neglect the policeman [Kas(?) . . .], and give him a commission seeing that a matter [. . .] and tell him, "Nobody is employed [. . . ." . . .] with my superior. There is no [*End lost*].

Address: The necropolis scribe Tjaroy to the scribe B[utehamon and the chantress of Amon Shedemdua].

312. *LRL No. 50*
(Dynasty 20: Year 10 of Renaissance)

[The scribe of the great and noble necropolis Dhutmose to . . . and the chantress of Amon Shed]emdua: In life, prosperity and health and in the favor of Amon-Re-Harakhti when he rises and sets! Every single day I am calling upon [Horus of Kub]an, who dwells in this mountain to give you life, prosperity and health, a long lifetime, and a good ripe old age, to let [Amon of the Thrones of the Two Lands], my lord, keep me safe that I may return and fill my embrace with you while I am alive. Indeed you are (the object of) my prayer [to the gods] in whose vicinity I now am. And may I find that Amon has kept you safe [. . . that] I [may be] one among you while you are still alive, prospering and healthy. And further:

How are you? How are [Hemesheri and her] girl? How are the scribe Meniunefer, the scribe Amenhotep, Takemene the younger, Shedsumut, [. . .], Tainedjeme, and Tapeses? Call upon Amon of the Thrones of the Two Lands, Mereseger, Amenophis, [Nofretari, Amon of the] Beautiful [Encounter], Hathor, mistress of the West, Amon, Holy of Place, and the great and [august] Ogdoad to bring me back prospering and let me arrive back home down [in] Egypt from the far-off land (Nubia) [in] which I am, [and you (the gods) shall] see me standing in your forecourt, after you (the gods) have rescued [me], so you should tell them (the gods).

A further [communication to the scribe Bu]tehamon: Look here please, what's the meaning of the things that you are saying to me, they being words of reply [. . .]? You [haven't] explained any of them. As for the coppersmith Hori's job which you and I received [. . .], you [haven't] written me about it, namely its order comprising the seventeen spears that you mentioned. I have caused [. . .] the place [where] the general is. Now you have mentioned the business of the spears, but you don't send the boat [. . .]. You haven't yet named the person to whom you entrusted it, (that is) the business of the spears; for although it was the Sher[den Hori who brought] them to me, I don't know the person to whom you gave them nor do I know the boat which [. . .] a letter bearing the general's name concerning them. What sort of business is this? I shall not keep silent to you about it [. . .] me while I was in Pahedj[. . .]mehty. i received them, and I found all the [. . .] to be in good condition. But the business of the spears is what I have (concern about), for it is not all right [. . .] to write a letter like this again.

Now regarding the affair of the policeman Kasy about whom I [wro]te to you but you failed to answer me, is what you have done with him like the affair of the [. . .] you Amenpanefer, concerning whom you never wrote me what you did with him? Did you bring him back or didn't you bring [him] back? [. . .].

Now you should give your personal attention to my(?) mother(-in-law?) Tanettabekhen, and(?) the girl . . . take(?) her [. . .] all the children. Don't neglect [. . .] their [. . . nor] neglect Shedemdua, seeing that God gives [. . .] in them(?), I would be like one who is yonder (i.e., dead). You know that [. . .], and you shall look after the children who are in your [house(?)] and have them brought [. . . without] delay, although you have not joined up with him concerning greatness(?) [. . .] letter to your superior. It's all right, this which you have done.

Now as soon as you learn [that he is writing to you, you shall se]nd (it) to him also. He should write you a letter first, for it is better if you do not [write a] letter first until he has written to you. Now as soon as you learn that he is writing you, you shall [send (it) to] him. Indeed I shall not keep silent to you about this business of the spears [about] which you haven't written [me whether you sent] them to him.[5]

Now you haven't written a letter in your handwriting to be sent [to] the general, your [superior, . . .] which [bears] the agents' names as well [. . .] so that it may serve you [as testimony(?) . . .] for us(?) also. Farewell!

313. LRL No. 9
(Dynasty 20: Year 10 of Renaissance)

[The scribe of the great and noble Necropolis of Millions] of Years of Pharaoh, l.p.h., [Dhutmose to] the necropolis scribe Butehamon, the chantress of Amon Shedemdua, and Hemesheri: In life, prosperity and health and in the favor of Amon-Re, King of the Gods, Mut, Khonsu, and all gods of Thebes! [And further]:

I am calling upon Horus of Kuban, Horus of Aniba, and Atum, the lord of the earth, to give you life, prosperity and health, a long lifetime, and a good ripe old age and to let Amon of the Thrones of the Two Lands, my good lord, bring me back alive [from] the wilds, the place where I am abandoned in this far-off land (of Nubia), and let me fill [my] embrace with you. And further:

This letter of yours reached me by the hand of the retainer Dhuthotep in Year 10, first month of the third season, day 25. I received it and inquired about you from him, and he told me that you are alive and that you are all right. My heart became alive; my eyes opened, and I lifted up my head whereas I had been ill.

Now regarding the mention you made of the matter of those letters of yours about which you inquired, "Have they reached you?" so you asked, they have all reached me except this letter which you gave to the (Nubian) foreigner Seti, the brother of the fisherman Paneferemneb. This is the only one which was not delivered to me.

Now I am doing quite well with my superior; he does not neglect me. He has caused one *maziktu*-jug to be fixed for me every five days, five ordinary loaves daily, and one ewer, which holds five *hin*-measures of beer, daily from his wages. And it (the beer) has dispelled the illness which was in me. Do [not] worry about me because of the fact that the children who were with me have returned.

And say in (your) hearts, "There must be some sort of reproach against Tja[roy]," so you should say. Indeed I know the nature of your thoughts. Don't worry about me in any matters. I am all right. Call upon Amon, United with Eternity, Amenophis, Nofretari, Mereseger, my mistress, and Amon, Holy of Place, to bring me back alive. And submit (my case) before (the oracles of both) Amon, United with Eternity, and Amenophis and ask them, "Will you bring him back alive?" And call upon Amon of the Thrones of the Two Lands to rescue [me].

Weave many kilts(?) which shall be for my [. . .] with him in these hills. Now you have wished to speak saying, "I am much interested in the matter of the documents which are deposited [in] the stairwell(?)." Now as for the documents upon which the rain had poured in the house of the scribe Horsheri my (grandfather), you brought them out, and we discovered that they had not become erased. I said to you, "I shall unbind them again." You brought them down below, and we deposited [them] in the tomb of Amennakht, my (great-grand)father. You have wished to say, "I am much interested."

And you are not to neglect your brethren(?) nor your commissions concerning which your superior has written to you and the captains who are with you. And take care to reprimand anybody who has quarreled with another, until Amon brings [me] back safe.

Now as for your failure to write me about what you have done for the son of Iunefer, as soon as I return, his affair will be (at least) partly under my control. Moreover, don't show neglect to the policeman Kas, but give him rations and have him weave the fabrics. And give your attention to the chariot donkeys and to the men who are in the fields as well. And dispatch the policeman Hadnakht and send him to me quickly — and don't let him linger. I have already written to you for him through the Sherden Hori. And I have spoken with Heramenpenaf as well saying, "Send him on to me."

And you shall order the coppersmith to make spears, you forming a single party with Kar. There is copper there at your disposal. And you shall communicate to me in writing whatever you are going to do concerning your superior's commissions and concerning all matters about which [I've written] you.

And you shall tell the carpenter Amenhotep son of(?) . . . , "Make the shaft which he (text: I) told you to make! He (text:I) shall give you payment for it," so you shall tell him.

Now I have spoken with Heramenpenaf concerning your superior's commission. Let him himself speak with you, but you both shall keep it secret from me. And don't talk in the presence of another, for you will be glad only if you don't talk with anyone until I return.

And you are to look after Neferti's ass's foal and train it. And give your personal attention to the daughter of the fowler and do for her all that which ought to be done. And tell her my condition and ask her to call upon Amon to bring me back.

(This is) testimony to let you know that I am much interested [in] the copper which I gave to the coppersmith Hori and from which he made the four spears and of which I told you to use the remainder as the overlays, exactly according to the sketch that I gave him, and about which he promised, "I shall make it according to its proper shape," concerning the 19.5 (*deben*) of copper that I gave him. Kar gave him 10.5 (*deben*) when you again(?) gave him a job. Farewell!

Now as for the piece of wood that you put inside a (rolled) letter, I have put it back in there [to] have it returned to you.[6]

Address: The scribe [of] the great and noble necropolis Tjaroy [to] the necropolis scribe Butehamon and the chantress of Amon Shedemdua.

314. LRL No. 16
(Dynasty 20: Year 10 of Renaissance)

The scribe of the great and noble Necropolis of Millions of Years of Pharaoh, l.p.h., Dhutmose from the necropolis scribe Butehamon, the chantress of Amon-Re, King of the Gods, Shedemdua and the chantress of Amon Hemesheri: In life, prosperity and health and in the favor of Amon-Re,

King of the Gods! Every single day we are calling upon Amon-Re, King of the Gods, Mut, Khonsu, and all gods of Thebes, upon Pre-Harakhti in his rising and in his setting, upon Amon, United with Eternity, upon Amon of Djeme (Medinet Habu), upon Amon of the Throne(s) of the Two Lands, upon the great and august Ogdoad that rests in Kheftehinebos, upon Mereseger, mistress of the West, upon Hathor, mistress of Deir el-Bahri and mistress of the hills in which you are, upon Amenophis, l.p.h., and Nofretari, l.p.h., and upon Amon of the Beautiful Encounter as I stand in his forecourt daily without becoming fatigued, praying in their names and saying, "Give him (text: you) very many favors before the general, his (text: your) lord. Indeed as long as he is favored with you (the gods)," so I keep telling them, "he shall be well-off in whatever place." And may the gods of the land in which you are rescue you from every danger of this land (Nubia) and hand you over to Amon of the Throne(s) of the Two Lands, your lord, and we fill our embrace with you. And further:

I've taken note of all matters concerning which you have communicated to me through the mouth of the workman Heramenpenaf, saying, "Don't neglect taking water to Amon of the Throne(s) of the Two Lands." I am doing so two to three times per decade (a period of ten days); I don't neglect taking water to him. Now it is appropriate for you to be considerate toward him (Amon) so that he may be considerate toward you without becoming angry.

As for your saying, "I won't keep silent to you about the business of the spears," so you said, I wrote the letter and gave it to the guardian Karoy regarding the order for spears while he was dwelling in Ne (Thebes). I said to him, "I won't forge for myself while I am dwelling here. I have drawn up the order for spears. Find out the boat and the man to whom you shall give this letter and write his name on it," so I said to him. And he answered me, "It was to Pa[y]shuuben that I entrusted them," so he answered me. Am I to know what he has done with them?

As for your mentioning the matter of the necropolis policeman Kasy, nobody has interfered with him. He is working on his commission. Don't worry about him.

As for your mentioning the matter of this son of Iunefer saying, "You haven't written me about his condition," I have taken up his case with his man. He is with them. Don't worry about him.

Now the little children are all right. Hemesheri and her girl are all right. No harm has befallen them. All your people are alive, prospering and healthy. It is you whom they are calling upon Amon of the Thrones of the Two Lands to bring back alive, prospering and healthy so we may fill our embrace with you. I am writing to let you know through the policeman Hadnakht.

The first month of the third season, day 20, arrival of Heramenpenaf.

Address: The scribe of the great and noble necropolis Tjaroy from the necropolis scribe Butehamon.

315. LRL No. 28
(Dynasty 20: Year 10 of Renaissance)

The fan-bearer on the king's right, royal scribe, general, high priest of Amon-Re, [King of the Gods], vice[roy] of Kush, overseer of southern foreign lands, granary overseer of Pharaoh's granaries, and [leader] of Pharaoh's troops, [Pi]ankh [from] the two foremen, the necropolis scribe Butehamon, the guardian [Kar], and [. . .]: In life, prosperity and health and in the favor of Amon-Re, King of the Gods! Every single day we are calling upon Amon-Re, King of the Gods, Mut, Khonsu, and all gods of Thebes, upon Pre-Harakhti in his rising and in his setting, upon Amon, United with Eternity, and his ennead, upon the great and august Ogdoad that rests [in] Kheftehinebos, upon Mereseger, mistress of the West, and upon the gods of the land (Nubia) in which you are to give you life, prosperity and health, a long lifetime and a good ripe old age, to give you [very many] favors [in the presence of] Amon-Re, King of the Gods, your lord, l.p.h., and may Amon bring you back safe and you fill your embrace with Ne (Thebes) and we fill our eyes with the sight of you when you have returned alive, prospering and healthy. And further:

We've taken note of all matters our lord wrote us about. As for his having sent us this letter by the hand of Hori the Sherden, this retainer of our lord, the scribe Butehamon ferried across and received it from him in the first month of the third season, [day] 18. I assembled the two foremen, the scribe Butehamon, the guardian Kar, and the necropolis workmen. I stood in their midst and read it out to them. They replied, "We will do, we will do according to what our lord has said," including the oldest and the youngest of them. Now as I was walking about in Ne (Thebes) to bring back the men who had settled there, I met the workmen Amenpanefer and Heramenpenaf, those two men who used to be there in the company of their lord in the south land (Nubia). They said to me, "We have returned. It is our lord who has sent us to where we now are, having caused us to bring a letter."

I, the scribe Butehamon, took the letter. I summoned the two foremen, this guardian, and the necropolis personnel who are under their supervision, including the oldest and the youngest of them, and I read it out to them. They replied, "We will do, we will do according to what our lord has said," it being in the first month of the third season, day 20, that this letter reached us.

Now we have taken note of our lord's message to us saying, "Don't be neglectful of this commission," so said our lord — and he did not say, "In what way did I write you previously when I was south?" — and saying, "Have some of the handy clothes sent. It is after I have departed that you shall send them after me," so said our lord.

Is the necropolis scribe Dhutmose unable to report to you about our having searched for a transport ship and having failed to find (one) right away? He just about passed away when we reached Ne (Thebes) and was told that you had departed before we had reached our mistress. She said to the necropolis scribe Tjaroy, "He (the general Piankh) told you to follow him." We delivered the clothes to our mistress, but she said to the scribe Tjaroy, "Aren't you going with the clothes, for it is you who should deliver [them] to your lord?" so our mistress told him. Even if there are some ten thousand servants belonging to our lord, would they obey him like us? Indeed we are accomplishing all our lord's commissions. We are attentive to him. Don't we respect all commissions of his which we are carrying out? Then shall Amon-Re, King of the Gods, your lord, grant us favor before you as well. Is it not out of our heart's desire that we work for you? We are writing to let our lord know.

A further communication from the workmen of the great and noble necropolis to our lord. We've taken note of all matters our lord wrote us about. As for what our lord wrote us, saying, "Go and carry out a certain (building) commission for me if you have not already gotten to it, and look to it until I reach you," so said our lord, what does it mean—the place which we know about, since we were already in it? "Leave it be. Don't tamper with it," so said our lord.

As for this scribe who used to be here in charge of us, it being he who can give (advice) since he is an experienced person, and who knows about a certain marker concerning which his father had testified, he is with you. Now as soon as he submits the evidence before us also, we shall spend from ten to twenty days, while he looks for a marker daily until he finds (one).

Now see, you have written saying, "Uncover a tomb among the ancient tombs and preserve its seal until I return," so said our lord. We are carrying out commissions. We shall enable you to find it fixed up and ready—the place which we know about. But you should send the necropolis scribe Tjaroy to have him come so that he may look for a marker for us, since we get going and go astray not knowing where to put our feet.

May Amon-Re, King of the Gods, do for you everything good, and you not be lacking in anything. I am writing to inform our lord through the necropolis policeman Hadnakht in the first month of the third season, day 29.

Address: The general of Pharaoh, l.p.h., [from] the captains of the necropolis.

316. *LRL No. 10*
(Dynasty 20: Year 10 of Renaissance)

The scribe of the great and noble Necropolis [of Millions] of Years of Pharaoh, l.p.h., Tjaroy to the guardian of the great and noble necropolis of Pharaoh, l.p.h., [K]aroy and to the scribe of the great and noble necropolis Butehamon: In life, prosperity and health and in the favor of Amon-Re, King of the Gods, your good lord! To wit:

Every single day I am calling upon Khnum, Satis, and Anukis to keep you alive, to keep you healthy, and to cause you to be invigorated. Before your missive reached me, I had already sent you the letter which I wrote to you concerning the spears. You are not to cease writing me about your condition. When the scribe Pentahunakht came to you to say, "Give it [to] Hori, who has been put to work," you refused to give it to him. The general has said, "Put him to work on the spears and give him copper to let him work on the spears." Farewell [in] favor(?)!

A further communication from the scribe Kenykhnum [to] the scribe Buteh[amon]. Every day [I am calling upon the gods] of the land to keep you alive, to keep you healthy, and to cause you to be invigorated. And further:

[Really], what's the meaning of this your failure to write me what is [on] your mind? May Amon be before you! If only Hemesheri were here concealed that you might write to me. And do [not] cease writing me about your condition. Farewell [in] favor(?)!

Address: The scribe of the great and noble necropolis [of Pharaoh, l.p.h.], Tjaroy to the guardian of the great necropolis Karoy.

317. LRL No. 29
(Dynasty 20: Year 10 of Renaissance)

The prophet of Hathor, lady of Agny, and troop captain Shedsuhor from the necropolis scribe Butehamon: In life, prosperity and health and in the favor of Amon-Re, King of the Gods! I am calling upon Amon-Re-Harakhti when he rises and sets to give you life, prosperity and health, and very many favors in the presence of the general, your lord, and may Amon bring you alive, prospering and healthy back down [to] Egypt and I fill my embrace with you, the gods of the land (of Nubia) in which you are having rescued [you]; and may they hand you over [to] the gods of your town and you become satisfied within Ne (Thebes) and Ne become satisfied with you.

Indeed you are kind, and you are responsible for my father. Be a pilot for the necropolis scribe Tjaroy. You know that he is a man who lacks experience, for he has never before made such expeditions as he is now on. Assist him in the boat. Keep watch over [him] vigilantly in the evening as well while you are around him, since you are traveling unimpeded(?). Now a person is childlike when he has become troubled, never yet having seen a fearful face (i.e., experienced danger).

Now all your people are alive. No harm has befallen them. I am writing to inform you. Farewell!

Address: It is for the scribe Tjaroy and Shedsuhor.

318. LRL No. 15
(Dynasty 20: Year 10 of Renaissance)

The scribe of the great and noble Necropolis of Millions of Years of Pharaoh, l.p.h., Dhutmose from the prophet of Amenophis Amenhotep son of Amennakht of the noble necropolis: In life, prosperity and health and in the favor of Amon-Re, King of the Gods! Every single day I am calling upon Amon-Re, King of the Gods, Lord of the Thrones of the Two Lands and Foremost of Karnak, upon Pre-Harakhti in his rising and in his setting, upon Atum, Lord of the Two Lands the Heliopolitan, upon Khnum, who has fashioned the great and august Ogdoad that rests in the Promontory of Kheftehinebos, l.p.h., and who made for them the hills in which you are, upon Amon of Djeme (Medinet Habu), upon Hathor, mistress of the West, upon Amenophis, l.p.h., and Nofretari, l.p.h., and upon Amon of the Beautiful Encounter, the King, l.p.h., who wears the White Crown and who rests in Kheftehinebos, l.p.h., to give you life, prosperity and health, a long lifetime, a good ripe old age, and very many favors in the presence of the general, your lord; and may Amon bring you back alive, prospering and healthy and we fill our embrace with you. And further:

When my letter reaches you, don't go out to observe a melee, since it is not as a combat soldier that you have been called up nor is it as a mere henchman that you have been called up. It is in order that advice may be sought of you that you have been taken along. Stay put in this boat, protecting yourself against arrows, spears, and sto[nes], and don't abandon us all, since you know that you are a father to all of us. There is no one here from whom we may seek advice about our livelihood. I am standing in the presence of Amenophis, l.p.h., daily, being pure, calling upon him to bring you back alive, prospering and healthy. I am writing to let you know. Pennestitowy, Pentaumte, Paby, Heramenpenaf, Sedjaa, Pahertahanakht, and all your brethren, both male and female as well, are calling upon Amon of the Thrones of the Two Lands to bring you back alive, prospering and healthy.

A further communication from the necropolis scribe Butehamon: I am calling upon the gods of the land in which you are to bring you back alive, prospering and healthy and to hand you over to Amon of the Thrones of the Two Lands since you are his useful servant. And I don't neglect taking water to him. I am writing to let you know.

As soon as my letter reaches you, you shall [write] me a letter in your own handwriting that I may know that you are still alive. Indeed my eyes are going blind since they cannot see you. Now all your people are alive, prospering and healthy. No harm has befallen them, from young to old.

Address: It is for the scribe of the great and noble necropolis Tjaroy.

319. LRL No. 30
(Dynasty 20: Year 10 of Renaissance)

The general of Pharaoh, l.p.h., [to] the two foremen, the scribe Buteha-mon, the guardian Kar, and all the necropolis workmen. Quote:

The necropolis scribe Tjaroy and the troop captain and prophet Shedsuhor have reached me; they have rendered report to me of all you've done. What you've [done] is all right, joining up and carrying out this assignment which I charged you to do and writing me about what you've done. As soon as my letter reaches you, you shall fetch the remainder of the chariot poles which are in the place from which Shedsuhor got the poles for me. It is lying there outside your place that you shall [let] me find them on my return from the South. But don't proceed to install a single one thereof there.

Now as for this matter of these five maidservants whom I gave, they are yours, all of them, from the captains down to all the workmen. But don't let one person tyrannize another among you. And don't give Heramenpenaf any of them, for I've already given to him. But if you haven't received them, you shall go to where Herere is and receive them from her. And you shall not be neglectful of any affairs of mine. And you shall preserve my letter so that it may serve you as testimony.

A further communication to the scribe Butehamon and the guardian Kar. Please join up with Heramenpenaf and receive the copper from him and [send] it to the coppersmith Tutuy and the coppersmith Hori, when he finishes, and to the two coppersmiths of mine. And have them make this knife and two lamp-pots(?). There is tin there at your disposal to add to the copper.

320. LRL No. 45
(Dynasty 20: Year 10 of Renaissance)

[Beginning lost of the Temple] of the King of Upper and Lower Egypt, Usermare-miamon (Ramesses III's mortuary temple) [in the Estate of] Amon: In life, prosperity and health and [in the favor] of Amon-Re, King of the Gods! Every single day I am calling upon Amon-Re, King of the Gods, upon [Mut], Khonsu, and all the gods and goddesses of Thebes, upon Amon, United with Eternity, and his ennead, upon Mereseger, mistress of the West, upon Amon, Holy of Place, the lord of the West, and upon every god and every goddess whom I visit daily, upon Amon of Luxor at each and every tenth day, when he comes [to] offer water [to] the Great Living Ba's, who rest in the place of Amon, United with Eternity, residing in the place of the tenth day processional appearance, to give you life, prosperity and health, a long lifetime, a good ripe old age, and very many favors in the presence of the general, your lord, and to preserve you in his charge. And may Amon-Re, King of the Gods, bring you back safe and alive and I fill my embrace with you. To wit:

You wrote to the army scribe Pentahunakht, saying, "Take thought concerning my people and also my serfs," so you said. Your people are all right. They are alive, prospering and healthy. Don't worry about them. It is you whom they long to see and whose condition they wish to hear about daily.

Now see, it is a second campaign that you are now with your superior, and you haven't yet written me about your condition. I am inquiring about you [. . . from] all persons who come north from there (where you are), and they tell me that you are all right. "He is happy in the presence of his superior," so they keep telling me (in) testifying to me.

You have sent three papyrus letters to the scribe Butehamon, but you haven't written me about your condition. As soon as my letter reaches you, you shall write me about your condition through the retainer Pentahunakht. Farewell!

Address: [. . .] of the necropolis.

321. LRL No. 31
(Dynasty 20: Year 10 of Renaissance)

The general's singer Pentahu[res, . . . of] Amon, the scribe Butehamon, [. . .] the confidant(?) Akhmenu, the carpenter [. . . , the chantress of Amon-Re], King of the Gods, Hemesheri, and the chantress [. . . : In life, prosperity and health and in the favor] of Amon-Re, King of the Gods! To wit:

Every day I am calling upon Amon-Re-Harakhti when he [rises] and sets, upon Khnum, Satis, Anukis, and all gods of Elephantine to give you life, prosperity and health, a long lifetime, and a good ripe old age. And further:

You (woman) are to look after the little children. Don't do them wrong. And don't be neglectful of my father. And you (woman) shall cause this spear which I said to have made to be made. And you shall have some confections prepared so that they produce one *muziktu*-jugful before his arrival.

Statement for the scribe Butehamon; to wit:

Your father had the letter brought to me, saying, "Let it be taken to you." And he wrote me saying, "As for all letters which your brother caused to be brought to me, your name is on them," so he said. "Have someone there take them to him," so he said. Now I have caused his (case) to be submitted before (the oracle of) Khnum, and he (Khnum) has answered saying, "He shall prosper," so he has responded to the chantress of Amon Tuia and the scribe Hori. It is every brother of mine who turns the face [to] my(?) [. . .] to them. Receive Taymedjay [. . .]; write me about the children [. . .] in the presence of Khnum. He (Khnum) has said, "I shall . . . [End lost].

Address: The singer Pentahures [. . .].

322. LRL No. 43
(Dynasty 20: Year 10 of Renaissance)

[Beginning lost the servant in the Place [of Truth . . . : In life, prosperity and health and in the favor of Amon-Re], King of the Gods! We are calling upon

Amon-Re, King of the Gods, to bring you back rescued from every sort of danger which is in the land above (Nubia) in which you are [sojourning].

Write us about your condition. Are you still alive? [And write us] about the condition of the necropolis scribe Tjaroy through the policeman Hadnakht. And assist Tjaroy in the boat. And look after him vigilantly in [the day and] evening. And be a pilot for him. Then shall Amon be a pilot for you. It is on a day like this that a man is tested. Now you are his man. I am writing to inform you through Akhmenu.

What's the meaning of what you wrote me, saying, "It was only when Hemesheri was here that you sent a letter"? You wouldn't write me a lie! I in fact wrote you two letters, but they failed to give them to you just like those which I caused to be taken to the scribe Tjaroy and which they failed to give to him.

323. LRL No. 7
(Dynasty 20: Year 10 of Renaissance)

The scribe of the great and noble Necropolis of Millions of Years of Pharaoh, l.p.h., Dhutmose to the guardian Kar: In life, prosperity and health and in the favor of Amon-Re, King of the Gods! Every single day I am calling upon every god and every goddess by whom I pass to give you life, prosperity and health, a long lifetime, and a good ripe old age, and to give you favor in the presence of gods and people. And further:

I have taken note of what you wrote to look into my condition. It is Amon, Pre, and Ptah who shall look into your condition and do you good. Please give your personal attention to Shedemdua and her little children to prevent another from doing wrong to them. And call upon Amon to bring me back safe [from] the wilds, the place where I am abandoned.

A further communication to the chantress of Amon Tauhenu: I am calling upon Amon and all the gods to give you life, prosperity and health. How are you? How are my people? Please write me about your condition. Farewell!

Address: It is for the guardian of the necropolis Kar.

324. LRL No. 38
(Dynasty 20: Year 10 of Renaissance)

The principal of the harem of Amon-[Re, King of] the Gods, Herere, to the troop captain Peseg. Quote:

What's this about the personnel of the [great] and noble necropolis [concerning whom] I wrote to you, saying, "Give them rations," that you haven't yet given them any? [As soon as my let]ter reaches you, you shall look for the grain which [I wrote you] about and give them rations from it. Don't make [. . .] complain to me again. Have them prepared [for] people [. . .] commission them. You know [. . .]. I am writing to inform [you. *End lost*].

Address: The principal of the harem of Amon-Re, King [of the Gods], Herere, to the troop captain Peseg.

========= **Miscellaneous Letters** =========

325. *LRL No. 6*
(Dynasty 20: Renaissance)

The scribe of the great and noble Necropolis of Millions of Years of Pharaoh, l.p.h., Dhutmose to the necropolis scribe Butehamon and to the chantress of Amon Hemesheri: In life, prosperity and health and in the favor of Amon-Re, King of the Gods! Every day I am calling upon the gods who are in my vicinity to give you life, prosperity and health, a long lifetime, and a ripe old age and to give you favor in the presence of gods. And further:

I am all right, I am in health. Don't worry about me. It is you whom I long to see and whose condition I wish to hear about daily. As soon as my letter reaches you, you shall call upon Amon to bring me back alive.

A further communication to the chantress of Amon Baki and the chantress of Amon Shed[em]dua: In life, prosperity and health and in the favor of Amon-Re, King [of the Gods]! Every day I am calling upon the gods who are in my vicinity to give you life, to give you health, and to give you favor in the presence of gods and people. And further:

I am all right. I am in health. Don't worry about me. It is you whose condition I wish to hear about daily. As soon as my letter arrives, you shall call upon Amon to bring me back. Farewell!

Address: The [necropolis] scribe Tja[roy] to the scribe Butehamon and to the chantress of Amon Hemesheri.

326. *LRL No. 11*
(Dynasty 20: Renaissance)

The necropolis [scribe Tja]raroy [from the] necropolis administrator Heramenpenaf: In life, prosperity and health and in the favor of Amon-Re, King of the Gods! Every day I am calling upon Amon-Re, King of the Gods, Amon-Re, King of the Gods (*sic*), Mut, Khonsu, and all gods of Thebes to keep you alive, to keep you safe, and to give you [favor in] the presence of the general, and to let you return alive, prospering and healthy [and I fill] my embrace with you. And further:

As soon as my letter reaches you, [you shall] look for Amenkeni and seek him out. Now don't worry [about any] people of yours. They are all right. And you shall write me about your condition.

Address: The necropolis [scribe Tja]raroy [from] the administrator Heramenpenaf.

327. LRL No. 32
(Dynasty 20; Renaissance)

It is [the general] who addresses the necropolis administrators. Quote:
As soon as my letter reaches you, you shall join up with the chief taxing master and fence in this pasturage. Don't be negligent. And may it (this letter) serve you as testimony.

328. LRL No. 48
(Dynasty 20: Renaissance)

[*Beginning lost*]. Every day [we are calling upon every] god and [every] goddess to give you life, prosperity and health and many favors in the presence of [. . .], your(?) superior. And further:
We've taken note of all matters you wrote us about. As for the mention [you] made of [the] matter of the grain and the fenugreek(?) which you told me the vizier is enregistering, we shall rejoice [. . .] that you are aware of this damage which was done to them. You will assess their loss [. . .] and write in order to instruct us to store whatever thereof we have found still usable.
Now when [we] were engaged in this commission until it was accomplished, it was you who saw to the [. . .] grain, and it is you who shall render report to the vizier concerning them. Farewell!

329. LRL No. 41
(Dynasty 20: Renaissance or later)

The *wab*-priest of Khonsu and scribe of the king's victuals Bakenkhons to the necropolis scribe Ankhef: In life, prosperity and health and in the favor of Amon-Re, King of the Gods! May he (Amon-Re) give you life, prosperity and health and favor in the presence of gods and people every day. And further:
I've heard the account of the words you wrote apropos of this false testimony which I had said against this man, it being slander against him. Don't make me write you millions of words. You are to [go and] see them. Keep a firm hand on these sixteen loaves. Let them be preserved and don't listen to any words they might say to you apropos of them. Farewell!

Address: The *wab*-priest of Khonsu and scribe Bakenkhons to [the necropolis] scribe Ankhef.

330. P. Bankes II
(Dynasty 20: Renaissance)

The scribe Butehamon: As soon as this letter for Peterpayneb reaches you, you shall read [this] letter that has been brought for Peterpayneb and take it and read it out to him, and you shall take it back and deposit it in your box, and you shall tell him such words as get right to the point.

Address: The scribe of the great and noble necropolis Tjaroy to the necropolis [scribe] Butehamon.

===== **A Daughter to Her Mother's Paramour** =====

331. P. BM 10416
(end of Dynasty 20)

To wit: Your people, including the eldest of them and the youngest of them, both male and female, have moved off by dark of night. They were coming saying, "We are going to beat her and her people up." [It was] the steward who said to them, "What means your going [to the house(?)] of my scribe in order to beat up my(?) people, while she isn't there?" And he held them at bay and said to them, "Was it your man who was encountered there as an emissary? Tell me the one whom you found fit to go and beat up.[7] Please tell him to me," so he said to them. And they answered saying to him, "It is eight whole months till now that he has been having sex with this woman while he is not a married man. [Now] if he were a married man, would he not then swear off your woman?" so they said to him.

And the steward sent word to my mother in the presence of Audjar, this workman from whom you took counsel as well, saying, "As for Nesamenemope, why did you accept him as your sexual partner [and so] gain for yourself adversaries? If only [they had not gone] by dark of night to deliver the things of a nice fledgling-child saying, 'We are going to [. . .] also,' so they said. If this man yearns for you, let [him] enter the court together with his wife and let him swear off [her (his wife)] and come to your house. But if not, he will be one who has to find the way for you to put your lips in touch with his lips. Even if I held them at bay on this occasion, I won't hold them at bay again," so he said.

When my letter reaches you, you shall refuse to go to the woman Neferti[8] in this m[anner].

Notes

1. An aphorism.
2. Or simply, "the matter of the new vessels."
3. So Ward (1985: 331), instead of "upper chamber," "loft."
4. Meaning the casualties anticipated in the war in Nubia against Panehsy.
5. The restoration is due to Mr. Gary Greig.
6. The insertion of a stick inside a rolled papyrus may have served as some sort of signal. On exhibit in the Botanical Museum at Kew Gardens, London, there is an example of a papyrus rolled around a stick.
7. Or, "The one whom we found going to beat up."
8. Perhaps the writer's mother.

XI

Twenty-first Dynasty Letters

Introduction

The death of Ramesses XI marked the end of the New Kingdom and the Renaissance era. Smendes, a potentate at Tanis in the northeastern Delta, founded the Twenty-first Dynasty, which ruled at Tanis. Concomitantly Thebes was governed by a line of high priests of Amon descended from the general Piankh. His son, the high priest Pinedjem I, assumed the kingship at Thebes much as Herihor had previously done early in the Renaissance era. Cordial relations existed between Tanis and Thebes, and Pinedjem I's son, Psusennes, whose name means "The star has arisen in Thebes," became king at Tanis. The kings and high priests of the Twenty-first Dynasty were of Libyan background and had at their disposal Libyan mercenaries, who had been settled in tribal cantons in the Delta and Middle Egypt.

The Theban realm extended north to El-Hiba, whose fortress was strategically situated on the Nile south of the approaches to the Fayum. At El-Hiba there was an encampment of Libyan mercenaries. With the exception of No. 339, all the letters of Part XI have to do with El-Hiba, whose god Amon was called "He of the Camp." Although these letters, published by Spiegelberg (1917a) and Posener (1982a), were purchased in Luxor, their probable provenience is El-Hiba.

Despite the Libyan origins of the Twenty-first Dynasty, letters of this period betray very little that can be regarded as distinctively Libyan, apart from the Libyan name of the high priest of Amon Masahert in No. 337. Indeed the existing monumental evidence and funerary iconography suggest that the Libyan kings and priests of the Twenty-first Dynasty had undergone significant acculturation in adopting Egyptian mores, particularly in the area of religion. The approach to the god Amon revealed in letters Nos. 337 and 338 continues the Ramesside tradition that viewed god as a master of destiny to whom petition could be made.

Letter No. 339, of unknown provenience, was certainly written at Thebes and mailed to some location, probably not too far distant, where there was a temple of Osiris.

================ Fugitive Servants ================

332. P. Strassburg 39
(Dynasty 21)

The communication of the god's father priest of Onouris and scribe Bakkhons which is destined for the god's father priest and temple scribe Horkhebe of "He of the Camp":

Bakenhor, this servant of Ankhef, this attendant who is responsible to you, has run away. He is in the Promontory (El-Hiba), your town. Now I have dispatched him (Ankhef) that I might send him on to you in order to take charge of him (Bakenhor), for I have been told that he is in the house of Aay, the laundryman. Have a retainer who is responsible to you go in pursuit of him (Bakenhor). Have him apprehended and brought before you and then turn him over to Ankhef, this attendant who is responsible to you.

If you don't find him, you shall seek out those people to whom Ankhef shall tell you to administer an oath, and you shall take them to the forecourt of their god so they can swear by him (the god).

333. P. Strassburg 26
(Dynasty 21)

The god's father priest of Amon-Re, King of the Gods, the administrative scribe of the Estate of Amon-Re, King of the Gods, and the general's [scribe] Pashed to the god's father priest and temple scribe Hor[penese of] "He of the Camp": In life, prosperity and health and in the favor of Amon-Re, King of the Gods! May he (Amon-Re) give you life, prosperity and health, a long lifetime, [a good ripe old age] and favors in the presence of gods and people every day. And further:

As soon as my letter reaches you, you shall [seek out(?)] those servants of Padiamon, this god's father priest of Amon, who took flight and came [. . . to the] Promontory (El-Hiba) where you are, in order to apprehend them wherever they are. [And] you shall hand them over [to . . .]amon, his servant, in order to have him take them south speedily.

Address: The god's father priest of Amon and the general's scribe Pashed to the god's father priest and temple scribe Horpenese.

================ An Eviction ================

334. P. Strassburg 31
(Dynasty 21)

The god's father priest and temple scribe Horpenese of "He of the Camp" [to . . .]tjpakaemkeme: In life, prosperity and health and in the favor of

Amon-Re, King of the Gods, your good lord! To wit:

Every day I am calling upon Amon-Re-[Harakh]ti when he rises and sets and upon Amon, Content of Heart, the great god, [. . .], to give you life, prosperity and health, a long lifetime, a good ripe old age and very many favors in the presence of gods and people. To wit:

[I've taken] note of [this] messsage you sent through Besbes, this weaver, saying, "Evict all people belonging to the military leader who are in this house of Saupaankh," so you said. [. . .] you to your good lord(?). I will do so, I will do so. See to those people, for I have sent someone to evict them from the house. Now I have come north here(?) to the Promontory (El-Hiba), and I will stay tomorrow.

Address: The god's father priest and temple scribe Horpenese of "He of the Camp" [to . . .]tjpakaemkeme . . . of the Camp.

═══════ Horses and a Watch on the Walls ═══════

335. P. Strassburg 33
(Dynasty 21)

The god's father priest and temple scribe Horpenese of "He of the Camp" to the captain of shield-bearers(?) Shepti: In life, prosperity and health and in the favor of Amon-Re, King of the Gods, your good lord! To wit:

Every single day I am calling upon Amon-Re-Harakhti when he rises and sets to keep you safe, to give you life, prosperity and health, a long lifetime, a good ripe old age, and favor in the presence of gods and people.

I've taken note of this message you sent by the hand of Horpesh, saying, "Write me whether any horses have come to you." No horses have come to us. Pay attention to us! At the time when some horses do arrive, we shall write to you, and you shall send us some men.

Furthermore still, see to those warriors of Neshyet(?) who are living [at] the Promontory (El-Hiba). Treat them with all severity. Send a watch onto the ramparts since a name-list has been delivered to us with the words, "Don't send anybody out [to] the countryside, be he a soldier, a weaver, or a person of any sort."

Address: The god's father priest and temple scribe Horpenese to the captain of shield-bearers(?) Shepti.

═══════════════ Fowlers ═══════════════

336. P. Strassburg 25
(Dynasty 21)

[Name lost to the god's father priest and] temple [scribe] Horpenese of "He of the Camp": In life, prosperity and health and in the favor of Amon, your

good lord! May he (Amon) give you life, prosperity and health and very
many favors in the presence of gods and people, while you are alive, prospering and healthy [. . .] every single day.

The divine votaress of Amon, my mistress, has dispatched Horiutowy, this
fowler of migratory birds. He has been sent downstream to where you are,
following the fowlers of migratory birds. As soon as he reaches you, you
shall commit them to his charge, but don't let him depart. Give him men who
are fit for assignment, namely, the reliable men who were in his charge once
before. And dispatch him so as to send him on very speedily without letting
him delay. See, it was in the second month of the second season, day 15, that
I dispatched him so as to send him on to you. Mark the date when you shall
dispatch him to have him return south and put it in writing in your letter
which you shall have him bring.

Address: [Name lost to] the god's [father] priest and temple scribe
Horpenese of "He of the Camp."

The High Priest of Amon's Illness

337. P. Strassburg 21
(Dynasty 21: Pontificate of Masahert)

[*Beginning lost* Masahert, the ser]vant [of] "He of the Camp," [who is] ill,
saying, "Preserve him, make him well, remove all illness that is in him completely in the presence of "He of the Camp," my lord, through his preserving
Masahert, making him well, granting him life, prosperity and health, a long
lifetime and a ripe old age, and hearkening to the plea of Masahert, his
(Amon's) son and his (Amon's) ward." And may he preserve (my) brother, this
servant of his, make him well and give him back to me by (my) petition just
like every good [turn] that my lord has done [for me].

Address: This noble prophet of "He of the Camp," the great god residing
in [the Camp].

Amon's Good Planning

338. P. Moscow 5660
(Dynasty 21: Pontificate of Menkheperre)

[This noble prophet of "He of the] Camp," the great god residing in [the
Camp from] his (Amon's) [belo]ved son, the high priest of [Amon]-Re, King
of the Gods, the generalissimo of Upper and Lower Egypt, and leader
Menkheperre, who is at the head of the great armies of all Egypt.

I've taken note of the account of the good decisions [. . .] great [. . .] which he (Amon) has proclaimed apropos of me, and I [*End lost*].

======= Tillage Rights =======

339. *P. Berlin 8523*
(Dynasty 21)

The troop captain and scribe Shedsukhons of the Temple of Khonsu to the Kushite cadet Painebenadjed: In life, prosperity and health and in the favor of Amon-Re, King of the Gods, your good lord! May he (Amon-Re) give you life, prosperity and health. And further:

It was after I had told you I would not let you have further tillage rights that I returned to Ne (Thebes). But see, my wife, this mistress of my house, has said to me, "Don't withdraw this landholding from Painebenadjed's charge. Restore it to him. Let him cultivate it."

As soon as my letter reaches you, you shall attend to this landholding and not be neglectful of it. And you shall remove its halfa grass and plow it and farm one aroura of land [in] vegetables at this well. Now as for the person who may dispute with you, you shall go before Serdjehuty, this grain-reckoning scribe of the Temple of Osiris, taking this letter in your hand, since I have entrusted to him my holding of the fresh land and my holding of this mud flat as well. And you shall preserve my letter so that it may serve you as testimony.

Address: It is for the Kushite [cadet] Painebenadjed.

XII

Letters to the Dead
and to Gods

Introduction

In keeping with the Egyptian view that the afterlife was to a certain extent a prolongation of this life, it is not unusual that ancient Egyptians sought to communicate with deceased relatives. Egyptian letters to the dead were not written simply to convey greetings but were prompted by some unfortunate situation in which the writer or close relative has found himself. The deceased recipient or some other person in the beyond is charged with being at the root of these misfortunes. Letters to the dead have a legalistic flavor, for according to Egyptian beliefs there existed a netherworld tribunal, made up of deceased spirits, presided over by the Great God, that could be invoked to deal with cases involving the dead and the living. The deceased recipient of such a letter is either requested to desist from exerting malign influences or to institute legal proceedings in the beyond against a fellow spirit (*Akh*) suspected of creating problems for the writer. In an attempt to persuade the spirit, the writer frequently argues how well he has acted in the recipient's best interest, both in life and in death. Generally inscribed on bowls filled with some sort of offering, letters to the dead were deposited at the tomb, where the dead person would be sure to read the letter. The basic edition of most of the letters to the dead is that of Gardiner and Sethe (1928), a work penetratingly reviewed by Gunn (1930). French translations of the corpus of letters to the dead have been provided by Guilmot (1966) in his discussion of this epistolary genre.

Although letters to the dead have a long history extending from the Old Kingdom to the New Kingdom, letters to the gods appear to be a more recent development, first attested in the Ramesside period. They are basically petitions to a god cast in epistolary form. The practice became more widespread in the Persian and Ptolemaic periods. Letter No. 337, translated in Part XI, has been considered by Černý (1962: 46) to be a petition in letter form, addressed directly to the Amon of El-Hiba rather than to the god's priest. His reading of the address is not shared by Posener (1982a: 136).

======== **A Wife and Son to Her Deceased Husband** ========

340. *Cairo Linen CG 25975*
(Dynasty 6)

It is a sister (i.e., wife) who addresses her brother (i.e., husband), and it is a son who addresses his father:

Your condition is like that of one who lives innumerable times. May Ha, lord of the West, and may Anubis, lord of burial, help you, as we both (text: he and she) desire.

This is a reminder of the fact that Behezti's agent came for leather while I was sitting by your head, when Irti's (i.e., my) son Iy was caused to be summoned to vouch for Behezti's agent[1] and when you said, "Keep him hidden for fear of Iy the elder! May the wood of this my bed which bears me rot(?), should the son of a man be debarred from his household furniture."

Now, in fact, the woman Wabut came together with Izezi, and they both have devastated your house. It was in order to enrich Izezi that she removed everything that was in it, they both wishing to impoverish your son while enriching Izezi's son. She has taken Iazet, Iti, and Anankhi away from you, and she is taking away all of your personal menials after removing all that was in your house. Will you remain calm about this? I had rather that you should fetch [me] away to yourself so that I might be there beside you than to see your son dependent upon Izezi's son.

Awaken your father Iy against Behezti! Rouse yourself and make haste against him! You know that I [have] come to you here about litigating with Behezti and Aai's son Anankhi. Rouse yourself against them, you and also your fathers, your brothers, and your relations and overthrow Behezti and Aai's son Anankhi.

Recall what you said to Irti's (i.e., my) son Iy, "They are the houses of ancestors that need to be sustained," when you (also) said, "It is a son's house and then (his) son's house." May your son maintain your house just as you maintained your father's house.

O Sankhenptah, my father, may it please you to have Ini summoned to you in order to regain possession of the house of Anankhi, born to Wabut.

======== **A Son to His Deceased Parents** ========

341. *Kaw Bowl, interior*
(late Old Kingdom)

It is Shepsi who addresses his father, Inekhenmut:

This is a reminder of your going to the prison to the place where Sen's son Hetepu is when you brought the foreleg of an ox, when I, your son, came with Enwaf, and when you said, "Welcome to me, both of you. Sit down and eat meat." Is it in your presence that I am being injured by my brother even though there is nothing that I, your son, did or said? Although three *khar*-measures (i.e., thirty *hekat*) of Upper Egyptian barley were charged against him as a loan (from me): a bolt of cloth, a mace(?), six *hekat*-measures of Upper Egyptian barley, a bundle(?) of flax, and a cup,[2] and although he had done what ought not to have been done, I prepared him for burial, brought him back from the city of I . . . , and interred him among his necropolis companions. Since you had said regarding me, your son, "It is in my son Shepsi that all my property shall be vested," he has done this against me, your son, very wrongfully.

Now my fields have been taken possession of by Sher's son Henu. Now that he (my brother) is with you in the same city (of the dead), you must institute litigation with him since you have witnesses at hand in the same city. Can the man who wields the javelin be joyful while his rulers are repressed?[3]

342. *Kaw Bowl, exterior*
(late Old Kingdom)

It is Shepsi who addresses his mother, Iy:

This is a reminder of the fact that you said to me, your son, "You shall bring me some quails that I may eat them," and I, your son, then brought you seven quails and you ate them. Is it in your presence that I am being injured so that my children are disgruntled and I, your son, am ill? Who, then, will pour out water for you?

If only you might decide between me and Sobekhotep, whom I brought back from another city to be interred in his own city among his necropolis companions after tomb clothing had been given to him. Why is he injuring me, your son, so wrongfully, when there is nothing that I said or did? Wrongdoing is disgusting to the gods!

=========== **A Son to His Deceased Father** ===========

343. *P. Naga ed-Deir N 3737*
(Dynasty 9)

It is a servant who speaks unto his lord; it is his [son] Heni who says:

Attention a million times! It is profitable to give attention to one who cares for you on account of this which your own servant Seni is doing because of my, your humble servant's, being made to see him[4] in a dream in the same city (of the dead) [together with] you. Now it is his own character that has done him in, whereas it was not through action on my, your humble servant's, part that this which happened to him occurred, nor is it the end of all that can happen. Besides, it is not I who was responsible for inflicting wounds [against him]; others did it in my, your humble servant's, presence.

Indeed, let his lord take heed so that he (Seni) no longer creates disturbance. He should be guarded until he has ceased to visit me, your humble servant, once and for all.[5]

Address: The hereditary noble and count, the overseer of priests, Meru [from] Heni.

=============== To Two Deceased Parents ===============

344. P. Naga ed-Deir N 3500
(Dynasty 9)

A letter to Hetepnebi and Tetisoneb:

Haven't you observed these remonstrances? The two of you are there (in the beyond), while it is only for your own self-interest that each of you is diligent there. Both of you, preserve(?) your offspring! Indeed, seize hold of this dead man or this dead woman so that neither may regard a single fault of his because no one has been vociferous against the two of you there.

=============== A Son to His Deceased Father ▬▬▬▬▬▬▬

345. Chicago Jar Stand
(First Intermediate Period)

This is a reminder of the fact that I told you regarding myself, "You know that Idu said regarding his son, 'As for what may be in store in the beyond, I won't let him suffer from any affliction.' Please do the like thereof for me."

Now I have brought this jar stand over which your mother should institute litigation. May it be agreeable for you to support her. Moreover, let a healthy son be born to me, for you are an able spirit. Now as for those two maidservants, Nefertjentet and Itjai, who have caused Seny to be afflicted, confound them! And banish for me whatever afflictions are directed against my wife, whom you know I have need of. Banish them completely!

As you live for me, may the Great One (Hathor?) favor you and the face of the Great God be kindly disposed toward you and he give you pure bread from his two hands.

Furthermore, it is for your daughter that I am begging a second healthy son.

=========== **A Husband to His Deceased Wife** ===========

346. *Berlin Bowl*
(First Intermediate Period)

An offering which the king gives to Osiris and Anubis, who is upon his mountain, that invocation offerings may be made to the revered . . . tjat. It was without any discontentment on your part against me that you were brought here to the city of eternity. If it is the case that these injuries are being inflicted with your knowledge, see, the house is held by your children, and yet misery is renewed.

If it is the case that they are being inflicted against your will, your deceased father remains influential [in] the necropolis. If there is a reproach in your heart, forget it for the sake of your children. Be gracious, be gracious that all the gods of the Thinite nome might be gracious to you.

=========== **A Mother to Her Deceased Son** ===========

347. *Louvre Bowl E 6134*
(First Intermediate Period)

O Mereri, born to Merti (the writer), may Osiris, Foremost of Westerners, provide for you millions of years by giving you breath in your nose and by giving you bread and beer in the presence of Hathor, lady of the horizon. Your condition is like that of one who lives innumerable times by the command of the gods who are in heaven and earth. May you make obstruction against male and female enemies who are evilly disposed toward your household, toward your brother and toward your mother.

It is a mother who addresses her able son Merer[i]:

As you were one who was excellent upon earth, so you are one who is in good standing in the necropolis. For you invocation offerings shall be made; for you the *haker*-feast shall be celebrated; for you the *wag*-feast shall be celebrated; and to you shall be given bread and beer from the offering table of the Foremost of Westerners (Osiris). It is in the evening bark that you shall sail downstream, and it is in the morning bark that you shall sail upstream. To you shall justification be awarded in the presence of every god. Be in your own interest the most praiseworthy of my male and female dead. You know that he said to me, "It is I who shall report against you and your children." Report against this since you are in the place of justification.

============== A Sister to Her Deceased Brother ==============

348. *Hu Bowl*
(First Intermediate Period)

It is a sister who addresses her brother, the sole companion Nefersefekhi:
Much attention—it is profitable to give attention to one who cares for
you—on account of this which is being done [against] my daughter very
wrongfully, although there is nothing that I did against him.[6] I did not consume his possessions, nor did he have to give a thing to my daughter. It is
for the sake of interceding on behalf of a survivor that invocation offerings
are made to a spirit. So punish the one who is doing what is distressing to
me since I will triumph over whatever dead man or woman is doing this
against my daughter.

============== A Husband to His Deceased Wife ==============

349. *Letter on a Stele*
(First Intermediate Period)

A communication by Merirtyfy to Nebetiotef:
How are you? Is the West taking care of you [according to] your desire?
Now since I am your beloved upon earth, fight on my behalf and intercede
on behalf of my name. I did not garble [a spell] in your presence when I
perpetuated your name upon earth. Remove the infirmity of my body! Please
become a spirit for me [before] my eyes so that I may see you in a dream
fighting on my behalf. I will then deposit offerings for you [as soon as] the
sun has risen and outfit your offering slab for you.
A communication by Khuau to his sister:
I have not garbled a spell in your presence nor have I withdrawn offerings
from you. Rather I have emptied out(?) [for you my coffers(?)]. Fight on my
behalf, and fight on behalf of my wife and children.

============== A Man to a Deceased Relative ==============

350. *Cairo Bowl*
(early Dynasty 12)

What Dedi sends to the priest Iniotef, born to Iunakht:
What about the maidservant Imiu, who is ill? Aren't you fighting on her
behalf night and day with whoever, male or female, is acting aginst her? Why

do you want your domicile desolated? Fight on her behalf anew this day that her household may be maintained and water be poured out for you. If there is nought (i.e., no help) from you, your house shall be destroyed. Can it be that you are unaware that it is this maidservant who keeps your house going among people?

Fight on [her] behalf: Watch over her! Rescue her from(?) whoever, male or female, is acting against her. Then shall your house and your children be maintained. It is good if you take notice.

A Man to Deceased Relatives(?)

351. *Oxford Bowl*
(late Dynasty 17 or early Dynasty 18)

Addressed by Tetiaa, son of Neni:
Meniupu has come in flight. My father and my mother will support him since he is . . . from(?) his wife Teti. If he dies, my mother shall bury him, for it is her husband Neni who told her to bury him and to perform the duties of an heir for him.

A Husband to His Deceased Wife

352. *P. Leiden I 371*
(Dynasty 19)

To the able spirit Ankhiry:
What have I done against you wrongfully for you to get into this evil disposition in which you are? What have I done against you? As for what you have done, it is your laying hands on me even though I committed no wrong against you. From the time that I was living with you as a husband until today, what have I done against you that I should have to conceal it? What [have I done] against you?[7] As for what you have done, it is the reason for my laying a plaint against you, although what have I done against you? I shall contend at law with you in the presence with the words of my mouth, that is, in the presence of the ennead of the West, and it shall be decided between you and [me through] this letter because a dispute with you is what I've written about.

What have I done against you? I took you for a wife when I was a youth so that I was with [you] while I was functioning in every office and you were with me. I did not divorce [you], nor did I cause you to be vexed. Now, I took you (for a wife) when I was a youth, and I functioned in every important office for Pharaoh, l.p.h., without my divorcing [you], saying, "She has got

to be with [me]," so I would say. And when any visitors(?) came to me in your
presence, did I not receive them out of consideration for you, saying, "I will
do according to your desire"?

Now look, you aren't letting my mind be at ease. I shall litigate with you,
and right shall be distinguished from wrong. Now look, when I was instructing officers for Pharaoh's infantry and his chariotry, I [had] them come
and prostrate themselves before you, bringing every sort of fine thing to set
before [you]. I concealed nothing at all from you during your lifetime. I did
not let you suffer discomfort [in] anything I did with you after the manner
of a lord, nor did you find me cheating on you after the manner of a field
hand, entering a strange house. I did not let an upbraider find fault with me
[in] anything I did with you.

And when I was assigned to the post in which I now am,[8] I became unable
to go out as had been my habit. I got to doing what someone who is in the
same situation as I does when he is [at] home [regarding] your oil, your
bread, and your clothes; and they would be brought to you. I didn't direct
them elsewhere, but said, "The woman is still with me(?)," so I would say and
not cheat on you.

Now look, you are disregarding how well I have treated you. I'm writing
[you] to make you aware of the things you are doing. When you became ill
with the disease which you contracted, I [sent for] a chief physician, and he
treated you and did what you told him to do.

Now when I went accompanying Pharaoh, l.p.h., in journeying south, this
condition (i.e., death) befell you, and I spent these several months without
eating or drinking like a normal person. When I arrived in Memphis, I
begged leave of Pharaoh, l.p.h., and [came] to where you were. And I and
my people wept sorely for you before [you] (i.e., your body) in my quarter(?).
I donated clothing of fine linen to wrap you up in and had many clothes
made. I overlooked nothing good so as not to have it done for you.

Now look, I've spent these last three years without entering (another)
house although it is not proper that one who is in the same situation as I be
made to do this. Now look, I've done this out of consideration for you. Now
look, you don't differentiate good from evil. One will judge between you and
me. Now look, as for those sisters in the household, I have not entered into
a one of them (sexually).

=========== **A Husband to His Deceased Wife** ===========

353. O. Louvre 698
(Dynasty 21)

O you noble chest of the Osiris chantress of Amon Ikhtay, who lies at rest
beneath you, hearken to me and transmit my message. Say to her since you

are near to her, "What is your condition? How are you?" It is you who shall say to her, "Alas, [Ikhtay] no longer prospers," so says your brother (i.e., husband), your partner. Alas, you with the beautiful face, like whom there is no other, I have found no instance of [any] ugliness [on your part to] hold against you. I called at any time [upon] you too(?), and [you] answered [me in response(?)]. My mother, father, brother and sister are well disposed to me. They have come, but you have been taken from me so it is as serious as what I (text: he) have described(?).

Alas, Ikhtay no longer prospers, you whose [. . .] has been taken away [. . .] from me, while my(?) [townsfolk say], "The fool is still weeping for her," and while my(?) [. . .] embraces [. . .] without ever having become satisfied [. . .].

[Alas], Ikhtay [no longer prospers], you who apportioned your plot [and . . .] in three withdrawals(?) comprising fifty-two *oipe*-measures, after having divided your(?) [. . . to] make you satisfied with them.

Alas, [Ikhtay] no longer [prospers], you who brought your cattle home. They didn't let you do [. . . after] you had made an offering of their offspring.

Alas, I[khtay] no longer prospers, [you who looked after] our many fields, [. . .] took them(?) [. . .] did not [. . .] say(?) to do it.

O, Ikhtay no longer prospers; O, [. . .], when the sky (i.e., weather) was windy and waves of water [. . .] descend from . . . , while you were burdened with all sorts of heavy loads although there was no carrying pole with which to carry them nor a spot in which to set (them) down. They are in [. . .] your (text: her) partner [. . .] youngster [. . .] after your [. . .] had taken [. . .] village(?) [. . .] and the enclosure wall was built [for you(?)] while things proceeded according to your wish [. . .] did not see you.

Alas, Ikhtay no longer prospers, the [. . .] Ikhtay, you who have departed so that your role is [. . .] approaching the one who approached you [. . .] make to prosper [. . .] you (text: she) stopped [to] see them.

O Ikhtay, [you] who are gracious as a woman, you who have been taken away while you were at my side(?), you never held your brother (i.e., husband) back(?) in any . . . that were in your heart.

Statement by the necropolis scribe Butehamon to the chantress of Amon Ikhtay:

Pre has departed and his ennead following him, the kings as well, and all humanity in one body following their fellow beings. There is no one who shall stay alive, for we shall all follow you. If I can be heard where you are, tell the lords of eternity to let your brother (i.e., husband) come to [you] that you may be his support in their midst(?), be they great or small. It is you who should speak well within the necropolis since I committed no abomination against you while you were on earth.

So then may you grasp my situation. Swear to god in every manner saying, "It is according to what I have said that things shall be done." I won't deceive your heart in anything I have said until I come to you. [Behave] toward [me in] every good manner, if I can be heard.

============= **Letters to Gods** =============

354. O. Gardiner 310
(Dynasty 19: Ramesses II)

Addressed by Hornefer to his god Amon-Re, Lord of the Thrones of the Two Lands:

If I see that you let success be with me, I shall provide you with an amphora of date-brew of (the type of) Kode (Kizzuwatna) and also a jar of beer, and likewise my man (shall come) with [kylles]tis-loaves and white bread.

355. P. Nevill
(late Dynasty 20)

When I was looking for you (the god) to tell you some affairs of mine, you happened to be concealed in your holy of holies, and there was nobody having access to it to send in to you. Now as I was waiting, I encountered Hori, this scribe of the Temple of Usermare-miamon (Ramesses III's mortuary temple), and he said to me, "I have access." So I am sending him in to you.

See, you must discard seclusion today and come out in procession in order that you may decide upon the issues involving seven kilts belonging to the Temple of Haremhab and also those two kilts belonging to the necropolis scribe. The vizier does not accept these garments, saying, "It is because you must make up their number in full."

Now as for one who is in the same position as you, being in a place of seclusion and concealed, he sends forth his pronouncements, but you haven't yet communicated anything at all to me. See here, you let eleven (garments) accrue to the woman Eseye, your [devotee(?)], by your intervening on account of them, but now it happens that your pronouncements no longer come forth as though (confined in) the netherworld for a million years. Farewell!

Notes

1. Or, "to be commended to Behezti's agent," but the same expression with the dative occurs in Letter No. 67, where the translation "vouched for" is beyond doubt.

2. The value of the total loan is expressed in terms of Upper Egyptian barley, three *khur*-measures being approximately four bushels at this period.

3. Probably an aphorism.

4. Taking "him" to refer to Seni, who may be deceased because of the wounds inflicted on him. On the other hand, the "him" could be the writer, who uses the third person, "your humble servant," to refer to himself.

5. Seni visits the writer by means of dreams.

6. An unnamed malefactor.

7. Or possibly without emending, "What ails you?"

8. Or following the suggestion of Mr. Gary Greig, "And when you were placed in the tomb in which you now are."

Sources

In order to keep the list of sources of reasonable length, it has not been possible to include all editions and translations. In particular, partial translations have only rarely been indicated. For additional information on the papyri there exists the detailed bibliography of Bellion (1987), and Allam (1973a) provides excellent bibliographical data on many of the Ramesside ostraca. Under Editions are indicated the basic textual publications whether or not accompanied by translations. If no previous translation has been made, this fact is noted after Translation. The numbers in sequence correspond to the numbers assigned to the letters in the main portion of the book.

1. **Edition:** Posener 1951: pls. 1–21.
   Translations: Kaplony 1974; Barta 1978.
2. **Edition:** Sethe 1932–33: 179–80.
   Translation: Roccati 1982: 78–79.
3. **Edition:** Sethe 1932–33: 62–63.
   Translations: Breasted 1906–7: 1:273; Roccati 1982: 126.
4. **Edition:** Sethe 1932–33: 60–61.
   Translations: Breasted 1906–7: 1:271; Roccati 1982: 125.
5. **Edition:** Sethe 1932–33: 61–62.
   Translations: Breasted 1906–7: 1:272; Roccati 1982: 125.
6. **Edition:** Sethe 1932–33: 128–31.
   Translations: Breasted 1906–7: 1:351–53; Lichtheim 1973: 26–27; Roccati 1982: 206–7; Lalouette 1984: 171–73.
7. **Editions:** Sethe 1932–33: 300–1; Goedicke 1967b: 184–89.
8. **Editions:** Blackman 1932: 31–32; Barns 1952: unnumbered plates [6–7], pp. 18–21.
   Translations: Pritchard 1969: 20–21; Simpson 1973: 67–68; Lichtheim 1973: 229–30.
9. **Editions:** Blackman 1932: 33–35; Barns 1952: unnumbered plates [7–9], pp. 21–27.
   Translations: Pritchard 1969: 21; Simpson 1973: 68–70; Lichtheim 1973: 230–31.
10. **Editions:** Schäfer 1904: 9–14; Sethe 1924: 70–71.
    Translations: Breasted 1906–7: 1:663–65; Pritchard 1969: 329; Lichtheim 1973: 123–24; Lalouette 1984: 173–74.

11. **Editions:** Hayes 1955: 71-85, pl. 5; Helck 1983: 11.
    Translation: Théodoridès 1960: 113-16.
12. **Editions:** Hayes 1955: 72-85, pl. 6; Helck 1983: 12.
    Translation: Théodoridès 1960: 108-13.
13. **Editions:** Petrie 1896, pl. 8; Sethe 1924: 98; Helck 1983: 73-74.
    Translation: Breasted 1906-7: 1:773-80.
14. **Editions:** Habachi 1972: 39-40, pl. 7; Helck 1983: 94.
    Translations: Stadelmann 1965; Pritchard 1969: 555; Smith and
    Smith 1976: 61.
15. **Editions:** Sethe 1906: 79-81; Lacau 1909-26: 11-13, pl. 5.
    Translations: Breasted 1906-7: 2:54-60; Sethe 1914: 41-42.
16. **Editions:** Helck 1955; Helck 1955-58: 1343-44; Manuelian 1987:
    155-58.
    Translations: Helck 1961: 50; Cumming 1982: 45-46.
17. **Editions:** Griffith 1898: 1:91-92, 105; 2: pl. 38; Sandman 1938:
    147-48.
    Translations: Löhr 1975: 142-44; Wente 1980.
18. **Edition:** Černý 1930-35: 76*, pl. 74.
    Translation: none.
19. **Editions:** Tresson: 1922: 10, pl. 3; Kitchen 1968-: 2:359.
    Translation: Breasted 1906-7: 3:292.
20. **Editions:** Kuentz 1928-34: 312-19; Kitchen 1968-: 2:90-95.
    Translations: Gardiner 1960: 13-14; Lichtheim 1976: 71; Fecht
    1984: 321-22; Lalouette 1984: 118; Way 1984: 328-37.
21. **Editions:** Berlin 1911: pls. 31-31a; Kitchen 1968-: 3:145-46.
    Translation: Kitchen 1982: 132-33.
22. **Editions:** Janssen 1960: 39, 45-47, pl. 14; Bakir 1970: pls. 16-17 and
    XXII; Kitchen 1968-: 2:894-95.
23. **Editions:** Janssen 1960: 38-39, 44-45, pls. 8, 13; Bakir 1970: pls.
    15-16 and XXI; Kitchen 1968-: 2:911-12.
24. **Editions:** Janssen 1960: 37-38, 44, pls. 11-12; Bakir 1970: pls. 14-15
    and XIX-XX; Kitchen 1968-: 2:910-11.
25. **Editions:** Janssen 1960: 37, 42-43, pls. 9-10; Bakir 1970: pls. 12-13
    and XVII-XVIII; Kitchen 1968-: 3:232-33.
26. **Editions:** Janssen 1960: 36-37, 42, pls. 7-8; Bakir 1970: pls. 11-12
    and XVI; Kitchen 1968-: 3:231-32.
27. **Editions:** Janssen 1960: 35-36, 41, pl. 5; Bakir 1970: pls. 10-11 and
    XIV; Kitchen 1968-: 2:926-27.
    Translation: Kitchen 1982: 111.
28. **Editions:** Möller 1910: 12-13; Janssen 1960: 35, 40, pls. 3-4; Bakir
    1970: pls. 9 and XII; Kitchen 1968-: 3:230.
29. **Editions:** Möller 1910: 11; Janssen 1960: 36, 42, pl. 6; Bakir 1970:
    pls. 11 and XV; Kitchen 1968-: 3:231.

30. **Editions:** Janssen 1960: 35, 40-41, pl. 4; Bakir 1970: pls. 10 and XIII; Kitchen 1968-: 3:233-34.

31. **Edition:** Gardiner 1937: 15-16.
    Translations: Caminos 1954: 48-50; Erman 1966: 280; Assmann 1975: 497.

32. **Edition:** Gardiner 1937: 46-47.
    Translations: Caminos 1954: 176-81; Erman 1966: 203.

33. **Editions:** Daressy 1927: 174-75; Kitchen 1968-: 4:339.

34. **Editions:** Griffith 1898: 1:94-95; 2: pl. 39; Gardiner 1948a: 14-15.
    Translation: Gardiner 1953.

35. **Editions:** Helck 1967: 137-40, 147; Kitchen 1968-: 6:518-19.

36. **Editions:** Helck 1967: 144-45, 151; Kitchen 1968-: 6:522.

37. **Editions:** Helck 1967: 135-37, 146; Kitchen 1968-: 6:517-18.

38. **Editions:** Helck 1967: 140-44, 148-50; Kitchen 1968-: 6:519-22.

39. **Editions:** Pleyte and Rossi 1869-76: 1:89-92; 2: pls. 66-67; Möller 1910: 6-7; Bakir 1970: pls. 24-25 and XXXI; Kitchen 1968-: 6:734-35.
    Translation: Breasted 1906-7: 4:595-600.

40. **Editions:** Gunn 1925; Gardiner 1927.
    Translations: Grdseloff 1948; Roccati 1982: 293-94; James 1984: 165 (partial).

41. **Edition:** Simpson 1965: 20-21, pls. 7-7a.

42. **Edition:** Simpson 1965: 21-22, pls. 8-8a.

43. **Edition:** Simpson 1965: 22-23, pls. 10-10a.

44. **Editions:** Černý and Gardiner 1957: pls. 30-30a; Kitchen 1968-: 3:29-30.
    Translation: Vernus 1986: 145-47 (partial).

45. **Editions:** Gardiner 1913: 16d-e, m-o; Kitchen 1968-: 3:31.

46. **Editions:** Černý and Gardiner 1957: pl. 54 (3); Kitchen 1968-: 3:30-31.
    Translation: Allam 1973a: 167.

47. **Editions:** Gardiner 1913: 16b, f-g; Kitchen 1968-: 3:40-41.

48. **Editions:** Gardiner 1913: 16b-c, g-k; Kitchen 1968-: 3:41-43.

49. **Editions:** Gardiner 1913: 16d, k-m; Kitchen 1968-: 3:43-44.
    Translation: Kitchen 1982: 196 (partial).

50. **Editions:** Černý 1930-35: 120*, pls. 120-21; Kitchen 1968-: 3:44-45.
    Translation: none.

51. **Editions:** Černý 1937a: 1, pls. 1-1a; Kitchen 1968-: 3:45-46.
    Translations: Allam 1973a: 91-92; Kitchen 1982: 196.

52. **Editions:** Gardiner 1935: 1:24-26; 2: pls. 11-12a; Kitchen 1968-: 4:85-88.

53. **Editions:** Goedicke and Wente 1962: pl. 43; Kitchen 1968-: 4:178.
    Translation: none.

54. **Editions:** Černý 1930-35: 119*, pl. 119; Kitchen 1968-: 4:361.
    Translation: none.
55. **Editions:** Černý and Gardiner 1957: pls. 72 (2) and 115 (4); Kitchen 1968-: 5:583-84.
    Translation: Allam 1973a: 224.
56. **Editions:** Wente 1961; Kitchen 1968-: 5:559-60.
    Translation: Allam 1973a: 76-77.
57. **Editions:** Černý and Gardiner 1957: pl. 67 (1); Kitchen 1968-: 5:563-64.
    Translation: Borghouts 1982a.
58. **Editions:** Černý and Gardiner 1957: pl. 58 (1); Kitchen 1968-: 6:79.
    Translations: Allam 1973a: 163-64; Groll 1970: 99 (partial).
59. **Edition:** Černý 1986: 5, pls. 18-19a.
    Translation: none.
60. **Editions:** Černý 1978: 25-26, pls. 29-29a; Kitchen 1968-: 6:524.
61. **Editions:** Maspero 1875: 110-13 and unnumbered plate; Kitchen 1968-: 6:523.
62. **Editions:** Möller 1927: pl. 1 (2); Posener-Kriéger and Cenival 1968: 37, pls. 80-80a (A).
    Translations: Posener-Kriéger 1976: 2:451-65; Roccati 1982: 285-86.
63. **Edition:** Posener-Kriéger and Cenival 1968: 37-38, pls. 80-80a (B,C).
    Translations: Posener-Kriéger 1976: 2:465-72; Roccati 1982: 286-87.
64. **Editions:** Baer 1966; Goedicke 1967a.
    Translation: Roccati 1982: 291-92.
65. **Edition:** Roccati 1968.
    Translation: Roccati 1982: 289-90.
66. **Edition:** Posener-Kriéger 1980: 83-85, pl. 6.
67. **Editions:** Berlin 1911: pls. 2-3a; Smither 1942.
    Translation: Roccati 1982: 288-89.
68. **Editions:** James 1962: 12-31, pls. 1-4; Goedicke 1984: 38-76, pls. 4-7.
    Translations: Baer 1963: 2-6; Callender 1975: 121-22.
69. **Editions:** James 1962: 31-45, pls. 5-7; Goedicke 1984: 13-37, pls. 1-3.
    Translation: Baer 1963: 6-9.
70. **Editions:** James 1962: 45-50, pls. 8-9; Goedicke 1984: 77-85, pl. 8.
71. **Editions:** James 1962: 50-52, pl. 9; Goedicke 1984: 98-101, pl. 13.
72. **Edition:** James 1962: 80-83, pl. 21.
73. **Editions:** James 1962: 92-94, pls. 26-27; Bakir 1968.
    Translation: Lichtheim 1971: 69-70 (partial).
74. **Edition:** Frandsen 1978.

75. **Edition:** James 1962: 89-92, pls. 24-25.
76. **Edition:** James 1962: 94-97, pls. 27-28.
77. **Edition:** James 1962: 98-101, pl. 30.
78. **Edition:** Griffith 1898: 1:67-70, 2: pls. 27-28.
79. **Edition:** Smither 1945: 6-7, pls. 2-2a.
80. **Edition:** Smither 1945: 7-8, pls. 3-4a.
81. **Edition:** Smither 1945: 8-9, pls. 4-5a.
82. **Edition:** Smither 1945: 9, pls. 5-5a.
83. **Edition:** Smither 1945: 10, pls. 6-6a.
84. **Editions:** Borchardt 1899: 99; Möller 1909: 19; Sethe 1924: 96-97.
    Translation: Redford 1986: 97-98.
85. **Editions:** Borchardt 1899: 97; Möller 1909: 18; Sethe 1924: 96;
    Gardiner 1957: 255-56.
86. **Editions:** Borchardt 1899: 98; Möller 1909: 18; Sethe 1924: 97.
87. **Editions:** Borchardt 1899: 91; Möller 1909: 18; Sethe 1924: 97;
    Möller 1927, pl. 4.
88. **Edition:** Scharff 1924: 27-28, pl. 2.
89. **Edition:** Scharff 1924: 28-30, pls. 3-4.
    Translation: Biedenkopf-Ziehner 1983: 161.
90. **Editions:** Scharff 1924: 24-27, pl. 1; Möller 1927: pl. 5.
91. **Edition:** Scharff 1924: 35-36, pl. 8.
    Translation: Green 1987: 54-55.
92. **Edition:** Scharff 1924: 32-33, pls. 5-6.
93. **Edition:** Scharff 1924: 33-35, pls. 6-7.
94. **Editions:** Scharff 1924: 30-31, pls. 4-5; Luft 1983.
95. **Edition:** Möller 1909: pl. 20.
    Translation: none.
96. **Edition:** Grdseloff 1949.
97. **Edition:** Griffith 1898: 1:75; 2: pl. 31.
98. **Editions:** Griffith 1898: 1:72; 2: pl. 29; Möller 1909: 19; Sethe
    1924: 97.
99. **Edition:** Griffith 1898: 1:73-74; 2: pls. 30-31.
100. **Edition:** Griffith 1898: 1:77-78; 2: pl. 33.
101. **Edition:** Griffith 1898: 1:75-76; 2: pl. 32.
102. **Edition:** Griffith 1898: 1:78-79; 2: pl. 34.
103. **Edition:** Griffith 1898: 1:70-71; 2: pl. 28.
104. **Edition:** Griffith 1898: 1:72-73; 2: pl. 30.
105. **Edition:** Griffith 1898: 1:76-77; 2: pl. 32.
106. **Edition:** Griffith 1898: 1:71-72; 2: pl. 29.
107. **Edition:** Griffith 1898: 1:79; 2: pl. 35.
108. **Edition:** Griffith 1898: 1:82-83; 2: pl. 37.
109. **Edition:** Griffith 1898: 1:78; 2: pl. 34.
110. **Edition:** Griffith 1898: 1:80; 2: pl. 35.

111. **Editions:** Hayes 1957: 81, 89–90, pl. 13 (2); Hayes 1959: 178, fig. 99.
112. **Edition:** Hayes 1960: 35, pls. 10–10a (No. 7).
113. **Edition:** Glanville 1928: 297–302, pls. 31–32, 35.
Translation: James 1984: 174–75.
114. **Edition:** Glanville 1928: 303–4, pls. 32–33, 35.
Translation: James 1984: 172.
115. **Edition:** Glanville 1928: 304–6, pls. 33, 35.
Translation: James 1984: 176.
116. **Edition:** Peet 1926: 70–71, pl. 17.
Translation: James 1984: 175 (partial).
117. **Edition:** Peet 1926: 71–72, pl. 17.
Translations: Green 1980: 46–47 (partial); James 1984: 176.
118. **Edition:** Caminos 1963.
Translations: James 1984: 178; Manuelian 1987: 161.
119. **Edition:** Berlin 1911: pls. 30–30a.
Translation: none.
120. **Editions:** Berlin 1911: pls. 30–30a; Černý and Gardiner 1957, pl. 42 (4).
Translation: none.
121. **Edition:** Černý 1930–35: 74*, pl. 71.
Translation: none.
122. **Edition:** Černý 1930–35: 74*, pl. 71.
Translation: Kroeber 1970: 126 (partial).
123. **Edition:** Peet 1930: 82–91, pls. 18–19, 22–25, 30.
124. **Edition:** Peet 1930: 92–97, pls. 20–21, 26–30.
125. **Edition:** Pendlebury 1951: 1:160–61; 2: pl. 84.
126. **Edition:** Pendlebury 1951: 1:161; 2: pl. 84.
127. **Edition:** Pendlebury 1951: 1:161; 2: pl. 84.
128. **Edition:** Gardiner and Sethe 1928: 27–28, pl. 9.
129. **Editions:** British Museum 1842: pls. 35–62; Gardiner 1911: 1*–34*, 2–81; Fischer-Elfert 1983.
Translations: Erman 1966: 214–34; Pritchard 1969: 475–79 (partial); Fischer-Elfert 1986.
130. **Editions:** Möller 1910: 8; Allam 1973b: pl. 86; Kitchen 1968–: 1:238.
Translations: Helck 1960–69: 501; Allam 1973a: 287–89.
131. **Editions:** Bakir 1970: pls. 6 and VIII; Kitchen 1968–: 3:156; Allam 1985: 24–28, pls. 3–4.
Translation: Helck 1960–69: 483.
132. **Editions:** Barns 1948: 35–40, pls. 9–10; Kitchen 1968–: 1:239–40.
133. **Editions:** Bakir 1970: pls. 1 and I–II; Kitchen 1968–: 1:322; Allam 1987: 5–12, pls. 1–2.
Translation: Kitchen 1982: 140 (partial).

134. **Editions:** Bakir 1970: pls. 2-3 and III-IV; Kitchen 1968-: 1:323-24; Allam 1987: 13-20, pls. 3-4.

135. **Editions:** Bakir 1970: pls. 3-4 and V-VI; Kitchen 1968-: 1:324-25; Allam 1987: 20-24, pl. 5.

136. **Editions:** Gunn 1933: 1:94; 2: pls. 90, 92; Kitchen 1968-: 1:128.

137. **Editions:** Lieblein 1873: 31-34, pl. 6; Bakir 1970; pls. 19 and XXV; Kitchen 1968-: 3:489-90.

138. **Editions:** Lieblein 1873: 34-35, pls. 6-7; Bakir 1970: pls. 19-20 and XXVI; Kitchen 1968-: 3:490.

139. **Editions:** Bakir 1970: pls. 4-5 and VII; Kitchen 1968-: 3:254-55; Allam 1985: 19-23, pls. 1-2.

140. **Editions:** Bakir 1970: pls. 6-7 and IX; Kitchen 1968-: 3:251-52; Allam 1983.

141. **Editions:** Černý and Gardiner 1957: pls. 81-82; Kitchen 1968-: 3:138-40.
Translations: Helck 1960-69: 467-68; Kitchen 1982: 131-32 (partial).

142. **Editions:** Černý and Gardiner 1957: pl. 107; Kitchen 1968-: 3:637-39.
Translation: none.

143. **Editions:** British Museum 1842: pls. 140-42; Bakir 1970: pls. 28-32 and XXXVI-XXXVII; Kitchen 1968-: 3:499-504.
Translation: Groll 1982: 17-26 (partial).

144. **Editions:** British Museum 1842: pl. 143; Bakir 1970: pls. 32-35 and XXXVIII; Kitchen 1968-: 3:504-8.
Translation: none.

145. **Editions:** Bakir 1970: pls. 17-18 and XXIII-XXIV; Kitchen 1968-: 3:250-51.
Translation: none.

146. **Editions:** Pleyte and Rossi 1869-76: 1:26-27; 2: pl. 16; Möller 1910: 7-8; Bakir 1970; pls. 26-27 and XXXIII.
Translation: Allam 1973a: 318-19.

147. **Editions:** Möller 1910: 9-11; Wolf 1930; Kitchen 1968-: 4:78-81.
Translation: Gardiner 1948b: 115 (partial).

148. **Edition:** Černý and Gardiner 1957: pl. 90.
Translation: Känel 1984: 66-69.

149. **Edition:** Černý 1986: 7, pls. 23-23a.
Translation: none.

150. **Editions:** Grdseloff 1942: 35-39, pls. 7-8; Goedicke and Wente 1962: pl. 93.

151. **Editions:** Maspero 1870: 49-51, pls. 3-4; Bakir 1970: pls. 21 and XXVII-XXVIII; Kitchen 1968-: 6:65-66.

152. **Editions:** Maspero 1870: 51-53, pls. 5-6; Bakir 1970: pls. 22-23 and XXIX-XXX; Kitchen 1968-: 6:67-68.
     Translation: Helck 1960-69: 943 (partial).
153. **Edition:** Posener-Kriéger 1978.
154. **Edition:** Edwards 1982: 127-32, pl. 12.
155. **Edition:** Gardiner 1950: 125-27, 132-33.
156. **Editions:** Gardiner 1948a: 72-73; Gardiner 1950: 115-24, 128-31.
     Translation: Gardiner 1948b: 205-6.
157. **Editions:** Černý 1930-35: 92*, pl. 94; Kitchen 1968-: 3:573.
     Translation: none.
158. **Edition:** Eyre 1984.
159. **Edition:** Černý 1951: 26, pl. 26.
     Translation: none.
160. **Editions:** Berlin 1911: pls. 32-32a, Kitchen 1968-: 3:161.
     Translation: Kitchen 1982: 125.
161. **Edition:** Černý 1951: 6, pl. 5.
     Translation: none.
162. **Edition:** Allam 1973b: pl. 97.
     Translation: Vernus 1986: 146 (partial).
163. **Editions:** Černý 1951: 24, pl. 23; Kitchen 1968-: 6:156.
     Translation: none.
164. **Edition:** Černý 1986: 5, pls. 20-20a.
     Translation: none.
165. **Editions:** Pleyte and Rossi 1869-76: 2, pls. 112-13; Bakir 1970: pls. 27 and XXXIV-XXXV.
     Translation: none.
166. **Edition:** Černý 1937b: 9, pl. 16.
     Translation: none.
167. **Editions:** Černý 1939a: 23-24, pl. 29; Kitchen 1968-: 3:535.
     Translations: Allam 1973a: 116-17; Kitchen 1982: 193.
168. **Editions:** Allam 1981; Kitchen 1968-: 7:194.
169. **Editions:** Pleyte and Rossi 1869-76: 1:167-68; 2: pl. 128; Bakir 1970: pls. 25-26 and XXXII; Allam 1973b: pl. 111; Kitchen 1968-: 6:598-99.
     Translation: Allam 1973a: 317-18.
170. **Editions:** Ayrton, Currelly, and Weigall 1904: 38, pls. 54-55; Černý 1930-35: 75*, pl. 72.
     Translation: Allam 1973a: 67-68.
171. **Edition:** Kitchen 1968-: 7:200-1.
     Translation: none.
172. **Editions:** Černý 1937a: 4, pl. 8; Kitchen 1968-: 3:557.
     Translations: Helck 1960-69: 661 (partial); Allam 1973a: 97-98; Kitchen 1982: 199.

173. **Edition:** Sauneron 1959: 1, pls. 1-1a.
     Translation: Allam 1973a: 126.
174. **Editions:** Černý 1937a: 3-4, pls. 6-7; Kitchen 1968-: 5:565-66.
     Translation: Allam 1973a: 95-96.
175. **Editions:** Černý 1939a: 2, pl. 2; Kitchen 1968-: 5:566.
     Translation: Walsem 1982: 193-95.
176. **Editions:** Černý 1939a: 2, pl. 2; Kitchen 1968-: 5:566.
     Translation: none.
177. **Editions:** Černý and Gardiner 1957, pl. 18 (1); Kitchen 1968-:
     6:211.
     Translation: Allam 1973a: 152-53.
178. **Edition:** Černý 1978: 13-15, pls. 18-18a.
179. **Edition:** Černý 1978: 26, pls. 30-30a.
     Translation: Posener 1982b.
180. **Edition:** Černý 1930-35: 91*, pl. 93.
     Translation: Borghouts 1980: 33 n. 3.
181. **Edition:** Černý 1937a: 5, pl. 9.
     Translation: Allam 1973a: 98.
182. **Edition:** Černý 1939a: 3, pl. 3.
     Translations: Edwards 1960: 1:xxii n. 4; Allam 1973a: 112; Green
     1979: 113; Borghouts 1982b: 15.
183. **Edition:** Černý and Gardiner 1957: pls. 16 (1), 114 (1).
     Translation: Borghouts 1982b: 20.
184. **Editions:** Letellier 1980; Kitchen 1968-: 7:257-58.
185. **Editions:** Berlin 1911: pls. 35-35a; Kitchen 1968-: 3:532-33.
     Translation: Posener 1982b: 122-23 (partial).
186. **Edition:** Kitchen 1968-: 7:214.
     Translation: none.
187. **Editions:** Sauneron 1959: 7, pls. 16-16a; Kitchen 1968-: 3:536.
     Translation: Allam 1973a: 137-38.
188. Unpublished.
189. **Editions:** Černý 1937a: 4, pl. 7; Kitchen 1968-: 3:532.
     Translations: Allam 1973a: 97; Green 1976; Kitchen 1982: 205.
190. **Editions:** Černý 1930-35: 47, 68*, pl. 63; Kitchen 1968-:
     4:330-31.
     Translation: none.
191. **Editions:** Černý 1939a: 20, pl. 21; Kitchen 1968-: 3:537.
     Translation: Kitchen 1982: 197.
192. **Editions:** Berlin 1911: pls. 38-38a; Kitchen 1968-: 3:545.
     Translations: Baer 1965: 141; Allam 1973a: 33-34.
193. **Editions:** Sauneron 1959: 3, pls. 6-6a; Kitchen 1968-: 3:658.
     Translation: Allam 1973a: 131-32.

194. **Editions:** Černý and Gardiner 1957, pl. 47 (2); Kitchen 1968–: 3:542.
    Translation: Allam 1973a: 166.
195. **Editions:** Černý 1939a: 13, pl. 13; Kitchen 1968–: 4:416.
    Translation: none.
196. **Edition:** Černý and Gardiner 1957: pl. 88.
    Translation: Allam 1973a: 48–49.
197. **Edition:** Kitchen 1968–: 7:190–91.
    Translation: none.
198. **Editions:** Sauneron 1959: 3, pls. 7–7a; Kitchen 1968–: 3:539.
    Translations: Allam 1973a: 132; Kitchen 1982: 198.
199. **Edition:** Černý and Gardiner 1957: pl. 23 (4).
    Translations: Helck 1960–69: 337; Allam 1973a: 242–43; Valbelle 1985: 238.
200. **Edition:** Černý and Gardiner 1957: pl. 70 (2).
    Translation: Allam 1973a: 246.
201. **Edition:** Černý 1939a: 8, pl. 8.
    Translation: none.
202. **Edition:** Černý 1951: 27, pl. 26.
    Translations: Allam 1973a: 124; Borghouts 1981; Kitchen 1982: 199.
203. **Editions:** Černý and Gardiner 1957: pl. 28 (3); Kitchen 1968–: 3:540.
    Translation: Satzinger 1976: 87 (partial).
204. **Editions:** Černý 1939a: 16, pl. 18; Kitchen 1968–: 3:534.
    Translations: Černý 1973: 337; Allam 1973a: 114; Kitchen 1982: 194.
205. **Edition:** Černý 1939a: 23, pl. 28.
    Translation: none.
206. **Editions:** Möller 1910: 9; Berlin 1911: pls. 33–33a; Kitchen 1968–: 6:155–56.
    Translations: Schott 1950: 114; Guilmot 1965; Černý 1973: 212–13.
207. **Edition:** Černý and Gardiner 1957, pl. 36 (3).
    Translation: none.
208. **Edition:** Černý 1937a: 4–5, pl. 8.
    Translation: none.
209. **Editions:** Černý 1978: 15–17, pls. 19–20a; Kitchen 1968–: 6:264–65.
210. **Editions:** Černý 1978: 18–19, pls. 21–21a; Kitchen 1968–: 6:265–66.
211. **Editions:** Černý 1978: 19, pls. 22–22a; Kitchen 1968–: 6:266–67.
212. **Editions:** Goedicke and Wente 1962: pl. 42; Kitchen 1968–: 6:254.
    Translation: none.

213. **Edition:** Černý and Gardiner 1957: pl. 42 (1).
     Translation: Allam 1973a: 245.
214. **Edition:** Černý and Gardiner 1957: pl. 33 (2).
     Translation: Allam 1973a: 201.
215. Edition: Černý 1978: 19, pls. 23-23a.
     Translation: none.
216. **Edition:** Černý and Gardiner 1957: pl. 27 (5).
     Translation: Allam 1973a: 154.
217. **Editions:** Černý 1951: 27, pl. 26; Kitchen 1968-: 3:639.
     Translations: Helck 1960-69: 696; Allam 1973a: 125.
218. **Editions:** Černý and Gardiner 1957: pl. 54 (4); Kitchen 1968-:
     3:533-34.
     Translations: Helck 1960-69: 938 (partial); Allam 1973a: 72-73;
     Janssen 1975: 510 (partial).
219. **Edition:** Sauneron 1959: 8, pls. 20-20a.
     Translation: Allam 1973a: 140-41.
220. **Editions:** Černý 1951: 29, pl. 27; Kitchen 1968-: 2:383.
     Translations: Kitchen 1978-79: 19-20; Kitchen 1982: 182 (partial).
221. **Editions:** Černý 1939a: 20-21, pl. 22; Kitchen 1968-: 3:537-38.
     Translation: none.
222. **Editions:** Černý 1937a: 2, pls. 4-4a; Kitchen 1968-: 3:538.
     Translation: Kitchen 1982: 192.
223. **Editions:** Černý and Gardiner 1957: pl. 32 (4); Kitchen 1968-:
     3:541.
     Translation: none.
224. **Edition:** Černý 1939a: 22, pl. 26.
     Translation: none.
225. **Edition:** Černý 1930-35: 81*, pl. 77.
     Translation: none.
226. **Edition:** Černý 1970: 13, pl. 21.
     Translation: none.
227. **Editions:** Černý 1937a: 1-2, pls. 3-3a; Kitchen 1968-: 3:540.
     Translation: Allam 1973a: 93-94.
228. **Edition:** Černý 1937a: 2, pls. 3-3a.
     Translation: Kitchen 1982: 198.
229. **Editions:** Černý 1937a: 4, pls. 6-6a; Kitchen 1968-: 3:543.
     Translation: Allam 1973a: 96.
230. **Editions:** Černý 1939a: 22, pl. 27; Kitchen 1968-: 3:538-39.
     Translation: none.
231. **Editions:** Černý 1939a: 17, pl. 18; Kitchen 1968-: 3:543.
     Translation: Allam 1973a: 114-15.
232. **Editions:** Černý 1937a: 5, pl. 10; Kitchen 1968-: 3:558.
     Translation: Allam 1973a: 99-100.

233. **Editions:** Černý and Gardiner 1957: pl. 69 (3); Kitchen 1968–:
     3:541–42.
     Translation: Allam 1973a: 247.
234. **Editions:** Grdseloff 1941; Kitchen 1968–: 3:542.
     Translation: Kitchen 1982: 193.
235. **Editions:** Černý 1939a: 22, pl. 25; Kitchen 1968–; 3:544.
     Translation: Allam 1973a: 116.
236. **Editions:** Černý 1937a: 2, pls. 4–4a; Kitchen 1968–: 3:535.
     Translations: Baer 1965: 140 (partial); Allam 1973a: 94–95; Sat-
     zinger 1976: 86 (partial).
237. **Edition:** Černý and Gardiner 1957: pl. 34 (3).
     Translation: none.
238. **Edition:** Allam 1982: 55–56, pl. 4.
239. **Edition:** Sauneron 1959: 3–4, pls. 8–8a.
     Translation: Allam 1973a: 133.
240. **Edition:** Černý and Gardiner 1957: pl. 35 (2).
     Translation: none.
241. **Edition:** Sauneron 1959: 11, pls. 25–25a.
     Translation: none.
242. **Editions:** López 1978: 41–42, pls. 48–48a; Kitchen 1968–: 4:436.
     Translation: none.
243. **Editions:** Goedicke and Wente 1962: pl. 59; Kitchen 1968–: 4:415.
     Translation: Allam 1973a: 213.
244. **Editions:** Černý 1937b: 10, pl. 17; Kitchen 1968–: 4:416.
     Translation: Allam 1973a: 106–7.
245. **Edition:** Sauneron 1959: 2, pls. 3–3a.
     Translations: Allam 1973a: 128–29; Davis 1973: 160 (partial).
246. **Edition:** Sauneron 1959: 4, pls. 8–8a.
     Translation: none.
247. **Edition:** Černý 1970: 5, pl. 9.
     Translation: none.
248. **Edition:** Goedicke and Wente 1962: pl. 44.
     Translation: none.
249. **Edition:** Černý 1937a: 5, pl. 10.
     Translation: Allam 1973a: 99.
250. **Edition:** Černý 1951: 6, pls. 5–5a.
     Translation: Allam 1973a: 117.
251. **Edition:** Sauneron 1959: 1, pls. 1–1a.
     Translation: none.
252. **Edition:** Černý and Gardiner 1957: pl. 46 (3).
     Translation: none.
253. **Edition:** Černý 1970: 1, pl. 2.
     Translation: none.

254. **Edition:** Sauneron 1959: 12, pls. 27-27a.
Translation: none.
255. **Editions:** Černý 1937a: 3, pls. 5-5a; Kitchen 1968-: 5:565.
Translations: Allam 1973a: 95; Davis 1973: 67-68 (partial).
256. **Edition:** Allam 1973b, pls. 10-11.
Translations: Allam 1973a: 35; Černý 1973: 351.
257. **Editions:** Černý 1951: 21, pl. 20; Kitchen 1968-: 5:567.
Translation: Allam 1973a: 121.
258. **Editions:** Černý and Gardiner 1957: pl. 45 (3); Goedicke 1963-64: 4, pl. 9; Kitchen 1968-: 5:563.
Translation: Allam 1973a: 255.
259. **Editions:** Černý 1939a: 25, pl. 32; Kitchen 1968-: 5:567.
Translation: none.
260. **Editions:** Černý 1937a: 1, pls. 2-2a; Kitchen 1968-: 6:448.
Translations: Allam 1973a: 93; Davis 1973: 143-44 (partial).
261. **Edition:** Černý 1951: 6, pl. 6.
Translation: none.
262. **Edition:** Černý 1986: 6, pls. 21-21a.
Translation: none.
263. **Edition:** Černý 1937a: 3, pls. 6-6a.
Translations: Groll 1970: 73 (partial); Bakir 1983: 82 (partial); Černý and Groll 1984: 318 (partial).
264. **Edition:** López 1980: 9, pls. 51-51a.
Translation: none.
265. **Edition:** Černý 1937a: 3, pls. 5-5a.
Translation: none.
266. **Edition:** Černý 1970: 10, pl. 18.
Translation: none.
267. **Edition:** Černý 1970: 16, pl. 24.
Translation: none.
268. **Edition:** Černý and Gardiner 1957: pl. 56 (4).
Translation: none.
269. **Edition:** Černý and Gardiner 1957: pl. 20 (6).
Translation: none.
270. **Edition:** Černý and Gardiner 1957: pl. 73 (2).
Translation: Allam 1973a: 243.
271. **Edition:** Černý 1951: 3, pl. 2.
Translation: none.
272. **Editions:** Sauneron 1959: 11, pls. 25-25a; Kitchen 1968-: 5:568.
Translation: Allam 1973a: 142.
273. **Editions:** Berlin 1911: pls. 39-39a, Kitchen 1968-: 5:564.
Translation: Allam 1973a: 27.
274. **Editions:** Berlin 1911: pls. 39-39a; Kitchen 1968-: 5:565.
Translation: none.

275. **Editions:** Černý 1951: 26-27, pl. 26; Kitchen 1968-: 6:157.
     Translation: none.
276. **Editions:** Černý 1951: 21, pl. 20; Kitchen 1968-: 6:156.
     Translation: Allam 1973a: 120.
277. **Edition:** Černý 1951: 7, pl. 6.
     Translation: none.
278. **Edition:** Sauneron 1959: 9, pls. 21-21a.
     Translation: none.
279. **Editions:** Černý 1951: 21, pl. 20; Kitchen 1968-: 6:254-55.
     Translation: Allam 1973a: 120.
280. **Editions:** Černý 1978: 23-24, pls. 26-27a; Kitchen 1968-:
     6:268-69.
281. **Editions:** Goedicke 1963-64: 2-3, pl. 3; Kitchen 1968-: 6:255.
     Translation: none.
282. **Edition:** Černý 1986: 1, pls. 1-1a.
     Translation: none.
283. **Editions:** Černý 1978: 20, pls. 24-24a; Kitchen 1968-: 6:671.
284. **Editions:** Černý 1978: 20, pls. 24-24a; Kitchen 1968-: 6:671-72.
285. **Editions:** Černý 1978: 21-22, pls. 25-25a; Kitchen 1968-: 6:672.
286. **Editions:** Černý 1978: 22-23, pls. 26-27a; Kitchen 1968-:
     6:672-73.
287. **Editions:** Černý 1978: 24-25, pls. 28-28a; Kitchen 1968-: 6:674.
288. **Edition:** Černý 1939b: 68-70.
     Translation: Wente 1967: 81-82.
289. **Edition:** Černý 1939b: 67-68.
     Translation: Wente 1967: 79-81.
290. **Edition:** Černý 1939b: 57-60.
     Translation: Wente 1967: 71-74.
291. **Edition:** Černý 1939b: 55-56.
     Translation: Wente 1967: 70-71.
292. **Edition:** Černý 1939b: 23-24.
     Translations: Roeder 1959: 305-9; Wente 1967: 44-45.
293. **Edition:** Černý 1939b: 42-43.
     Translation: Wente 1967: 58-59.
294. **Edition:** Černý 1939b: 41-42.
     Translation: Wente 1967: 57-58.
295. **Edition:** Černý 1939b: 1-2.
     Translation: Wente 1967: 18-19.
296. **Edition:** Černý 1939b: 27-28.
     Translation: Wente 1967: 46-47.
297. **Edition:** Černý 1939b: 9-11.
     Translation: Wente 1967: 27-31.

298. **Edition:** Černý 1939b: 37-39.
Translations: Wente 1967: 55-56; Biedenkopf-Ziehner 1983: 162-63.
299. **Edition:** Černý 1939b: 39-40.
Translation: Wente 1967: 56.
300. **Edition:** Černý 1939b: 35-36.
Translation: Wente 1967: 52-53.
301. **Edition:** Černý 1939b: 36-37.
Translation: Wente 1967: 53-54.
302. **Edition:** Černý 1939b: 53-54.
Translation: Wente 1967: 69.
303. **Edition:** Černý 1939b: 54-55.
Translation: Wente 1967: 69.
304. **Edition:** Černý 1939b: 34.
Translation: Wente 1967: 52.
305. **Edition:** Černý 1939b: 35.
Translation: Wente 1967: 52.
306. **Edition:** Černý 1939b: 37.
Translation: Wente 1967: 54-55.
307. **Edition:** Černý 1939b: 33-34.
Translation: Wente 1967: 51.
308. **Edition:** Černý 1939b: 7-8.
Translation: Wente 1967: 24-27.
309. **Edition:** Černý 1939b: 5-7.
Translation: Wente 1967: 21-24.
310. **Edition:** Černý 1939b: 13-17.
Translation: Wente 1967: 33-37.
311. **Edition:** Černý 1939b: 2-5.
Translation: Wente 1967: 20-21.
312. **Edition:** Černý 1939b: 71-74.
Translation: Wente 1967: 83-85.
313. **Edition:** Černý 1939b: 17-21.
Translation: Wente 1967: 37-42.
314. **Edition:** Černý 1939b: 31-33.
Translation: Wente 1967: 49-51.
315. **Edition:** Černý 1939b: 44-48.
Translation: Wente 1967: 59-65.
316. **Edition:** Černý 1939b: 21-22.
Translation: Wente 1967: 42-43.
317. **Edition:** Černý 1939b: 48-49.
Translation: Wente 1967: 65.
318. **Edition:** Černý 1939b: 28-30.
Translation: Wente 1967: 47-49.

319. **Edition:** Černý 1939b: 50–51.
     Translation: Wente 1967: 65–67.
320. **Edition:** Černý 1939b: 65–67.
     Translation: Wente 1967: 78–79.
321. **Edition:** Černý 1939b: 51–52.
     Translation: Wente 1967: 67–68.
322. **Edition:** Černý 1939b: 64.
     Translation: Wente 1967: 76–77.
323. **Edition:** Černý 1939b: 13.
     Translation: Wente 1967: 32–33.
324. **Edition:** Černý 1939b: 60–61.
     Translation: Wente 1967: 74.
325. **Edition:** Černý 1939b: 12.
     Translation: Wente 1967: 32.
326. **Edition:** Černý 1939b: 22–23.
     Translation: Wente 1967: 43–44.
327. **Edition:** Černý 1939b: 53.
     Translation: Wente 1967: 68–69.
328. **Edition:** Černý 1939b: 70.
     Translation: Wente 1967: 82.
329. **Edition:** Černý 1939b: 62.
     Translation: Wente 1967: 75–76.
330. **Edition:** Edwards 1982: 132–33, pl. 13.
331. **Edition:** Janssen 1988.
332. **Editions:** Spiegelberg 1917a: 20–21, pl. 1; Allam 1973b: pls. 104–5.
     Translation: Allam 1973a: 307–8.
333. **Edition:** Spiegelberg 1917a: 9–11, pl. 3.
334. **Edition:** Spiegelberg 1917a: 6–7, pl. 1.
335. **Edition:** Spiegelberg 1917a: 7–9, pl. 2.
336. **Edition:** Spiegelberg 1917a: 11–13, pl. 4.
337. **Edition:** Spiegelberg 1917a: 13–14, pls. 5–6.
     Translation: Černý 1962: 46.
338. **Edition:** Posener 1982a.
339. **Editions:** Möller 1910: 12; Spiegelberg 1917b; Allam 1973b: pls.
     76–77.
     Translations: Erman and Krebs 1899: 92–93; Théodoridès 1963;
     Allam 1973a: 274–75; Harari 1983: 51–53.
340. **Edition:** Gardiner and Sethe 1928: 1–3, pls. 1–1a.
     Translations: Gunn 1930: 148–50; Roeder 1961: 263–67; Guilmot
     1966: 9–11; Théodoridès 1976: 35–44; Roccati 1982: 295–97.
341. **Edition:** Gardiner and Sethe 1928: 3–4, pls. 2–2a.
     Translations: Roeder 1961: 273–77; Roccati 1982: 297–98.
342. **Edition:** Gardiner and Sethe 1928: 4, pls. 3–3a.
     Translations: Roeder 1961: 277–78; Roccati 1982: 298.

343. **Edition:** Simpson 1966; Roccati 1967.
    Translations: Fecht 1969; Gilula 1969 (partial); Simpson 1970: 62.
344. **Edition:** Simpson 1970.
    Translation: Goedicke 1972.
345. **Edition:** Gardiner 1930.
    Translations: Roeder 1961: 269-73; Guilmot 1966: 16-18; Brier 1980: 202.
346. **Edition:** Gardiner and Sethe 1928: 5-7, pls. 5-5a.
    Translations: Schott 1950: 148 (partial); Roeder 1961: 278-81; Guilmot 1966: 15-16; Fecht 1969: 114-15 (partial).
347. **Edition:** Piankoff and Clère 1934.
    Translations: Roeder 1961: 267-69; Guilmot 1966: 11-13; Brier 1980: 200-1.
348. **Edition:** Gardiner and Sethe 1928: 5, pls. 4-4a.
    Translations: Gunn 1930: 151-52; Schott 1950: 148; Guilmot 1966: 13-14; Simpson 1966: 43; Roccati 1967: 327.
349. **Edition:** Wente 1975-76.
350. **Edition:** Gardiner and Sethe 1928: 7-8, pls. 6-6a.
    Translations: Guilmot 1966: 19-21; Brier 1980: 204.
351. **Edition:** Gardiner and Sethe 1928: 26-27, pl. 9.
    Translation: Gunn 1930: 153-54.
352. **Editions:** Möller 1910: 13-15; Gardiner and Sethe 1928: 8-9, pls. 7-8; Schneider [1981]: 14, 45.
    Translations: Schott 1950: 150-51; Pestman 1961: 53-54 (partial); Roeder 1961: 281-87; Guilmot 1966: 21-26; Guilmot 1973; Brier 1980: 203-4.
353. **Edition:** Černý and Gardiner 1957: pls. 80-80a.
    Translation: Černý 1973: 369-70 (partial).
354. **Editions:** Černý and Gardiner 1957: 50 (2); Kitchen 1968-: 3:797.
    Translation: Allam 1973a: 190-91.
355. **Edition:** Barns 1949.
    Translation: Roeder 1960: 252-55.

Bibliography

Allam, Schafik
  1973a   *Hieratische Ostraka und Papyri aus der Ramessidenzeit.* In *Urkunden zum Rechtsleben im alten Ägypten:* Vol. 1, *[Text].* Tübingen: Independently published by Schafik Allam.
  1973b   *Hieratische Ostraka und Papyri: Transkriptionen aus dem Nachlass von J. Černý.* In *Urkunden zum Rechtsleben im alten Ägypten:* Vol. 1, *Tafelteil.* Tübingen: Independently published by Schafik Allam.
  1981   "Ostracon Berlin P. 12398." *MDAIK* 37: 9-13.
  1982   "Einige hieratische Ostraka der Papyrussammlung der staatlichen Museen zu Berlin." Pp. 51-61 in Staatliche Museen zu Berlin, *Forschungen und Berichte:* Vol. 22, *Archäologische Beiträge.* Berlin: Akademie-Verlag.
  1983   "Papyrus Boulaq XIV und die Silber-Schrift." *Die Welt des Orients* 14: 22-29.
  1985   "Trois lettres d'affaires (P. Caire *CG* 58056, 58058, 58060)." Pp. 19-30 in *Mélanges Gamal eddin Mokhtar,* vol. 1. Cairo: Institut Français d'Archéologie Orientale.
  1987   "Trois missives d'un commandant (Pap. *CGC* 58053-5)." *ASAE* 71: 5-25.
Assmann, Jan
  1975   *Ägyptische Hymnen und Gebete.* Zurich: Artemis Verlag.
Ayrton, E. R., C. T. Currelly, and A. E. Weigall
  1904   *Abydos:* Pt. 3 *1904.* London: Egypt Exploration Fund.
Baer, Klaus
  1963   "An Eleventh Dynasty Farmer's Letters to His Family." *JAOS* 83: 1-19.
  1965   "Temporal *wnn* in Late Egyptian." *JEA* 51: 137-43.
  1966   "A Deed of Endowment in a Letter of the Time of *Ppjj* I?" *ZÄS* 93: 1-9.
Baines, John, and C. J. Eyre
  1983   "Four Notes on Literacy." *GM* 61: 65-96.
Bakir, Abd-el-Moḥsen
  1968   "The Middle-Kingdom Cairo Letter: A Reconsideration (Papyrus 91061 = CGC No. 58045)." *JEA* 54: 57-59.

1970   *Egyptian Epistolography from the Eighteenth to the Twenty-first Dynasty. BdE* 48. Cairo: Institut Français d'Archéologie Orientale.

1983   *Notes on Late Egyptian Grammar: A Semitic Approach.* Warminster: Aris & Phillips.

Barns, John

1948   "Three Hieratic Papyri in the Duke of Northumberland's Collection." *JEA* 34: 35-46.

1949   "The Nevill Papyrus: A Late Ramesside Letter to an Oracle." *JEA* 35: 69-71.

1952   *The Ashmolean Ostracon of Sinuhe.* Oxford: Griffith Institute.

Barta, Winfried

1978   "Das Schulbuch Kemit." *ZÄS* 105: 6-14.

Bellion, Madeleine

1987   *Catalogue des manuscrits hiéroglyphiques et hiératiques et des dessins, sur papyrus, cuir ou tissu, publiés ou signalés.* Paris: Epsilon Reproduction.

Berlin, Königliche Museen zu

1911   *Hieratische Papyrus:* Vol. 3, *Schriftstücke der VI. Dynastie aus Elephantine, Zaubersprüche für Mutter und Kind, Ostraka.* Leipzig: J. C. Hinrichs.

Biedenkopf-Ziehner, Anneliese

1983   *Untersuchungen zum koptischen Briefformular unter Berücksichtigung ägyptischer und griechischer Parallelen. Koptische Studien,* vol. 1. Würzburg: Gisela Zauzich.

Bierbrier, Morris

1982   *The Tomb-builders of the Pharaohs.* London: British Museum Publications.

Blackman, A. M.

1932   *The Story of Sinuhe. BAe* 2. Brussels: Fondation Égyptologique Reine Élisabeth.

Borchardt, Ludwig

1899   "Der zweite Papyrusfund von Kahun und die zeitliche Festlegung des mittleren Reiches der ägyptischen Geschichte." *ZÄS* 37: 89-103.

Borghouts, J. F.

1980   "The Ram as a Protector and Prophesier." *RdE* 32: 33-46.

1981   "Monthu and Matrimonial Squabbles." *RdE* 33: 11-22.

1982a   "A Deputy of the Gang Knows His Business (*Hier. Ostr.* 67, 1)." Pp. 71-99 in *Gleanings from Deir el-Medîna.* Ed. by R. J. Demarée and Jac. J. Janssen. Leiden: Nederlands Instituut voor het Nabije Oosten.

1982b "Divine Intervention in Ancient Egypt and Its Manifestation (*b3w*)." Pp. 1–70 in *Gleanings from Deir el-Medîna*. Ed. by R. J. Demarée and Jac. J. Janssen. Leiden: Nederlands Instituut voor het Nabije Oosten.

Breasted, James Henry
1906-7 *Ancient Records of Egypt*. 5 vols. Chicago: University of Chicago Press.

Brier, Bob
1980 *Ancient Egyptian Magic*. New York: William Morrow.

British Museum
1842 *Select Papyri in the Hieratic Character from the Collections of the British Museum*. London: W. Nicol.

Bryan, Betsy M.
1984 "Evidence for Female Literacy from Theban Tombs of the New Kingdom." *Bulletin of the Egyptological Seminar* 6: 17–32.

Callender, John B.
1975 *Middle Egyptian*. Malibu: Undena Publications.

Caminos, Ricardo A.
1954 *Late-Egyptian Miscellanies*. London: Oxford University Press.
1963 "Papyrus Berlin 10463." *JEA* 49: 29–37.

Černý, Jaroslav
1930-35 *Ostraca hiératiques*. Cairo: Musée des antiquités égyptiennes.
1937a *Catalogue des ostraca hiératiques non littéraires de Deir el Médineh. Vol. 2. (Nos 114 à 189)*. DFIFAO 4: 1–24, pls. 1–53.
1937b *Catalogue des ostraca hiératiques non littéraires de Deir el Médineh. Vol. 3. (Nos 190 à 241)*. DFIFAO 5: 1–15, pls. 1–24.
1939a *Catalogue des ostraca hiératiques non littéraires de Deir el Médineh. Vol. 4. (Nos 242 à 339)*. DFIFAO 6: 1–26, pls. 1–33.
1939b *Late Ramesside Letters*. BAe 9: 1–81.
1951 *Catalogue des ostraca hiératiques non littéraires de Deir el Médineh. Vol. 5. (Nos 340 à 456)*. DFIFAO 7: 1–34, pls. 1–30.
1962 "Egyptian Oracles." Chapter 6 in *A Saite Oracle Papyrus from Thebes in the Brooklyn Museum [Papyrus Brooklyn 47.218.3]*. By Richard A. Parker. Providence: Brown University Press.
1970 *Catalogue des ostraca hiératiques non littéraires de Deir el-Médineh, Nos 624-705*. DFIFAO 14: 1–18, pls. 1–28.
1973 *A Community of Workmen at Thebes in the Ramesside Period*. BdE 50:1–383. Cairo: Institut Français d'Archéologie Orientale.
1978 *Papyrus hiératiques de Deir el-Médineh. Vol. 1. [Nos I-XVII]*. Ed. by Georges Posener. DFIFAO 8: 1–27, pls. 1–30a.
1986 *Papyrus hiératiques de Deir el-Médineh. Vol. 2. [Nos XVIII-XXXIV]*. Ed. by Yvan Koenig. DFIFAO 22: 1–7, pls. 1–24a.

Černý, Jaroslav, and Alan H. Gardiner
1957 *Hieratic Ostraca*, vol. 1. Oxford: Griffith Institute.

Černý, Jaroslav, and Sarah Israelit Groll
1984   *A Late Egyptian Grammar.* 3d ed. Rome: Biblical Institute.
Cumming, Barbara
1982   *Egyptian Historical Records of the Later Eighteenth Dynasty.* Fasc. 1. Warminster: Aris & Phillips.
Daressy, Georges
1927   "Quelques ostraca de Biban el Molouk." *ASAE* 27: 161-82.
David, A. R.
1986   *The Pyramid Builders of Ancient Egypt: A Modern Investigation of Pharaoh's Workforce.* London, Boston, and Henley: Routledge & Kegan Paul.
Davis, Virginia Lee
1973   *Syntax of the Negative Particles* bw *and* bn *in Late Egyptian. Münchner ägyptologische Studien* 29. Munich and Berlin: Deutscher Kunstverlag.
Edel, Elmar
1970   *Die Felsengräber der Qubbet el Hawa bei Assuan.* II. Abteilung. *Die althieratischen Topfaufschriften* 1. Band. *Die Topfaufschriften aus den Grabungsjahren 1960, 1961, 1962, 1963 und 1965.* 2. Teil. *Text (Fortsetzung).* Wiesbaden: Otto Harrassowitz.
Edwards, I. E. S.
1960   *Hieratic Papyri in the British Museum.* 4th Series, *Oracular Amuletic Decrees of the Late New Kingdom.* 2 vols. London: British Museum.
1982   "The Bankes Papyri I and II." *JEA* 68: 126-33.
Erman, Adolf
1966   *The Ancient Egyptians: A Sourcebook of Their Writings.* Trans. by Aylward M. Blackman. Introduction to the Torchbook edition by William Kelly Simpson. New York: Harper & Row.
Erman, Adolf, and Fritz Krebs
1899   *Aus dem Papyrus der Königlichen Museen.* Berlin: W. Spemann.
Eyre, Christopher J.
1984   "A Draughtsman's Letter from Thebes." *SAK* 11: 195-207.
Fecht, Gerhard
1969   "Der Totenbrief von Nag' ed-Deir." *MDAIK* 24: 105-28.
1984   "Das 'Poème' über die Qadeš-Schlacht." *SAK* 11: 281-333.
Fischer-Elfert, Hans-Werner
1983   *Die satirische Streitschrift des Papyrus Anastasi I: Textzusammenstellung.* Wiesbaden: Otto Harrassowitz.
1986   *Die satirische Streitschrift des Papyrus Anastasi I: Übersetzung und Kommentar. Ägyptologische Abhandlungen* 44. Wiesbaden: Harrassowitz.
Frandsen, Paul John
1974   *An Outline of the Late Egyptian Verbal System.* Copenhagen: Akademisk Forlag.

1978   "A Fragmentary Letter of the Early Middle Kingdom." *JARCE* 15: 25-31.

Gardiner, Alan H.

1911   *Egyptian Hieratic Texts*. Series 1: *Literary Texts of the New Kingdom*. Pt. 1. *The Papyrus Anastasi I and the Papyrus Koller together with the Parallel Texts*. Leipzig: J. C. Hinrichs.

1913   "Hieratic texts." In *University of Toronto Studies: Theban Ostraca*, pt. 1. Ed. by Alan H. Gardiner, Herbert Thompson, and J. G. Milne. London: H. Milford.

1927   "An Administrative Letter of Protest." *JEA* 13: 75-78.

1930   "A New Letter to the Dead." *JEA* 16: 19-22.

1935   *Hieratic Papyri in the British Museum:* 3d Series, *Chester Beatty Gift*. 2 vols. London: British Museum.

1937   *Late-Egyptian Miscellanies*. BAe 7. Brussels: Fondation Égyptologique Reine Élisabeth.: 1-142a.

1948a   *Ramesside Administrative Documents*. London: Oxford University Press.

1948b   *The Wilbour Papyrus:* Vol. 2, *Commentary*. Oxford: Oxford University Press.

1950   "A Protest against Unjustified Tax-demands." *RdE* 6: 115-33.

1953   "The Harem at Miwēr." *JNES* 12: 145-49.

1957   *Egyptian Grammar*. 3d ed., rev. Oxford: Griffith Institute.

1960   *The Ḳadesh Inscriptions of Ramesses II*. Oxford: Griffith Institute.

Gardiner, Alan H., and Kurt Sethe

1928   *Egyptian Letters to the Dead, Mainly from the Old and Middle Kingdoms*. London: Egypt Exploration Society.

Gilula, Mordechai

1969   "Negative Sentences in a Letter to the Dead." *JEA* 55: 216-17.

Glanville, S. R. K.

1928   "The Letters of Aaḥmōse of Peniati." *JEA* 14: 294-312.

Goedicke, Hans

1963-64 "Hieratische Ostraka in Wien." *Wiener Zeitschrift für die Kunde des Morgenlandes* 59/60: 1-43.

1964   "Diplomatic Studies in the Old Kingdom." *JARCE* 3: 31-41.

1967a   "Ein Brief aus dem Alten Reich (Pap. Boulaq 8)." *MDAIK* 22: 1-8.

1967b   *Königliche Dokumente aus dem alten Reich*. Ägyptologische Abhandlungen 14. Wiesbaden: Harrassowitz.

1972   "The Letter to the Dead, Nag' ed-Deir N 3500." *JEA* 58: 95-98.

1984   *Studies in the Hekanakhte Papers*. Baltimore: Halgo, Inc.

1988   *Old Hieratic Paleography*. Baltimore: Halgo, Inc.

Goedicke, Hans, and Edward F. Wente

1962   *Ostraka Michaelides*. Wiesbaden: Otto Harrassowitz.

Goldwasser, Orly
    1981   "Hekanakhte and the 'Boat Metaphor.'" *GM* 40: 21-22.
Grdseloff, Bernhard
    1941   "Une missive minuscule de Deir el Medineh." *ASAE* 40: 533-36.
    1942   *Les débuts du culte de Rechef en Egypte.* Cairo: Institut Français d'Archéologie Orientale.
    1948   "Remarques concernant l'opposition à un rescrit du vizir." *ASAE* 48: 505-12.
    1949   "A New Middle Kingdom Letter from el-Lāhūn." *JEA* 35: 59-62.
Green, Michael A.
    1976   "The Passing of Harmose." *Orientalia* 45: 395-409.
    1979   "*B3w* expressions in Late Egyptian." Pp. 107-15 in *Glimpses of Ancient Egypt: Studies in Honour of H. W. Fairman.* Ed. by John Ruffle, G. A. Gaballa, and Kenneth A. Kitchen. Warminster: Aris & Phillips.
    1980   "Notes on the Words *wšbt* and *šbt.*" *GM* 41: 43-50.
    1987   *The Coptic* share *Pattern and Its Ancient Egyptian Ancestors: A Reassessment of the Aorist Pattern in the Egyptian Language.* Warminster: Aris & Phillips.
Griffith, F. L.
    1898   *The Petrie Papyri: Hieratic Papyri from Kahun and Gurob.* 2 vols. London: B. Quaritch.
Groll, Sarah Israelit
    1970   *The Negative Verbal System of Late Egyptian.* London and New York: Oxford University Press.
    1974   Review of Edward F. Wente, *Late Ramesside Letters. RdE* 26: 168-72.
    1982   "Diachronic Grammar as a Means of Dating Undated Texts." Pp. 11-104 in *Egyptological Studies.* Ed. by Sarah Israelit-Groll. *Scripta Hierosolymitana,* vol. 28. Jerusalem: Magnes Press.
Guilmot, Max
    1965   "Une lettre de remonstrances, l'ostracon Berlin P. 10627." *Chronique d'Egypte* 40: 235-48.
    1966   "Lettres aux morts dans l'Egypte ancienne." *Revue de l'histoire des religions* 170: 1-27.
    1973   "Lettre à une épouse défunte (Pap. Leiden I, 371)." *ZÄS* 99: 94-103.
Gunn, Battiscombe
    1925   "A Sixth Dynasty Letter from Saqqara." *ASAE* 25: 242-55.
    1930   Review of Alan H. Gardiner and Kurt Sethe, *Egyptian Letters to the Dead, Mainly from the Old and Middle Kingdoms. JEA* 16: 147-55.

1933   "The Graffiti and Ostraka." In *The Cenotaph of Seti I at Abydos,*
           vol. 1, chap. 10; vol. 2, pls. 88-93. By H. Frankfort, A. de Buck,
           and Battiscombe Gunn. *Memoir of the Egypt Exploration Society*
           39.

Habachi, Labib
1972   *The Second Stela of Kamose and His Struggle against the Hyksos Ruler
           and His Capital. Abhandlungen des Deutschen Archäologischen
           Instituts Kairo. Ägyptologische Reihe* 8. Glückstadt: Augustin.

Harari, Ibram
1983   "La capacité juridique de la femme au Nouvel Empire." *RIDA,*
           3d Ser., 30: 41-54.

Hayes, William C.
1955   *A Papyrus of the Late Middle Kingdom in the Brooklyn Museum
           [Papyrus Brooklyn 35.1446].* Brooklyn, NY: The Brooklyn
           Museum.
1957   "Varia from the Time of Hatshepsut." *MDAIK* 15: 78-90.
1959   *The Scepter of Egypt,* vol. 2. Cambridge, MA: Harvard Univer-
           sity Press.
1960   "A Selection of Tuthmoside Ostraca from Der el-Bahri." *JEA* 46:
           29-52.

Helck, Wolfgang
1955   "Eine Stele des Vizekönigs *Wśr-Śt.t.*" *JNES* 14: 22-31.
1955-58   *Urkunden der 18. Dynastie.* Berlin: Akademie-Verlag.
1960-69   *Materialien zur Wirtschaftsgeschichte des Neuen Reiches. Abhand-
           lungen der Akademie der Wissenschaften und der Literatur in Mainz.
           Geistes- und socialwissenschaftlichen Klasse,* nos. 2 and 3 (1963), no.
           4 (1964), nos. 4 and 13 (1969). Wiesbaden: Steiner.
1961   *Urkunden der 18. Dynastie: Übersetzung zu den Heften 17-22.*
           Berlin: Akademie-Verlag.
1967   "Eine Briefsammlung aus der Verwaltung des Amunstempels."
           JARCE 6: 135-51.
1983   *Historisch-biographische Texte der 2. Zwischenzeit und neue Texte der
           18. Dynastie.* 2d ed. Wiesbaden: Otto Harrassowitz.

James, T. G. H.
1962   *The Hekanakhte Papers and Other Early Middle Kingdom Documents.*
           Publication 19. New York: Metropolitan Museum of Art
           Egyptian Expedition. 146 pp.
1984   *Pharaoh's People: Scenes from Life in Imperial Egypt.* Chicago:
           University of Chicago Press.

Janssen, Jac. J.
1960   "Nine Letters from the Time of Ramses II." *Oudheidkundige
           Mededelingen uit het Rijksmuseum van Oudheden te Leiden* 41: 31-47.
1975   *Commodity Prices from the Ramessid Period: An Economic Study of the
           Village of Necropolis Workmen at Thebes.* Leiden: Brill.

1986   "A Notable Lady." *Wepwawet: Research Papers in Egyptology* 2: 30-31.

1987   "On Style in Egyptian Handwriting." *JEA* 73: 161-67.

1988   "Marriage Problems and Public Reactions (P. BM 10416)." Pp. 134-37 in *Pyramid Studies and Other Essays Presented to I. E. S. Edwards.* Ed. by John Baines, T. G. H. James, Anthony Leahy, and A. F. Shore. London: Egypt Exploration Society.

Känel, Frédérique von
1984   *Les prêtres-ouâb de Sekhmet et les conjurateurs de Serket.* Paris: Presses universitaires de France.

Kaplony, Peter
1974   "Das Büchlein Kemit." In *Akten des XIII. Internationalen Papyrologenkongresses Marburg/Lahn, 2.–6. August 1971.* Ed. by Emil Kiessling and Hans-Albert Rupprecht. Munich: Beck.

Kaplony-Heckel, Ursula
1971   *Ägyptische Handschriften. Pt. 1. Verzeichnis der orientalischen Handschriften in Deutschland,* vol. 19/1. Wiesbaden: Franz Steiner.

Kemp, Barry J.
1989   *Ancient Egypt: Anatomy of a Civilization.* London and New York: Routledge.

Kitchen, Kenneth A.
1968–   *Ramesside Inscriptions: Historical and Biographical.* 8 vols. Oxford: B. H. Blackwell.

1978-79 "Some Ramesside Friends of Mine." *Journal of the Society for the Study of Egyptian Antiquities* 9: 13-20.

1982   *Pharaoh Triumphant: The Life and Times of Ramesses II, King of Egypt.* Warminster: Aris & Phillips.

Kroeber, Burkhart
1970   *Die Neuägyptizismen vor der Amarnazeit: Studien zur Entwicklung der ägyptischen Sprache vom Mittleren zum Neuen Reich.* Ph.D. dissertation, Eberhard-Karls-Universität, Tübingen.

Kuentz, Charles
1928-34 *La bataille de Qadech. Mémoires publiés par les Membres de l'Institut Français d'Archéologie Orientale du Caire* 55. Cairo: Institut Français d'Archéologie Orientale.

Lacau, Pierre
1909-26 *Stèles du Nouvel Empire.* 2 vols. Cairo: Musée des antiquités égyptiennes.

Lalouette, Claire
1984   *Textes sacrés et textes profanes de l'ancienne Egypte.* [Paris]: Gallimard.

Letellier, Bernadette
1980   "La destinée de deux enfants, un ostracon inédit." Pp. 127-31 in *Livre du Centenaire, 1880–1890, Institut Français d'Archéologie*

Orientale. Ed. by Jean Vercoutter. Cairo: Institut Français d'Archéologie Orientale.

Lichtheim, Miriam
1971   "On the Iterative Use of the Particle *mk*." *JNES* 30: 69-72.
1973   *Ancient Egyptian Literature. A Book of Readings:* vol. 1, *The Old and Middle Kingdoms.* Berkeley, Los Angeles, and London: University of California Press.
1976   *Ancient Egyptian Literature: A Book of Readings:* vol. 2, *The New Kingdom.* Berkeley, Los Angeles, and London: University of California Press.

Lieblein, J.
1873   *Die aegyptischen Denkmäler in St. Petersburg, Helsingfors, Upsala und Copenhagen.* Christiana: A. W. Brøgger.

Löhr, Beatrix
1975   "Aḫanjāti in Memphis." *SAK* 2: 139-87.

López, Jesús
1978   *Ostraca ieratici N. 57001-57092. Catalogo del Museo Egizio di Torino.* Serie seconda — Collezioni. Vol. 3, fasc. 1. Milan: Istituto Editoriale Cisalpino — La Goliardica.
1980   *Ostraca ieratici N. 57093-57319. Catalogo del Museo Egizio di Torino.* Serie seconda — Collezioni. Vol. 3, fasc. 2. Milan: Istituto Editoriale Cisalpino — La Goliardica.

Luft, Ulrich
1982   "Illahunstudien, I: Zu der Chronologie und den Beamten in den Briefen aus Illahun." *Oikumene* 3: 101-56.
1983   "Illahunstudien II: Ein Verteidigungsbrief aus Illahun: Anmerkungen zu P Berol 10025." *Oikumene* 4: 121-79.

Manuelian, Peter Der
1987   *Studies in the Reign of Amenophis II. Hildesheimer ägyptologische Beiträge* 26. Hildesheim: Gerstenberg.

Maspero, G.
1870   "Le Papyrus Mallet." *Recueil de travaux relatifs à la philologie et à l'archéologie égyptiennes et assyriennes* 1: 47-59.
1875   *Mémoire sur quelques papyrus du Louvre.* Paris: A. Franck.

Matzker, Ingo
1986   *Die letzten Könige der 12. Dynastie.* Frankfurt am Main, Bern, and New York: Peter Lang.

Möller, Georg
1909   *Hieratische Lesestücke für den akademischen Gebrauch:* Vol. 1, *Alt- und mittelhieratische Texte.* Leipzig: J. C. Hinrichs.
1910   *Hieratische Lesestücke für den akademischen Gebrauch:* Vol. 3, *Musterbriefe und geschäftliche Texte des Neuen Reiches.* Leipzig: J. C. Hinrichs.

1927   *Hieratische Paläographie:* Vol. 1, *Bis zum Beginn der Achtzehnten Dynastie.* Leipzig: J. C. Hinrichs.

Moran, William L.
1992   *The Amarna Letters.* Baltimore and London: Johns Hopkins University Press.

Peet, T. Eric
1926   "Two Eighteenth Dynasty Letters: Papyrus Louvre 3230." *JEA* 12: 70-74.
1930   "Two Letters from Akhetaten." *Annals of Archaeology and Anthropology,* University of Liverpool 17: 82-97.

Pendlebury, J. D. S.
1951   *The City of Akhenaten:* Pt. 3, *The Excavations of Tell El-Amarna during the Season 1926-1927 and 1931-1936.* 2 vols. *Memoir of the Egypt Exploration Society* 54.

Pestman, Pieter Willem
1961   *Marriage and Matrimonial Property in Ancient Egypt.* Leiden: Brill.
1982   "Who Were the Owners, in the 'Community of Workmen,' of the Chester Beatty Papyri?" Pp. 155-72 in *Gleanings from Deir el-Medîna.* Ed. by R. J. Demarée and Jac. J. Janssen. Leiden: Nederlands Instituut voor het Nabije Oosten.

Petrie, W. M. F.
1896   *Koptos.* London: B. Quaritch.

Piankoff, A., and J. J. Clère
1934   "A Letter to the Dead on a Bowl in the Louvre." *JEA* 20: 157-69.

Pleyte, W., and F. Rossi
1869-76   *Papyrus de Turin.* 2 vols. Leiden: Brill.

Posener, Georges
1951   *Catalogue des ostraca hiératiques littéraires de Deir el Médineh:* Vol. 2, fasc. 1 (Nos 1109 à 1167). DFIFAO 18: 1-16, pls. 1-35a.
1956   *Littérature et politique dans l'Egypte de la XIIe Dynastie.* Paris: Libraire ancienne Honoré Champion.
1982a   "Un papyrus d'el Hîbeh." *JEA* 68: 134-38.
1982b   "Un voeu d'abstinence." Pp. 121-26 in *Studies in Egyptian Religion Dedicated to Professor Jan Zandee.* Ed. by M. Heerma Van Voss et al. Leiden: Brill.

Posener-Kriéger, Paule
1976   *Les archives du temple funeraire de Néferirkarê-Kakaï (Les papyrus d'Abousir).* 2 vols. BdE 65/1 and 65/2. Cairo: Institut Français d'Archéologie Orientale.
1978   "A Letter to the Governor of Elephantine." *JEA* 64: 84-87.
1980   "Fragments de papyrus provenant de Saqqarah." *RdE* 32: 83-93.

Posener-Kriéger, Paule, and Jean L. de Cenival
1968   *Hieratic Papyrus in the British Museum:* 5th Series, *The Abu Sir Papyri.* London: British Museum.

Pritchard, James B., ed.
1969   *Ancient Near Eastern Texts Relating to the Old Testament.* 3d ed. Princeton: Princeton University Press.

Redford, Donald B.
1986   *Pharaonic King-lists, Annals and Day-books.* Mississauga: Benben Publications.

Roccati, Alessandro
1967   "Due lettere ai morti." *Rivista degli studi orientali* 42: 323-28.
1968   "Una lettera inedita dell'Antico Regno." *JEA* 54: 14-22.
1982   *La littérature historique sous l'Ancien Empire égyptien.* Paris: Cerf.

Roeder, Günther
1959   *Die ägyptische Götterwelt. Die ägyptische Religion in Texten und Bildern,* vol. 1. Zurich and Stuttgart: Artemis-Verlag.
1960   *Kulte, Orakel und Naturverehrung im alten Ägypten. Die ägyptische Religion in Texten und Bildern,* vol. 3. Zurich and Stuttgart: Artemis-Verlag.
1961   *Der Ausklang der ägyptischen Religion mit Reformation, Zauberei und Jenseitsglauben. Die ägyptische Religion in Texten und Bildern,* vol. 4. Zurich and Stuttgart: Artemis-Verlag.

Romer, John
1984   *Ancient Lives: Daily Life in Egypt of the Pharaohs.* New York: Holt, Rinehart and Winston.

Sandman, Maj
1938   *Texts from the Time of Akhenaten.* BAe 8. Brussels: Fondation Égyptologique Reine Élisabeth.

Satzinger, Helmut
1976   *Neuägyptische Studien: Die Partikel ir. Das Tempussystem.* Vienna: Verlag des Verbandes der wissenschaftlichen Gesellschaften Österreichs.

Sauneron, Serge
1959   *Catalogue des ostraca hiératiques non littéraires de Deir el-Médineh (Nos 550-623).* DFIFAO 13: 1-19, pls. 1-32.

Schäfer, Heinrich
1904   "Die Mysterien des Osiris in Abydos unter König Sesostris III: Nach dem Denkstein des Oberschatzmeisters I-cher-nofret im Berliner Museum." *Untersuchungen zur Geschichte und Altertumskunde Aegyptens* 4, 2: 1-42.

Scharff, Alexander
1924   "Briefe aus Illahun." *ZÄS* 59: 20-51.

Schneider, Hans D.
[1981] *Een brief voor Anchiry.* Zutphen: Uitgeverij Terra.

Schott, Siegfried
1950   *Altägyptische Liebeslieder.* Zurich: Artemis-Verlag.

Seeber, Christine
1979   "Kornbraut." *Lexikon der Ägyptologie* 3: 743–44.
Sethe, Kurt
1906   *Urkunden der 18. Dynastie.* Leipzig: J. C. Hinrichs.
1914   *Urkunden der 18. Dynastie. Übersetzung zu den Heften 1-4.* Leipzig: J. C. Hinrichs.
1924   *Aegyptische Lesestücke zum Gebrauch im akademischen Unterricht.* Leipzig: J. C. Hinrichs.
1932-33 *Urkunden des alten Reichs.* 2d ed. Leipzig: J. C. Hinrichs.
Simpson, William Kelly
1965   *Papyrus Reisner II: Accounts of the Dockyard Workshop at This in the Reign of Sesostris I.* Boston: Museum of Fine Arts.
1966   "The Letter to the Dead from the Tomb of Meru (N 3737) at Nag' ed-Deir." *JEA* 52: 39–52.
1970   "A Late Old Kingdom Letter to the Dead from Nag' ed-Deir N 3500." *JEA* 56: 58–62.
Simpson, William Kelly, ed.
1973   *The Literature of Ancient Egypt.* New ed. New Haven and London: Yale University Press.
Smith, H. S.
1976   *The Fortress at Buhen: The Inscriptions. Excavations at Buhen,* vol. 2. London: Egypt Exploration Society.
Smith, H. S., and Alexandrina Smith
1976   "A Reconstruction of the Kamose Texts." *ZÄS* 103: 48–76.
Smither, Paul C.
1942   "An Old Kingdom Letter concerning the Crimes of Count Sabni." *JEA* 28: 16–19.
1945   "The Semnah Despatches." *JEA* 31: 3–10.
Spiegelberg, Wilhelm
1917a   "Briefe der 21. Dynastie aus El-Hibe." *ZÄS* 53: 1–30.
1917b   "Varia: 10. Eine zurückgezogene Pachtkundigung." *ZÄS* 53: 107–11.
Stadelmann, Rainer
1965   "Ein Beitrag zum Brief des Hyksos Apophis." *MDAIK* 20: 62–69.
Sweeney, Deborah
1985   "Intercessory Prayer in Ancient Egypt and the Bible." Pp. 213–30 in *Pharaonic Egypt: The Bible and Christianity.* Ed. by Sarah Israelit-Groll. Jerusalem: Magnes Press.
Théodoridès, Aristide
1960   "Du rapport entre les parties du *Pap. Brooklyn 35.1446.*" *RIDA,* 3d Ser., 7: 55–145.
1963   "Propriété, gérance et mandat dans le *Papyrus Berlin 8523.*" *RIDA,* 3d Ser., 10: 91–113.

1976   "Le droit matrimonial dans l'Egypte pharaonique." *RIDA*, 3d Ser., 23: 15-55.

Tresson, Paul

1922   *La stèle de Koubân. BdE* 9. Cairo: Institut Français d'Archéologie Orientale.

Valbelle, Dominique

1985   *"Les ouvriers de la tombe": Deir el-Médineh à l'époque Ramesside. BdE* 96. Cairo: Institut Français d'Archéologie Orientale.

Valloggia, Michel

1976   *Recherche sur les "messagers" (*wpwtyw*) dans les sources égyptiennes profanes.* Geneva and Paris: Librairie Droz.

Ventura, Raphael

1986   *Living in a City of the Dead: A Selection of Topographical and Administrative Terms in the Documents of the Theban Necropolis. Orbis Biblicus et Orientalis* 69. Freiburg, Switzerland: Universitätsverlag.

Vernus, Pascal

1985   "Etudes de philologie et de linguistique (IV)." *RdE* 36: 153-68.

1986   "Etudes de philologie et de linguistique (V)." *RdE* 37: 139-47.

Walsem, R. van

1982   "The God Monthu and Deir el-Medîna." Pp. 193-214 in *Gleanings from Deir el-Medîna.* Ed. by R. J. Demarée and Jac. J. Janssen. Leiden: Nederlands Instituut voor het Nabije Oosten.

Ward, William A.

1985   "Late Egyptian 'r.t: The So-called Upper Room." *JNES* 44: 329-35.

1986   *Essays on Feminine Titles of the Middle Kingdom and Related Subjects.* Beirut: American University of Beirut.

Way, Thomas von der

1984   *Die Textüberlieferung Ramses' II. zur Qadeš-Schlacht. Hildesheimer ägyptologische Beiträge* 22. Hildesheim: Gerstenberg.

Wente, Edward F.

1961   "A Letter of Complaint to the Vizier To." *JNES* 20: 252-57.

1967   *Late Ramesside Letters. Studies in Ancient Oriental Civilization* 33. Chicago: University of Chicago.

1975-76   "A Misplaced Letter to the Dead." *Orientalia Lovaniensia Periodica* 6/7: 595-600.

1980   "The Gurob Letter to Amenhotep IV." *Serapis* 6: 209-15.

Wolf, Walther

1930   "Papyrus Bologna 1086." *ZÄS* 65: 89-97.

Glossary

Akuyta. A gold-mining region in the eastern desert of Nubia.

Amenophis. The Greek form of the name of King Amenhotep I, who was posthumously venerated as a god at Thebes.

Amon. The major god of Thebes and the preeminent deity in the New Kingdom.

Amon-Re. The solarized form of Amon.

Amon, United with Eternity. The Amon of Ramesses III's mortuary temple of Medinet Habu, with whom the deceased king was identified.

Ankhtowy. The western sector of Memphis.

Anubis. The jackal-headed god of embalming.

Anukis. A goddess of the First Cataract region, linked with Khnum and Satis.

aroura. A measure of area, equivalent to 2,756.5 square meters, or roughly two-thirds of an acre.

Arsaphes. The ram-headed creator god of Heracleopolis.

Aton. The solar disk that was the sole god of the heretic pharaoh Akhenaton.

Atum. The creator god of Heliopolis, considered as the evening form of the sun-god.

Ba. Often loosely translated "soul," the *Ba* was a manifestation of power of a deity or deceased person.

Byblos. The principal Lebanese seaport on the Mediterranean Sea.

Construction Site. The royal tomb under construction in the Valley of the Kings in western Thebes.

cubit. A measure of length equivalent to 52.5 centimeters.

deben. A weight of approximately 91 grams.

Deir el-Bahri. The site of Queen Hatshepsut's mortuary temple in western Thebes.

Deir el-Medina. The sector of the Theban necropolis where the village and tombs of the necropolis workmen were situated.

digit. A measure of length equivalent to 1.875 centimeters.

ennead. A grouping of deities, generally nine in number.

gezira. An Arabic term for land situated between the high and low water marks of the Nile, often an island.

God's Land. An expression designating lands outside Egypt, especially Punt, Arabia, and the Lebanon.

Great Place (of Pharaoh). The Theban royal necropolis.

Harakhti. The falcon god Horus as he relates to the horizon.

Hathor. A major goddess with bovine attributes, associated with the sun-god and also worshiped as a goddess of the necropolis.

hebnet-measure. A liquid measure of unknown size.

hekat. A grain measure equivalent to 4.8 liters.

hin. A measure of capacity equivalent to .48 liter.

Horus. The celestial falcon god, whose earthly manifestation was the king.

Iam. A land in the Sudan.

Ka. A vital force or persona, possessed by deities, kings, and humans.

Kadesh. A city located strategically on the Orontes river in Syria.

Karnak. The sector of Thebes where the Temple of Amon was situated.

Kedem. A territory located in the wooded hinterland of Byblos in Lebanon.

khanto-land. Crown land administered by a temple.

khar. A grain measure equivalent to 48 liters in the Eleventh Dynasty Hekanakht letters and to 76.8 liters in the New Kingdom.

Khatti. The Hittite kingdom in Asia Minor.

Khnum. A ram-headed creator god, especially venerated in the region of the First Cataract.

Khonsu. A lunar god, the third member of the Theban triad together with Amon and Mut.

kite. A weight equivalent to 9.1 grams.

Kush. The land south of Egypt comprising Nubia and the Sudan.

Maat. A goddess personifying order, harmony, justice, and truth, the daughter of the sun-god Re.

Maher-warrior. A soldier of officer status who served as a scout in preparing the way for the advancing army.

Maryan-warrior. A chariot warrior.

Medinet Habu. The site of Ramesses III's mortuary temple in western Thebes.

Medjay. A Nubian desert people who eventually served as police in Egypt during the New Kingdom.

Mereseger. Depicted in serpent form, this goddess, whose name means "She loves silence," was revered as the mountain peak that protected the Theban necropolis.

Min. An ithyphallic god of fertility with major cult centers at Akhmim and Coptos, but also revered as an aspect of Amon at Thebes.

Montu. The god of the Theban nome and patron of warfare.

Mut. The consort of Amon at Thebes.

Naarin. A Semitic designation for warriors.

Ne. Meaning "The City," this was the common designation of Thebes during the New Kingdom and later was the biblical No.

Nofretari. King Amenhotep I's mother, who was posthumously venerated as a goddess in Thebes.

nome. An administrative district, there being twenty-two nomes in Upper Egypt and twenty in Lower Egypt.

Ogdoad. The group of eight primordial deities, believed to be buried in the Eighteenth Dynasty temple at Medinet Habu in western Thebes.

oipe. A grain measure equivalent to 19.2 liters.

Opet. The ancient designation of the Temple of Luxor, to which the Amon of Karnak made an annual visit.

Osiris. The god who ruled the underworld and with whom a deceased person became identified.

phyle. A corps of priests that served in monthly rotation.

Pi-Ramessu-miamon. The great Ramesside capital in the northeastern Delta.

Place of Beauty. The Valley of the Queens in western Thebes.

Place of Pharaoh. The Theban royal necropolis, including the workmen's village of Deir el-Medina.

Place of Truth. The Theban necropolis, including the workmen's village of Deir el-Medina.

Pre. A New Kingdom designation of the sun-god Re.

Pre-Harakhti. The sun-god in falcon form.

prophet. A higher order priest.

Ptah. The primary creator god of Memphis.

Punt. A land yielding exotic products, probably Somaliland.

Re. The sun-god.

Residence. A term for the capital where the king normally resided.

Retenu. A designation of Syro-Palestine.

Sacred Marriage Chapel. A chapel where the symbolic union of the king with the goddess Hathor took place on the occasion of the jubilee.

Sakhmet. A lioness goddess, with a primary cult center at Memphis, but also broadly venerated as a deity who could both inflict and cure disease.

Satis. A goddess of the First Cataract region, linked with Khnum and Anukis.

setem-priest. A priest, clad in a leopard skin, who functioned in the Memphite cult and at funerals.

Seth. A god of confusion, who was represented as a fabulous animal and regarded as the antithesis of Horus. Despite his negative qualities, Seth was much venerated by Ramesside kings.

Sherden. An ethnic appellative applied to a person whose origin was from one of the mercenary colonies of Sea Peoples established in Egypt during the Ramesside period.

Sobek. A crocodile god, endowed with regenerative power through his association with water, possessing cult centers in the Fayum area and in Upper Egypt at Kom Ombo and Crocodilopolis.

Sokar. A Memphite falcon god of craftsmanship and of the necropolis.

Sopdu. A god of the eastern region who possessed a temple at Kahun.

Southern City. A designation of Thebes.

Stolist. A priest responsible for clothing the god's image.

Tatenen. The god of the deep earth, often combined with Ptah of Memphis.

Thinite nome. The eighth Upper Egyptian nome in which Abydos was located.

Thoth. A lunar god, depicted as an ibis or a baboon and regarded as the patron of writing.

Two Ladies. The goddesses of Upper and Lower Egypt, who appear as protectors in the king's titulary.

Village of Pharaoh. The workmen's settlement of Deir el-Medina in western Thebes

wab-priest. A lower order lay priest who served in the temple periodically.

West. The region of the dead.

Indexes

I. Deities

Amenophis, 50, 136, 139, 140, 150², 157, 160, 171², 179², 189, 191², 193, 193, 196, 197

Amon, 23, 26, 32³, 33, 37, 39, 45², 46, 48, 50², 66, 90, 113, 114, 117, 118, 119, 124, 125, 126, 127, 129, 130², 131, 133, 136², 137, 139, 140, 142, 144, 147, 150, 151², 154, 157, 158, 160, 162, 164, 166, 167, 173, 174², 175, 176², 177, 178, 179², 180, 181², 182, 185², 188, 189³, 191³, 192², 193², 194, 196, 197², 198, 199², 200², 201², 206, 207², 208², 217, 218

Amon-Harakhti, 175

Amon-Kamutef, 126

Amon-Pre-Harakhti, 182

Amon-Re, 29, 32², 33², 38², 39, 45, 50, 90², 91², 113, 117, 118, 125, 126, 127, 128, 129², 131, 134, 135, 137², 138, 140, 141, 142, 144, 146, 147, 149², 150, 152, 153, 155, 159, 160, 161, 165, 166, 167², 168, 169², 172, 174, 175, 176², 177, 178, 179², 180, 181², 182², 183, 185, 187, 188³, 191, 192, 194, 195³, 196, 197, 198, 199², 200, 201², 202, 207³, 209², 219

Amon-Re-Harakhti, 129, 131, 173, 174, 179, 180, 181, 182, 185, 186, 189, 196, 199, 207

Amon-Userhat, 187

Anath (f.), 127

Anubis, 69, 73, 100, 211, 214

Anukis (f.), 131, 195, 199

Arsaphes, 62, 63, 64, 87, 178, 180

Aton, 94, 95², 96

Atum, 23, 85, 90, 191, 197

Bastet (f.), 15, 100

Djed-pillar, 55

Edjo (f.), 109

Ha, 211

Harakhti, 128, 129, 169

Haroeris-Re, 23

Hathor (f.), 20, 23², 50², 56², 63, 65, 66, 70, 84, 101, 110 n.13, 130, 134, 135, 139, 167, 168, 169, 189, 193, 196, 197, 213, 214

Heket (f.), 85

"He of the Camp" (Amon of El Hiba), 206², 207², 208²

Horus, 23³, 26, 27², 45, 58, 65, 66, 79, 104, 105, 109, 126, 189, 191

Isis (f.), 34

Khentikhtai, 79

Khnum, 37, 131, 195, 197, 199

Khonsu, 29, 45, 50, 129, 134, 137, 141, 147, 150, 160, 169, 174, 177, 179, 181, 187, 188, 193, 194, 198, 201, 202, 209

Maat (f.), 28, 34, 39, 51, 102, 123, 145

Mereseger (f.), 140, 141, 158, 167, 169, 178, 189², 191, 193, 194, 198

Min, 21, 25, 26, 38, 154

Min-Horus, 23
Montu, 15, 23², 38, 60, 64, 65, 66, 87, 109, 110 n.18, 139, 148, 176, 185
Mut (f.), 29, 37, 45, 50, 129², 134, 137, 141, 147, 150, 160, 169, 174, 175, 177, 179, 181, 187, 188, 191, 193, 194, 198, 201

Nebetuu (f.), 175
Nefertum-Horus, 126
Nehemawayet (f.), 103, 135
Neper, 101
Nofretari (f.), 50, 136, 151, 179, 189, 191, 193, 197
Nut (f.), 23

Ogdoad, 189, 193, 194, 197
Onnophris, 100
Onouris, 104, 206
Osiris, 24, 209, 214², 217

Pre, 30, 34, 35, 36, 45, 46, 48, 124², 125, 129, 147, 164, 176, 181, 200, 218
Pre-Harakhti, 29, 31, 32, 33², 50, 113, 125, 128, 140, 150, 167, 169, 187, 193, 194, 197
Ptah, 15, 28, 29, 31², 32, 33², 34², 35, 45, 55, 62, 63, 64², 65, 91, 92, 102², 113, 116, 117, 125, 134, 151,

154², 160², 164, 166, 169, 176, 200
Ptah-Sokar, 126
Ptah-Tatenen, 123

Re, 18, 20, 22, 23², 25, 28, 30, 31, 34, 35, 46, 56², 90, 120, 123³
Re-Harakhti, 90
Re-Harakhti-Sopdu, 85

Sakhmet (f.), 70, 117, 126
Satis (f.), 131, 195, 199
Sekhayet-Hor (f.), 101
Selket (f.), 142
Seshat (f.), 90, 99
Seth, 33, 130, 141, 172
Shesmetet (f.), 70
Shu-Onuris, 100
Sobek, 65, 66, 70², 73, 76, 79, 81, 83, 85, 86, 140, 170 n.4, 177²
Sobek-Re, 23
Sokar, 69, 100, 126, 151
Sopdu, 23, 80, 85
Sothis (f.), 73

Tatenen, 29, 37, 123
Tayet (f.), 22, 101
Thoeris (f.), 143, 170 n.5
Thoth, 90, 91, 99, 102³, 103, 114, 123, 125³, 135, 165, 175, 178, 180

Wepwawet, 125

II. Selected Personal Names
(Principally writers, recipients, and rulers)

Aau, 64²
Akhenaton (King) (see also Amenhotep IV), 94, 95, 96
Akhpe, 117²
Ahmose, 90, 91²
Ameke, 154
Amenemhat, 94, 155
Amenemhat III (King), 70, 71², 72², 74², 75, 76², 77, 78, 79², 83

Amenemhat IV (King), 69, 80, 81
Amenemone, 160
Amenemope, 49, 100, 144, 165
Amenemwia, 157²
Amenhotep, 158, 179, 196
Amenhotep II (King), 27, 92
Amenhotep III (King), 96, 126
Amenhotep IV (King) (see also Akhenaton), 28²

Amenkhau, 51, 129, 130
Amenmose, 135, 142, 150, 163, 166, 167, 168², 169
Amennakht, 139, 150, 163, 167
Amenpanefer, 186
An, 160
Anurkhau, 46, 52
Ankhau, 156
Ankhef, 202
Ankhiry (f.), 216
Ankhtify, 70, 87
Ankhu, 24, 25
Apophis (King), 26
Apy, 28²
Au, 16²

Bakenamon, 124, 127
Bakenkhons, 127, 128, 202
Bakenmut, 178
Baki, 92, 93, 158, 159, 161
Bakkhons, 206
Bennakhtef, 137
Burekhtuinuf, 160
Butehamon, 179, 180, 185, 186², 187, 188, 189, 190, 192, 193, 194, 195, 196, 198, 199², 201², 202, 218

Dedi, 215
Dhutemhab, 120, 121, 122
Dhutmose (see also Tjararoy Tjaroy, Tjertja, Tjuroy), 112, 158, 178, 179, 180, 185², 186, 187, 188, 189, 190, 192, 196, 200, 201
Djashe, 69
Djedkare-Izezi (King) see also Izezi, 18, 19, 55, 56
Djehuty, 90
Djoser (King), 53 n.1

Ernute (f.), 32²

Gereg, 63

Harkhuf, 20²
Hat, 115, 116²
Hathor (f.), 33, 162

Hatia, 119
Hatshepsut (Queen), 90², 91², 92, 94
Hay, 50, 139, 140, 150²
Hekaib, 69
Hekanakht, 58, 60, 62
Hekanefer, 181, 182²
Hemenetjer (f.), 154
Hemesheri (f.), 185, 190, 192, 199, 201²
Hemnetes, 162
Heni, 212, 213
Henuttowy (f.), 174
Henutudjebu (f.), 156
Heramenpenaf, 186, 201
Herere (f.), 200, 201
Herunefer, 62, 63
Hetepe (f.), 60, 61²
Hetepnebi, 213
Hordedef, 103
Horemhab, 157
Horemsaf, 74², 75, 76, 77²
Horemsai, 56
Horemwia, 147
Hori, 36, 49, 91, 100, 118, 122, 134, 166, 176, 177
Horkhebe, 206
Hormin, 134, 135, 167
Hormose, 93, 145
Hornefer, 219
Horpenese, 206, 207², 208
Horwerre, 70
Huy, 117, 123, 148, 155, 161
Huynefer, 147

Iatib, 70
Idi, 21
Ikhernofret, 24
Ikhtay (f.), 217, 218
Imbu, 77, 78
Imisiba, 140
Inekhenmut, 211
Inerwau (f.), 141
Inetsu, 66
Iniotef, 215
Iniotef (King Nubkheperre), 25
Iniotefoker, 43, 44

Inpuherkhenet, 70
Inushefenu, 44
Ipi (f.), 60, 61
Ipu, 157
Ipuy, 127
Irer (f.), 82, 83
Iruremtju, 58²
Iryaa, 128
Irypersen, 83, 84
Irysu, 80, 81
Isis (f.), 157, 161
Isisnofre (Princess), 33
Iuferankh, 69
Iufersep, 69
Iy (f.), 212
Iye (f.), 147
Iyemiatib, 85, 86
Iyib, 79, 80²
Izezi (King) see also Djedkare-Izezi,
    18, 19², 20², 21, 55, 56

Kaha, 134
Kamose (King), 26
Kar (see also Karoy), 197, 198, 200²
Karoy (see also Kar), 195, 196
Kay, 65²
Kemny, 86²
Kenamon, 93
Kenhikhopeshef, 47, 48, 141, 149,
    163, 167
Kensety, 165
Kenyamon, 123
Kenykhnum, 183², 186
Kenymin, 163
Khabekhene, 137
Khaemwase (Prince), 31
Khaemwia, 152
Khau, 215
Khay, 31, 45, 46, 47², 128, 129, 140,
    142, 155, 157
Khemem, 81, 82
Khendjer (King), 24, 25
Khenememuskhet, 96
Khonsu, 50, 140
Khor, 159
Kinen, 25

Kynebi, 163

Maanakhtef, 52, 152, 167², 168²,
    169², 170 n.17
Maaninakhtef, 137
Maatptah (Prince), 31, 32
Maiseti, 114, 115, 116², 127
Masahert, 208
May, 96
Meh, 94, 95, 96, 113, 114
Mehy, 143, 158
Memi, 57²
Menkheperre, 208
Menmarenakht, 130
Mentuhotep, 90, 91
Mentuhotep (King Sankhkare), 58,
    60, 62, 63
Merenptah (King), 34, 48, 49, 124
Merenptah (Prince), 31
Merenre (King), 57
Mereri, 56, 214
Merirtyfy, 215
Merisu, 58, 61²
Meritaton (Prince), 94, 95³, 96
Meron, 130
Mermaat, 32, 33
Merrenakht, 58, 67 n.1
Mersuiotef, 34²
Merti (f.), 214
Meru, 213
Meryiotef, 32²
Meryre, 47, 143, 163
Mesha, 113
Minemhat, 25
Minhotep, 155
Mininuy, 46
Minmose, 126, 159
Montuhikhopeshef, 128, 129
Montumose, 143
Montuser, 43, 44
Montusu, 66
Mose, 45, 162
Mutenope (f.), 175, 176
Muwatallis (Hittite King), 29

Naia (f.), 117

Nakht, 64[2]
Nakhtamon, 145
Nakhtsobek, 150
Nakhtsobeki, 46
Neb, 96
Nebetiotef (f.), 215
Nebeton (f.), 156
Nebhimaat (f.), 156
Nebiemon, 118
Nebmarenkht, 52, 170 n.17
Nebnefer, 47, 134
Nebnetjeru, 155
Nebre, 45, 138, 145
Neferabu, 118
Neferhotep, 25, 49, 50, 139, 143, 162,
  165, 166
Neferiu, 76
Neferkauhor (King), 21
Neferkhay, 147
Neferronpe, 37, 51, 135, 148
Nefersefekhi, 215
Nehsi, 65
Nehyu, 70
Nekhemmut, 52, 136, 149, 162, 163
Neni, 79[2], 80, 86
Nesamenope, 174, 176[2]
Nodjme (f.), 183
Nofretkha (f.), 140
Nubemnu (f.), 157
Nubemshas (f.), 156
Nubkhaure, 73

Pabaki, 137
Pahemnetjer, 163, 165
Pahen, 130
Paherypedje, 126
Pahy, 155
Painebenadjed, 209[2]
Painefernefer, 177[2]
Paiuten, 127
Paneb, 159
Panehsy, 40, 48[2], 118, 185
Panetyni, 86
Paser, 44, 45[2], 120, 134, 154
Pashed, 207
Paukhed, 33, 127

Pay, 143, 153
Payiry, 112
Payshuuben, 183
Penbuy, 159
Peniaty. 90, 91, 92
Pennebu, 143, 145, 156
Pennesettowy, 161
Penhensu, 66
Pentahunakht, 176
Pentahures, 185[2], 199[2]
Pentawere, 33, 48, 159
Pepi I (King), 56, 57
Pepi II (King), 20[2], 57[2]
Pepu, 84, 85
Pepyankhu, 57
Pepyhotep, 73
Peseg, 200, 201
Peterpayneb, 203
Petersuemhab, 34
Piankh, 194
Piay, 113, 142, 143, 166
Preemhab, 138, 142, 153, 157
Prehotep, 149, 158
Ptahpuwah, 86
Ptahshed, 143
Ptahu, 91, 92

Ramesses I (King), 112, 113
Ramesses II (King), 29-34, 36, 40
  n.9, 44, 45[2], 46[2], 47, 99, 110 n.12,
  116, 117[2], 118[2], 119, 120, 122, 123,
  133, 134, 137[2], 138, 139, 142[2], 143,
  144[2], 145, 146, 147, 148, 153[2],
  154[2], 155, 156[2], 157[2], 158
Ramesses III (King), 50[2], 52, 238,
  139, 149, 150, 162, 163, 165, 166
Ramesses IV (King), 52, 127, 128,
  135, 140, 163, 166
Ramesses V (King), 150, 151[2], 167
Ramesses IX (King), 37[2], 38[2], 52,
  130, 137, 152, 167, 168[2], 169[2]
Ramesses XI (King), 39, 52, 130, 172,
  173
Ramesses (Prince), 32
Ramesses-Maatptah, 31
Ramessesnakht, 37, 38

Ramose, 94, 95, 119, 120, 122², 124, 134, 153, 154, 158
Rashepses, 18
Re, 58, 67 n.1, 70
Renakht, 160
Renisoneb, 69
Resti (f.), 93
Rudefneheh, 32, 33

Sabni, 58
Sahnufe, 130
Sankhenptah, 211
Sankhuire, 65, 66
Sebtyemptah, 34²
Sehetepib, 79²
Senebni, 76
Senebtify, 70
Senedjemib, 18, 19
Senenmut, 90
Sennofer, 92, 93
Senu, 94
Senwosret, 74
Senwosret I (King), 22², 43², 44
Senwosret II (King), 77, 82, 83, 86
Senwosret III (King), 24, 73²
Ser, 70
Setemhab, 127
Seti I (King), 113, 114, 115, 116²
Seti II (King), 35, 36², 124, 143
Shedemdua (f.), 180, 185, 188, 189, 190, 192
Shedsuhor, 196
Shedsukhons, 209
Shemai, 22
Shemsenptah, 34
Shepsi, 211, 212
Shepti, 207²
Sheri, 141
Sherire (f.), 95
Sheritre (f.), 138
Sikaiunu, 80, 81
Sinuhe, 22²
Siptah (King), 145, 160
Sitnebsekhtu (f.), 63
Sobekhotep, 126
Sobekhotep (f.), 84, 85

Sonbu, 87
Soneb, 70
Su(?), 116
Sul, 31, 131 n.4
Suty, 30

Takhentyshepse (f.), 147
Tanetdjesere (f.), 147
Taysennofre (f.), 155
Tel (f.), 33
Teti, 91
Tetiaa, 216
Tetisoneb, 213
Tey, 92
Thutmose I (King), 27²
Tit, 90
Tjararoy (see also Dhutmose, Tjaroy, Tjertja, Tjuroy), 184, 201
Tjaroy (see also Dhutmose, Tjararoy, Tjertja, Tjuroy), 176, 177, 178, 179, 183, 184, 185, 189, 192, 194, 195, 196², 197, 201, 203
Tjel, 37
Tjertja (see also Dhutmose, Tjararoy, Tjaroy, Tjuroy), 181, 182
Tjuroy (see also Dhutmose, Tjararoy, Tjaroy, Tjertja), 182
To, 50²
Turo, 146
Turoi, 27
Tutuia (f.), 154

Uhem, 63
Usekhnemtet, 127
User, 166
Userhat, 93, 150
Usersatet, 27

Wehemmesut, 69
Wel (f.), 147
Wenenamon, 129, 130
Wernemty, 116, 117

Yey, 87, 113, 114, 131 n.4
Ynes, 40

III. Places

Abu Simbel, 72
Abydos, 24, 100², 102, 110 n.3
Achshaph, 107
Acco, 107
Adumim, 107
Adurun, 107
Agny, 196
Ahetmer, 77
Aiyanin, 109
Akhetaton (Amarna), 94
Akhset, 94
Akuyta, 29, 38, 39
Alalakh, 27
Aleppo, 106
Aniba, 191
Ankhtowy, 28, 33, 92, 117
Aperel, 120
Aradus, 125
Araphka, 27
Armant, 176
Asher, 108
Assiut, 96
Aswan, 20
Atfih, 84
Athribis, 79
Avaris, 118
Azaya, 107

Babylon, 27
Beirut, 107
Bethshan, 107
Beth-Sopher, 107
Bigga, 120
Bilbeis, 100
Black Land, 148, 170 n.8
Bubastis, 16, 110 n.2
Busiris, 100
Byblos, 27, 70, 107

Camp, the (El-Hiba), 209
Canaan, 109
Coptos, 21, 25, 26, 38, 146, 149
Crocodilopolis, 70, 79

Dagal, 107
Dagal-El, 107
Dapur, 107
Deir el-Bahri, 90, 94, 193
Deir el-Medina (see also Village,
    Village of Pharaoh), 132–170
Delta (see also Lower Egypt), 23, 53,
    109, 110 n.2, 110 n.9, 118
Dendera, 130
District of Horus, 79
Djahy, 106
Djedisut (Memphis), 59
Djeme (Medinet Habu), 185, 187,
    193, 197
Djeseret, 94

Edfu, 131
Egypt, 22, 26, 30, 35, 39², 108, 123,
    189, 196, 208
Elephantine, 23, 27, 72, 109, 120,
    128, 129, 130, 185, 188, 189, 199
El-Hiba (see also Camp, Promontory),
    181, 183, 206, 207
El-Lahun (see also Kahun), 77, 78

Faras, 71
Fenkhu, 23

"Garden of the Prince," 80
Gaza, 109, 127
Giza, 18, 19
God's Land, 16
Great Place (of Pharaoh), 46², 48², 49

Hamath, 107
Hazor, 107
Head of the South, 27
Heberet, 109, 110 n.17
Heliopolis, 15, 35, 39, 85, 90², 103,
    121
Heracleopolis, 31, 62, 63, 64, 80, 87,
    178
Hermon, 107
Hermopolis, 99, 103, 178, 180

Hieraconpolis, 71
Hieraconpolite nome, 57
Hikuptah (Memphis), 117, 146
Hu (See Hu-Sekhem)
Husayin, 109
Hu-Sekhem, 92, 93, 167², 168², 169, 215
Huthaa, 62
Hutnebes, 80²
Hutnesu, 44

Iaku-quarries, 81
Iam, 20²
Ibesgeb, 109
Ibhayet, 71
Ibirta, 106
Iken (Mirgissa), 71
Imiotru (Rizeiqat), 57
Island of Debu, 116
Island of Pekha, 113
Islands of the Sea, 23
Iusobeku, 63

Joppa, 108
Jordan (river), 107

Ka, 105, 110 n.9
Kadesh, 29, 106, 107
Kahun (see also El-Lahun), 68, 69
Karnak, 28, 91, 134, 142, 187, 197
Kaw, 211, 212
Kedem, 22, 23
Kehkeh, 38
Keshu, 23
Khadum, 106
Khalsu, 107
Khatti, 30, 106
Kheftehinebos, 193, 194, 197
Khepesheyet, 59, 62
Kheriu, 127, 128
Khor, 127
Kina, 107
Kiriath-Anab, 107
Kuban, 189, 191
Kur-Marruna, 107
Kush, 26, 29, 39, 120, 194, 209²

Litani (river), 107
Lower Egypt, 62, 63, 83, 126
Luxor, 198

Magara, 106
Medja, 58
Megiddo, 107
Meha, 72
Memphis, 28, 31, 40 n.7, 59, 113, 114, 115, 117, 119, 121, 124, 125, 146, 217
Middle Egypt, 178
Mirgissa, 71
Mount Shawe, 106
Muked, 38, 39

Naga ed-Deir, 212, 213
Naharin, 27
Namekhay, 178
Ne (Thebes), 47, 48, 129, 137, 142, 153, 167, 176, 178², 181, 187, 193, 194³, 196, 209
Nebeseyet, 59, 60, 62
Nekhes, 109
Neshyet(?), 207
Northern Promontory (El-Hiba), 181
Northern Region, 114, 115, 118, 123, 175
Nubi, 23, 24, 27, 58, 115, 176, 183, 185², 188, 189, 191, 193, 194², 196, 200

Oasis Land, 35²
Ombi (Kom Ombo), 131²

Pahedj[. . .]mehty, 190
Pakhaty, 27
Peniufneri, 176
Perbener, 118
Perhaa, 58, 59, 60, 61, 62
Perhebit, 53
Perkheny, 82
Permeten, 128
Perunefer, 40 n.7

Pi-Ramessu-miamon, 31, 32³, 33, 34²,
    117, 121, 125, 199
Place of Beauty (Valley of the
    Queens), 50
Place of Pharaoh, 36, 47, 52
Place of Truth, 30, 45, 46, 47, 149
Poker, 100
Promontory (El-Hiba), 206², 207²
Punt, 16, 20, 21, 23

Qus, 93

Raphia, 109
Red Mountain, 105²
Red Sea, 38
Rehob, 107
Retenu, 22, 23, 110
Rizeiqat, 57
Rosehwy, 81, 83, 85, 86

Sakkara, 18, 53 n.1
Sarepta, 107
Seba-El, 109
Second Cataract, 71
Sekhempehty, 125
Semna, 70², 73
Sepatmat, 63
Settlement Town, 76
Shechem, 107
Shenaut, 69
Sheneset, 130
Siagerteb, 43²
Sidiputu, 107
Sidon, 107
Silsila, 70
Simyra, 106
Sinai, 21
Southern City (Thebes), 24, 25, 40
    n.7, 92, 93, 118

Southern Heliopolis (Thebes), 28, 147
Southern Region, 40, 123
Sudan, 40 n.2
Sumenu, 23

Taanach, 163
Takhsy, 27, 107
Taminta, 107
Tell el-Balamun, 114
Theban nome, 16, 23², 60, 64, 65, 66
Thebes (see also Ne), 24, 25, 28², 40
    n.7, 45, 141, 150, 160, 167, 174,
    177, 179, 181, 187², 191, 193, 194,
    198, 201
Thinite nome, 24, 43, 44, 214
Tirek-El, 107
Tjebu, 72
Tjel, 110 n.15
Tubikhi, 106
Tura, 42, 56
Tyre, 107²

Upe, 106, 107
Upper Egypt, 21², 30, 45, 126
User, 107
Usu (Old Tyre), 107

Valley of the Kings, 40 n.8, 134, 152,
    169 n.1
Village, the (Deir el-Medina), 50, 51,
    136, 138, 150, 151², 153, 160
Village of Pharaoh (Deir el-Medina),
    45²

Wawat, 58

Yagadiya, 106
Yan, 107

IV. Subjects

accession, 27
adultery, 148, 203
agent(s), 16, 32, 56², 75, 101, 120, 147, 190
ale(?), 64
allowance, 59, 60, 61, 104
amphora, 160, 219
amulets, 146, 153
Apiru-laborers, 124
apprentices, 36, 99
armory, 35, 103, 108
army, 25, 30, 40, 100, 102, 106², 107, 115², 117, 126, 208
arrears, 28, 44, 48, 78
Asiatic(s), 22, 80, 82, 107
assignment (see also commission), 31, 45, 47, 48, 114², 121², 145, 164, 165, 180, 184, 198, 208
authorization, 37, 130

Ba, 100, 108, 173, 198
bandages, 22, 182
barge (see also boat, ship), 42, 65, 66, 120, 121, 183
bark (divine), 72, 100, 214
barley, 43, 57, 59², 60, 61², 62, 63, 65, 69, 80, 92, 119, 122, 126, 131², 138, 144, 148, 169, 212
bartering, 70, 72
basket, 49, 138, 144, 152, 154², 155², 157, 158, 161, 162², 164, 183
battle (see also fighting, war), 30, 107
beams, 90, 104, 160
beans, 138, 162
bed, 49, 138, 140, 162, 167, 168², 211
Beduin, 38, 39, 106², 107, 108
beef (see also meat), 76
beer, 71, 95, 101, 148, 149, 155, 161², 167, 185, 186, 191, 214
bird(s) (see also fowl), 103, 119², 158, 208
birthday(?), 16
blindness, 142, 173, 197

boat (see also barge, ship), 40, 43, 44, 49, 52, 59, 70, 79, 80, 82, 93, 94, 114, 121, 135, 156, 160, 174, 175, 180², 185, 190, 193, 196, 197, 200
box, 138, 146, 162, 203
boy(s), 44, 60, 118, 122, 123, 125, 126, 127, 156, 164, 180
bread (see also loaves), 30, 39, 71, 76, 87, 95, 101, 106, 108, 121, 139², 148, 149, 151, 155, 156, 161, 162, 167, 184², 185, 186, 187, 213, 217, 219
bricks, 105
brother, 38, 87, 91, 94, 95², 147, 151, 152, 154, 156, 157, 173, 177, 181, 199, 208, 212, 214, 215, 218²
brush, 142, 165
bull, 61, 75², 78, 105, 122, 131 n.3, 140
burial, 22, 87, 212
business, 48, 58, 148, 190±, 193

cadet, 16, 56, 209
cakes, 64, 106, 158, 160
calf, 30, 162, 169, 176
campaign (see also expedition), 199
candles (see also torch), 133
cannibalism, 67 n.3
cargo (see also freight), 43, 80, 120, 121², 125, 131 n.7
carpenter, 44, 96, 109, 140, 167, 168², 169², 199
carrying-stand, 40
castration, 169
cattle, 30, 31, 45, 93, 103², 113, 119², 120, 122², 123, 126, 127, 134, 218
chantress, 32², 33², 100, 114, 117, 174, 175, 176, 179, 180, 185, 187, 188, 189, 190, 192, 199², 200², 201²
charcoal, 128, 180
chariot, 106, 107, 108², 109, 114, 117, 192, 198
charioteer, 123²
chariotry, 217

chest (*see also* box), 104, 105, 137, 138, 165, 174, 217
child, 92, 100, 151, 203
children, 22², 34, 61, 66, 77, 120, 149, 152, 158, 169, 179², 180, 181, 186, 187², 190, 191, 199, 200, 212, 214², 215², 216
cloth, 49, 58, 59, 64, 83, 84², 87
clothes (*see also* garments), 47, 82, 87, 107, 118, 133, 144, 151, 182, 194, 195, 217²
clothing, 42, 62, 119, 164, 167, 180, 212, 217
coffin, 153, 162², 165, 168
colossus (*see also* statue), 105
commission, 38, 40², 133, 134, 169, 172, 173, 184, 186, 187, 189, 191, 192, 194², 195², 202
companion(s), 16, 21, 24, 51, 57, 58², 62, 151², 168, 212²
conscripts, 80², 81
Construction Site, 47, 50, 52, 133
copper, 50, 53, 62, 117, 119, 145², 146³, 156, 192², 196, 198
coppersmith, 185, 188, 189, 192², 198
corvée, 74, 82, 83, 85, 128
country, 95, 180
countryside, 46, 118, 177, 207
courier, 35, 37
court, 18, 19², 24, 25, 43, 44, 56, 91, 96, 101, 113, 124, 125, 145², 175, 203
Court of Horus, 58
cow, 122, 152, 161
crew, 30, 43², 45, 46², 48, 49, 58, 72, 100, 115, 121, 122, 124, 134, 136, 147
crewmen, 42, 120², 121
crime, 148
cult, 76, 123, 138
cult image, 24
cultivator (*see also* field hand), 25, 92, 118, 119, 125², 126², 127

dance, 20, 22
dancing-girl, 16

danger, 179, 293, 196, 200
date-brew, 138, 142, 164, 219
daughter, 63, 65, 92, 95, 96, 147, 180, 181, 186², 187, 192, 203, 214, 215
dead, 190, 215
dead man, 76, 213, 215
dead person, 84
dead woman, 213, 214
death, 72, 141, 143, 144, 217
debts, 145
deficit (*see also* arrears), 75
deliveries, 38, 74, 77
dependents, 25, 59, 113
desert, 23, 38, 71, 72
deserters (*see also* fugitives), 118
destiny, 141
dirt, 51, 160
dispatch, 37, 40, 47, 70, 71², 72, 105, 136
dispute, 84, 152, 216
diviner, 141
divorce, 97, 148, 173, 216
dockyard, 44, 120²
document, 52, 72, 126, 135, 165², 191
dog(s), 23, 43², 140
donkey, 39, 53, 70, 72, 112, 119², 137, 138, 149, 180, 192
door, 64, 91, 138, 141, 148, 167
drawing(s) (*see also* sketch), 52, 134, 139, 166
dream, 23, 151, 212, 215
duck(s), 64, 161
dung, 161
duties, 73
dwarf, 20, 21

ebony, 66, 140
emmer, 53, 57, 59², 60, 62², 80, 117, 126, 138, 145, 148, 159, 174²
enemy, 38², 102, 107, 108, 124, 214
estate, 21², 45, 57, 80, 112, 113, 120, 123
Estate of Amon, 38, 39, 118, 119², 127, 133, 142, 149, 158, 174, 176², 207

Estate of Ptah, 31
evidence, 128, 195
evil, 59, 85, 217
expedition (see also campaign), 20,
  182, 188, 196
eye-paint, 37²

family, 26, 56, 96, 146, 148
farm, 57, 60
farmer (see also cultivator), 58
farmland, 58, 59, 113, 127
fat, 76, 140², 161, 164
fate, 168
father, 16, 26, 28, 30, 35, 46, 109,
  122, 142, 146, 155, 158, 166, 169,
  173, 196, 197, 199, 211³, 212, 214,
  216, 218
fault, 36, 45, 46, 52, 92, 95, 102, 124,
  173, 184, 217
feast, 16, 50, 75, 105, 119, 120, 139,
  140, 144, 153, 163, 214
Feast of Opet, 119, 120
Feast of the Valley, 139, 145
festival, 27, 105, 126, 127, 142, 144
field (see also land), 46, 61, 66, 79,
  125, 127, 131, 147, 179, 180², 186,
  187, 192, 212, 218
field hand (see also cultivator), 76, 126,
  217
field workers, 91
figs, 157
fighting (see also battle, war), 27, 58
firewood, 46, 51, 134
fish, 16, 30, 46, 51, 81, 107, 109, 120,
  121, 131 n.7, 134, 143, 148, 160
fishermen, 119, 120², 121², 129, 160,
  172, 174, 180, 191
fishing, 81
flax, 60, 92, 212
fleet, 44, 119
flight, 22, 23, 83, 206, 216
flood (see also inundation), 102, 128,
  180
flowers, 40, 93, 100
food, 26, 59², 62², 70, 75, 78, 79, 82,
  87, 97, 100, 103, 104, 106, 108, 144

food allowance, 59, 61², 104
food provisions, 82
food rations, 61, 79, 87, 97
foreign countries, 22, 23, 27, 58, 110
foreigners, 36, 100, 109
fortress, 38, 70, 71², 72³, 109, 120²,
  125
fowl (see also birds), 16, 63, 74, 75
fowler, 119, 186, 192, 207, 208
freeman, 173
freewoman, 156
freight (see also cargo), 121
frit, 47, 84²
frontier, 71, 72, 107
fruit, 30, 53, 157, 167, 176
fuel, 128
fugitive (see also deserters), 25, 130,
  206
funeral, 22

galena, 37², 38, 142
galley, 66
garments (see also clothes), 140, 180,
  219
garrison, 114, 125, 127
geese, 64, 69
general, 31, 34, 40 n.9, 65, 114, 175,
  179², 181, 182, 183, 184², 187, 199,
  190³, 193, 194, 195², 196², 197,
  198, 199, 201, 206
Generalissimo, 31, 208
girl(s), 32, 77, 144, 179, 189, 190, 193
goat, 53, 73, 106, 118, 140, 143, 154,
  158², 161, 163
gold, 22, 24, 29, 39, 103, 119, 131
gold-washing, 38, 39
goods, 80, 86, 119, 147, 157, 159
grain (see also barley, emmer), 46, 51,
  58, 70², 74, 75, 81, 101, 119, 123,
  124, 125, 126², 131, 134, 135, 138,
  139, 142, 144, 145, 147, 155², 157²,
  159, 169, 172, 173, 174², 180², 181,
  186, 187, 200, 202
granary, 40, 51, 57, 102, 103, 119,
  120, 125, 126, 145, 147, 174, 175²,
  180, 194

grass, 161, 164, 209
groom, 100, 107, 115
guidance, 23, 95, 96
gum, 47, 53
gypsum, 47, 48, 49, 96, 134, 146

handwriting, 190, 197
harem, 36
harvest, 31, 60, 126, 131, 178
heir(s), 26², 30, 216
heliacal rising (of Sothis), 73
herald, 23, 125²
herders, 118, 119²
herdsmen, 93, 122², 123, 127, 181
hide(s), 62, 73, 152, 155
high priest, 37, 38, 46, 47, 90, 134,
    194, 208²
hire, 112
homeland, 23
honey, 56, 100, 101, 129², 142, 164
horses (see also steads), 46, 101, 106,
    107, 108, 124, 207
house, 35, 60², 62, 64, 79², 91, 92,
    93, 94², 126, 131, 135, 138², 143,
    146, 147, 149, 151, 153, 160, 167,
    168, 176, 180, 181, 183², 190, 191,
    203, 206, 207, 209, 211, 214, 216,
    217²
household, 25, 56, 60, 61, 62, 63,
    65², 79, 86, 87, 144², 173, 177, 211,
    216, 217
housemaid (see also maid servant), 60
hunger, 51, 61², 72, 144, 173
husband, 148, 211, 214, 215, 216, 217,
    218²
Hyksos, 26

illness, 137, 142, 143, 179, 181, 191,
    208, 215, 217
incense, 129, 139, 141, 145, 153, 164,
    168
infants, 71, 72, 141
ink, 75, 114, 143, 154, 165
instructions, 36, 50, 92, 109, 156
instructor (see also teacher), 16, 99

inundation (see also flood), 58, 60, 61,
    102

jail (see also prison), 31, 114
job, 176, 185, 190, 192
joke, 173²
jubilee, 19, 20, 29, 50, 123, 154

Ka, 15, 20², 22, 31, 32, 33, 34, 38,
    62, 63, 64, 65, 80, 85, 102², 125
kilt, 16, 39, 49, 153, 159, 161, 191,
    219
knife, 39, 49, 146, 155, 198

labor, 43, 88, 76, 82, 119, 124, 127,
    180
laborers (see also workmen), 25, 44,
    85, 115, 124, 176
lake, 19², 101, 104
land, 26, 58, 59, 60, 61, 62, 92, 108,
    131², 176, 209
landholder, 56
lapis lazuli, 22, 40
laundry, 144
laundryman (see also washerman), 139,
    144², 160, 206
law, 24, 25, 43, 44, 56, 216
lease, 58, 62
leather, 108, 109, 152, 163, 211
Libyans (see also Meshwesh), 35, 53
litigation, 57, 91², 212², 213, 217
loan, 212, 219 n.2
loaves (see also bread), 30, 39, 44, 106,
    121, 139, 152, 155, 156, 158, 160,
    162, 163, 191, 202, 219
loincloth, 49, 147, 153, 157, 160, 164

magazine, 75, 78, 93, 96, 105, 128,
    165, 180
magistrate(s), 21, 22, 56², 57, 78, 91,
    95, 96
Maher-warriors, 106, 107², 108⁴
maid servant, 57, 61, 91, 92, 129,
    198, 214, 215, 216
market place, 143, 156, 161
Maryan-warrior, 107

mat(s), 80, 90, 119, 139, 144, 145,
    152, 162, 164
matting, 90
mayor, 26, 35, 47, 76, 84, 90, 91, 92,
    93, 114, 120, 129, 130, 134, 178²
meat, 26, 30, 78, 155, 163, 212
Medjay, 53, 71², 72
merchant, 129², 130
Meshwesh, 53, 106, 177, 305²
messenger (see also courier), 29, 101,
    188
milk, 70, 93, 134, 159
money, 50, 114, 117, 118, 140
mortuary priest, 58, 60, 61, 62, 77²
mother, 16, 26, 27, 50, 63, 87, 92,
    124, 141, 146, 148, 154², 180, 203,
    212, 213, 214, 216, 218
mountain, 29, 45, 102, 103², 104,
    107, 108, 150, 189, 214
mummy, 22
musical troop, 77

Naarin-warriors, 106, 109
natron, 70, 119
nets, 86
netherworld (see also underworld),
    100, 219
Nile, 60, 61, 102, 110 n.9, 118
nome, 21, 57
nourishment, 122
Nubians, 28, 28, 38, 39, 70, 71, 72,
    106, 191

oath, 27, 50, 113, 131, 206
obelisk, 105
obligations, 74, 78, 92
occupation, 52, 94, 142
ochre, 47, 84, 142
offense, 35², 186²
offerings, 22, 26, 27, 28, 74, 75², 78²,
    94, 101, 119, 126², 127, 139², 174²,
    214, 215², 218
officer(s), 74, 108, 114, 125, 217
official(s), 25, 28, 36, 114, 135, 173,
    175

oil, 22, 51, 53, 63, 64, 143, 153, 154,
    155, 161², 163, 167, 169, 175, 186,
    217
ointment, 129, 161, 167
old age, 15, 22, 62, 63, 64, 65, 100,
    131, 137, 141, 150, 151, 152, 158,
    166, 167, 168, 173, 174, 176, 177,
    178, 179, 180, 181, 182, 185, 189,
    191, 194, 197, 198, 199, 200, 201,
    206, 207², 208
old man, 46, 90
oracle, 152, 179, 184, 191, 199, 219
order(s), 21, 25, 31, 43, 47, 49, 52,
    53, 57, 115², 128², 190, 193²
orphan, 16, 149, 151, 166
ox, 22, 56, 123, 131, 140, 149, 157,
    160, 162, 181, 211

paint, 139
palace, 19², 20, 22, 23, 24, 25, 28, 30,
    31, 35², 37, 40, 43, 44, 45, 72, 103
palette (scribal), 104, 165²
papyrus, 16, 26, 77, 100, 102, 104,
    114, 117, 119, 121², 136, 138, 142,
    163, 165², 184, 199, 204 n.6
patrol, 35², 72²
payment, 56, 83, 91, 92, 93, 117, 129,
    177, 188, 192
peace, 22, 28, 30
personnel, 49, 73, 90, 114, 118, 123,
    177, 194
petition, 25², 26, 208
phyle, 56, 57, 73², 7, 78
physician, 37², 217
pig, 140
pigeons, 75, 158
pigments, 47, 140
pilot, 38, 153, 177, 196, 200
pine, 66, 106, 121
police, 46², 53, 123
policeman, 39, 46, 146, 127, 145, 180,
    183², 189, 192, 193
possessions, 58, 107, 215
pottery, 46, 134, 145
prayer, 23, 189, 193
price, 145, 153, 163

priest(s) (*see also* prophets), 21, 25, 37, 45, 56, 57, 64, 73², 78, 116, 117, 134, 141, 142, 175, 176, 206², 207, 208, 213, 215
prince(s), 31², 32, 5 0, 105
princess, 33
prison (*see also* jail), 116², 211
prisoners, 24
procession, 55, 74, 125, 157, 163, 179, 198, 219
produce, 60
products, 21, 38, 104
promissory note, 118
property, 26, 58, 63, 73, 103, 117, 144, 145, 212
prophet(s), 21², 37, 47, 76, 118², 124, 125, 130, 175, 176, 177², 178, 181, 182³, 196², 198, 208
provisions, 21, 65², 82, 100, 103, 106
punishment, 35
pupil, 24
pyramid complex, 57
pyramid temple, 73
pyramid town, 73, 75, 76, 78, 79

quarries, 42, 56, 81, 105
quay, 43, 80², 82, 105
queen, 22

rags, 103, 153
raisins, 69, 70
ramp, 104
rations (*see also* allowance), 46, 49, 61², 62, 78, 87, 97, 101, 104, 106, 114, 124, 134, 143, 162, 175, 184², 187, 192, 200
reconnaissance, 35²
records, 100, 120, 125
Red Crown, 26, 187
rent, 59, 62
report, 28, 44, 48, 49, 52, 109, 187, 202
requirements, 49, 56, 100, 156
Residence, 16, 20, 21, 22, 23, 25², 38, 42, 43, 57, 84, 118
rings, 144, 146

river, 23, 101, 106, 107², 118, 121, 177, 188
riverbank, 43, 92, 105
robbery, 58
rope, 116, 119
rushes, 196, 104, 121, 137, 165

Sacred Marriage Chapel, 19, 57
sacred relic, 26²
sailor, 91, 121²
salt, 119, 175
sand, 35, 101, 105, 107, 108
sandals, 28, 73, 127, 145, 152, 154, 158, 159, 160, 161, 163², 164
sandal-maker, 74, 152
school, 180
scow, 107, 120, 175
seal, 32, 52, 84², 87, 102, 115, 146, 174, 195
seed, 57, 58, 59, 61, 79
seed-order, 125
serfs, 120, 130, 198
servant, 15, 16, 28, 29, 32, 39, 45², 46, 56, 57, 77, 85, 92, 95², 99, 124, 127, 130, 134, 146², 179, 194, 196, 206², 208, 212
service, 95, 114, 122, 142², 162
setem-priest, 31, 145², 175
shawl, 49, 157
sheep, 22, 106, 108
Sherden, 106, 190, 192, 194
ship (*see also* barge, boat), 19, 21, 66, 117, 120², 125, 127, 173, 194
silver, 24, 29, 118, 119, 120, 121, 131 n.7, 146, 183
sister, 16, 52, 93, 95, 96, 124, 130, 154, 157, 187, 211, 215², 217, 218
sketch (*see also* drawings), 192
skins, 22, 157
slander, 173, 202
slave, 83, 86², 91, 113, 124, 125, 129
slave-boy, 51
slave-girl, 43
slave-woman, 82, 129, 144
soldier, 30, 72, 101, 104, 106², 109, 113, 115², 117², 124, 125, 154, 180, 185, 197, 207

soldier-scribe, 106
son, 16², 20, 21, 24, 25, 26¹, 30, 32, 38, 60, 74, 102, 122, 129, 130, 141, 149, 208, 211, 212, 213, 214
sorcerer, 28
spears, 188, 189, 190², 193², 196, 197, 199
speech, 22, 149
spikes, 29, 48, 146
spirit, 213, 215², 216
stable, 100, 101, 103, 104, 110 n.8, 115, 123, 124, 126
stalls, 45, 103, 146
standard, 52, 125
standard-bearer, 114, 115², 116, 117, 127
statue (see also colossus), 50, 94, 120
steeds (see also horses), 100, 115
stele, 24, 25, 26, 27, 29, 141
stipend, 26, 124
stone, 51, 57, 64, 108, 137, 146, 181, 197
storehouse, 51, 147
storerooms, 90
straw, 122, 161
summer, 71, 126
supplies, 21, 38, 39, 51, 52, 82, 87, 134
sycamore, 101, 129
sycamore figs, 157
Sycamore Shrine, 16
Syrian, 125², 126, 167

tallow, 47, 51
tariff, 113
task, 137
taxes, 119, 156
teacher (see also instructor), 104
temple, 21, 25, 26, 28, 37, 52, 56, 70, 73², 74, 75², 76, 80, 82, 85, 86, 94, 114, 16, 118, 124, 125², 126, 129, 130², 133, 142, 145, 158², 167, 168², 174, 175, 176³, 186, 198, 206², 207², 209², 219
tenant, 56, 131
tent, 21

testimony, 128, 173, 190, 192, 198, 202², 209
texts, 16², 165, 166
thief, 84
timber(s), 44, 121, 129
tin, 176, 198
Tjukten, 35²
tomb, 22, 29, 47, 50, 100, 102, 133, 191, 212
tools, 49, 146²
torch (see also candles), 76
track, 71, 72
transactions, 153
treasury, 26², 37, 47, 48², 51, 86, 103, 118, 119, 128, 131, 146², 153², 175, 177²
tree(s), 106, 108, 180, 181
trial, 83
tribunal (see also courts), 158
troop(s), 38, 39, 40, 42, 58², 70, 72, 104², 106², 109, 129, 194, 209
Tuhir-troops, 129
tunic, 39, 108, 156, 161, 175

underworld (see also netherworld), 29, 103
unguent, 94, 95, 96, 100, 101, 151²

varnish, 153, 168
vegetables, 46², 51, 123, 128, 134, 139, 143², 154, 156², 159², 161, 186, 187, 209
viceroy, 27², 29, 39, 120
vizier, 18², 21, 24, 25, 31, 36, 37, 38, 42, 43, 44², 45², 46², 47², 48², 49, 50², 51, 52², 125, 134, 135, 136, 137, 147, 168, 173, 174, 175, 202
wab-priest, 51, 52, 64, 93, 94, 96, 118, 126, 129, 163, 165, 174, 180, 202
wab-priestess, 82
wages, 30, 44, 45², 46, 47, 48, 49, 52, 80, 134, 191
war (see also battle, fighting), 186
warfare, 30, 110 n.18
warrant, 24

warriors, 71, 72, 106², 107³, 108,
109², 207
washerman, 84
watchposts, 45, 46², 47, 48, 50
water(s), 21, 23², 29, 46, 64, 67 n.4,
100, 107, 108, 124, 128, 137, 144,
149, 152, 155, 176, 180, 181, 183²,
189, 193, 197, 212, 216, 218
weapons, 35, 176
weavers, 82, 207²
weaving, 36, 82
well, 29, 71, 110 n.6, 124, 181, 209
wheat, 43, 60
White Crown, 26, 197
wicks, 47, 50, 133
widow, 50, 124
wife, 16², 60, 62², 65, 97, 117, 143,
148², 149, 173, 203, 20, 211, 214,
215, 216², 217
wine, 74, 75, 101, 106, 139

wisdom, 16, 24
witnesses, 122, 212
woman, 27, 71, 76, 82, 93, 94, 95,
129, 173, 187, 203, 216, 218
wood, 38, 46, 51, 66, 93, 116, 128²,
129, 135, 137, 138, 145, 153, 156,
159, 176, 180, 192, 211
wool, 120, 121², 131 n.7, 156
work, 42, 48, 50, 51, 60, 92, 94, 101,
121, 137, 149, 169, 172², 178
workers (see also laborers), 76, 93,
109, 137
workforce, 104, 105²
workman, 46, 48, 94, 115, 178², 194,
198, 203
writing(s), 16, 24, 26, 53, 58, 90, 91,
99, 110 n.1, 115, 129, 138, 149,
162, 165, 174, 192, 198, 208
writing board, 165

CPSIA information can be obtained
at www.ICGtesting.com
Printed in the USA
FFOW02n1603241117
43612864-42428FF